THE
SECRET
MASTER

Praise for *The Secret Master*

'This carefully researched and highly readable book seamlessly blends three distinct literary genres. It is at once a memoir, of a serious and curious student of our classical music; a biography, of the tortuous personal journey of a great and greatly underrated musician; and a cultural history, of the evolution of that sublime and enduringly appealing art form, khayal gayaki. Finely observed, vividly rendered, suffused with love and learning, *The Secret Master* deserves, and shall surely get, a wide readership across regions and generations.'

– Ramachandra Guha, historian, writer and columnist

'A good khayal performance intertwines an awareness of tradition and respect for the guru with the musician's unique personal expression. In *The Secret Master*, Sumana Ramanan similarly pushes the boundaries of literary non-fiction, lovingly combining personal narrative, biography and history in a virtuoso performance that redefines what writing about music can achieve. A stunning accomplishment.'

– Warren Senders, khayal singer, educator and world music expert

'This wonderful book brings into its ambit the world of gurus and shagirds, of musical cultures ranging from national-level festivals to small baithaks, of research spaces and archives, of the worlds of recording studios and popular forums and more. This is an ambitious project indeed, but Sumana Ramanan does justice and more to the task she sets herself. Focusing on Mumbai and its hinterland, the story she tells is at once the life of a single musician, her guru, juxtaposed skilfully with the spaces and cultures of performance, the connections between students and teachers, of organisers and listeners, and of the histories and politics of music. The book raises questions about patronage, pedagogy, training of both singers and listeners, changing spaces and audiences, and much more. At every stage you sense the quiet yet tenacious presence of this writer and committed student of music, her passion and devotion, her painstaking research, above all her deep love for khayal gayaki and her dedication to and respect for her guru and for all those masters, secret or otherwise, known or unknown, who have shaped and continue to shape the form. An absolute tour de force, this is a must-read for anyone who loves music!'

– Vidya Rao, thumri singer, editor and author of
Heart to Heart: Remembering Nainaji

'With the passion of a rasika, the curiosity of a prize-winning reporter and the fluid storytelling abilities of a novelist, Sumana Ramanan leads the reader on a sonorous journey through the universe of khayal. Much writing about Indian classical musicians is hagiographic, clouded by extravagant reverence for its subjects. *The Secret Master* distinguishes itself with its clear-eyed portrayal of Arun Kashalkar's quest for perfection. Demonstrating how tradition is never static, Ramanan deftly describes how political and economic transformations are impacting the stage and the music room. In a world brimming over with flashy distractions and seductions, *The Secret Master* reminds us that there are still mavericks spending their lives in single-minded pursuit of their art—for its own sake.'

– Naresh Fernandes, editor of *Scroll.in* and author of *Taj Mahal Foxtrot: The Story of Bombay's Jazz Age* and *City Adrift: A Short Biography of Bombay*

'The world of Hindustani classical music is marked by plurality and complexity, contradictions and anxieties. Equally, a lot remains hidden and invisible, with many unnoticed efforts and hard struggles towards its vibrant creativity and rich imagination. In this well-researched and well-written biographical narrative about Arun Kashalkar, Sumana Ramanan shines a light on a singular and significant life in music. Interestingly, she also explores and analyses the institutional, personal and public ethos relating to music, its inadequacies and constraining factors. A revealing, sometimes provocative, and deeply insightful work, it is a significant addition to a rather small body of literature on music.'

– Ashok Vajpeyi, Hindi poet-critic and art lover

'Within the true artist lies the eternal seeker who has embarked on his quest for the raga, drowning in and sharing from within its soundscape. Yet, the musician in him also needs validation, and this is determined by social power dynamics. Sumana Ramanan's thoughtful investigation of this chasm brings these two realities into conversation. She portrays this intense tension in the life of Arun Kashalkar, the protagonist of this book, with great sensitivity. *The Secret Master* courageously calls out the normalised opacity in the business of classical music, asking serious questions about respect and success. It also uncannily reveals another truth: through the description of the innumerable tugs and pulls within classical music and its cultural ethos, the book subtly informs us that the classical music universe rarely engages with the larger world that it inhabits.'

– T.M. Krishna, Carnatic vocalist, writer and activist

THE SECRET MASTER

Arun Kashalkar *and*
a Journey to the Edge of Music

SUMANA RAMANAN

cntxt

Published by Context, an imprint of Westland Books, a division of Nasadiya Technologies Private Limited, in 2025

No. 269/2B, First Floor, 'Irai Arul', Vimalraj Street, Nethaji Nagar, Alapakkam Main Road, Maduravoyal, Chennai 600095

Westland, the Westland logo, Context and the Context logo are the trademarks of Nasadiya Technologies Private Limited, or its affiliates.

Copyright © Sumana Ramanan, 2025

Sumana Ramanan asserts the moral right to be identified as the author of this work.

ISBN: 9789371979658

10 9 8 7 6 5 4 3 2 1

The views and opinions expressed in this work are the author's own and the facts are as reported by her, and the publisher is in no way liable for the same.

All rights reserved

Typeset by Jojy Philip
Printed at Thomson Press (India) Ltd

No part of this book may be reproduced, or stored in a retrieval system, or transmitted in any form or by any means, electronic, mechanical, photocopying, recording, or otherwise, without express written permission of the publisher.

To Jaikumar, my life's shadja.

All that we don't know is astonishing.
Even more astonishing is what passes for knowing.
— Philip Roth

Contents

MYSTERY

CHAPTER 1
- ◇ Underground — 3

CHAPTER 2
- ◇ Rabbit Hole — 6

CLUES

CHAPTER 3
- ◇ Fakir — 17
- ◈ Storm: 1970 — 26
- ◆ Alchemy — 28

CHAPTER 4.
- ◇ Verdict — 31
- ◈ Sea: 1965–68 — 39
- ◆ Concert — 53

CHAPTER 5.
- ◇ Ride — 55
- ◈ Roots — 58
- ◆ Palace — 73

CHAPTER 6.
- ◇ Fringe — 75
- ◈ Shore: 1969–72 — 82
- ◆ Architect — 98

CHAPTER 7.
- ◇ Black Box — 101
- ◈ Backwaters: 1943–57 — 112
- ◆ Sport — 128

CHAPTER 8.
- ◇ Counterweights — 131
- ◈ Travels: 1958–64 — 144
- ◆ Sound — 151

CHAPTER 9.
- ◇ Society — 154
- ◈ Mountain: 1973–80 — 160
- ◆ Rope — 174

IDEAS

CHAPTER 10.
- ◇ Garden — 179
- ◈ Cusp: 1981–85 — 190
- ◆ Language — 205

CHAPTER 11.
- ◇ Movie — 207
- ◈ Fire: 1986–95 — 213
- ◆ City — 230

CHAPTER 12.
- ◇ Carnival — 232
- ◈ Susegado: 1996–97 — 240
- ◆ Time — 251

CHAPTER 13.
- ◇ Colours — 255
- ◈ Beauty: 1998–2000 — 264
- ◆ Drama — 277

PATHS

CHAPTER 14.
- ◇ Reception — 281
- ◈ Arun, Mandaar, Ravi: 2001–05 — 289
- ◆ Quality — 301

CHAPTER 15.
- ◇ Cult — 303
- ◈ Arun, Vishal, Mukul: 2003–14 — 313
- ◆ Weave — 325

CHAPTER 16.
- ◇ Boutique — 328
- ◈ Arun, Sugandha, Ketaki: 2010–15 — 339
- ◆ Story — 350

CHAPTER 17.
- ◇ Puzzle — 352
- ◈ Arun, Omkar: 2012–15 — 365
- ◆ Word — 374

CHAPTER 18.
- ◇ Voice — 378
- ◈ Light: 2001–14 — 388
- ◆ Feeling — 391

CHAPTER 19.
- ◇ Flame — 393
- ◈ Tailwinds: 2015 — 398
- ◆ Spiral — 400

TRUTH

CHAPTER 20.
- ◈ Love — 405

Notes — 409
Interviews — 438
Bibliography — 442
Acknowledgements — 448
Sound and Image — 452

MYSTERY

Music fills the infinite between two souls.
— Rabindranath Tagore

1

◇ **Underground**

SHORT, DARK AND PORTLY, RAMBHAU PAWAR, EIGHTY-NINE years of age, sat cross-legged on the floor of a green room, spotlighted by the sun streaming in from a window.[1] An electronic tanpura's drone filled the room.[2] The instrument's shadja, notated as Sa,[3] the anchoring note from which all others blossom, was set to the pitch C#.[4] A young man tuned an acoustic tanpura lying lengthwise on the floor, its side silhouette resembling a massive ladle. With his right hand, he plucked the four strings that ran along the instrument's long neck and were wound around tapered wooden tuning pegs emerging from holes at the end. With his left hand, he rotated each peg's knob to align the corresponding string's pitch with the electronic tanpura's. The pegs, snug in their holes, squeaked.

Rambhau's nephew tuned his tabla, tapping a steel hammer above and below the braided leather rim of the instrument's round top surface. Rambhau, too, tuned his vocal cords, by humming softly to align them to the shadja. About ten of us settled down on satranjis spread out on the floor, our anticipation whetted by these familiar sights and sounds. Yet this was no rehearsal. It was a performance of khayal, the most widespread of the three Hindustani art music genres, the other two being dhrupad and thumri. This vocal performance unfolded on the sidelines of a music festival due to start the following morning, in Aundh, a remote town in southern Maharashtra. The Aundh Sangeet Mahotsav was a rare twenty-four-hour music event that took place every year a week before Diwali. Since 1940, it had presented superbly trained khayal musicians who epitomised high classicism, many of whom had only a meagre presence on mainstream stages.

I had been going to Hindustani music concerts since I was a teenager, but I was attending this festival for the first time, in October 2016. It was off the beaten track, patronised by aficionados who were insiders in a world that I, then in my forties, had only recently entered like a wide-eyed child. At that time, I knew only the bare outlines of Rambhau's life. He had grown up abjectly poor, herding cattle. He had developed a taste for khayal as a child while passing by the home of a master vocalist every day and hearing him teach his son.[5] That vocalist was Anant Manohar Joshi, or Antubuwa, the festival's founder, who had been a court musician in Aundh, a princely state in British India. In all, Rambhau had formally learnt khayal for only about six months.

The tuned tanpura's heady sound filled the room.

'Let's start,' said the tanpura player.

Rambhau launched into a stately aalaap, the slow, meditative opening of a raag, or raga, rendition. The raag form is a melodic framework for improvisation. Rambhau had a strong, resonant voice with a gravelly edge, textured but not harsh. His voice boomed as the walls amplified the sound.

'Bhimpalas,' said one man, a couple of seconds later.

'Yes,' replied Rambhau.

Raag Bhimpalas blends strains of melancholy on the ascent with effervescence on the descent, allowing a musician to play with contrasts of light and shade. Rambhau sketched the popular raag with a few distinctive phrases, like a skilled draughtsman capturing the essence of a person's face with the fewest possible ink marks. Appreciative waahs, ahas and ohos sprung into the air like colourful balloons. Adjusting his Gandhi cap, Rambhau followed his aalaap by singing a drut bandish, or fast composition, accompanied by the tabla player. Rambhau then sang another composition in Bhimpalas and again improvised.

'What next?' asked a man.

We shifted around on the satranjis and made ourselves more comfortable. Rambhau sang raag Bhoop and raag Yaman, which like

Bhimpalas, are foundational and popular. He went on to present brief portraits of more specialised raags: Miyan ki Todi, Multani, Puriya Dhanashree and Shankara. He brought these varied raags to life within minutes, while also demonstrating his command over a range of taals, which are various rhythmic cycles expressed on the tabla. In the final rendition, he outdid himself by singing a devotional song that he himself had set to raag Lalita Gauri, belonging to a category of complex raags. I shook my head in wonder.

'Kya baat hai!' exclaimed a listener.

'Bahut khhoob!' cried another.

In each raag, Rambhau sang only fast compositions, skipping the majestic slow compositions that typically open a raag rendition. But even this was remarkable for someone who had essentially taught himself. His music had not been polished and chiselled under a guru's supervision, and exhibited some rough edges. Yet it exuded raw power and originality. One listener told me that Rambhau had regaled visitors for years on the festival's sidelines. His singing as well as the warmth and knowledge with which the audience received his impromptu recital belonged to a musical culture radically different from any that I had experienced.

Classical music is a niche activity. But by then, I knew that beyond its public manifestation lay a rich multitude of worlds, including this vibrant counterculture—thin on resources but thick in substance, low on hype but high on passion. It was a world in which a cattle grazer without training could hold his own on the strength of his art. This counterculture nurtured the equivalent of underground music, a term originally used for Western popular forms that resisted mainstream trends. Underground music is characterised by 'sincerity, intimacy [and] freedom of creative expression, in opposition to … practices deemed formulaic or commercially driven.'[6]

Rambhau's music certainly lived up to this definition. His green room recital was one of the high points of a dreamy journey that I had embarked upon several months earlier after falling into a rabbit hole.

2

◇ Rabbit Hole

NINE MONTHS EARLIER, IN JANUARY 2016, AT A PRIVATE venue in South Mumbai, a very different kind of musician performed a full-length khayal concert. The venue was the foyer of the Homi Bhabha Auditorium at the Tata Institute of Fundamental Research, where my husband, Jaikumar, worked. The performer, Arun Kashalkar, was a superbly trained Brahmin musician in his early seventies. I had never heard him before.

I had heard *of* him, several times in the preceding four months, after I began writing a column for an influential tabloid, *Mumbai Mirror*. In the column, I was covering different facets of Hindustani music in Mumbai, which has been the epicentre of the art form for more than a century, a fact that surprises many people, including long-standing residents of the city. Two veteran listeners had praised Arun-ji's singing, while two others had told me that he had taught hundreds of people. I had run into two of his current students. I also learnt that Arun-ji had trained under three great musicians, namely Gajananrao Joshi, or Gajananbuwa, who was Antubuwa's son, Rambhau Marathe and Shrikrishna 'Babanrao' Haldankar. Arun-ji, I was told, had a command over three of the twenty-first century's six most widespread gharanas, or stylistic traditions: Agra, Gwalior and Jaipur, the other three being Kirana, Patiala and Rampur-Sahaswan. As a journalist always on the prowl for something new, I had made a note against his name: 'Seems to be a hidden city institution, fix up to meet him.' Equally intriguing was the fact that he was the eldest brother of the well-known Ulhas Kashalkar, established as one of the finest khayal singers. Ulhas-ji was twelve years younger than Arun-ji, the last of six brothers and someone whose music I had admired for nearly two decades. Where had his eldest brother been hiding all these years? This tantalising question had to wait because two finely tuned tanpuras had begun suffusing the room with their mutually reinforcing tones and overtones.

The recital was a baithak, a chamber concert. Most listeners sat on a huge carpet in front of the stage, while a few chose benches and chairs at the back. Lean, tall and dressed in an eye-catching cobalt blue silk kurta, Arun-ji sized the audience up from a low stage. His white hair and beard framed a rectangular face with small twinkling eyes and an aquiline nose. His skin was unusually fair. He looked down and tentatively sang the shadja.

'I take time to warm up,' he said, looking up after a few seconds. 'Please bear with me.'

Two youngsters sat behind him on either side at an angle, playing a tanpura each. Arun-ji softly sang two phrases of raag Dhanashree, a favourite of Agra gharana musicians. Was this septuagenarian up to the task? Within minutes, I got the beginning of an answer. His voice steadied as he plunged into a nom-tom aalaap, or nom-tom for short, which are strings of sonorous syllables, such as ri-da-ta-na-nom, sung without any percussion accompaniment. I was agog because by the turn of the twenty-first century, the nom-tom had become an endangered species in khayal. Arun-ji increased the nom-tom's pace in stages and ended the final, fast segment with a flourish. This slow-to-fast progression is a key feature of a raag rendition.

The audience let the music sink in. Arun-ji then opened the second part of Dhanashree by starting the vilambit bandish, or slow composition, a raag rendition's highlight. Arun-ji sang the sthayi, the first verse, and then started doing bol ka kaam, or improvisation using lyrics, an Agra gharana speciality. Like with the nom-tom, the musician moves from a slow to a fast tempo: from the languid bol aalaap, followed by bol laykari, or rhythmic play, to lightning bol taans, climactic passages of rapid-fire improvisation that showcase virtuosity.

Arun-ji spun out variation upon variation on the initial line. His voice had a husky edge, but this receded from my consciousness because the music had become so compelling. After a while, he hit the taar, or upper, shadja, and sang the antara, the second verse. He then increased the tempo and returned to the first verse, before launching into bol laykari. After a while, he again increased the tempo and began singing bol taans as well as aakaar taans, those using the sound 'aa'.

'I am singing Nivruttibuwa-style off-beat taan patterns,' he said in English at one point, referring to Nivruttibuwa Sarnaik, a Jaipur gharana vocalist and tabla player who infused his singing with mind-boggling rhythmic designs.

In a while, Arun-ji began the third part of his rendition: the fast composition. Here too, musicians can gradually increase the pace as much as they wish to. But Arun-ji chose to maintain the initial tempo, doing a lilting lyrical improvisation that resembles the bol banaav of thumri, in which a singer uses vocal modulation and dynamics to evoke shades of meaning. I was hooked.

Arun-ji sang the second raag, Gaud Malhar, in a sweet yet vigorous vein, presenting the traditional composition, *Maana na karori* (Don't sulk),[1] first in the sixteen-beat Teentaal and then in the seven-beat Roopak. He then announced an interval. I went up to the stage.

'Did you learn from Nivruttibuwa?' I asked him.

'No, although I wanted to,' Arun-ji replied in English. 'But we knew each other well. I analysed his music. It took me a long time to understand what he was doing and many more years of practice to replicate it.'

I was surprised by how fluently he spoke English, in contrast with most Hindustani musicians of his generation, including Ulhas-ji. They had both grown up in a small town in eastern Maharashtra. Equally, for a Hindustani musician, I found him unusually approachable and forthright. After finishing his cup of tea, he turned to his right and exchanged a few words with his student, Vishal Moghe, who was providing vocal support.

'Darbari,' Arun-ji then announced.

'Aha,' I thought to myself, just as someone I knew who was sitting ahead of me turned around and made big eyes, signalling the same anticipatory thrill that I felt. Many people believe that Tansen, the celebrated singer at the court of the sixteenth-century Mughal emperor Akbar, adapted Darbari Kanada, often called just Darbari, to the north Indian idiom from Carnatic music. In contrast with the frisky charm of the Carnatic raag, the Hindustani version has a slow, majestic gait. I had not often heard it live maybe because of Hindustani music's time convention for raags, which Carnatic music does not have. This convention, which musicians rarely flout, slots Darbari deep into the night, when all is still and quiet. But the number of late-night programmes had declined in the new millennium perhaps because of a Supreme Court judgement in 2005 banning the use of loudspeakers in public places after 10 p.m. and before 6 a.m. All-night music concerts, common in my youth, had all but disappeared in Mumbai. Further, not many women vocalists, who account for a big proportion of khayal singers in Maharashtra, sing this raag, probably because it has been viewed as a male prerogative. As its name suggests, the raag was directly linked to the darbar, the Mughal court, whose rulers were all male, and was sung in its majlis, an exclusive gathering of male patrons.[2] But this raag might be daunting even for male musicians because of legends about old masters' great renditions.

As Arun-ji plunged into another nom-tom, I began emitting with increasing frequency that characteristic sound that South Indians use to signal appreciation: tch-tch-tch. His music spoke to me from a distant past like a lost treasure, but appearing alone and vulnerable, it also made me sad. Arun-ji himself was far from morose. He had noticeably good chemistry with Vishal, joking with him and giving him considerable air time. Vishal, in turn, gave rousing support to his guru, expressing spontaneous appreciation for his leaps of imagination, echoing his phrases and sometimes expanding on them in a robust voice that was tailor-made for classical music. Towards the end of the nom-tom's last and fastest segment, Arun-ji repeated the final phrase of a sequence in sargam form, i.e., using the names of notes.

'Re Re Sa ni Pa ma Re Sa ni Sa,' he sang. Vishal repeated it. Arun-ji then looked pointedly at Siddhesh Bicholkar, the harmonium player. Betraying the barest puzzlement, the much younger Bicholkar looked up.

'Ha pan rasta ahe,' Arun-ji told him with a playful smile. This is also a way.

Bicholkar naturally deferred to Arun-ji and reproduced the phrase, but his hesitation was understandable: this phrase did not contain either ga or dha, Darbari's two key notes. Yet it sounded right. I, too, was baffled. I made a mental note to ask Arun-ji about it later. He continued singing several passages, finishing each one with the same phrase and then turning towards Bicholkar, who faithfully followed while still looking perplexed. Arun-ji had given his young accompanist an amusing musical riddle in the middle of a concert.

Before every concert, audiences often wonder which raags the performer will present. Once the performer announces the raag, many listeners wait to see which composition he or she will sing.

'ma Pa dha___,' Arun-ji sang in eekar, vocalising with the sound 'ee', before launching into the composition.

'Haz-a-ra-ta Tu ...,' he sang, while the tabla player Praveen Karkare played a flurry of opening beats before starting Tilwada, a sixteen-beat taal. The composition, *Hazrat Turkman* (Hazrat Turkman), is a eulogy to the eponymous thirteenth-century Sufi saint. I had heard Gajananbuwa singing the composition in an online recording, but I had never heard it live. Darbari, a nom-tom *and* a regal composition from the traditional repertoire. I was floating.

Arun-ji filled one avartan—the rhythmic cycle that repeats throughout a rendition—after another with inspired improvisations and arrived on each sam, or first beat of the rhythmic cycle, with razor-sharp crispness, slowly pulling listeners into the heart of Darbari. In addition to the evening's other revelations, it was becoming clear to me that I was listening to a master of rhythm. In some avartans, I even thought that I heard a kathak dancer's ghungroos tinkling. Arun-ji gradually wove in more and more musical matter into each avartan, building up to a climax of taans. Like the increase in tempo, this progression of musical density is an important feature of khayal singing.

I was still digesting the slow composition when he opened the raag rendition's third part: the fast composition, this time his own creation, *More aangan* (My courtyard). Set to the twelve-beat Ektaal, it had a catchy lilt, its appeal enhanced by Karkare's delicate accompaniment. The tune was alluring, but the highlight was Arun-ji's improvisation on sargams. Some purists frown upon the use of sargams in concerts because they are also used as a pedagogical tool. Yet Arun-ji's sargam improvisations had a texture that I had not heard in Hindustani singing. Rhythmic and layered were words that came to mind, but I could not tell how he was achieving those effects.

I had noticed time and again that khayal singers peak right after the interval. Perhaps by then they have adapted to the venue's acoustics and temperature, their voices have warmed up and they have established a rapport with the audience. Where would Arun-ji's concert go from here? I was prepared for an anti-climax. But Arun-ji followed Darbari with a sparkling Kedar. In the first composition, he again showed the potential of sargam improvisation and in the second, he did delicate bol banaav. But my biggest epiphany came in the tarana, a form that, like the nom-tom, uses a group of special syllables, but is set to a taal.[3] Arun-ji improvised relentlessly on the tarana, producing passages with new combinations of the original syllables. I had simply not heard a tarana being presented like this in a live concert. How could such a musician have gone missing in action for all these years? The plot thickened.

For the final piece, in Bhairavi, a raag that often closes a concert, Arun-ji chose another one of his own compositions: the tender and plaintive *Kaahe kinhi mose barajori* (Why are you forcing me?). After he sang the last note, a meditative silence filled the hall for several seconds before applause broke out. As I watched the musician quietly gathering his notebooks, I knew that he was much more than a city institution. Many of us in the audience kept sitting, not wanting to break the spell. Eventually, a few of us got up and gathered around him. I met four more of his students. He seemed to have a loyal coterie around him. I left the venue pondering the mystery of the man, his music and his apparent marginalisation.

For a whole week afterwards, I savoured the concert's after-effects. Combining soulfulness with high energy, Arun-ji's music had a startlingly novel sound, one infused with rhythm. It had an imposing architecture with a variety of finely etched elements. It reminded me of a huge South Indian temple, with its ornate entrance tower containing relief sculptures of different depths: high, low and sunken. Arun-ji's compositions resembled Mughal miniatures, exuding a variety of moods, from playful to plangent.

I tried to look for his music online. I found just a handful of recordings, including renditions of raags Sar Nat and Shree. They did not carry a date, but Arun-ji sounded much younger and the singing was full-throated, including no-holds-barred taan segments that revealed impressive virtuosity. His voice bordered on the aggressive. Was it just me who had somehow missed his performances over the past three decades during which I had been an active concert-goer?

Arun-ji's concert had come about because one of my husband's colleagues, a diehard music lover, had run into the vocalist a month earlier. If Arun-ji's private concert by the sea in downtown Mumbai was a world apart from Rambhau's recital in the green room in the rural hinterland, Ulhas-ji inhabited a different universe from both. He was a fixture on many high-profile stages and a favourite of several wealthy patrons. Less than a year earlier, I had attended a private concert of Ulhas-ji's hosted by Nilima Kilachand, a prominent benefactor in Mumbai. It took place at her palatial mansion—once owned by the maharaja of Patiala—on Napean Sea Road, one of the city's swishest neighbourhoods. But the mainstream, too, had a spectrum. Ulhas-ji was more frequently seen in long-standing festivals and forums dedicated to khayal rather than in gaudy variety shows featuring a clutch of lesser musicians who mixed genres.

Ultimately, the mainstream as a whole was visible. I was, therefore, curious about what was hidden. I wanted to find out more about the musical culture around Arun-ji and why his trajectory had been so different from his youngest brother's. Both were soft-spoken and refined in speech and manner, but their personalities were like chalk and cheese. A year earlier, I had spent a week in Kolkata, where Ulhas-ji lived, interviewing him for a long magazine profile on the occasion of his sixtieth birthday.[4] He eventually opened up, but was instinctively cautious and laconic. Arun-ji appeared to be the polar opposite: spontaneous and loquacious. Given how Arun-ji's career seemed to have gone, I also found his geniality intriguing.

Soon after the concert, I donned my metaphorical detective's hat and embarked on a journey of discovery. Like the intertwining of melody, rhythm and text in khayal, what follows is a three-stranded story of my expedition. In the first strand, I chronicle my adventures in Mumbai's Hindustani music underground as a learner for nearly a decade, interspersed with my perspectives on mainstream Hindustani music and its cast of characters. In the second strand, I tell the tale of one musician's magnificent obsession with his art and describe his innovations, viewed in light of Hindustani music's history. In these two narratives, I include smatterings of musical examples, which I have often visually formatted to convey a pattern. Readers can absorb whatever they can or skip over these portions without any loss of continuity. In the third strand, I offer brief explanations about khayal, one of the world's most exciting vocal genres, not as an expert, but in the spirit of a music lover periodically whispering into the ears of a friend during a concert. Any explanation, however, is likely to be incomplete because khayal is a living idiom whose limits its leading practitioners are constantly testing and pushing outwards. Indeed, this story's three layers capture how this music lives and evolves, through a process in which a musician inflects what appears to be an unchanging idiom while passing it on to the next generation.

When I began my journey, I had already been involved with khayal for more than three decades, as a listener and, intermittently, as a learner. But in the mid-2010s, the genre acquired a significance for me that went beyond its artistic value. As a living testament to the Indian subcontinent's tradition of religious syncretism, it flew in the face of crude and cynical narratives about the past propagated by an ascendant Hindutva, an ethno-majoritarian political project that worried me both as a citizen and journalist. Khayal resembled a beautiful tapestry woven from the warp of Hinduism and the weft of Islam.[5] One could not pull the threads of one culture out without destroying the whole. Khayal also resisted the homogenisation and quick results valued by the dominant global economic orthodoxy of neoliberal capitalism. This music entailed an unhurried unfolding and savouring of ideas and demanded a high degree of improvisation. It accommodated a variety of stylistic approaches and required decades of training to master. Khayal was the ultimate slow music, which, like slow food and slow fashion, represented an alternative way of living. For those who submitted to its lure, it could become both a salve and a salvation.

To start unravelling the ball of tangled mysteries, I had to visit the secret master.

CLUES

> To pursue beauty to its lair.
> To never simplify what is complicated
> or complicate what is simple.
> To respect strength, never power.
> — Arundhati Roy

3

◇ Fakir

ON A WEEKDAY MORNING A FORTNIGHT AFTER THE CONCERT, I took a train to Mulund, where Arun-ji lived, at a walking distance from the station. I had never visited this locality, Mumbai's northernmost one in the east, as far-flung as possible from my home on the city's southern tip. I planned to sit in on Arun-ji's master classes for about a month and interview him for a newspaper profile. He held these classes three times a week, from 10 a.m. to noon, attended by students at the intermediate level all the way to professionals. At Mulund railway station, I took the eastern exit: Mumbai's three railway lines cleave all localities they pass through into eastern and western parts.

I stepped into a long, busy street, where women of all ages and a few elderly men were buying vegetables from footpath vendors. A couple of stalls displayed greens that I'd never seen in South Mumbai's markets. I passed old-fashioned family-owned grocery stores, a couple of modern supermarkets, pharmacists, hardware stores, a shop dedicated to lingerie, a cavernous Udupi restaurant and a snack shop where customers were inspecting fresh dhoklas, kachoris and samosas heaped on trays set on a glass-topped counter. I spotted a Bata shoe outlet, but did not see retailers for other big international brands. The commercial landscape here suggested a more subdued gentrification than what had steamrolled other parts of the city in the decades following India's embrace of a market economy in 1991.

At the end of this street, I turned left into a wide avenue called Ninety Feet Road. Passing a shed housing the local Shiv Sena branch, I turned right into a quiet, leafy lane. With fewer high-rise buildings and cars as well as more open footpaths and pedestrians than many localities, Mulund East had managed partly to retain the feel of a calm, cohesive neighbourhood. I did not see the same frenzy of vehicles clogging the streets and hodge-podge of shops encroaching the footpaths like in many other areas. A hundred metres into the lane, on the right, I saw a nameplate hanging from the grill of a window on the ground floor of a three-storey building: 'Arun Kashalkar' it said in Devanagari, but used the special Marathi letter for the retroflex 'l' in his last name. I walked further down the road and rounded the gate to his flat.

I began to get mild jitters. Why? He had come across as particularly down-to-earth in a field that encouraged cults of personality. I had also been comforted by the fact that he spoke fluent English, the language in which I was most at ease. Several pairs of slippers and sandals lay in a heap outside his door, which was ajar. I heard the sound of a tanpura. I peered in and stood tentatively outside. Arun-ji was sitting on the floor facing the door, with his back against the far, short side of an oblong living room. After the glare outside, the room appeared dim and felt cool. Several people were seated in a half-ellipse around him. I saw a tableau, of a sage in his cave with his disciples.

'Welcome!' the sage called out brightly.

I stepped in.

As I set up my laptop next to Arun-ji, he introduced me to his students. Among them was Bhavik, whom I had met before the concert. He was the one who had uploaded the few recordings of Arun-ji's that I had found online.

'We're doing Bihagada today,' Arun-ji said.

He began singing the canonical slow composition *Pyare pag hol* (My dear, tread softly), in Teentaal. Arun-ji was streaming the iTabla app's tanpura and tabla through a Bose speaker. Bihagada, a variation of the more common Bihag, was rendered by vocalists of many styles, but the Jaipur gharana's interpretation of it had become particularly influential. I had not learnt this raag and melted into the background. When I had arrived, a bit past 10 a.m., I had counted seven students, but people continued to trickle in over the next hour, by the end of which the number of students had doubled. They were of all ages. I felt anxious merely imagining how it would be to sing here. I wondered how Arun-ji managed such a large and disparate group.

For the first five minutes, Arun-ji sang the composition several times.[1] After that, each student got a turn to try. After each student's attempt, Arun-ji sang, switching between the roles of teacher and performer. For the next half an hour or so, students attempted to reproduce the composition's tune. A few of them then tried to improvise on it, while the rest continued to sing the basic tune. Arun-ji calibrated a student's airtime to his or her ability, but gave even the more fluent ones not more than about five minutes in each round. One student said that she wished to merely listen for a few rounds. Skipping a turn seemed to be an honourable option.

Arun-ji regularly intervened to correct students. If they had managed to improvise, he showed them how to advance their elaborations. He spoke in Marathi to most students, switching to Hindi for a couple and English for one.

'I don't know Bihagada,' one female student said in Marathi.

'You know Bihag, right?' Arun-ji answered. 'For a start, sing Bihag without the sharp Ma, then add Ga ma ni__ Dha_ Pa_ . Keep singing the composition and you will gradually begin to get a feel for the other twists from Bihag. A composition that has stood the test of time will give you an outline of the raag.'

To a young man who began hesitating after singing a few avartans, he asked: 'You've exhausted your stock?'

Everyone laughed.

'Some musicians say that we should stick to Ga-ma-Pa Ga____ Sa____ in Bihagada and avoid the phrase Ga-ma-Pa ma-Pa__ Ga____ Sa____ because it appears in Savani,' Bhavik said in Hindi.

The only difference between the two phrases is the ma-Pa___ in the second phrase after the initial Ga-ma-Pa.

'Ga-ma-Pa ma-Pa___ Ga___ Sa___ is indeed a typical Savani phrase, but one can also use it in Bihagada because …' Arun-ji replied and launched into an explanation about what were two unknown entities to me, for I had not learnt Savani either.

Arun-ji sang to illustrate his explanation.

'Wah!' Bhavik exclaimed.

Such fine distinctions, I knew, contributed to creating a raag's ambience. I decided to later ask Arun-ji about this nuance, along with his use of the non-standard Darbari phrase at the concert. What also struck me was that Bhavik felt free to offer his opinion. In a traditional learning environment presided over by a Great Man, disciples are expected only to follow instructions, not to ask questions.

After more than an hour of going around, Arun-ji began singing taans.

'These are off-beat patterns, like Nivruttibuwa's,' he said. 'After one sings them, the challenge is to end on a beat and land smoothly on the sam.'

These offbeat patterns were evidently a favourite of his. The class was turning out to be as much of a revelation as the concert. I knew enough to grasp the lesson's high musical level and impressive scale in terms of size and diversity. While surgically examining his students' attempts and losing himself in his improvisations, Arun-ji managed to evoke a festive atmosphere. At 11:30 a.m., his wife, stocky, with her white hair tied in a bun, appeared in the room for the first time, carrying a tray with mini cups of steaming tea.

'This is the cup without sugar,' she said to an elderly student sitting on the sofa, pointing to it on the tray.

She then handed the tray to a student, went inside and returned with a cup of coffee for someone else and a large plate of kothimbir vadi. Bespoke beverages and a snack! The class was beginning to feel like a family gathering. After this five-minute refreshment break,

Arun-ji moved to a fast composition in Bihagada, his own, *Kaise aaun piya mein tore paas* (How do I come to you, my love?). Those who knew the composition sang it together several times. After that, Arun-ji got students to take turns improvising.

'What is the notation of what you just sang?' he asked a student who had attempted an aakaar taan. 'Your notes are blurring into one another. Sing it first in sargam form. You should know the spelling of what you are singing.'

People laughed. After several rounds, everyone sang the composition together one last time. At noon, Arun-ji brought the class to an end.

'It is time for all of you to go back to your piyas,' he said.

Everyone again laughed, recognising his reference to his own composition, the one they had all been singing.

⁂

A few students lingered. Ketaki, one of the best singers that day, wanted advice about what to present for an upcoming music competition. As I waited for Arun-ji to get free, I looked around the room. On the wall to the right of him hung a photo of Gajananbuwa. On another wall hung two photos of Arun-ji and his wife, taken, it appeared, when they were about a decade younger. In one, it appears as though she is laughing at a joke that he has just cracked. In the other, he has his arm around her and both are smiling broadly. I found this public display of affection unusual for a middle-class Indian of Arun-ji's generation. In that photo, too, he looks unusually fair, but has some brown patches on his face. I assumed that he had sustained a skin condition of some kind, perhaps leucoderma.

After the last student had left, Arun-ji's wife came in to the living room with two plates of lunch. He and I continued to sit on the floor, while she sat on the armchair sofa close by.

'I have a problem with my knees,' she explained.

The meal she had made consisted of the usual daily fare—dal, sabzi and roti. But like her husband's music, the dishes felt fresh and their flavours subtle, a sign that she took pride in her cooking. I was brimming with questions, but I knew that it would take me time to penetrate the enigma of his art and his life. I began by asking him about what I thought was the central conundrum.

'I have been listening to music for years in Mumbai,' I said. 'Why haven't I heard you before?'

'While learning from my gurus, I performed for many years,' he replied in English. 'I thought this would continue. It did not occur to me that after my training there was no straight line to a full-fledged performing career. It is not that I did not want concerts, but I did not know that I had to make a special effort to get them. I am from an older generation, where such things were not expected of artists. I didn't struggle financially: we had enough for two square meals. I did suffer mentally though. I knew that I had trained for decades under great gurus and, deep down, this must have troubled me. Others should not go through what I did. But after a certain age and stage, I felt that it was not dignified to approach organisers.'

He paused.

'Instead, I have kept singing in my home—for people who understand classical music and love it deeply. The atmosphere is friendly and lively. I also perform whenever people invite me. I have never bothered about the money.'

His wife shook her head as if to say, 'Don't I know that.'

An intent observer, she made her presence felt, but unlike her husband, she was not a conversationalist.

'My gurus did not advertise themselves or try to network with influential people,' Arun-ji continued, pointing to Gajananbuwa's photo.

His eyes dilated, making his gaze intense.

'I have no regrets,' he continued. 'I have never stopped investing in my music. My search has been artistic, like that of my gurus.'

The obvious next question was: why had concert organisers not approached him?

'You should ask them,' he replied, smiling once again.

He presented me a copy of *Swar Archana*, his book and CD of about 150 compositions.

'I'd like to hear more about your life and musical journey,' I told him.

'You can ask me anything,' he replied. 'I have nothing to hide.'

That gave me the opening I was looking for. As I packed my belongings, his wife got a video call from their son in Singapore. The son's infant daughter came into the frame.

'Hello, Nisa, ch-ch-ch,' Arun-ji's wife clucked.

On that day, as I took the long and winding road back home, I was charmed once again by Arun-ji's humble demeanour and openness, his wife's quiet hospitality and their simple lifestyle but meaningful life. Together, they were running an informal gurukul, a tradition of passing on knowledge in which students become part of the teacher's household. I felt lucky to have made my way to it.

Later, I realised that on the first day I had learnt everyone's name in class, but not his wife's. As a feminist, I was uneasy about thinking of her just as the patriarch's wife. In many ways, Arun-ji was unconventional, but some aspects of his household were also traditional.

A month later, I heard Arun-ji again, at the home of a couple who lived in his locality. About two dozen listeners, including several of Arun-ji's students, sat on the floor of the living room. A student opened the evening with a tarana, as a sort of appetiser. As Arun-ji then started singing, a couple whom I knew, Devina Dutt and Pepe Gomes, walked in. They had recently founded First Edition Arts, a start-up for promoting classical music. Devina had been a journalist in my cohort and Pepe a rock musician and an ad filmmaker. They had not heard of Arun-ji.

In this intimate gathering, he seemed at ease right from the start. Supported by a long-time student, Mandaar, he sang raag Maru Bihag, presenting a nom-tom, the slow composition *Pari mori naav* (My boat has capsized),[2] and his own fast one, *Jai bajrang* (Victory to Hanuman), another eminently catchy tune dedicated to the eponymous monkey god, who rarely features in khayal compositions. Arun-ji's improvisations flowed effortlessly and apparently inexhaustibly. But I saw that one of his strengths was a highly developed sense of proportion. He never belaboured a point, moving on well before the listener became sated. In this way, he made the elaboration so engrossing that I realised only at the end that he had sung for nearly an hour. He concluded with Bhairavi, singing *Mahadev*, a meditative ode to Shiva that he had composed. His students joined in, creating an intense ambience.

In this intimate setting, the music had an even more profound effect on me. I had never heard a Maru Bihag rendition at once so mellifluous and lively. I still could not digest the fact that such wonderful music was being made in a home hidden away in the outer reaches of Hindustani music's longtime capital, unknown to the majority of its aficionados.

The hosts served snacks, and I mingled with the guests. I had long admired Maharashtra's literary, theatrical and musical traditions, but this milieu of mostly Marathi speakers was new to me, an instance of how Mumbai contained many subcultures. Until then, I had moved in cosmopolitan and linguistically heterogeneous circles where the lingua franca was English. In my English-medium school, Hindi was the second language and, for the third language, I learnt Sanskrit for a few years and then French. I later learnt the state language for two years at the Mumbai Marathi Sahitya Sangh and on the job as a journalist.

Finally, Devina, Pepe and I trooped back with Arun-ji to his home, where Devina plied him with the same questions that had dogged me.

'I consider myself a music lover,' she said. 'Why haven't I heard you before?'

Arun-ji explained to her that he had performed regularly at home for anyone who wanted to drop in and had gone wherever people invited him.

'When I was learning from him,' he said, looking up at Gajananbuwa's photo, which, by then, I had seen him doing several times, 'upcoming singers' reputations spread by word of mouth. Music circles asked prominent gurus to recommend promising students. Initially, I did get several opportunities. Yet, even in my forties, I did not break into the big league. But I am content. Over the years, I have gathered at least two hundred listeners who appreciate my music. I sing for them.'

The conversation wound down past 11 p.m.

'I'd like to present you a few times,' Devina told Arun-ji.

The music had apparently stirred her too.

'As you wish,' he replied.

After we left his home, Devina looked at me and said, 'What a fakir.'

Arun-ji may have transcended worldly goals, but we felt that his absence from the wider music scene was a loss to listeners like us, who would have savoured his music's freshness and beauty.

'His music has a molten quality,' Devina told me a week later. 'I thought, here is someone who takes me past blandness into a journey of discovery. I was very grateful for that.'

Arun-ji's physical location far away from Mumbai's centre mirrored his relegation to the margins of the city's concert scene. But the secrecy surrounding him had a whiff of romance and his life story a hint of heroism. Tucked away in a quiet suburb, far from centres of pelf and power, Arun-ji was relentlessly exploring khayal's full potential with undimmed curiosity and conveying his excitement to others. His music, jazzy and full of verve, was anything but placid.

◈ Storm: 1970

ON A HOT MORNING, ARUN, TWENTY-SEVEN YEARS OLD, LAY curled in bed, drifting between sleep and wakefulness when an idea wafted into his head. He let it float there for a minute, then sat up, both elated and frightened. An hour later, he was riding a train to downtown Bombay from his home outside the city limits. Lulled by the train's steady rhythm, Arun went over all that had happened to him in the previous month. He had lost his job at National Machinery Manufacturers. He had been forced to move from Dombivli, a town north-east of Bombay, further out of the city, to Ulhasnagar because housing rents were lower there. His job recruiting workers, although humdrum, had provided a steady income that supported his ambitions of making a mark as a khayal singer in Bombay, the art form's epicentre.

'There's a positive side to this,' he had thought. 'I can earn a living by teaching music, working in Marathi musicals and giving khayal performances.'

He had been teaching music since he was a teenager. That very day, he was headed to the home of one of his students. He had also acted in several Marathi musicals and had been performing khayal since he was a pre-teen. For the past five years, he had been training under a master khayal singer.

'My income might go up and down, but I will be immersed in music all my waking hours,' he had told his sweetheart, Sayli.[3]

'That's true,' she had said.

The couple had felt it was time to get her parents' consent to marry. Right from the start, her father had been ambivalent about the liaison but had not outright discouraged it. When she had broached the subject with him, he had grilled her about Arun's educational and family background. She had given him the details.

'That's fine,' he had replied. 'Where does Arun work?'

'He doesn't have a job,' Sayli had replied. 'He wants to make a living from music.'

The answer had dropped like a stone. She had been taken aback by her father's strident silence. Wasn't he a music lover?

'What will he earn?' he had finally asked, to which Sayli had found no answer.

She had tearfully narrated the episode to Arun, admitting that in the end her father was averse to her marrying a full-time musician.

'He thinks that it's a risky career,' she had said.

Arun had waited for her to add that she would either reason with or defy him, but she had said nothing more. How easily she had caved in! Arun had poured his anguish into poetry.

> When words evanesce, the story does too
> And nothing of our love is left behind.
>
> Two minds were woven each to each
> With memory's flowers twined in the breach
> Purified, they slipped from our reach.
>
> Spring blossomed in our touch
> The scents of flowers spread everywhere
> Today, all that is desolate.
>
> Even the histories of those bonds are gone.
> Why does my mind reach into the past?
> Those quivering lips are shrivelled now.[4]

Arun realised just how low a musician's stock was in his social milieu's marriage market, even among lovers of art. Then had landed the coup de grâce.

'I plan to suspend classes for the rest of the year,' his beloved guru, Gajananbuwa, had told his students. 'I am suffering from high blood pressure and need rest. But you can come a couple of times a week to listen to me sing.'

His guru was offering a flower bed after barricading his lush garden, serving a snack in the place of a sumptuous repast.

'Why now, when I have just begun inhabiting his style?' Arun had thought.

The train rumbled on. Arun looked gloomily out of the window. He smelt rain on a light breeze, which momentarily relieved the smouldering heat of May. Was it a sign? Of what?

'What are you brooding about?' asked a man sitting next to him.

Startled, Arun turned to him. He looked familiar. Until a couple of years ago, the two of them had often caught the morning train together at Dombivli and chatted on the way to downtown Bombay, where they worked. The man must have got on the train when Arun was replaying the unfortunate events of the previous month in his mind for the umpteenth time.

'I am going to give up music,' Arun abruptly replied, surprised that he had so starkly articulated his hazy early morning rumination.

'Why?' asked the man, almost shouting.

Arun could not bring himself to explain. Because of music, he had looked for minimally demanding jobs. Now he could cast his net wider. Because of music, he had lost Sayli. His marriage prospects would surely improve. The man remained silent for several seconds.

'What else will you do?' he finally asked.

Arun knew that he would find a job. But as a lover of poetry, he heard the subtext. Will you turn your back on all those years that you invested in music? What will give you meaning in life?

From the age of five, Arun's life had revolved around music. Without it, he would be like Bombay without the sea, bereft of the life force that had sculpted the shape of his being. Yes. What else would he do?

◆ Alchemy

LIKE ALCHEMISTS OF YORE, KHAYAL SINGERS ARE ON AN eternal quest to make miraculous transformations. Just as alchemists sought to produce gold and silver from base metals like lead and copper, khayal singers strive to create hours of scintillating music from a small core of composed material. Unlike alchemists, they mostly succeed. Moreover, khayal singers work their magic not tucked away in a lab, but in public, and on the spur of the moment. Khayal's very name, which means idea, thought or imagination, boldly proclaims its artistic ambition.

Khayal is one of three Indian art music genres that focus on improvising within a raag. The other two are dhrupad and Carnatic music. Khayal and the older dhrupad have roots in North India and are together called Hindustani classical vocal music. Carnatic music originated in South India and does not have sub-genres. I use the label 'classical' to describe such raag music.[5] Khayal uses a core of about a hundred raags. The broader category of Hindustani vocal music, without the 'classical' label, includes thumri and allied genres, which use a small subset of raags and aesthetically break raag grammar. For this reason, they are considered semi-classical genres. Hindustani and Carnatic music have instrumental branches as well.

To become a khayal singer, a person must become tuneful and fluent in numerous raags, gain control over several taals, be able to present different compositional forms and employ several improvisation techniques. Singers across gharanas share a core set of raags, taals, compositional forms and improvisation methods. Beyond that, their repertoires in all these categories depend on the traditions in which they have trained. Across styles, singers use a composition a few minutes long as the kernel from which to improvise within a raag for up to an hour. A khayal singer can thus create fresh music even when starting from the same composition each time, enabling listeners to be surprised by the unfamiliar within the familiar.

A person needs to train for years to become an alchemist who can make these seemingly magical transformations.

'Every khayal musician attempts to achieve flow while improvising. When a musician produces ideas that have a forward momentum, he creates a feeling of flow. Flow is what you see in a river. Its moving water might encounter natural obstructions, like a boulder, but finds a way around it. Similarly, a musician might even stall, but should find a way to continue smoothly. Flow partly reflects a singer's control over rhythm. Without flow, a rendition sounds like a patchwork. Every style has mediocre musicians who produce such patchwork.' —AK

4

◇ Verdict

AFTER VISITING ARUN-JI A FEW MORE TIMES, I WAS SUDDENLY nagged by doubt: was he really a hidden gem? I may not have heard him, but I had not gone to concerts for long stretches. I may have liked his music, but who was I to judge? I felt it was time to get comments from knowledgeable people who had heard his music. But the most visible commentators on the Hindustani scene in Mumbai had not heard him. I finally struck lucky with an old colleague, Vithal Nadkarni, a former science journalist and seasoned listener of Hindustani music. He had heard Arun-ji for decades.

'He's monumentally good,' Vithal said. 'He's got the aesthetic vision and the technical chops to back it.'

'Then why has he been so elusive?' I asked.

'There are barriers to excellence,' Vithal replied. 'We have all had a hand in spreading mediocrity. The terrible thing about this music is that it demands so much not just of performers, but also of listeners. Yet Arun-ji has persevered with his thing and hasn't lost heart. He's one of the sanest people I know. I respect him very much.'

I found two connoisseurs outside Mumbai who confirmed Vithal's opinion. They had listened to thousands of hours of khayal in a variety of styles and had a long track record of quiet service in the field. The first was Amlan Das Gupta, a former professor of English literature at Jadavpur University in Kolkata and a scholar of Hindustani classical music who had built an excellent archive of music at his institution. He was a tabla player and a diehard fan of Mallikarjun Mansur. Amlan-da had heard only the few renditions of Arun-ji's that were online, so I sent him a recording of the January concert.

'His raag renditions are extremely thoughtful,' Amlan-da replied via email. 'They are very compact. He has an economy of style and avoids excess and repetition. He is very discerning in his choice of bandishes. Technically all around, he appears to be very strong. He must have worked hard on developing his Agra gayaki because he sings the nom-tom aalaap, which not all singers from this gharana do.'

'It's sad,' Amlan-da added, referring to Arun-ji's absence from the mainstream concert scene.

The other person was Chandra, a passionate music archivist with a state-of-the-art studio in Pune who wanted me to use just his first name. He had built the studio on principles that he believed created the ideal acoustic environment for Indian classical music—a far cry, he said, from most performance spaces in the country, which were designed for visual spectacles. The studio replicated many aspects of stone temples and palaces, in which Indian classical music evolved and flourished.[1] Chandra had been close to the vocalist Bhimsen Joshi, but over the years had recorded a wide variety of musicians at his studio, including Arun-ji. I had a long conversation with him over the phone.

'Arun Kaka is a phenomenal musician,' Chandra told me. 'He has taken the essence of multiple styles, synthesised them and made them his own. The Agra-Gwalior-Jaipur combination in his taans is amazing. His approach of embedding the raag swaroop in the laykari is also amazing. For him, laykari is not something you do once in a while; it's part of the melodic structure. His laykari is brilliant, at a level of mastery that's beyond most singers. His repertoire is enormous and he composes brilliantly. He has given his life to mastering the khayal form.'

At that point, I could only intuitively grasp what Chandra meant by Arun-ji 'embedding the raag swaroop in the laykari', just as I could only sense that the vocalist's sargam style was original but could not say why.

'Then why has he been virtually invisible?' I asked.

'Much of the intended audience has not spent the time and resources developing its sensibilities,' Chandra replied. 'Ordinary folks have very little time to search for what is the best. Folks with money go for the branded artists, good or not, no matter by what means they have developed their brands—via film music, garish video performances and so on. Once they get the limelight, often anything goes. It's also the era of mass consumption of standardised products. Even tomatoes have to look uniform. You can get away with consistently delivering packaged fare that's just about good enough, but you can't have down days even if you are brilliant most of the time.'

'So Arun-ji has down days?' I asked.

'Well, he is sensitive to the canvas he paints on,' Chandra replied. 'These large-format programmes do not suit his nuanced and delicate presentations. You have to have the ear to hear the detailing of his style. How can you serve gourmet food in a buffet for a thousand people?'

Like most listeners, these connoisseurs had their favourites, but I respected them for evaluating Arun-ji's music on its merits.[2]

I also asked them about his voice. Until his late forties, Arun-ji's voice had been intensely sweet, Vithal told me. In the next phase, as a result of his Agra gharana training, it had become broad and powerful, as evident in the online recordings. Subsequently, a little roughness might have crept in as he tried to integrate styles, Chandra said. In addition to all the other threads in the mystery, I would have to follow this one too.

These verdicts also served a practical purpose. For five years, I had been learning from Asavari Phadke, a singer about ten years younger than me with impeccable antecedents harking back to Mogubai Kurdikar, mother and guru of the celebrated vocalist Kishori Amonkar, known as Kishori-tai in the music world. In this period, I had a full-time job, so I had just a weekly one-hour solo lesson with Asavari-ji on Saturday morning. But a few months before Arun-ji's January concert, I had begun freelancing because I wanted to scale up my music training and spend more time with my son and daughter, twins who were soon likely to leave home for college. After a long break, I had started attending concerts every week, but yearned for a community of music lovers. The sudden appearance of a secret master presenting music that appealed to my tastes and who had a large band of students was, therefore, like a rare alignment of stars in the night sky. I nervously told Asavari-ji that I wanted to learn from Arun-ji. Gentle and generous, she made it easy for me.

'Yes, sure,' she said without hesitation, even adding that one of her neighbours was his student.

By then I had learnt that Arun-ji had taught more than three hundred people over the past three decades. How in the world had he remained a secret, I wondered anew. Among his students was Madhavi, who had accompanied him to the January concert. She and her husband, Yogesh, who were around my age, lived near Arun-ji.

'A few years ago, Madhavi and I drove from Mumbai to Kolhapur with Arun Kaka,' Yogesh told me. 'We listened to Gajananbuwa and Vilayat Hussain the whole way. It was such fun.'

He was referring to the Agra gharana maestro Vilayat Hussain Khan. A more kindred group of music aficionados I would have been hard-pressed to find. The evolutionary psychologist Robin Dunbar lists a shared taste in music as one of seven attributes that foster friendships between people.[3] When that music represents what one might call a difficult pleasure, this sense of kinship can be strong. I decided to learn from Arun-ji for two years and then, depending upon my work commitments, take a call on whether to continue.

I felt like I had been building up for years to learn from him. Growing up in Mumbai, I had learnt various performing arts in fits and starts, the lack of continuity being a result of my parent's moves and what was locally available. From the time I was a toddler to the time I left home for college, hardly a day went by when my father did not sing Carnatic music, which is seeped in rhythm. He taught me, but instead of practising, I played langadi and climbed trees. He let me be. Starting at age seven, I learnt bharatanatyam for about three years, during which one of my teachers remarked on my flair for rhythm. My family then moved to the US for two years, when I took free optional lessons in Western classical violin that my school offered.

By the time we returned to Mumbai, the dance school's branch where I had learnt bharatanatyam had shut. By then, my younger sister had begun learning Carnatic vocal music from a local teacher, and later trained with some well-known musicians. When I was thirteen, I began learning to play the Hindustani flute after being mesmerised by an LP of Pannalal Ghosh in my parents' collection. My teacher, Ronu Majumdar, was just out of his teens at the time and went on to become a celebrated flautist. After two years, when Ronu-ji began focusing on his performing career, I learnt for two more years from Ghanshyam Vyas, a student of the stalwart Hariprasad Chaurasia. For college, I went to the US, where I began taking lessons with a Kirana gharana singer, Kalpana Mazumdar, but gave up after a few months because travelling to her place was arduous.

On returning to India, I could not find a flute teacher, so I shifted once and for all to vocal music, learning first from Namdeo Panchal and then Asavari-ji. Panchal-ji had learnt from several gurus: the Agra-Khurja gharana's Azmat Hussain Khan, the Delhi gharana's Inayat Khan and the Gwalior gharana's Ramakrishnabuwa Joshi. He was a generous teacher but did not have a fleshed-out pedagogy, especially to teach taal. He came from a working-class background, managing to learn because of his passion and his gurus' generosity. His sur was wonderful and he had a taste for high-brow khayal. He was the one who introduced me to Gajananbuwa and Vilayat Hussain Khan.

All along, I kept working as a journalist, which meant late hours, six-day working weeks and almost no holidays, so I practised in snatches—and dreamt. In my late twenties, I fantasised about begging Kishori-tai to teach me. I was not remotely at a level where she would have considered it, so this was sheer navel-gazing. By my late thirties, I had become a fan of Ulhas-ji's, to whose music Panchal-ji had introduced me. I occasionally dreamt about becoming Ulhas-ji's student, an equally outlandish proposition because by then I had twins and a demanding but fulfilling job. Fantasising, after all, is pleasurable because it allows us to transcend reality. In my late forties, when the opportunity to learn from a master came my way, I felt that I could not let it go.

Two months after my first visit to Arun-ji's home, I began schlepping one-and-a-half hours each way to his morning masterclasses. In his eyes, my learning had begun the very first time I visited him. 'Listening is half of learning,' he said. 'If someone with no background but with a musical ear regularly sits in my class for five years without producing a single note, by the end, that person will begin singing.' When I asked him what he meant by 'singing', because many people can sing, at least after a fashion, he said that he was referring to presenting khayal with some improvisation. This sounded like an audacious claim. But, because I had heard on the student grapevine of dramatic transformations in his class, I reserved judgement.

In one lesson, Guruji, as 'Arun-ji' had now become, again took up raag Bihagada. Like other students, I also began calling his wife Kaku, or aunt. After the usual tea break, instead of moving to a fast composition in the same raag, he switched to Sughrai.

'Bhavik, sing *Kaho mero man* (Heed what I am saying),' he said, referring to one of Vilayat Hussain Khan's fast compositions in Teentaal.

Bhavik was a storehouse of compositions, because of which he had earned the nickname Bhatkhande, after V.N. Bhatkhande, a musicologist active at the turn of the twentieth century who had collected compositions from hereditary musicians and compiled them in a series of books. After Bhavik finished singing the composition several times, Guruji improvised. Ketaki quickly picked up key phrases and pulled off a few rounds. Most others decided to sit this one out.

Shortly, a former student who had switched to learning dhrupad, dropped in.

'Sing something you know,' Guruji said.

The former student began singing *Tu kartar* (You are the maker), in raag Bhairav, set to the ten-beat Sooltaal, used in dhrupad. Bhavik and Ketaki quickly picked up the tune and chimed in.

'Never a dull moment,' I thought.

The next week, I arrived in class to find that Guruji had begun Nat Bihag, another complicated Bihag variety, with a slow composition set to the sixteen-beat Teentaal. I was recording all the lessons, so I tried to learn the composition at home. But in the next class, Guruji began singing the same composition in the twelve-beat Ektaal. A few students caught on at once, but I struggled, missing the sam several times, because the avartan, or rhythmic cycle, now had four fewer beats. Despite my alleged childhood aptitude for rhythm, I was not able to adjust the first verse on the spot to fit the new taal.

A few days later, Vishal, the student who had given Guruji vocal support in the January concert, arrived from Pune, where he lived. Guruji continued with Nat Bihag but dispensed with the electronic tabla because Vishal was playing the dagga, the bass drum in the pair that makes up the tabla. The other member of the pair is the treble drum, also called the tabla. One can play only bare-bones versions of taals on the dagga, but in the era before electronic tablas, vocal students learnt to keep time on this bass drum so that they did not have to depend upon a tabla player to accompany them while practising. Even after high-quality electronic tablas became available, many students learnt to play the dagga to enhance their rhythmic control. I have heard of musicians playing the tanpura with one hand and the dagga with the other during their riyaaz.

It takes a while for students to figure out how to follow live accompaniment even in this pared-down form because most of them use electronic tablas both in class and while practising. The best electronic tablas produce only a fixed number of variations of each taal, but tabla players dynamically vary their strokes.[4] Therefore, a singer cannot assume that each beat will sound exactly the way it did in the previous cycle or even that the time intervals between two successive beats in a cycle will be precisely the same. Scholars have measured these intervals and they do in fact vary.[5] But percussionists must also follow the singer: it is an essential part of the skill of accompaniment. Thus, both parties must be alert to each other as they move through each avartan and attempt to arrive on the sam at the same split second, like a pair of people running a three-legged race and breasting the tape together.

I had not practised much with live accompaniment, so I strained to follow Vishal. More fundamentally, I could barely believe that I was sitting in the same class as him. The phrase 'scaling up my training' took on a new meaning.

A few weeks later, I stayed back to interview Guruji, and another student decided to listen in. Kaku, whose name I learnt was Dhanashree, was visiting her sister in Nashik, a city north of Mumbai. But Guruji nevertheless invited us to join him for lunch.

'Jyoti will be coming as usual,' he said, referring to the thirty-something house help, who walked in a little after noon.

'You look tired,' Guruji, sitting in his usual spot on the floor, told her.

'I queued up all night to enter Siddhivinayak Temple in the morning,' she replied, standing to his right.

It was a Tuesday, when the famous temple dedicated to Lord Ganesh in central Mumbai opened at about 3 a.m., two hours earlier than usual. Guruji and Jyoti continued chatting about how often she went to the temple, whom she usually went with and so on. Then, tired of standing, Jyoti sat down on the armchair sofa to Guruji's right and continued talking. I did a double take, but my phone pinged just then, so I tuned out to read the message. I perked up again when I heard Jyoti saying, 'I will prove that you are wrong.'

To which Guruji laughed and replied, 'Then I will admit defeat.'

I had not paid attention to what they had been sparring about, but I had noticed the ease in their interaction.

'In which Indian household would a male employer sit on the floor and chat with a much younger house help sitting on the sofa?' I thought.

Of course, there was an implicit power equation, for when she finally got up, Guruji told her to make three bhakris. But even as a surface interaction, I found the exchange striking.

◈ Sea: 1965–68

ARUN'S TRAIN PULLED INTO DOMBIVLI STATION. HE squeezed himself and his suitcase past a group of men standing at the entrance of his carriage and got off, only to find himself pressed into another horde, moving in the opposite direction, trying to get on to the train. Tall and slender, he struggled against the tide of people, a couple of whom cursed him for blocking their way. Extricating himself from the throng, he looked around the platform. People everywhere.

It was peak commuting time in the morning, when trains ferried office-goers from Bombay's northern suburbs and beyond to office districts in the southern-most part of the long, narrow peninsular city, protruding into the Arabian Sea like a finger. Earlier that morning, he had arrived at a long-distance rail terminus from Nagpur, in eastern Maharashtra, and switched to a local train to get to Dombivli.

It was July 1965. Five years earlier, after a fierce agitation, Bombay had become the capital of the new state of Maharashtra. But it was now politically a relatively peaceful time. The weather, however, was stormy. The south-west monsoon was in full swing. It was not raining, but the air hung heavy with moisture and a charcoal sky glowered. Standing on the railway platform in a crumpled kurta, Arun felt a wave of despondency wash over him.

'This ocean of humanity is Bombay,' he thought. 'But I don't know a single soul. I am like a thirsty man at sea, surrounded by water that I cannot drink.'

Arun had moved to the city on the advice of an older colleague in the Nagpur office of All India Radio, the public broadcaster where he had been working. He had applied to a few positions in Bombay, finally receiving an interview call for an entry-level position as a clerk at the accountant-general's office, which audited the accounts of various government projects. Arun had travelled to Bombay for the first time, without a clue about his chances of getting the job. What did he have to lose except the railway fare?

'Your certificates show that you are a classical musician,' the interviewer, a Tamilian, had said, leafing through Arun's application. 'Is that why you have come here?'

Arun had a BA with distinction in music and a Sangeet Alankar, the equivalent of a master's degree in music granted by the Gandharva Mahavidyalaya.

'Yes,' Arun had said without hesitation.

Fortunately, the man had viewed this favourably.

'Very good,' he had said. 'I will give you the job on one condition. The office teems with union activity. You should not get involved in any of it. Focus on your work. Your salary will be about two hundred rupees a month.'

'He's probably a music lover,' Arun had thought with relief, before realising that his income would be barely enough to get by. Still, it would give him a footing in Bombay. Arun had returned to Nagpur to pack up his belongings. Another acquaintance had arranged for him to stay as a paying guest in the eastern part of Dombivli, a quiet town with a majority of middle-class Marathi speakers. That morning, Arun headed to his new lodgings to begin his life in Bombay.

Arun stood hesitantly at the doorway of a room on the ground floor of a chawl.

'Come in,' a woman greeted him, ushering him through the kitchen into the only other room, pointing to a corner where he could store his suitcase. Arun was taken aback by how small the place was. But even as early as the 1960s, Bombay had become notorious for its inflated real estate prices and small living spaces. At night, Arun slept on a single cot along with the landlady's son. She, her husband and two daughters slept on mattresses on the floor in the same room. Squashed in with a stranger, Arun could not sleep. When he rose to use the chawl's communal toilet, he nearly stepped on one of the sleeping bodies.

The next morning, he woke up exhausted and disoriented. Where was he? He heard the chatter of children and smelt roasted garlic and onions. Bombay! Soon he was on a train from Dombivli to Victoria Terminus, or VT, the last stop in downtown Bombay on one of the commuter railway lines. He had been pushed into the train by the same human current that he had defied the previous morning. As the train approached VT station, Arun estimated that he would be spending nearly four hours commuting each day.

At the office, a senior colleague desultorily explained to him the nitty-gritty of his job. After lunch, left to his own devices, Arun began wondering how to initiate his music training. His supervisor in Nagpur had given him a letter of introduction to Chidanand Nagarkar, an Agra gharana singer. A few months earlier, Arun had also been introduced to Gajananbuwa, a Gwalior gharana singer and violinist, when the musician had visited the All India Radio office in Nagpur in his capacity as adviser to the public broadcaster.

'Arun is learning from Rajabhau Kogje,' Arun's colleague had told Gajananbuwa, referring to a khayal and thumri singer who lived in Nagpur.

'If you are ever in Bombay, come and see me,' Gajananbuwa had told Arun on his way out, giving the young man his address. Arun had not paid much attention then, but he now realised that Gajananbuwa, too, lived in the eastern part of Dombivli. It had been a sheer coincidence that Arun had found a place to stay in the same locality.

Arun had heard Gajananbuwa singing and playing the violin only on the radio, but had not listened closely because in his mid-teens he had become besotted with the celebrated singer Bhimsen Joshi. But Arun now decided to visit the musician and play it by ear.

⁂

It was dark when Arun approached Gajananbuwa's house. He heard a man singing. Pushing open a door that was ajar on the ground floor, he saw Gajananbuwa sitting cross-legged at the far end of a small room. The musician nodded, seemingly in recognition, and continued singing. Arun sat on the floor near the entrance and looked around. There were four or five other people. One was playing the tabla and another the tanpura. Gajananbuwa was singing the first verse of a slow composition, in raag Chhayanat, set to the fourteen-beat Jhoomra taal. The 'x' marks the position of the sam.

x	
Karata ho moso neha ki	You keep spinning
Jhoothi jhoothi batiya banaye	False tales of love.

'A huge chasm divides a radio broadcast from live music, especially when one hears it at close quarters,' Arun thought.

In contrast with the soothing tones of some musicians that immediately appealed to the lay listener, Gajananbuwa's voice had a raw timbre. Yet it was so tuneful and resonant that he seemed to be hitting every note's sweet spot. His singing throbbed with rhythmic energy. Arun had never heard khayal singing that created such an intense atmosphere.

He had endured a tiring day. He had not imagined that he would be commuting for so many hours in such insalubrious conditions. His living arrangements were barely tolerable. Sitting there, mesmerised by the way Gajananbuwa moved through each avartan and arrived at the sam, he forgot about his difficulties. For decades afterwards, he could recall the visceral effect of his first close encounter with Gajananbuwa's music.

After a while, Gajananbuwa went around the room, calling upon each student. When it was Arun's turn, he began tentatively singing the first line but fumbled at the sam. Gajananbuwa took over. In the following rounds, he skipped over Arun. After each person had attempted a few avartans, Gajananbuwa sang for several minutes. Arun looked on apprehensively. He knew more than five dozen raags and could give a two-hour concert. He may have had few original musical ideas, but impressed many listeners with his glittering imitation of Bhimsen Joshi. But he just could not grasp the melodic and rhythmic patterns that Gajananbuwa was unfurling.

Arun felt chastened, but also elated that fate had led him to a musician whose art was like an impenetrable fortress. Arun was grateful that at least he had enough training to recognise the musician's depth. He had found this great guru on the day after arriving in Bombay. How lucky was that?

After a few classes, Arun figured out that the man who played the tanpura and sang fluently with a sweet voice was Madhukar, or Madhu, Gajananbuwa's middle son of three, and the tabla player was Narayan, his youngest son, who had learnt from the peerless Ahmed Jan Thirakwa. Arun also learnt that Madhu, like his father, played the violin.

'I'm in illustrious company,' Arun thought.

At the end of the month, Arun asked Gajananbuwa what he should pay him.

'Do you have savings?' Gajananbuwa asked him.

'Um ...'

'Let us talk about this later,' Gajananbuwa interrupted. 'Keep coming and listening to the music. After several months, you will get a better feel for my style. If you progress, then you can continue.'

As Arun walked back to his flat, he began to feel more upbeat about Bombay. If Gajananbuwa lived in this city, then it must really be a great centre of music.

Arun had arrived in the right place at the right time. By the mid-twentieth century, Bombay had become khayal's economic and artistic centre when two long-term trends on the Indian sub-continent converged: the disintegration of royal courts and the emergence of the western port city as the country's leading industrial hub and commercial entrepôt.[6] The Delhi region had been an important centre for khayal for more than two centuries after the genre's emergence sometime in the late sixteenth to early seventeenth century. Yet many khayal singers also kept migrating out of Delhi in waves, spurred by Aurangzeb's proscription of music in 1667, the decline of the Mughal empire after his death in 1707, the British East India Company's subsequent brutal suppression of the 1857 rebellion, and finally, the dissolution of princely states after Independence in 1947. These musicians first made their way to numerous regional states in the north and other areas, from where many eventually migrated to Bombay. Kolkata probably had the edge in instrumental music because after 1857, Wajid Ali Shah, the arts-loving ruler of Awadh, one of those regional states that was a magnet for musicians, fled to Bengal. His retinue had dozens of instrumentalists and singers of thumri, which had flowered under his rule.[7] But many instrumentalists and thumri singers also made

Bombay their home. Dhrupad exponents, too, made their way to both cities.

Bombay's industrial and commercial wealth spurred the entertainment sector, a big component of which was initially Parsi theatre, which was performed in Hindi, Gujarati and Urdu,[8] and Marathi musicals. These theatrical troupes hired classical musicians to train actors to render raag-based songs. Hindustani musicians thereafter found work in the growing Hindi film industry, whose music composers drew heavily from raags. When recording technology came to India at the turn of the twentieth century, many prominent recording companies set up offices in Bombay, cementing the city's preeminent position in the Hindustani music world.[9]

A parallel development added momentum to Bombay's rise as a thriving centre for Hindustani music. Around the turn of the twentieth century, the scholar-singers V.N. Bhatkhande and V.D. Paluskar ushered in a democratic revolution in Hindustani music that dramatically expanded its base of listeners. Bhatkhande was born in Bombay and then based there throughout his life, while Paluskar spent many years in the city. Driven by nationalistic zeal and a desire to prove that India's music was as sophisticated as the West's, the two men contributed to formalising, institutionalising and disseminating a closely guarded musical system that had been transmitted orally for centuries within dynasties.

In the decades before and after the turn of the twentieth century, Bhatkhande travelled all over the sub-continent collecting compositions from hereditary musicians, and devised a notation system for Hindustani music. He tried to give a theoretical framework to what was until then an oral tradition and attempted to insert this tradition into an older history by connecting it to expositions in Sanskrit texts. He also helped set up the Marris College of Hindustani Music in 1926, later called the Bhatkhande Music Institute, with the goal of making music education accessible to the public. Paluskar, for his part, founded the first Gandharva Mahavidyalaya in Lahore in 1901 with the same aim. Several years later, he moved it to Bombay. The school gradually expanded into a pan-Indian network of institutions that held a series of examinations based on a common syllabus. Many students of Paluskar's schools became the audience for performances organised by neighbourhood music circles all over Bombay. Paluskar also came up with a notation system of his own.

The two men had their critics. Many musicians argued that their attempts to codify an oral tradition were well-intentioned but misguided. Their notation systems flattened and even distorted a host of vital musical information and nuances, their critics said. Paluskar's schools did not produce performers, they further pointed out. Paluskar's guru, Balakrishnabuwa Ichalkaranjikar, was scathing about his student. 'He has earned a name, but lost the art,' Balakrishnabuwa said.[10]

Paluskar and Bhatkhande came under criticism also for harbouring and propagating prejudices against hereditary musicians, the vast majority of whom were Muslim. Bhatkhande helped perpetuate the false stereotype that Muslim musicians were all illiterate, while Paluskar actively attempted to Hinduise khayal.[11] Nonetheless, the two men undoubtedly exposed a wider swathe of the population to Hindustani music than had access to it before.

Because of these developments, in the first half of the twentieth century Bombay became home to prominent vocalists from most gharanas. This was why Arun's colleague in Nagpur had kept urging him to move there.

※

About two months into his job, Arun sat at his desk in the office going over an expense account for a small bridge that the government had built. It was just mid-morning, but he was exhausted. He had slept fitfully on that narrow cot and had still not become inured to the long commute. Yet he wanted to live only in Dombivli, close to Gajananbuwa's home. He never missed his guru's daily morning and evening lessons. But was he doing justice to the classes? He desperately needed to do riyaaz, but could not in that chawl room. Gajananbuwa hardly called on him in class. As he had bluntly said early on, Arun was just to listen.

Out of the corner of his eye, Arun saw his boss approaching and went back to tallying figures. He had settled into his new job easily enough, but the work hardly set his blood racing. Among other tasks, he had to check that various government projects had bills to support the expenses cited in the accounts submitted by supervisors. On some days, he found the work so dull that he managed to get it done by singing in his head to relieve the tedium.

He looked forward to Sundays like a tryst with a lover. He and other students spent the whole day at Gajananbuwa's home. It was an open house. His guru began the day by singing. After lunch, he switched to playing the violin. After tea, he and his students went for a walk. He came back and held a short class. At night, Arun returned to the chawl as though in a trance, floating on air. He forgot about whether he would get a place to sit on the train the next morning, which files he would have to go through at work and what he would do for lunch.

It was now mid-week. The high from the Sunday fix of music had worn off. On the train in the evening, he felt weary. He gave himself a pep talk: you cannot afford to be despondent, you have no one and no money to fall back on. His father was a modestly successful lawyer in Pandharkowda, a small town in eastern Maharashtra, south of Nagpur. Although he was a sharp legal mind, he had deliberately kept his law practice low-key in order to devote time to teaching Hindustani vocal music to his sons and other children in the town. Arun was the eldest of six boys. Knowing that the family's finances were tight, he had not asked his father for any money since leaving home for college at the age of fifteen. On the contrary, he had helped with his younger brothers' education. He did not have relatives in Bombay. He had to make his way on his own.

In the pale pink light and crisp stillness of dawn, a year after moving to Bombay, Arun returned to his new lodgings after performing overnight at a well-known Ganesh temple nearby during the annual ten-day festival dedicated to the elephant-headed god. A few weeks earlier, he had moved to Thakurli, a village near Dombivli where the British had established a housing colony for railway employees. A foreman in the railways who lived in this village had been impressed by Arun's singing at a local event and offered the young singer the empty outbuilding behind his bungalow. Arun had moved there the next day.

It was a turning point in Arun's life in Bombay. Arun plunged into his riyaaz with great intensity, as if to make up for what he had not been able to do in his chawl room the previous year. He also fell in with about a dozen young singers, tabla players and harmonium players, who got together on weekends to practise. Very soon, Arun was performing almost every weekend in and around Dombivli, often getting the last slot, reserved for the most popular or accomplished singer. In public, Arun used a basic Gwalior gharana framework infused with a robust Kirana style that Bhimsen Joshi had made popular and that was in favour with local audiences. All the while, he continued to religiously attend Gajananbuwa's classes, doing riyaaz in his guru's mould. He did not find it strenuous to juggle his two musical lives, believing that the two would eventually merge.

Arun won the admiration and support of a group of older listeners in Dombivli. He could walk into their homes at any time and expect to be welcomed warmly and fed from their kitchens. He became a star performer at the Shreemant Sangeet Sabha, a monthly gathering of about three dozen music lovers. They met on the second Saturday of every month and each time about three or four of them performed. Many connoisseurs and occasionally, musicians attended these sessions of the Second Saturday Group, as the gathering was also called. On one occasion, Arun was honoured when on listening to him present Miyan Malhar at this forum, the well-known Agra gharana musician Jagannathbuwa Purohit invited him home for lunch.

Arun had many takers for his semi-classical music as well. One organiser would advertise his programmes thus: 'Arun Kashalkar—*Ravi mi ha chandra kasa,* Dinanath-style', referring to Dinanath Mangeshkar, a leading actor-singer in Marathi musicals. This title was a fragment of the first line of a song, *Ravi mi ha chandra kasa miravitase* (I am the sun, but look how this moon is preening). Listeners regularly wanted Arun to sing songs from the musical *Maan apmaan* (Honour and dishonour), and render the hit song *Bahut din nach bhetalo sundarila* (I haven't met my beloved for many days) from *Sangeet Saubhadra* (Musical about Subhadra) in the style of Chhota Gandharva, another leading actor-singer of that time. Arun sang devotional songs—bhajans and abhangs—with equal gusto, which added to his popularity. Audiences kept asking him to sing *Indrayani kathi* (On the banks of the Indrayani), an abhang made famous by Bhimsen Joshi. People began calling him a 'prati Bhimsen', a copy of Bhimsen, which, for a young musician, was no pejorative.

Dombivli, located in Thane district, was a vibrant cultural hub in the Bombay metropolitan area but did not have the visibility of its counterparts within the city's limits, such as Girgaum and Dadar. Dombivli's lower rents, however, attracted talent from not only outside Bombay but also the city itself. In the 1950s, Gajananbuwa's family had moved there from Girgaum. The Dombivli-Kalyan belt had a couple of big Hindustani classical music organisations, such as the Kalyan Gayan Samaj, that invited established artists such as Bhimsen Joshi and Kesarbai. But it also had many smaller forums, such as the Second Saturday Group, that played an important role in providing a platform for budding performers.

Around the mid-twentieth century, Dombivli was also home to many writers, lyricists, playwrights and poets, such as the prolific and fiery Savarkarite writer P.B. Bhave and short-story writer S.N. Navare. Art lovers were spoilt for choice on weekends: there were poetry readings, plays, music recitals and dance performances. Arun enjoyed Dombivli's cultural ambience, but aside from attending the occasional poetry reading, he spent most of his weekend at Gajananbuwa's home or doing riyaaz.

One Sunday, however, he skipped class to attend Bhimsen Joshi's recital. Arun had wondered how he would feel about the singer's music after about two years of relentless exposure to Gajananbuwa. Arun still found qualities in Bhimsen Joshi to admire but had developed a more balanced view of his music. The following day, Gajananbuwa looked pointedly at him.

'Where were you yesterday?' he asked.

'I went to listen to Bhimsen Joshi,' Arun replied.

'In your own interest, don't miss class,' his guru said.

Arun read the compliment in Gajananbuwa's admonition. His guru wanted him to be fully committed to learning his gayaki. For that, he had to immerse himself in it without distractions.

'Hee shravan vidya ahe,' Gajananbuwa often said. This is aural knowledge.

This is why when Gajajanbuwa began a raag that was unfamiliar to many students, for several classes, he sang for most of the time. For the first nine months, Arun had barely opened his mouth in class and his guru had hardly spoken to him. Gajananbuwa allowed students to sing only as much he thought they could with a modicum of control, as Arun had found out on his first day. Gajananbuwa did not speak much and had little interest in music theory and history.

'I have been trained to sing, not to talk,' he said many times.

Gajananbuwa did not ask his students what they wanted to learn and they did not have the gumption to offer suggestions. Unlike teachers who exclusively taught one raag for several months, Gajananbuwa mixed things up. He started a raag and pursued it for a few days. He sometimes introduced a new raag for a short while before moving on to one that he had already been teaching. Students had to juggle several raags, each at a different stage of pedagogical development. What bound the raags was Gajananbuwa's gayaki, or style. After a year, Arun had been astonished to realise that he could make a go at singing along Gajananbuwa's lines.

One evening, Arun approached his guru's bungalow with a spring in his step. To free up more time to practice, he had quit his job at the accountant-general's office, finding work much closer to Dombivli, at the National Machinery Manufacturers, at Kalva, just three stations away. His guru was singing the composition *Hazrat Turkman* in raag Darbari Kanada. When Arun entered the room, the music hit him like a physical force. Arun wondered how his guru, whom he had been listening to almost daily for three hours, managed to summon up such intensity each time he sang. Everyone was listening in hushed silence. Arun sat down and closed his eyes.

'All right,' Gajananbuwa said after a while. 'Begin.'

Madhu started off. Arun liked to hear Madhu, who was five years older, because he had absorbed so much from his father. Madhu, too, quickly had developed respect for Arun because he could see that the young man was transparently in love with Gajananbuwa's music and was rapidly picking up his style. When Arun's turn came, he fluently sang the composition. Gajananbuwa moved to the second phase, of singing sargam sequences. He had meticulously refined the chalans of the raags. Chalan, literally 'way of going', or gait, consists of the various phrase sequences that define a raag. For Darbari Kanada, Gajananbuwa sang a passage that went along these lines:[12]

```
ni Sa Re dha____ ni Pa____,
ma Pa dha____ ni Sa____,
Re Re Sa ni, dha ni Sa Re ga_ ga_____ ma____ Re Sa
     Re_____ Sa____,
ni Sa ma Re Sa dha_____ ni_____ Pa_____,
ma Pa dha____ ni Sa____,
dha____ ni Sa____,
dha____ ni Sa____ Re____,
```

Re Sa ṇi ḍha____ ṇi Sa____ Re_____,
Sa Re ga ma Re Sa ṇi Sa Re Sa ḍha_____,
ṇi Sa Re Sa ḍha_____,
Re Sa ḍha_____ ṇi Sa_____,
Re Sa Re ga____ ma Re_____ Sa_____.

By imbibing such sequences, students could gradually generate the equivalent of sentences and paragraphs in a raag, stepping stones to full-blown improvisation. After a while, the tabla player joined in. Now students had to mesh their singing with the taal. They sang one at a time, feeding off their guru and one another, spinning out one avartan after another.

'This is paradise,' Arun thought.

⁂

One day, during the Darbari phase, Arun came to class eager to see what would happen, the way a reader waits to see what will unfold in a detective story. Each lesson had several twists and turns in the great plot of Darbari. His guru was singing the composition's first verse. After completing the avartan, he sang the phrase ga_ ma_ Re Sa ṇi Sa_.

'Come on,' he said to Arun. 'Take this further.'

Gajananbuwa wanted Arun to use this phrase as a theme to generate more sentences. Arun began singing:[13]

ḍha ṇi Sa Re_ **ga_ ma_ Re Sa ṇi Sa_**,
ḍha ṇi Sa Re_ ga_ ma Pa, **ga_ ma_ Re Sa ṇi Sa_**,
ga ma Pa_ dha___ ni_ Pa___ ma Pa **ga_ ma_ Re Sa ṇi Sa_**,
ga ma Pa_ dha___ ni_ Pa___ ni ma Pa ni **ga_ ma_ Re Sa ṇi Sa_**,
ma Pa dha_ ni_ Pa_ ma Pa ni ga___ ma Pa_ ga ma Pa
                              ga_ ma_ Re Sa ṇi Sa_.

Linked by this theme phrase, the sentences grew longer and formed the equivalent of a coherent paragraph as Arun entered an advanced phase of improvisation called upaj, in which sequences emerge spontaneously one after the other, carrying the narrative forward.

He kept arriving at the sam with precision. When Arun ran out of ideas for building on one theme, he moved to a new phrase and began improvising around that.

For the next two years, Gajananbuwa kept returning to a trinity of raags—Darbari, Hem Kalyan and Jaitashree—through which he drew Arun deeper and deeper into his music.

◆ Concert

A CONTEMPORARY KHAYAL CONCERT NORMALLY CONSISTS of a singer rendering more than one raag, accompanied by a tabla player and a harmonium player. For every rendition, the tabla player marks out a taal. The person playing the harmonium, a type of reed organ, unobtrusively follows the singer's melody and, whenever the singer allows, plays brief solo passages. Traditionally, a sarangi player provided melodic accompaniment, a practice that began waning in the final decades of the twentieth century, possibly because the bowed string instrument is challenging to master. In the new millennium, the sarangi seems to be making at least a partial comeback. Occasionally, a violinist may accompany a performer.

In a concert's first raag rendition, the singer usually presents a vilambit bandish, or slow composition, followed by a drut bandish, or fast composition. A slow composition, set to a leisurely tempo, allows for the most extensive improvisation. It is therefore also called the bada khayal, literally meaning 'big idea', although 'elaborate idea' better captures its spirit. A fast composition, set to a brisk tempo, is correspondingly sometimes called a chhota khayal, which literally means 'small idea', although 'miniature idea' might be more appropriate, because the form is equally challenging to present: it is small only in terms of the time that a singer devotes to it relative to the slow composition. Compositions can also be presented in madhya laya, or medium tempo.

Some styles present an aalaap before the slow composition, without percussion accompaniment. The most elaborate of its kind is the nom-tom aalaap, which was adapted to khayal from the dhrupad genre.

Khayal singers also present other compositional forms, such as the tarana and, sometimes, items from the dhrupad repertoire, and use these as take-off points for improvising within a raag. Towards the end of a concert, some khayal singers present semi-classical genres and, to please lay listeners from specific language communities, songs from popular genres, such as natya sangeet, the repertoire of songs from Marathi musicals, and devotional songs such as Hindi bhajans, Marathi abhangs and Kannada vachanas, all of which are often loosely based on raags.

'People can enjoy art at different levels: in totality or by focusing on specific aspects of it. For example, a viewer of a portrait might admire the whole picture, another might appreciate the subject's expression and yet another the play of light.' —AK

5

◇ Ride

AFTER A FEW WEEKS IN MY NEW MUSIC CLASS, I BEGAN TO FEEL like a novice swimmer who had foolhardily ventured into the middle of the deep blue sea, enticed by its beauty and a yearning for adventure. I was used to a very different kind of teaching. Both Panchal-ji and Asavari-ji had given me solo lessons, working on one raag at a time for several weeks. I mainly repeated what they sang. Both taught people for whom music was a hobby. Guruji, however, taught groups that included professionals and whose size and composition were fluid. So was the content! Until we got to class, we had no idea which raag he would work on. Like the best khayal improvisations, the class was fluid and unpredictable.

For every raag, Guruji sang the slow composition and expected students to reproduce it as best they could. The composition became the medium through which students absorbed raag, taal, sur, or pitch, laya, or rhythm, and his gayaki, or style, all at once. As he and the advanced students sang the composition over and over again, others gradually picked it up. Now and then, he corrected students' pitches, sang the raag's key phrases, helped some of us with the taal, told us how to use laya to enhance our expression and suggested how we should practise in order to improve on each front, tailoring his advice to each one's level.

'I don't believe in starting students off by making them recite sa-re-ga-ma and practise alankars for months on end,' he later told me, referring to scales and related drills. 'That is not the most efficient or enjoyable way to learn. Students must, of course, later practise several patterns, but the trick is to create a context for them. Music is like human language. You learn to speak a language by speaking, not merely by learning the grammar and vocabulary. Children may copy adults around them, but they also come up with their own sentences because they have an urge to communicate. They may need to be corrected here and there, but over time, they begin speaking fluently. Singing is no different.'

Like Gajananbuwa, he used sargams to teach us a raag's key phrases. If students did not know a raag, they had to pick up what they could. Guruji's approach departed from straightforward imitation because it offered students a window of autonomy. When their turns came, they had to think on their feet and sing what they could muster. What else was this but a rudimentary form of improvisation? I found his method intimidating, but full of possibility. Guruji was fine if we took baby steps in improvising, stumbled and even fell, but we had to try. He was always there to help us get up and get on our way again. For him, improvisation was not a lofty goal for later, something students could attempt only after mastering the technicalities. They had to do so *while* acquiring these skills.

Guruji's performing experience was a huge bonus. By then, I knew that he had regularly performed in public till his mid-forties before gradually disappearing from the scene. Subsequently, he continued to perform at low-key festivals and events, and sang relentlessly for connoisseurs at his own home and at baithaks. He brought the weight of this experience to his teaching, encouraging every student to think like a khayal singer. To get the most out of his teaching, students had to be alert, fully engaged and daring, like most children naturally are. Students had to banish a fear of the unknown, a useful attitude to have in any field, but particularly so in an art form in which almost everything a performer sings is, in fact, unknown.

The similarities between Guruji's pedagogy and that of the most effective language teacher who taught me were uncanny. When I was working as a journalist in Jerusalem in the mid-1990s, I learnt spoken Arabic from Moin Halloun. Having studied several Indian and foreign languages in school and outside, I had many points of comparison. Halloun, who worked at Bethlehem University on the Israel-occupied West Bank, taught colloquial Palestinian Arabic to foreigners in the evenings in Jerusalem. Formal Arabic, called Fuṣḥā, is common to all Arabic-speaking nations, but every country has its own spoken dialect. To represent Arabic sounds, Halloun used Roman letters with diacritics, as in the very word Fuṣḥā, so that students did not get bogged down in learning a new script.

The lessons in his book consisted of dialogues between two people, so he paired the roughly twenty students in the class. He read aloud each conversation several times and each pair took turns to repeat them, looking at the book if needed. After each turn, he repeated parts of the dialogue that people found difficult. After a round, he discussed one or two grammatical points. Because a dialogue was repeated many times, it seeped into us. To this day, I remember the first one, which went as follows:

wēn ᵉBrahīm?	Where is Ibrahim?
ᵉBrahīm fi l-kafitērya.	Ibrahim is in the cafeteria.
wēn il-kafitērya?	Where is the cafeteria?
Il-kafitērya fi l-ǧāmʻa.	The cafeteria is in the university.
wēn il-ǧāmʻa?	Where is the university?
Il-ǧāmʻa fi Bētlaḥim.	The university is in Bethlehem.

Just as I began reproducing snatches of Bihagada and Nat Bihag in class, in Jerusalem I soon began using bits of colloquial Palestinian Arabic. After a few lessons, I uttered my first sentence to a native speaker when I lost my bearings in the Old City's labyrinthine streets.

'Wēn Bāb il-ʻAmūd?' I made bold to ask him, using the Arabic name for Damascus Gate, a leading landmark.

This period from my past echoed in other ways. Guruji's concert was, in musical terms, proving to be my road to Damascus, and his class a musical Jerusalem, a city in which three great traditions—Christianity, Islam and Judaism—merged.

Much later, I discovered that I was not alone in my bewilderment. Most students had experienced a culture shock on joining Guruji's class. Some people dropped out after a few months.

'I couldn't keep up,' one woman told another student.

His approach was not for the faint-hearted and could be dizzying for an amateur like me. But Guruji did not make such distinctions.

'One can never tell which student will take off when,' he told me.

By all accounts, his method was highly effective.

'I don't know what his secret is,' said Ramdas Bhatkal, a singer who had headed Popular Prakashan, a pioneering publisher of Marathi literature, for many years, and occasionally dropped into Guruji's classes. 'At least ten of his students are excellent singers.'

As an observer, I had found the group class thrilling. As a participant, I often felt like I was on a stomach-churning rollercoaster ride. As for a solo lesson with Guruji, the prospect began to appear terrifying.

◈ Roots

GAJANANBUWA'S GAYAKI, A COMPOSITE OF THE GWALIOR, Jaipur and Agra styles, reflected his deep and diverse training from four major gurus, two Hindu and two Muslim. Born in 1911 in Bombay, Gajananbuwa began learning the Gwalior style of khayal from his father Antubuwa at the age of about four. Much later, he went on to learn from Ramakrishnabuwa Vaze, another musician from the same tradition. Vazebuwa had travelled from Maharashtra's coast to Gwalior state to learn from a student of one of the gharana's leading figures.

'What did you learn from Vazebuwa?' Antubuwa once asked his son.

'Above all, I learnt how to analyse raags,' Gajananbuwa replied.

A voracious seeker of knowledge, Gajananbuwa later sought out great gurus from other traditions. He trained with Shamsuddin 'Bhurji' Khan, the son of Alladiya Khan, the Jaipur gharana's founder. So thoroughly did Gajananbuwa absorb this style that some connoisseurs joked that he had gone native. He then learnt from the Agra gharana's Vilayat Hussain Khan for several years. Gajananbuwa's bi-religious lineage reflected khayal's history of deep Indo-Islamic syncretism.

Historians have gleaned considerable details about the evolution of North Indian art music. Of the three genres in this category, dhrupad predates khayal, while the modern thumri emerged after it. The concepts of raag and taal, Indian art music's pillars, have ancient roots, but contrary to a common belief about dhrupad's antiquity, it originated only in the late fifteenth century, in Gwalior, in the court of Man Singh Tomar, a great music lover.[1] The great musicians in his court, called nayaks, were dhrupad's first performers.[2] After the fall of Gwalior in the second decade of the sixteenth century, these dhrupad singers, such as Nayak Bakshu and Tansen, dispersed to other courts.[3] Later, Akbar, the Mughal emperor who ruled in the second half of the sixteenth century, became a great patron of dhrupad. He appointed many nayaks who were still alive and successors of deceased nayaks to his court.[4] Tansen became the most celebrated of these dhrupad singers, who were known as kalawants in Mughal courts.[5]

Khayal later emerged independently of dhrupad, but was subsequently influenced by it. The history of khayal's early evolution has three main inflection points. The following abridged story reveals how musical cultures and society as a whole become richer when they organically absorb a variety of influences.

Khayal emerged as an independent genre sometime in the late sixteenth to early seventeenth century when Sufi musicians in the region between Delhi and Jaunpur began blending Persian genres that they sang in their devotional gatherings with regional genres that used one of many Hindi dialects.[6] The Persian forms included the qaul and tarana, while prominent among the regional genres was the cutkula,[7] an elite, court genre that was a love song consisting of four lines.[8] The cutkula was likely invented by the music-loving Sultan Hussain Shah Sharqi, who ruled Jaunpur in the second half of the fifteenth century.[9] The khayal form that emerged in this phase was probably a precursor to the drut bandish, or chhota khayal, and may have had rudimentary improvisation and some taan singing.[10]

In the early seventeenth century, khayal travelled from Sufi communities outside Delhi to the qawwals of Hazrat Nizamuddin Dargah in the city. The Delhi qawwals, as they came to be known, had inherited traditions associated with Amir Khusro, a polymath who lived in the late thirteenth and early fourteenth centuries.[11] They soon became associated with the most prestigious version of khayal being sung at around this time.[12] Until the early eighteenth century, the word qawwali, which originated from qaul, was an umbrella term for all Sufi genres, and consequently, a qawwal was anyone who sang the Sufi genres, including khayal. But thereafter, qawwals came to be *defined* by their specialisation in khayal singing.[13] The modern qawwali performance, which blends several Sufi genres, emerged much later.[14] Importantly, Indian Sufism in these centuries was hugely influenced by yoga and vaishnavism, with Sufi communities in North India routinely performing Hindu devotional songs such as vishnupads in their gatherings.[15]

By the seventeenth century, in addition to singing khayal in Sufi gatherings, qawwals began performing this genre in royal courts. They were one of four hereditary musician communities that performed in the Mughal majlis, an exclusive gathering of male patrons.[16] At these gatherings, qawwals presented khayal and tappa, a genre with roots in Punjab. Another group of hereditary musicians were the kalawants, elite soloists who sang or played an instrument. Specialising in dhrupad, been, rabab and sursringaar, the kalawants had been attached to Mughal courts from a much earlier era, going back to the reign of Akbar, starting in the mid-sixteenth century.[17] By one estimate, there were fifteen kalawant dynasties,[18] including a hugely influential one called the Senia lineage, which gets its name from the fact that it goes back to Tansen.[19] In the modern period, those who claim the Senia lineage as their heritage are mainly instrumental soloists, in particular sitar and sarod players,[20] but a few vocalists do so as well. Both kalawants and qawwals, who were all men, were considered practitioners of elite art music. The third group in the Mughal majlis consisted of hereditary groups of elite female courtesans.

The fourth group was made up of dhadhis, originally versatile performers from Rajasthan and Punjab, whose men sang dhrupad and battle songs as well as played the kingri, a string instrument, and the duff, a frame drum, and whose women sang at wedding and birthday celebrations. Men drawn from the dhadhi community accompanied the three other elite groups on percussion instruments and the sarangi,[21] but had a lower status than the solo artists.[22] 'The soloist is the artist ... The accompanist is an artisan,' writes Daniel M. Neuman, of practitioners of art music in North India.[23] The main reason accompanists had a lower status was that they also played for courtesans.[24] Over time, some sarangi and tabla players tried to improve their status by becoming vocalists, but they faced barriers. As accompanists, they knew the contours of many raags and tunes of compositions by ear, but that got them only so far. They needed formal training, which soloists would not impart, both because accompanists had a lower status[25] and because elite hereditary musicians guarded their knowledge even from one another like family heirlooms[26] and trade secrets.[27]

⁓

A second turning point in the evolution of khayal came in the early eighteenth century, when Niyamat Khan 'Sadarang', a famous kalawant who sang dhrupad and played the been, further developed the genre. He had close links with Sufis, including the descendants of the Delhi qawwals, called the qawwal bachche. Sadarang, the first known kalawant to sing khayal,[28] ushered in a number of innovations and prolifically composed. First, influenced by dhrupad, he spawned the bada khayal by slowing down the chhota khayal's tempo.[29] Sadarang's bada khayal 'was set in longer cycles and performed in slow medium tempo that provided a leisurely framework in which a detailed improvisatory treatment of the raga became possible, while retaining the textual identity of the composition'.[30] The bada khayal opened up the possibility of singers rendering compositions in a variety of speeds, from a leisurely pace, like in dhrupad, all the way to very fast, as with the tarana.[31] '[Everything was] first to be sung in vilambit laya [slow speed] and then the speed would be increased to medium and fast laya,' wrote the singer Vilayat Hussain Khan, referring to Sadarang's innovation.[32]

Second, Sadarang adapted to khayal the melodic movements of meend and gamak seen in dhrupad, which was intimately associated with the aalaap,[33] as well as more melodic ornaments present in Sufi genres but absent in dhrupad.[34] Meends are long glides and gamaks are heavy short oscillations. Third, he integrated the bol taan from dhrupad and elements of the hori,[35] a semi-classical form that the Sufis in his time may have sung. In other words, Sadarang incorporated into khayal what he thought were dhrupad's best features as well as hitherto untapped but attractive elements of Sufi genres. Fourth, Sadarang expanded the scope of improvisation by allowing a singer to 'explore the raag through aakaar, eekar and ookar' after singing the basic composition and fifth, he worked on the approach to the sam, according to Vilayat Hussain Khan.[36] Sadarang introduced 'increasing [and] decreasing ... vowel spaces in the words of compositions and of coming in an artistic way to the sam,' he wrote.[37]

Sadarang's innovations became mainstream, cemented khayal's status as art music[38] and 'raised the universal standard of contemporary musicality'.³⁹ By the time Muhammad Shah 'Rangila' became ruler in the early eighteenth century, Sadarang's bada and chhota khayals had become 'all the rage', being sung all over North India and the Deccan, by both kalawants and qawwals.⁴⁰ Many of Delhi's qawwal bachche also adopted Sadarang's style.⁴¹ As khayal increased in popularity, other kalawants also began composing in that genre and allied ones, while continuing to do so in their traditional genre of dhrupad.⁴²

When the British brutally suppressed the 1857 rebellion, some musicians were killed, while others dispersed from the Delhi region, seeking patronage in regional states such as Gwalior, Jaipur, Lucknow and Rewa.⁴³ This led to the third inflection point in khayal's evolution. This came in the middle decades of the nineteenth century in Gwalior, which was part of the Maratha empire. This was when khayal took its modern form. During this unstable era, kalawants and qawwals, who had migrated far from their home bases in and around Delhi, had to earn a living by beginning to teach people outside their families. Musicians from the qawwal bachche pedagogical lineage made their way to Gwalior and the nearby state of Rewa, following stints in Lucknow. In Gwalior, these qawwals taught numerous people, including several Hindus who spoke Marathi, the primary court language.

Among the qawwal bachche at the Gwalior court was Bade Mohammad Khan. He was among the best khayaliyas of his time,⁴⁴ incorporating the singing of intricate taans into khayal, a practice that became one of the genre's distinguishing features, clearly setting it apart from other North Indian art music genres. Some think of him as having founded the Gwalior style.⁴⁵ He had a big influence on the brothers Haddu and Hassu Khan, who had learnt from other qawwal bachche in Lucknow and had made their way to Gwalior. On seeing that others were copying his style, Bade Mohammad Khan moved to the princely state of Rewa, about four hundred kilometres south-east of Gwalior.[46] Some contend that it was Haddu and Hassu Khan, along with their contemporary, Nathu Khan,[47] who shaped what became the Gwalior idiom.[48] The trio also taught taranas to their students, which is why inheritors of the Gwalior style have a rich repertoire of this form. Since the qawwals also sang tappas, this, too, became part of repertoire of musicians from this tradition. By the end of the nineteenth century, the Gwalior style of khayal had become hegemonic.

The thumri, for its part, evolved from a song form that accompanied courtesans while they danced.[49] This was the bandish ki thumri, which was similar to the chhota khayal.[50] The name 'thumri' comes from the word 'thumak', a rhythmic hip movement in Indian dance. In the 1830s, in the state of Awadh, thumri came to include an improvisation method call bol baant, involving the rhythmic parsing of lyrics. But it continued to be associated with dance and retained its fast tempo. A few decades later, when Awadh fell to the British, this form of thumri began declining in popularity, partly because the colonisers stigmatised dance and its courtesan practitioners. In subsequent decades, another form of thumri emerged as an independent vocal genre, in Varanasi. This thumri had a slower tempo than the bandish ki thumri and came to include bol banaav, a rich method of lyrical improvisation. The bol banaav thumri is the form that has been prevalent since the start of the twentieth century.

Thumri compositions use only a small subset of raags in the khayal repertoire, and the singer is expected to deviate from the initial raag guided by precedent, principles and aesthetics, which form an important part of training in this genre. Modern thumri compositions are set to taals that are largely of folk origin. Given that courtesans originally specialised in thumri, most of the lyrics are romantic, sensuous or erotic. The singer uses vocal modulation and dynamics to evoke shades of emotions, a process akin to acting. In modern usage, the word 'thumri' refers to the bol banaav thumri and is also an umbrella term that includes several semi-classical forms, such as dadra, chaiti, hori, jhoola and kajri. Over time, two broad styles of bol banaav thumri developed. The Varanasi, or purab, or eastern, style of bol banaav thumri has a languid flavour, epitomised by Rasoolan Bai and Siddheshwari Devi. A more filigreed version was later popularised by Bade Ghulam Ali Khan, his brother Barkat Ali Khan and his son Munawar Ali Khan. This came to be known as the Punjabi style.

As we know, the Gwalior tradition of khayal incorporated intricate taan singing into renditions and had a vast repertoire of tappas and taranas. Its approach to improvisation also exhibited some key structural features, which one could call the traditional model.[51] One, this model viewed a raag as a set of linked phrases, together called the chalan, or way of walking or gait. Two, this traditional model took cues from the composition's melodic themes for improvisation. Finally, the model closely linked improvisations to the taal cycle. In sum, one can say that the traditional approach is chalan-based, bandish-directed and avartan-linked.

As the Gwalior approach was becoming dominant, another, heterodox model was emerging in the mid-nineteenth century due to the efforts of a musician called Behram Khan.[52] This model used the merukhand technique of raag elaboration. This technique involved creating permutations from groups of notes in a raag, moving from the bottom to the top of the octave. It could be applied across raags and compositions. Musicians were not meant to mechanically apply this method because not all permutations are consonant with a raag. Musicians had to use it as a tool during riyaaz, when they could sift the permutations to choose what they felt fit in with a raag's sound.[53] Individual musicians therefore had to make judgements, which left room for variability. Overall, the merukhand method tended to view a raag as a scale of notes, took a linear approach to elaboration, i.e., one starting from low notes and moving up, and was relatively delinked from the avartan. In a nutshell, one can say that the heterodox model is note-based, linear ascending and free-flowing or floating.[54]

How and why did Behram Khan pioneer this new approach to raag elaboration? The answer is likely to lie in North Indian cultural and political history. The following account draws from the work of both Daniel M. Neuman[55] and Dard Neuman,[56] who are father and son. In the cultural sphere, the quasi-caste system characterising the community of North Indian art musicians began partly disintegrating after the decisive collapse of the Mughal empire in the mid-nineteenth century. In the aftermath of this collapse, the trail of where many kalawants and qawwals—who were the elite, hereditary musicians of the Mughal courts—dispersed goes cold.[57] But historians know that some made their way to regional courts like Lucknow and Gwalior. This was a transitional period, in which the court framework sustaining old hierarchies no longer existed, but the attendant social relations did not altogether disappear. Born at the turn of the nineteenth century, Behram Khan came of age in this fluid environment. By Gajananbuwa's time, people talked of Khan as someone from an elite, vocal lineage, because he had learnt dhrupad and spawned the Dagar style. But oral history and family genealogies suggest that he actually came from a non-elite, dhadhi background.[58] This is not surprising, because even when some dhadhis managed to become vocalists after 1857, they often obscured their non-elite origins.

In what Dard Neuman sees as a creative act of resisting exclusion and hierarchy, Behram Khan came up with a new method of raag elaboration that did not depend on being trained by elite musicians. Posing as a Brahmin, he went to Varanasi to study music and Sanskrit treatises, including Sarangdeva's thirteenth century *Sangita Ratnakara*, which described the merukhand technique. He then zealously propagated this system to people of all backgrounds, including women and those from weaver communities.[59] Behram Khan was influenced by egalitarian spiritual movements that challenged power relations in society, whose leading figures include Guru Nanak, Kabir and Ravidas, Neuman says. During this period of change, at least some elite soloists began teaching those from non-elite backgrounds in order to earn a living. But many non-elite musicians also learnt Behram Khan's method, perhaps to hedge their bets. Dard Neuman calls the musicians linked to this trailblazer the Behram Khan 'biradari', or brotherhood, who further taught others. 'A network of musicians from outsider communities worked to disseminate musical knowledge more broadly to students from marginalised groups,' Neuman says.[60]

⁓

As singers from various backgrounds took to khayal in the nineteenth century, they were influenced to differing degrees by these prototypical models—namely the traditional one, represented by the paradigmatic Gwalior approach, and the heterodox one, pioneered by Behram Khan. It is important to note that these models are theoretical paradigms. In practice, when these singers went on to mould khayal in their unique ways, their styles fell on a spectrum between these two conceptual poles. In addition, these positions on the spectrum, far from being static, evolved over time, as many khayaliyas continuously drew from a variety of influences.

As shown by the following brief descriptions of the origins of gharanas,[61] their positions on this spectrum are a function of many parameters: one, the social status of their forbears; two, the proportion of vocal influences in their lineages versus instrumental ones; and three, the extent of training they received from Gwalior musicians versus how much they were influenced by Behram Khan's merukhand method.[62] Moreover, the extent to which a gharana was rooted in vocal lineages influenced how much its singers took to composing, probably because the linguistic skills required to render vocal music were passed on from generation to generation. Similarly, the extent to which a gharana's roots lay in instrumental lineages seems to have contributed to their singers' pin-pointed pitch and resonant tonality.

By Gajananbuwa's time, the Agra, Gwalior, Jaipur, Kirana, Patiala and Rampur-Sahaswan gharanas were becoming the most widespread gharanas. Of these, the Agra and Jaipur styles lean towards the Gwalior-moulded traditional precepts of elaboration. There are, however, deviations in specific areas of improvisation: the Agra gharana's nom-tom aalaap and the Jaipur style's aalaap within the taal cycle tend towards a linear ascending progression. But in other respects, they lean towards the traditional model.

The early singers of the Agra and Jaipur styles came from solo, and therefore elite, vocal lineages, and they trained almost exclusively with Gwalior khayaliyas, and were consequently not influenced much by Behram Khan or his biradari. Of the three other big gharanas, the Rampur-Sahaswan gharana falls mid-way between the traditional and the heterodox approaches, probably because its founder had roots in solo vocal lineages *as well as* a prominent instrumental lineage. The Patiala gharana hews closer to the heterodox end and the Kirana gharana even more so because their early singers had roots in sarangi-playing families.

A brief look at the influences on the founders of the six big gharanas can offer more insights into the historical underpinnings of their aesthetics. The Agra gharana took shape when Ghagghe Khuda Baksh, a dhrupad singer from an elite, kalawant lineage, took to khayal in the early nineteenth century.[63] He learnt from Nathan Pir Baksh, a leading exponent of the Gwalior style, for a dozen years.[64] While retaining the Gwalior approach's key principles, the Agra singers imbued khayal with their foundational training in dhrupad to create a distinct style. In particular, they adapted and extended dhrupad's nom-tom aalaap and bol work.[65] They also became prolific khayal composers.

The Jaipur gharana's founder, Alladiya Khan, also came from an elite dhrupad lineage.[66] He indirectly absorbed many aspects of the vocal style of Gwalior's Mubarak Ali Khan when they were both at the Jaipur court. Mubarak Ali Khan was the son of the influential Gwalior singer Bade Mohammad Khan. Later, Alladiya Khan's son, Manji Khan, was influenced by Gwalior's Rahimat Khan, Haddu Khan's son. Further, Alladiya Khan came to have links to the Agra singers via marriage. Specifically, both Agra and Jaipur singers were related to a clan of singers from Atrauli,[67] as a result of which the two streams shared musical material. At some point, the Agra gharana subsumed the Atrauli style. Alladiya Khan even lived for a while in the joint family home of the hereditary Agra gharana musicians in Mumbai. Building on his foundational training, Alladiya Khan went on to create his own style, raags and compositions. He adapted many dhrupad compositions to khayal with an 'extraordinary musical brilliance.'[68] In Jaipur, Alladiya Khan also interacted with Behram Khan, who was at the court at the same time, but likely did not fully explore the heterodox method. Still, the linear ascending progression of many Jaipur singers may be linked to this interaction.

The Rampur-Sahaswan gharana's early khayal singers had roots in both an elite vocal dynasty and the elite Senia instrumental lineage.[69] Two of its early singers, Haider Khan and Kallan Khan, learnt from Haddu Khan of Gwalior. Subsequently, Inayat Khan, who was active in the late nineteenth and early twentieth century, was considered the most influential, fusing the Gwalior style he had learnt with the instrumental strand of his lineage. The instrumental component in this fusion as well as later Rampur-Sahaswan singers' taste for some aspects of the Kirana style[70] might explain why it is slightly removed from the traditional, Gwalior model compared with the two other styles with roots in elite lineages, namely Agra and Jaipur. The Rampur-Sahaswan gharana also has a repertoire of finely crafted compositions, perhaps reflecting the vocal presence in its roots.

The Patiala gharana was shaped by multiple genres: the sarangi as well as vocal genres such as dhrupad, thumri, tappa and folk music. An important figure in the lineage was Miyan Kalu Khan, who was a rabab and sarangi player at the Patiala court. He learnt from Tanras Khan, an elite vocalist at the court of Bahadur Shah Zafar, whose father was a kalawant but had trained under a qawwal. Tanras Khan, the fountainhead of the Delhi gharana, escaped to the Patiala court during the 1857 uprising. Miyan Kalu Khan's son, Ali Baksh Khan, and a relative or friend, Fateh Ali Khan, became a duo called Alia-Fattu and learnt from the Gwalior musicians Haddu Khan and Mubarak Ali Khan, from Tanras Khan as well as from Behram Khan. Ali Baksh Khan's son was Bade Ghulam Ali Khan, who became a great exponent of this style.

The Kirana gharana got its identity in the twentieth century from the music of Abdul Karim Khan and Abdul Wahid Khan. Abdul Karim Khan trained as a sarangi player[71] but later learnt khayal from his father and a distantly related uncle. He was also influenced by the Gwalior style's Rahimat Khan.[72] Abdul Karim Khan had either a blood or pedagogical link to Bande Ali Khan, who played the been, which was played by elite kalawants. But Bande Ali Khan was likely also from a sarangi background.[73] Like Behram Khan, Bande Ali Khan fought back against the traditional social stratification of musicians by learning to play the been, marrying either Haddu or Hassu Khan's daughter,[74] and then teaching many people from outsider communities. He may have also married Behram Khan's daughter.[75] The Kirana gharana's Abdul Wahid Khan, for his part, learnt merukhand elaboration from a sarangi player who was Behram Khan's nephew and expanded its application to improvisation. Abdul Wahid Khan is also said to have also considerably slowed down the tempo of the bada khayal.

❦

Of about a dozen smaller gharanas, the old Delhi gharana, the Khurja and Visnhupur gharanas have roots in elite lineages. Many descendants of the old Delhi gharana's influential singer, Tanras Khan, who, as mentioned earlier, had both kalawant and qawwal links, moved to Pakistan, while those who remained in Delhi specialised in modern qawwali.[76] The Khurja gharana was similar: its musicians had kalawant roots and links with qawwals.[77] One of its great exponents was Zaoor Baksh 'Ramdas', and later, Azmat Hussain Khan and Aslam Khan. The Vishnupur gharana evolved from the elite Senia kalawant tradition,[78] which is why it produced both vocalists and instrumentalists. In the early eighteenth century, after Aurangzeb proscribed music, the arts-loving ruler of Vishnupur, in West Bengal, invited Bahadur Khan, a kalawant, to his court. Bahadur Khan went on to found the Vishnupur gharana.[79]

The smaller gharanas strongly influenced by Behram Khan's merukhand method are the modern Delhi gharana, whose stalwart was Mamman Khan, and the Indore gharana, whose fountainhead was Amir Khan.[80]

A large number of the smaller gharanas are hybrid. The Benaras gharana's progenitors learnt from Rampur-Sahaswan singers and perhaps others.[81] The Bhendi Bazaar style was influenced by the Rampur-Sahaswan tradition as well as the merukhand approach.[82] Similarly, the Mewati gharana had roots in the Gwalior tradition as well as in the Behram Khan biradari, in particular Bande Ali Khan and his been style[83], consequently incorporating the merukhand method into its approach to elaboration.[84] The eclectic Kunwar Shyam gharana, the only one not named after a place, was founded by Goswami Lalji Maharaj 'Kunwar Shyam', who was attached to a Radha-Govind temple in Delhi.[85] Not much is known about his musical antecedents,[86] but he composed and sang fast compositions that incorporated elements of dhrupad, tappa, bandish ki thumri—sung to accompany dance—and a folk form called dhawaroo.[87] He specialised in varieties of Malhar, especially compound ones.[88] Laksman Prasad Jaipurwale, who learnt from at least one of Laji Maharaj's students, began singing slow compositions. Both Jaipurwale and his son, Govind Prasad, admired Amir Khan, Bade

Ghulam Ali Khan and Salamat Ali Khan,[89] who all leaned towards the heterodox model. Jaipurwale's student, Rajaram Shukla, began using the merukhand method more systematically for improvising.[90] The relatively recent Kotali gharana was founded by Tarapada Chakraborty in the mid-twentieth century. The gharana's name comes from his birthplace, Kotalipara, now in Bangladesh.[91] Chakraborty's pedagogical lineage includes several traditional vocal styles, including Agra, Gwalior and Khurja as well as Rampur-Sahaswan.[92] It also includes an instrumental component: one of his teachers, Girija Shankar Chakravarty, in addition to training with many vocalists, learnt from the sarangi player Badal Khan.[93]

This short history amply bears out a key observation about khayal made by Amlan Das Gupta. He has pointed out that from its inception khayal has been a melting pot, capable of seamlessly assimilating a variety of distinct genres and influences into its framework. In this respect, khayal is like the novel form, which has proven flexible enough to incorporate various genres, Das Gupta has further said. 'Socially distinct genres can enter into the novel, get mixed up and lose their original purpose,' he said.[94] A similar process can be seen in khayal.

⁂

By the mid-twentieth century, Bombay, itself a melting pot, was a hub for about three-fourths of khayal gharanas. But in Gajananbuwa's milieu, when the cognoscenti talked about 'gharanedar' singers, they meant those trained in the Gwalior, Agra and Jaipur styles—those that adhered to chalan-based, bandish-directed and avartan-linked elaboration. In some structural respects, these styles are arguably closer to Carnatic music than the other khayal styles. These styles have a large repertoire of raags, including complex and compound raags, which are stubbornly chalan-based and resist being elaborated by the merukhand approach; they need to be learnt from a guru. Singers in these gharanas, on average, also use a greater number of taals than vocalists from the heterodox styles. Further, because of the traditional styles' roots in vocal music, they have a large store of compositions.

Nevertheless, the best musicians from the heterodox styles, such as Abdul Karim Khan, Amir Khan and Bade Ghulam Ali Khan, won universal admiration because they maintained the integrity of raags and because of their originality and quality of sur. Overall, the heterodox gharanas more systematically explored the lower octave and thus expanded the canvas of elaboration. They also focused on achieving a razor-sharp intonation and powerful resonance, qualities that, as earlier mentioned, might hark back to the instrumental component in these styles' heritage.

In fact, Arun had a theory that Gajananbuwa himself had such a sharp and resonant pitch because he was also an instrumentalist: he had taught himself to play the violin. While learning to produce precise frequencies on the violin, a fretless string instrument, Gajananbuwa's perception of pitch must have deepened and fed back into his singing, Arun surmised. His guru must similarly have absorbed the violin's resonance and channelled it into his voice.[95] Gajananbuwa had also taught himself to play the harmonium and learnt to play the tabla from the respected Vinayakrao Ghangrekar.

When Arun arrived in Bombay, his guru was admired by musicians for the way his ideas effortlessly and vigorously, sometimes explosively, surged forth, like a powerful river nourished by several tributaries. When he performed in and around Bombay, about a hundred of his fans routinely turned up, but he was not widely known among the lay public. To Arun, his guru was living proof that popularity was not a measure of musical merit.

◆ Palace

IN CONTEMPORARY USAGE, THE WORD GHARANA REFERS TO A pedagogical lineage and style.[96] The word, which literally means dynasty or blood lineage and is derived from the Hindi word 'ghar', or home, originates from a time when music styles were passed on and retained largely within musical families, who often competed with one another for royal patronage. A musician family's name became more or less synonymous with its style. But by the early twentieth century, musicians were moving to big cities to earn a living. In these new and unfamiliar urban environments, khayal musicians began branding themselves by the places that were their hometowns or where they or their ancestors had first established themselves as musicians.[97] By then, these musicians were teaching people outside their families, so the gharana names gradually began referring not to a musical dynasty but a distinctive style.

Each gharana renders typical raags, taals, compositional forms and compositions, and employs specific improvisation techniques. These are broad generalisations, because there are many overlaps. But each gharana does create an idiosyncratic sonic texture. One could compare these sonic textures to saree weaves such as Chanderi, Kanchipuram and Pochampally or modern Western art styles such as Henri Matisse's fauvism, Pablo Picasso's cubism and Salvador Dali's surrealism. To use yet another metaphor, if one thinks of khayal as a multi-storied palace, we could think of all gharanas as having the same ground floor, but each using a different plan to build the floors above it.[98] To a lay listener, these styles may initially all sound the same, but seasoned listeners can usually perceive many of the differences.

> 'Poetry has many styles. Each style might focus on a theme, such as nature, philosophy, love and death. Each style might also have a unique approach to using language: one style might indulge in word play, another might prefer a simpler form of expression. A person steeped in poetry will be able to distinguish among different styles and appreciate each one's special qualities.' —AK

6

◇ Fringe

THE CONCERT HALL'S LIGHTS DIMMED AS THE CURTAINS parted. Columns of marigolds hung on either side of a black backdrop, framing the musicians. The flowers in shades of sunshine indicated that this was a joyous occasion, but the stark backdrop spoke of shadows. First Edition Arts was presenting Guruji for the first time, a month after Devina and Pepe had met him. They had given this concert the cool label of 'Secret Masters Sessions', riffing on the jazz jam session, in which instrumentalists get together to improvise and experiment with the aim of creating edgy, original music. The venue, however, was the stodgy Karnataka Sangh Hall, its seats creaking as listeners leaned back. But the venue had a rich history because many great musicians had performed there, while the locality, Mahim, had the advantage of geography, located in the centre of Mumbai, easily accessible via all modes of transport.

That evening, the hall was brimming with anticipation. The first few rows were filled with well-known musicians, connoisseurs and art critics, including the Agra gharana vocalist Raja Miyan, Agra-Gwalior gharana singer Sanjeev Chimmalgi, Gwalior gharana singer Shrikant Waikar, violinist Kailash Patra, musicologist Deepak Raja, art critic Shanta Gokhale, patron Neelima Kilachand, leading publisher Ramdas Bhatkal and connoisseur Romit Chatterjee. Listeners can play a huge role in influencing a khayal performance. In intimate settings, they can even become co-creators of the music. I knew, therefore, that a hall full of connoisseurs and musicians guaranteed a high quality of listening and therefore, in all likelihood, of singing.

Guruji looked relaxed, wearing a spiffy raw-silk magenta kurta that my friend, Shirin, a fashion designer and an eternal good samaritan, had stitched for him. In the run-up to the concert, Guruji had smiled as Shirin's young female staff had fussed over him while they took his measurements. He had gamely posed for Pepe, an exacting photographer who wanted eye-catching images for the concert poster. While appreciating everyone's efforts, Guruji retained an amused detachment towards the sudden brouhaha over him, reminding me of an indulgent parent going along with his enthusiastic children's dopey schemes or a benevolent monk being patient with his worldly followers. That evening, when he finally walked on stage and looked around at the floral decorations, he had exclaimed, 'I feel like a bridegroom all over again!'

Guruji greeted people in the front row. Vishal and Mukul, another senior student of Guruji's who lived in Pune, sat on either side of him. As Guruji fine-tuned the tanpuras, I sat in silence until I heard sniffling. Kaku, who was sitting next to me, was dabbing her eyes with her palloo.

'He's finally getting a little of what he deserves, isn't he?' I asked softly.

'Haan, but all these years …,' she said, trailing off.

That bittersweet feeling. A splash of orange on black.

The sound of the tanpuras filled the hall. Music. The eternal balm. Guruji began with raag Bhoop. Only after starting to learn from him did I discover many subtleties in this pentatonic raag and realised how important it was to keep it distinct from the raags Deshkar, Shuddh Kalyan and Jait Kalyan. I was mighty pleased when after just a couple of months of knowing Guruji, I could apply to raags an aphorism that I had invented for my kids: nothing is hard, so don't be intimidated, but nothing is easy, so don't take any task lightly. Bihagada and Nat Bihag are not hard, Bhoop and Bhimpalas are not easy.

For about an hour, Guruji built another one of his temples, with an elaborate nom-tom as the foundation. The nom-tom typically has three segments: slow, medium-paced and fast, sometimes called respectively aalaap, jod and jhala, terms that are commonly used for a similar progression in instrumental music. Singers can speed the last segment up to the extent that they wish. The nom-tom's intrinsic rhythm and progression of tempos create a powerful narrative structure.

After presenting a stately Bhoop, he delivered a high-spirited Kedar, which I had already heard at the first concert. But this time, he sang it for twice as long, full of rhythmic bol work. After the interval, he created a completely different mood with a serene Sar Nat. Following this, he evoked a contrasting ambience with an animated Sughrai. It was almost as enjoyable to see Vishal appreciating Guruji with a string of 'ohos' at the end of each avartan as it was to listen to Guruji himself. For the concluding raag, Guruji created yet another mood with a shimmering Paraj Kalingada. At one point, when he was singing some interesting patterns, I saw Vishal turning to the tabla player and mouthing the words 'Vilayat Hussain', who had also invented the raag.[1] One could, I felt, learn a great deal from the responses of knowledgeable listeners.

Mukul and Vishal offered excellent stereophonic interventions, all the more alluring because of their contrasting personalities. Mukul had a soothing sweetness, Vishal a gutsy effervescence. They vividly illustrated the shifting balance between continuity and change across generations, and between conformism and individualism in khayal. The way Guruji wordlessly communicated with them painted a tender picture of the guru-shishya relationship.

I wondered how many in the audience would be able to see the treasure behind his ageing voice. Would some people's reception of his music be skin deep? After the concert, a large number of listeners poured onto the stage to talk to him, to shake his hand, to embrace him. He genially attended to each person while photographers wove in and out to capture this post-concert euphoria. Kaku and I watched quietly from our seats.

Guruji's concert attracted a flood of praise on social media. The punchiest review came from Yogesh, who was married to Guruji's student Madhavi. 'This was a masterful performance,' he wrote on Facebook. 'Let there be no secret about it.'

⁂

After this landmark concert, I realised that Guruji was not a secret for a circle of gharanedar musicians and hardcore connoisseurs because they had all spontaneously turned up to listen to him. I was also convinced that I had to hang on in Guruji's class at least until my self-imposed two-year trial period ended. In a recent class, Guruji had told us that 'you should sing as though you are dancing'. I had thought to myself, 'That's exactly what I want to try and do.'

But along with these realisations, I was also dismayed about another aspect of the world of Hindustani music, which, as an inveterate journalist and engaged citizen, I could not help noticing. I saw a large number of Hindustani musicians uncritically supporting the far-right, ethno-majoritarian agenda of the ruling Bharatiya Janata Party, or BJP, which had swept to power two years earlier. I also saw them deifying Narendra Modi, the highly controversial prime minister. The BJP had garnered about a third of the votes, but the proportion of Hindustani musicians who supported its ideology seemed, from strong anecdotal evidence, more than double this figure. I was disappointed that musicians whom I liked and respected were so susceptible to the far right's propaganda and were in thrall to a deeply divisive demagogue.

I understood that many people were fed up with the other main national party, the Congress, which had ruled the country for years, and that they wanted change. But I was taken aback by many musicians' elation about the BJP's victory. On social media, they came across as fans cheering a sports team rather than thinking citizens in a democracy, who ought to be cautious, if not sceptical, about all political parties, particularly the one in power. I also expected that people steeped in art would recognise our shared humanity and shrink from the far right's demonising of minorities, especially Muslims. Music especially is 'the arousal of tender sympathy in the heart', writes Faqirullah in *Raag Darpan*.[2] How did Hindustani singers, of all musicians, square the BJP's ethno-majoritarian agenda with their music's blended religious heritage? They routinely sang Muslim musicians' compositions, including those invoking Sufi saints and Allah himself. Many of their Hindu gurus had learnt from Muslim musicians and developed deep bonds with them. Examples of such guru-shishya relationships included the ones between Alladiya Khan and Bhaskarbuwa Bakhale, Burji Khan and Mallikarjun Mansur, and Vilayat Hussain Khan and Jagannathbuwa Purohit. When Haddu Khan, who helped shape the Gwalior gharana, died, Jayaji Rao Scindia, his patron, is reported to have fasted and not spoken for a week.[3] In this climate, I was curious about Guruji's views.

'I am not interested in politics,' he said.

'Hmm,' I replied.

The sudden spotlight on Guruji illuminated a larger habitat populated by many excellently trained and committed khayal musicians and their students who had little or no presence in the mainstream, revealing a larger pattern of marginalisation. In the Mumbai–Pune belt, in roughly Guruji's generation, these included Alka Deo Marulkar, Aslam Khan, Dinkar Panshikar, Madhukar Joshi, Narayan Bodas, Sharad Jambhekar and Sharad Sathe, among others. In the younger generation, there were Kedar Bodas, Pournima Dhumale, Pratima Tilak, Shalmali Joshi, Shubhada Paradkar and Vijaya Jadhav, to name a few. Each of these wonderful singers deserves his or her own saga, but I found the stories of two in the older generation to be particularly poignant.

One was Aslam Khan, about whom Panchal-ji, my first vocal guru, had told me in the mid-1990s. Like Panchal-ji, Aslam-ji had trained under Azmat Hussain Khan, who was also his brother-in-law. The few times that I had heard Aslam-ji in that period, I remember being impressed by his fluency in rare and specialised raags. He had then slipped off my radar. But in late 2015, I met his student, Vrinda Mundkur, who told me Aslam-ji was not doing well.

When Vrinda took me to meet him, I found him paralysed from the waist down, living alone in a run-down locality in Marve, a remote Mumbai suburb. He had earlier lived in South Mumbai, where he had enjoyed periods of relative financial stability. But Vrinda told me that the previous decade had been very unstable for him. His second wife and two sons had passed away, while his only daughter lived in Delhi. He was getting by with the help of a few students and patrons. I visited him several times to interview him and to watch him teach Vrinda rare raags such as Abiri Todi and Manjiri Bihag. He was articulate and witty. He had trained many people, including the playback singer Anwar and the ghazal artist Manhar Udhas, Vrinda told me. Through her efforts and those of other students, he managed to give a handful of concerts during that period. Despite Aslam-ji's failing health, his musicianship shone through. It was tragic to see this fine musician withering away in India's affluent hub for Hindustani music.[4]

The other musician was Madhukar Joshi, the second of Gajananbuwa's three sons. Madhubuwa was off the radar of most aficionados, but was a musical powerhouse. Like his father, he was both a top-notch vocalist and violinist, probably the only musician in his cohort to straddle vocal and instrumental music at such a high level. He infused a Van Gogh-like madness into his father's already blistering style, had composed several bandishes and had trained dozens of students. He lived in Dombivli, which by the twenty-first century had turned into a sprawling city. At some point, Madhubuwa had taken to drinking. But in Dombivli, this tragic genius's towering musical reputation and the fierce passion for khayal among the locality's Marathi-speaking intelligentsia meant that students went to great lengths to learn from him. Young men and women routinely sat patiently on the steps outside his flat, waiting for him to sober up so that they could take lessons with him. His students include his niece, Apoorva Gokhale, one of her generation's most accomplished khayal singers, and her very capable younger sister, Pallavi Joshi.[5]

―――

These musicians, their students and supporters all belonged to the Hindustani music underground, or fringe. The word 'fringe' with respect to the arts arose in a specific historical context. It was 'a performing arts tradition that started in Edinburgh, Scotland, in 1947, when eight performing groups were excluded from the mainstream annual arts festival ... [but] decided to perform anyway, finding inexpensive or free venues on the fringes of the city'.[6] The word gradually began referring to all art that was not at all, or only sporadically, represented in the mainstream, yet offered something unique and innovative. Fringe events were not for profit, were likely to be curated by artists, were free, used word-of-mouth publicity and social media rather than paid advertising, and got funding from a wide base of donors rather than a few big sponsors. Although the Hindustani music fringe was not a self-consciously constituted group, its members shared musical traditions, values and performing sites.

What, then, was the nature of the mainstream that had created this informal fringe? Along with learning from Guruji, I began looking for an answer to this question. In the first sections of the next three chapters, I narrate what I found, before resuming the story of my journey.

But whenever I asked Guruji why his career in Mumbai had ended up in the fringe after beginning in the mainstream, his most frequent answer was 'naseeb'—fate. This implied that a musician's trajectory was a random outcome, like a natural phenomenon or the result of divine will. In a grotesquely unequal society like

India's, moulded by an ancient and violent caste system overlaid by more recent, brutal class inequities, a society in which the accident of one's birth influenced many aspects of one's life, such fatalism is understandable. As a personal credo, it is even admirable, engendering an equanimous acceptance of one's circumstances. But it obscures human decisions and actions as well as the economic, political and social forces at play. Naseeb is like the black box in an air crash. It has to be opened and examined.

◈ Shore: 1969–72

SOFT SUNLIGHT SUFFUSED THE ROOM. WINTER WAS receding, but the early morning air was still cool. Arun ended his rendition of Miyan ki Todi. He had sung the slow composition *Bajo re Mohammad Shah* (Let's celebrate Mohammad Shah) in Jhoomra taal, followed by the fast composition *Langar kankariya jina maro* (Naughty one, don't throw pebbles)[7] in Teentaal, at the end of which he had unleashed a sparkling sequence of taans, the notes sharp and clear.

'Your taans may still have some Bhimsen in them,' an older listener told him as the two sipped tea afterwards. 'But I heard a lot of Gajananbuwa today.'

'Really?' Arun replied.

The man was among about two dozen people who had gathered for a session of the Second Saturday Group at a hall in Dombivli.

'I also think so,' said another elderly well-wisher of Arun's who was standing nearby. 'You've been learning from Buwa for more than three years, haven't you?'

Arun had been singing Todi in public since the age of ten. A deep, rich raag that uses all seven notes, it belongs to the Hindustani music canon's core repertoire, sung by all gharanas. After arriving in Bombay, Arun had sung Todi largely in the Kirana gharana manner, slowly developing the raag from the lower octave onwards, note by note. By now, he was doing so in the Gwalior style of his guru, whose improvisations were strongly linked to the rhythmic cycle, swung across the octave and used multiple speeds from the get-go. For the bulk of raags, in the opening phase singers usually finish a round of improvisation in the central octave by heading back down towards the shadja. Arun called this the avrohi tendency, or singing with a downward momentum. Gajananbuwa did this to powerful effect.

Arun's biggest epiphany under Gajananbuwa was the fundamental importance of being rooted in one gharana. Earlier, he had assumed that he could, magpie-like, pick up whatever he saw as attractive elements of all styles. Now he saw that this created a musical pastiche. The central paradox of genuine creativity was that it needed some constraints or rules within which it could take shape. Without such a framework, how would one even evaluate what constituted creativity? A gharana's rules, rather than being restrictive, enabled focused experimentation. Arun further saw that each gharana channelled creativity in particular musical areas and that Gajananbuwa's genius lay in the way that he had seamlessly merged the rules of different traditions.

Arun was pleased that a seasoned listener had detected his guru's influence in his singing.

One day, Gajananbuwa called out to Arun at the end of class.

'I am singing this Saturday,' Gajananbuwa said. 'You will sit on the tanpura.'

This was his way of asking Arun to provide vocal support.

Gajananbuwa rarely complimented his students. His pedagogy did not include regular feedback, let alone exams. Students had to extrapolate from his one-word reactions and non-verbal cues as well as develop internal gauges. But there were some explicit milestones of progress: a major one was when a student earned the privilege of accompanying him.

Arun began wondering which raags his guru would present. He had given support to his two previous gurus, but following Gajananbuwa in real time would be challenging. Gajananbuwa's composite style appeared deceptively simple to the ear but hid a complex machinery. Further, Arun's first outing with Gajananbuwa, nearly four years after he had begun learning from him, was in Hari Mahadev Vaidya Hall, in the Marathi cultural heartland of Dadar, and would attract many musicians.

At the concert, Gajananbuwa started with Lalita Gauri, singing the canonical composition *Peetam saiyaan* (My dear beloved). Jaipur singers had imbued this raag, like Bihagada, with their unique sensibility. The raag incorporates a key phrase of Lalit into one of two versions of Gauri. For the first ten minutes or so, Arun was silent, while Madhu, who was sitting on the other side, did the filling in. Madhu knew his father's music like the back of his hand. In the meanwhile, Arun began mentally singing his guru's phrases split-seconds after he had rendered them. At one point, Gajananbuwa sang along the following lines, folding a key phrase from Lalit into Gauri:

Ni__ re Ga_ re Ga Ma Pa__ Ma Pa Ma Ga, re Ga Ma Pa__,
Ga ma Ma ma_ Ga_ re Ga_ re (Lalit) Ga Ma Pa__,
Ma dha Ni dha Pa__.

After this sequence, as Gajananbuwa neared the end of the avartan, Arun and Madhu joined in singing 'peetam', which is the mukhda, or portion of the first line that is sung before the sam, and all three of them landed together on the sam with 'saiyan'. They could sing in unison because the mukhda was short and therefore did not lend itself to a lot of variation. Gajananbuwa then turned his head to Arun's side. Taking the cue, Arun began singing, and halfway through the cycle, hesitated, thinking his guru would take over, but Gajananbuwa said, 'Chalo.' Come on.

Arun completed the avartan. To take Gajananbuwa's earlier improvisation a bit further, he sang something like this:

Ga re Ga Ma Pa_ Ma dha Ni dha Pa_ Ma Ga re Ga___ ,
re Ga Ma Ga re Sa____ Ṇi ḍha Ṇi__ re Ga_ re Sa___ .

He arrived smoothly at the sam. Gajananbuwa glanced back with a hint of a smile. Arun began to relax. He got several more opportunities to sing. Towards the end of the rendition, Arun got a chance to sing a sequence of taans.

'Theek ahe!' Gajananbuwa exclaimed. All right!

Arun found that his perspective had literally and figuratively flipped from that of his usual stance of sitting in front of his guru in class. Arun felt reassured that Gajananbuwa presented the same phrases that he sang in class, similar to what someone learning a foreign language might feel on hearing a native speaker uttering phrases being taught in the classroom. The abstract became real, the theoretical became practical. In a state of heightened consciousness, Arun felt his mind penetrating the startlingly pure pitches of his guru's notes and registering his every phrase, pause, stress point, modulation of volume and fine division of beats. Arun also picked out the components of his guru's composite style. From the start, Gajananbuwa had begun generating characteristic Jaipur phrases, recognisable by their looping patterns with paired notes, like this:[8]

Pa-dha Pa-dha Ma-Pa Ma-Pa Ma Ga re Ga,
Dha-Ni Ni-dha Pa-Ma Pa-Ma Ga-re Ga-re Ga-re-Ga-Ma_,
Ga-re Ga-re Ga Ma Ga re Sa_____ .

Arun understood why some musicians said that his guru's renditions of Jaipur raags were up there with the best. Arun also noticed his guru's typical Gwalior swings up and down the octave and his sapaat, or straight, taans. Arun was particularly charmed by his guru's liberal use of the Agra gharana pukar, a manner of calling out either to the beloved or God, when he sang the words 'peetam saiyan', sounding now urgent, now plaintive, now desolate.

'Faiyaz Khan,' Gajananbuwa said to the audience, revealing the inspiration for this device, one of many instances when Hindustani musicians quote another musician within a rendition and immediately offer a reference for that quote. This self-referential practice, of musicians breaking character while performing, to talk to the audience about their music and lineage, is part of Hindustani music culture.

A few weeks later, Gajananbuwa again asked Arun to give him support. A couple of weeks after that, he asked Arun one more time. Arun saw a whole new world opening up. The nature of support depends upon the latitude that a guru affords the vocal accompanist. The supporter's musical strengths, temperament, previous training and experience in accompanying also plays a role. Madhu, while supporting his father, sometimes sang like his grandfather, Antubuwa, from whom he had also learnt for many years. 'Antubuwa', Gajananbuwa would say to audiences when Madhu did this, in another example of citation. Madhu, being an old hand, knew how far to push the limits. Arun realised that he would have to try and hoist himself up to his guru's level yet not overextend himself. In class, like all students, Arun closely followed Gajananbuwa. But on stage he had to take the improvisation further without breaching protocol, the precise contours of which could be discovered only in the moment. After Arun became comfortable in this new role, he became more daring. He sometimes sang a sargam sequence in the hope that his guru would elaborate on it. Gajananbuwa did not always take the bait, but when he did, Arun felt a small thrill.

Early one morning, Arun boarded the bus to Satara town, about three hundred kilometres south-east of Bombay, feeling a surge of excitement. He was on his way to the Aundh Sangeet Mahotsav. Attending this festival was a high point of the year for those in Gajananbuwa's circle. As the bus left Bombay for Satara, close to Aundh, Arun thought of all the wonderful musicians whom he had heard at the festival in previous years: Kanebuwa, Kanetkarbuwa, Limayebuwa, Nivruttibuwa. Run by Gajananbuwa and his sons, the festival took place in a Datta temple, dedicated to the Hindu holy trinity of Brahma, Shiva and Vishnu. The main programme usually began in the morning and went on till the following dawn. But every year, a smaller, informal mehfil took place on the previous evening, when Gajananbuwa's students and other young musicians performed. Since coming to Bombay about four years earlier, Arun had been singing every year in this evening session.

When Arun arrived at around lunch time, the small complex around the temple was buzzing with activity. He went straight to meet Gajananbuwa. After taking his guru's blessings, he mingled with the volunteers, music lovers and students who had begun arriving from nearby towns, Pune and Bombay. The temple complex had a kitchen, an open dining area and buildings with spartan rooms where people slept on mattresses laid on the floor. Arun was always moved by the ambience: the clean village air, the historical setting and the company of musicians.

When the sun set, it was time for the music to start. As Arun sat waiting for his turn, he was enraptured by the pristine music, the smell of incense, the tinkling bells, the faces of his guru, fellow students and music lovers, all arranged like a picture in the temple. When the time came for Arun to sing, he was in a trance. He sang Hem Kalyan, one of the trinity of raags through which he had discovered the secrets of his guru's style. Afterwards, Arun did not remember much. The music had flowed out of him like an independent spirit, of its own free will.

'Your taleem with Buwa is going very well,' Bachchu, Gajananbuwa's eldest son, told Arun.

'That was lovely,' Babanrao, who knew Gajananbuwa well, told him.

'If only I could enter this altered state of consciousness each time I sing,' Arun thought.

At night, wondering what he would get to savour the following day, he drifted into a blessed and blissful slumber.

~

A few months after the Aundh festival, halfway through class, Gajananbuwa ended his exposition of raag Jaitashree.

'Come on, listen to some tabla bols,' he said.

Gajananbuwa often told his students how his training in tabla had opened a rich world of rhythmic possibilities that he began using in his raag improvisations.

'You should all learn the basics of the tabla and its compositions,' he told them.

The tabla has an amazingly rich language, whose building block is the bol, or syllable, such as dha and dhin, each corresponding to a unique stroke or set of strokes on the instrument. These bols are divided into the equivalent of consonants and vowels, and reciting them goes hand in hand with learning to play. Similar to the notes in raags, these syllables can be grouped into the analogues of words, phrases and sentences, in accordance with the rules of tabla grammar. The tabla has many compositional forms, akin to poetic forms such as the haiku, limerick and sonnet. Each tabla form is governed by rules relating to the rhyme scheme, metre and syllables in a line. Some tabla forms, such as the chakradhar, paran and toda, are fully composed. Others, such as the peshkar, qaida and rela, entail improvisation on a core pattern, each with its own rules.

A qaida, the form that Gajananbuwa wanted to recite that day, has a basic pattern within a cycle of sixteen beats or multiples. This pattern has two symmetrical halves, the bhari and khali, meaning full and empty.[9] Gajananbuwa recited a famous qaida with thirty-two syllables.

Bhari: dha ti ta, dha ti ta, dha dha ti ta, **dha ge tin na ki na**,
Khali: taa ti ta, taa ti ta, dha dha ti ta, **dha ge dhin na gi na**.

The qaida has many rules governing improvisation: its very name means 'norms'. A percussionist can use only those syllables that appear in the initial pattern and must ensure that the variations follow the symmetry of the bhari and khali. This means that once a tabla player creates an improvised sequence in the bhari, he or she must transpose it in the khali. The percussionist must also end the variations with the same phrases found in the initial pattern, such as the boldfaced phrases above. The percussionist can create varieties in any multiple of sixteen beats, but cannot change the speed.

A stretch of improvisation usually progresses from simple to complex. The relatively simple variation below has sixty-four beats, double the length of the original qaida, and the additional, improvised sequence appears at the beginning, rendered in italics. One could think of the original qaida as a couplet and this variation as a related quadruplet.

Bhari: *dha ti ta, dha ti ta, dha dha, dha ti ta, dha ti ta, dha dha*
dha ti ta, dha ti ta, dha dha ti ta, **dha ge tin na ki na**,
Khali: *taa ti ta, taa ti ta, taa taa, taa ti ta, taa ti ta, taa taa*
dha ti ta, dha ti ta, dha dha ti ta, **dha ge dhin na gi na**.

Arun saw that by getting some control over these tabla forms, a singer could dramatically expand the canvas of improvisation.

─────

By his late twenties, Arun was performing all over Bombay, including at a range of gharana-focused programmes. Jagannathbuwa invited him to sing at an event in memory of the Agra maestro Vilayat Hussain Khan, in Dadar, at the Hari Mahadev Vaidya Hall, where he had first given vocal support to Gajananbuwa. That day, the audience included many musicians such as Ram Marathe, Vasantrao Kulkarni and Yashwantbuwa Joshi.

Arun also performed at a programme showcasing Jaipur raags at the home of Ratnakar Pai, who had a command over a host of uber-complex raags of that gharana, such as Baraari and Khat Todi.

The audience had many Jaipur musicians, including Arun's beloved Nivruttibuwa, who in his concluding speech commended his rendition of Bihagada. Arun sang at the Trinity Club in Girgaum, in the heart of South Bombay. The venue was a room in a chawl where intimate concerts had been taking place since the early twentieth century, after the great musician Bhaskarbuwa Bakhale had initiated them. Since Bakhale had been a beloved student of Alladiya Khan, Arun sang Nat Kamod, a Jaipur speciality. The audience included well-known connoisseurs, including Annasaheb Thatte, Balasaheb Tikekar and Bhaiyyasaheb Dhamankar. Arun was being noticed and watched.

Arun became an annual fixture at several prominent community festivals, such as the Ganeshotsav hosted by Dada Sawant at his home in Grant Road, in South Bombay, and the Satyanarayan pooja at the Khandekars in Matunga, in central Bombay. Sharad Jambhekar, who was known more for his natya sangeet but was also a fine khayal singer, attended the Khandekar's Satyanarayan pooja one year because he had heard that Arun was one of Gajananbuwa's most promising students. 'What sur, and what dazzling taans,' Jambhekar thought. 'How much practice he must have put in.'

'In the younger generation, the singer to hear is Arun Kashalkar,' Muralidhar Joshi, a discerning listener who regularly attended these community events, began telling people. 'He presents outstanding gharanedar music.'

Arun saw her entering the room. She took her place in the chorus, then quickly looked around. She caught his eye. He smiled. She did too. He had met Sayli three months earlier at a common friend's home, during an informal music session. After that, they had both started attending such gatherings every weekend. She had not learnt music formally, but wanted to, she told Arun. They fell in love. His weekends, already too short, whizzed by in a haze of music and the dance of courtship. He reached for his pen.

This night
I bathed in moonlight, my love.
I am drenched.

Alone, I wait for you,
Exuding fresh love.
The night jasmine laughs.
I am bewildered.

My eyes open to blue waters.
Embarrassed, I mumble.
Who left me this dream?
I am bemused.

I long to meet you.
I effloresce, I bloom.
Hold me close, my love.
I am impatient.[10]

❦

Arun arrived at Rambhau Marathe's bungalow in Thane, at about 8 p.m. one evening to find only the musician's wife at home.

'Make yourself comfortable,' she told Arun. 'I am just leaving to watch a play. You can practise in the music room till Rambhau returns from his rehearsal. You can have dinner with him too.'

'Right,' Arun said, wondering whether he should leave.

No, no, no. He would stay put. The previous month had been psychologically draining, following a perfect storm of setbacks. He had lost his job. His relationship with Sayli had ended. He had cut back on performing in public in order to accelerate his progress under Gajananbuwa. But soon afterwards, his guru had pared down his class schedule because of his declining health. At the end of a week of fitful sleep and disorienting dreams, Arun had even contemplated giving up music, announcing his decision to a fellow passenger on the train.

But right afterwards, he had attended one of the two weekly classes that Gajananbuwa was still holding. His guru had sung Kukubh Bilawal. It was so tuneful, rhythmic and imaginative that it had made Arun euphoric. Not for the first time had the power of Gajananbuwa's music led Arun to imagine the clear blue sky behind dark clouds. Eternally drifting, the clouds would eventually part, even if they drenched the earth before that. One had to stand firm during a downpour and not lose faith in the eternal light. Arun had decided to scout around again for jobs and to start learning from Rambhau, whom he already knew well. Fortunately, Arun had some savings to tide him over for about six months. Until he landed a job, he could devote all his free time to music.

Arun had heard Rambhau live for the first time in Yavatmal, when he had been touring eastern Maharashtra with the troupe of *Sangeet Mandaarmala* (Musical about Mandaar's life).[11] Rambhau was playing the lead role of Mandaar. He had a high pitch for a man, singing in F. For the first time, Arun had heard a musician singing super-fast taans with such clarity. After coming to Mumbai, Arun had got to know Rambhau well and, through osmosis, had absorbed aspects of his music. But he was looking forward to formally training with the musician. Like Gajananbuwa, Rambhau combined elements of the Agra, Gwalior and Jaipur styles, although in his own manner. He had a career in musical theatre, but was a respected khayal singer, a badshah of compound raags, such as Hindol Bahar and Kaunsi Kanada.

Arun spent two hours practising in Rambhau's music room. At about 10 p.m., Arun went back into the living room. Rambhau's wife was nowhere to be seen. Arun was famished, but hesitated to help himself to dinner. Rambhau finally returned at around midnight.

'Come on, come on,' he said, ushering Arun into the music room as soon as he walked in. 'Tune the tanpura. Let's sing.'

Didn't Rambhau want to eat? Arun began his first class in the dead of night, ravenous. Rambhau began singing a slow composition in Jait Kalyan set to Teentaal. Rambhau improvised for several avartans. Arun took over for a couple of cycles. They alternated for a whole hour, till Rambhau's wife appeared, apparently from thin air.

'Don't you want to eat?' she asked.

Arun looked expectantly at Rambhau, who, fortunately, stood up.

It was nearly 2 a.m. when they finished eating.

'Stay over and leave tomorrow,' Rambhau said.

The lesson boosted Arun's spirits. He needed that intense involvement with music to feel alive. The build-up had been fully worth it. Until Gajananbuwa's health improved, Arun decided he would absorb all that he could from Rambhau. But for years afterwards, whenever Arun heard Jait Kalyan, he began to feel hungry.

⁂

A few weeks later, Arun was singing taans when the harmonium player, Madhukar Pednekar, suddenly doubled his speed without warning. Arun stared at him, turned back to the listeners sitting in a small temple where they were performing, in the Masjid area of South Bombay, and correspondingly sped up his taans. The tabla player smiled knowingly.

After the crowd dispersed, Pednekar took Arun aside.

'Whom are you learning from?' he asked.

'Gajananbuwa.'

'Impressive, the way you managed to double the speed to match mine. Many vocalists stumble when I do that.'

Arun frowned, too annoyed by the man's antics to be flattered.

'Are you free tomorrow?' Pednekar continued. 'Come home for lunch. I live nearby.'

At lunch the next day, when Pednekar learnt that Arun was looking for a job, he offered to give him a letter of introduction to a top bureaucrat, an amateur harmonium player who had recently introduced classical music as a subject in government schools and was looking for teachers.

'You will certainly be hired,' Pednekar said.

A week later, while Arun was still debating whether to call the bureaucrat, he was invited by a tabla-playing friend to sing at his workplace, the State Bank of India.

'You will have to sing half a dozen ghazals along with Gajanan Bhave,' said the friend, referring to another singer from Dombivli. 'It will be a duet.'

A couple of days after the programme, the friend informed Arun that a senior executive at the bank wanted to offer him a job through its cultural quota. The State Bank of India often took part in various inter-bank music competitions and the executive wanted Arun to take part in a forthcoming competition of Marathi musicals. He accepted the offer. The job with the country's largest public-sector bank was much better than the teaching position. Looking back at his state of mind a few months earlier, he saw how outlandish the idea of giving up music had been. Even his train companion had seen through it as the ravings of a disturbed soul.

It was the second day of the three-day Sawai Gandharva festival, in the winter of 1971. The festival had been started by Bhimsen Joshi in 1953 in honour of his guru and had quickly mushroomed into a massive affair held in a huge open-air venue accommodating up to a thousand listeners. The vocalist Kishori Amonkar and the sarod player Amjad Ali Khan, both heavyweights, were in the last two slots of the day's line-up of ten artists.[12] As a new face, Arun was the second performer that day. Before starting to sing, Arun smiled at Shaikh Dawood Khan, a much older, well-known tabla player. Khan had heard Arun practising in the green room and told the organisers that he wanted to accompany the young man. Eknath Thakurdas was on the harmonium.

Arun opened with *Dhan dhan bhaag* (Blessed fortune), a slow composition in raag Gorakh Kalyan, pairing it with Ektaal. A few minutes into his rendition, Arun, who enjoyed connecting with listeners, realised that he could not see a single person because even the first row was far away from the stage. He focused on establishing a lively rapport with his accompanists. He moved on to a fast composition in the same raag and ended with a natya geet, or song from the Marathi musical repertoire. Among the receptive audience was Shrikant, Arun's brother, who had moved to Dombivli from Nagpur about two years earlier and was proud to see his elder brother making a mark.

'I am pleased to see how your music is progressing,' their normally restrained father had said in a letter to Arun on learning that he was to perform at the festival.

Arun had received the invitation from Y.D. Joshi (not related to Bhimsen Joshi), the festival committee's vice-president, who was taking lessons from Arun. Several months earlier, Arun had been invited to perform at a felicitation for Hirabai Barodekar, the great Kirana gharana singer, near Pune at which Bhimsen Joshi and Y.D. Joshi had also been present. Arun realised that his recital there had been a de facto audition for the Sawai Gandharva festival.

Arun did not talk about any of this to Gajananbuwa, whose students knew better than to bother their guru with trifling details about their fledgling careers. Arun was nevertheless pleased when a review appeared in the prominent *Kesari* newspaper. 'While singing the dhrut composition in Ektaal, [Kashalkar] rained down taans,' the report said. '[Arun's] natya geet charmed the audience and elicited applause.'[13]

In mid-1972, Arun began a performance of natya sangeet in Dombivli. The previous year, he had won a prize for his singing in a Marathi musical at the Maharashtra State Natya Mahotsava, a state-wide theatre festival. He had played the role of Ustad Jamnalal, a singer in *Panditraj Jagannanth*, a fictional depiction of doomed love between the eponymous Hindu scholar at Shah Jahan's court and the Mughal king's daughter.[14] Arun, encouraged by the harmonium player Govindrao Patwardhan, had spent time developing a unique style inspired by the actor-singer Chhota Gandharva. The casting director of Lalitkaladarsha Natak Mandali, a leading theatre company, had seen Arun's performance at the theatre festival and recruited him for its own production of the same musical. Arun had acted and sung for five full-house shows. 'You did a great job,' Bhalchandra Pendharkar, the energetic producer, had said.

Yet after that, Arun decided not to act in musicals because it diverted his attention from khayal, and restricted himself to presenting its songs, like that evening in Dombivli. That day, in the audience was a young woman called Sunanda, who was listening with lukewarm enthusiasm. She had little interest in music, let alone of the classical kind. She had merely accompanied a music-loving friend whose parents were eyeing Arun as a potential groom for their daughter. They had sent her to check him out.

'What happened?' Sunanda's mother asked her when she got home.

'She didn't fancy him,' Sunanda replied. 'I don't know why. He was nice.'

Sunanda's parents moved swiftly. Through an intermediary, her father communicated to Arun that he had a daughter of marriageable age. Soon afterwards, Arun and an elderly well-wisher visited the young woman's home for the customary chai-poha, or tea and snacks.

Her family had found out that Arun had a stable job at a big public-sector bank, was a rising vocalist and came from a respectable family. Even in arranged marriages, some initial chemistry helps tip the balance. Sunanda liked what she saw. Arun, too, gleaned information about her and her family. She was twenty-four years old and had three siblings—two brothers and a sister. She had grown up in Mahad, in Ratnagiri, one of three districts in the state's Konkan region, which lined the western coast south of Bombay. Her father had been in and out of low-paying jobs, even driving state-run inter-city buses for a while. After Sunanda finished high school, her family had moved to Dombivli after one of her brothers had found a job there. Sunanda was completing her bachelor's degree in commerce while working part-time in the accounting department of a firm in Dombivli. She was also helping her mother run the house after her elder sister had got married and left home.

Arun weighed his options. His family background was very different from hers. His father was not very well-off, but was a renaissance man, immersed in classical music and keenly interested in literature and philosophy. Yet Arun knew how his community viewed singers. He was pushing thirty. Like the vast majority of men of his generation, he wanted a wife who could cook and manage the home. On that front, the young woman was more than capable. Crucially, perhaps not fully realising all the implications, she was amenable to Arun's long-term plans: he had no intention of climbing the bank hierarchy; the job was merely a source of income to support his ambitions in music.

Arun's guardian strongly advised him to accept the proposal. He decided to take the plunge, but years later, to elicit laughs, he sometimes deliberately presented a one-sided version of what had happened.

'She saw me singing and grabbed me,' he would say.

The wedding was fixed for October. He had a secure job. A few months earlier, Gajananbuwa had come out of his semi-retirement and increased his hours of teaching. Arun found that stepping back had helped him process and integrate what he had learnt. The previous two years with Rambhau Marathe had added another dimension to his music. He had steadily gained performing experience. He had got to know many outstanding musicians from the older generation. Not a few people were saying that he was a singer to watch out for.

After the engagement ceremony, Shrikant, who had been staying with Arun, moved out of their one-room flat. Following a convention in Maharashtra according to which a woman took on not only her husband's last name but also a new first name of his choice, Arun decided that he would call his wife-to-be Dhanashree, the name of one of his favourite raags. In the weeks leading up to the wedding, Sunanda came over after work almost daily to cook Arun's dinner. Her initial attraction to him, when she had heard him performing, gradually gained an emotional texture as she basked in his sunny temperament. Her childhood had been austere. In a particularly tough period, she and her sister had made and sold flower garlands to earn money. Arun was the first person who could make her smile so much. After she had cooked for him, Arun walked her back home, about a kilometre away. Arun was by far the more talkative. She was mostly content to listen, but came clean to him that she did not care for classical music. He understood that her life had been one full of struggle, in a household barely getting by, but felt that he would be able to make her see the music's beauty.

On those leisurely walks, he began filling her in on his past, starting with his heartbreak and going all the way back to his childhood.

◆ Architect

ANYONE WHO ENTERS THE WORLD OF KHAYAL IS LIKELY TO soon encounter the word 'gayaki', which means vocal style. One can speak of this or that gharana's gayaki, the vocal style associated with a pedagogical tradition. One can also talk of a singer's gayaki, especially because khayal's culture puts a great premium on a performer developing his or her distinctive style within the discipline offered by the gharana. Ultimately, creatively ambitious khayal singers try to go beyond imitating their gurus through thoughtful innovation. This is why singers within the same gharana, while sharing many characteristics, can sound different from one another, at least to seasoned listeners. This drive for stylistic originality partly underlies the common belief among musicians that one cannot become a good khayal singer before one turns forty. One should not take this number literally. It merely symbolises the long time it takes for a singer to attain creative autonomy.

A particularly original singer or one who learns in more than one gharana and synthesises the principles of various traditions might build a new structure within the broad architectural style represented by the gharana palace. If this new style catches on, such a singer might be viewed as having founded a new gharana. For a new style to sustain, it must go beyond experimentation and embody well-defined principles that the inventor can teach to a new generation of students. As a rule of thumb, if such a new style is passed on for at least three generations, it can be considered a gharana.

Consequently, when students learn from a khayal singer, they do not learn a generic form of khayal but the guru's gayaki. However, some gurus might present their gayaki as normative, not just one of many approaches.[15] In the internet age, when students have easy and perennial access to a wide variety of styles, how important are concepts such as the gharana and gayaki? The gharana as a stylistic vision is essential for becoming a performer because it gives coherence and well-defined aesthetics to improvisations. A khayal style, after all, incorporates the thoughts, refinements and ideas of successive generations of musicians. If a student tries to use elements from different singers without first having undergone rigorous training exclusively under one guru, the outcome is likely to be a superficial mishmash. This, then, is khayal's artistic paradox: for many years, students must imitate and absorb the guru's gayaki, but eventually, to make a mark and demonstrate their individuality, they must break free, find their unique voices and perhaps even forge new styles.[16]

'While learning to write, every school child gets the same font as a model. The child practises copying it in an exercise book and gradually the formation of letters becomes disciplined. But within that discipline, each child develops a unique handwriting, which eventually becomes so characteristic of that individual that it is used to identify the person. Even with two children who practise equally hard, a common model leads to different expressions, depending upon each child's physical abilities, temperament, visual impressions and cultural background.' —AK

7

◇ Black Box

A FEW WEEKS AFTER THE SECRET MASTERS SESSIONS CONCERT featuring Guruji, someone brought to my attention a Facebook post put up by Art and Artistes, a Mumbai-based company that described itself as 'India's first Multi-media Music Programming Company working across all mass mediums'. This post shared a link to another post with the following introduction, 'A very simple yet comprehensive commentary on the next generation of Classical Music. Interesting aspects highlighted by Durga Jasraj, which would go towards the overall development of a performing artiste. Must read.' The link took me to a concert review by Durga Jasraj, the firm's founder and Hindustani vocalist Jasraj's daughter. The identity of the performer is irrelevant. 'GM my dear lovely friends ...,' her post began. 'Last evening attended #HindustaniClassical performance by [a] young Rising Star… She looked so elegant & beautiful with perfectly manicured nails with rings, subtle make up and accessories… Please note being pretty is an asset for a performing artiste… During her an hour long [sic] performance she presented Raag Kedar & Raag Saraswati… Firstly she is blessed with a very sonorous voice & as they say "Surel" has excellent grip over "Laykaari"… She has worked hard to have powerful "Taans" too… Her rendition of Raag Kedar was good but when she announced her 2nd Raag Saraswati my 1st reaction was like why is she singing yet another raag???? Maybe she could have sung the predictables a thumri or a bhajan… It was a brave decision & it paid off… She sang

Saraswati beautifully... She had fantastic co artistes... both these young men are good looking too!!!'[1]

Social media tends to encourage flippancy and instant pontificating, so one must cut people slack for what they say there. But when a company posts a comment on its official page, it presumably wants people to take it seriously. The review consequently gives us an inkling about the values that propel an influential part of the Hindustani music mainstream. For Art and Artists, founded in 1999, is one of three big private firms that have shaped this mainstream ecosystem since the turn of the millennium. The other two firms, founded in 1996, are Pancham Nishad Creatives and Banyan Tree Events.[2] The promoters of these firms spotted a business opportunity in organising concerts after the Indian government began transforming the economy in 1991 by opening up many sectors to the products, services and investment of local and global firms. These promoters began raising money both from ticket sales and a booming corporate sector that wished to market its brands to a burgeoning consumer class. Representing the fourth phase of patronage in khayal's history, this millennial ecosystem replaced one that evolved after Independence, in 1947, which was shaped primarily by state-run entities and non-profit groups. In the phase preceding that, from the late nineteenth to mid-twentieth century,[3] non-profit music clubs and circles emerged and coexisted with an older stream of patronage from rulers of British India's princely states. Before that, in the first phase, rulers of empires and kingdoms were the main patrons.

In the third phase, after Independence, among state-run entities, the All India Radio, or Akashvani, played an important role.[4] Until television channels proliferated in the 1990s,[5] state radio had a significant presence in people's lives. It aired hours of classical music every week and employed musicians as staff artists, producers and advisers, thus giving them financial stability. Inevitably, some musicians enjoyed a greater presence on the concert circuit than others. But All India Radio ensured that listeners heard a large and diverse set of worthy musicians. Like any large institution, the state broadcaster had its share of politics and controversies, including conflicts with musicians. But on balance, it was a force for the good. In the second category, among non-profit groups, SPIC MACAY, an acronym for the Society for the Promotion of Indian Classical Music And Culture Among Youth, worked across the country. In Mumbai, the large National Centre for the Performing Arts, or NCPA, many smaller non-profit organisations and neighbourhood music circles promoted Hindustani classical music.

By the turn of the millennium, the big private players became a powerful force, driven by commercial interests. Strictly speaking, these firms are not patrons, i.e., those who support an art form without any expectation of monetary returns. But in their early years, they were able to present artistically serious performers because many corporate sponsors and listeners belonged to the All India Radio era, recognised musicians' names and valued their music. In this period, the troika of private firms added scale and spectacle to Hindustani music. After a while, however, they had to deal with corporate sponsors and listeners who were increasingly from the post-All India Radio generation and were not familiar with the music. In a buoyant post-liberalisation India, in which the lines between art and entertainment were blurring, the troika of big firms and smaller entities in the Mumbai–Pune belt music therefore faced new compulsions.

'I am not there to impress the connoisseur,' Durga told me over a five-hour interview at her home office in Mumbai, where she came across as warm and hard-working. We even discovered that we had a friend in common. 'My responsibility is to make sure that khayal is not stuck in time and that the music is attractive so that the audience is lured. There is a reason why I get a huge audience and others don't. Sponsors don't care about the artist. They want audiences. By the grace of God, for my biggest projects, I have never signed a contract with artists' names on it.' In other words, in the new ecosystem, she could determine what the public heard through a process in which art and artists, the very name of her company, had become irrelevant.

※

Over the years, I spoke about a dozen times to Shashi Vyas, the founder of Pancham Nishad Creatives and son of the late khayal singer C.R. Vyas. Shashi-ji was a cheerful, forthright man who could be charming. A Marathi speaker who had grown up in Matunga, a South Indian hub in central Mumbai, he once took me by surprise by addressing me in fluent Tamil. Shashi-ji had several longstanding forums presenting good musicians, including youngsters, but over the years, they all got just a couple of opportunities each. For his big events, he tended to circulate the same clutch of musicians. When I asked him what was special about his favourites, he said, 'A star can touch the hearts of everyone in the audience. Stardom depends upon mass appeal ... Those who cannot present devotional or other musical forms will have limited popularity.' On another occasion he told me candidly, 'I am running a business. I have to ensure that tickets sell.' Yet another time, he said, 'This is my profession ... I can't take the approach of experimental theatre, where people try something new every time and put up plays irrespective of the consequences.'

Mahesh Babu, the founder of Banyan Tree Events, the third of the troika, had also presented fine musicians in his early days, but subsequently began focusing on a coterie of performers for his big-ticket events. At some point, he also diversified into Sufi music and jazz. During a four-hour interview that I did with him and his business partner, who is his wife, at their Mumbai office, I said that there were many excellent musicians of all ages who were not visible. 'We can create many more platforms,' said Babu, a soft-spoken man who had learnt to play the tabla for many years. But I did not discern a significant change in his flagship offerings.

It would be unrealistic to expect businesses to ignore market conditions and prioritise art over profits; it takes a rare visionary to nurture a niche music genre while remaining solvent.

~

Unfortunately, some of the mainstream stars, whom the public has been made to believe are the finest classical artists, fail to display the requisite depth, breadth and taste. They often indulge in gimmicks involving speed and volume, capitalising on the advent of electronic sound reinforcement and powerful microphones. In general, the mainstream favours musicians who are willing to tailor their art to the middling tastes of mass audiences or those who have name recognition either because they also sing popular genres or are related to established musicians. Once musicians become celebrities, impresarios can keep selling events to sponsors and the public on the strength of their names. Organisers probably feel this is a better business strategy than spreading their publicity budgets across a large number of performers without any guarantee that they will be able to fill large halls. 'The broader trend in Hindustani music today is avoidance by many musicians, especially the very famous, of delving deep into one's knowledge of the subject and creating music that is congruent to the aesthetic values of this art form,' Kedar Bodas, the late khayal singer, told the sarod player and music writer Arnab Chakrabarty, whom I got to know over the years.[6]

Devina had a similar view. 'For many reigning stars, it has now become less about the art and more about establishing a near monopoly on the very limited sponsorship pie assigned to this form, and the status and power that goes with it,' she said. 'But after years of operating in this manner, they must know that beneath the surface glitter, there is a growing void. They must be asking themselves, for whom do I sing or play? Ironically, the constant reminders of their status as successful artists often prevent them from seeing that there are other worthy musicians who remain hidden, whom, in an equitable and fair ecosystem, they might have regarded as their musical colleagues and equals, but whom they regard merely as people who didn't make it.'

A handful of khayal singers with depth and artistic integrity do have a presence in the mainstream, but mostly because they became known through other means or before the commercial imperative became entrenched. Yet the system does even these performers a disservice because it does not offer them the incentive to take creative risks. The big promoters' choices have a downstream effect. Because their favourite artists are so visible, it has become difficult for music festivals and smaller organisations to raise money from sponsors for non-celebrities. 'Almost the same musicians are chosen to perform in all the festivals,' Amarendra Dhaneshwar, critic, organiser and singer, told tabla player and historian Aneesh Pradhan.[7] Arvind Parikh, a sitar player and businessman who has for decades been closely associated with the NCPA, told me during a long interview at his home that the organisers of a leading music festival were willing to feature musicians if they brought along sponsors. 'This is the very, very difficult market now,' he said.

Duets and fusion music are also favourites among some promoters, but many of these events appear less as thoughtful experiments and more as one-time marketing ploys aimed at retaining the interest of listless consumers with an appearance of novelty. These events are arguably not classical music but 'viewable classical music-like shows', in the same way that highly processed foods are not food but 'edible food-like substances', as the food writer and activist Michael Pollan argues.[8] *Jalsa*, a television show with live audiences produced by Durga Jasraj, is a case in point. Aired first on state-run Doordarshan in 2008 and then on the private channel Zee TV in 2011, the show had more than a hundred episodes featuring performers of non-film Indian music, including classical, semi-classical and folk genres. Each episode had one musician, sometimes two, performing a short item, then chatting with Durga and another host, and finally taking questions from the audience. With its loud stage décor and dramatic editing, the series unabashedly emulated show business.

'Over the last two decades and more, we had begun to feel disillusioned with the way concerts were presented …,' Devina and Pepe wrote in an essay.[9] 'In the newly unleashed neoliberal fantasy world that was to become the India Story, ICM [Indian classical music] concerts, had … begun to acquire a loud, exhibitionistic and brassy sheen. [They were] being repackaged and marketed in a manner that seemed more suited to a competitive high-stakes sport than a subtle, exquisite and quiet art form.' A 'high-stakes sport' was precisely one of Durga's benchmarks. 'At some point, *Jalsa* was beating the TRPs of repeat telecasts of IPL,' she told me. 'That is my contribution to Indian classical music.'

Yet the setting of a khayal performance can play a major role in shaping the quality of music. The gradual unfolding of a raag needs a relaxed and calm ambience in which both the performer and audience can immerse themselves. Further, the quality of *listening* can significantly influence the outcome. This is why so many descriptions of memorable Hindustani music concerts list the musicians and connoisseurs in the audience. The ideal forum for a khayal performance is a baithak, which allows the performer to make eye contact with the audience. Even the proscenium stage, especially in large venues, may be a compromise. A flashy television set that fragments everyone's attention might actually be counterproductive. In theatre, actors performing in large halls often wear excessive make-up because its effect gets diluted at the distance at which viewers sit. The make-up serves an artistic purpose: it is one of the ways in which the actor conveys the character's attributes. But when Hindustani musicians give their performances the equivalent of garish make-up in order to get applause from every last listener in a large hall, they often end up distorting the art form.

Market-driven packaging grips many creative fields, such as films and publishing, but in most cases the stakeholders do recognise the distinction between sales and quality. In Hindustani music, many factors contribute to muddying the waters. For one, many listeners have little exposure to alternatives. For another, art music is an acquired taste. Informed listeners look at the quality of musicians' sur, the depth of their raag elaborations, their control over and creative use of rhythm, their command over various improvisation techniques and, especially for khayal, the originality of their styles. The way musicians handle raags is particularly important. 'For a seasoned listener of Hindustani music, it is ... being able to bring out the spirit of a raag, and then, to maintain it throughout a performance, that matters the most,' Arnab wrote.[10] T.M. Krishna, a leading Carnatic musician, writer and activist, has said that in a trained listener's mind 'the raga exists ... even before it is heard'.[11] I had, however, noticed that even lay listeners responded sensitively to honest music presented in tasteful, appropriate settings.

Just as the public's health deteriorates when empty calories and addictive ingredients of aggressively marketed fast and processed food crowds out nutritious fare, audiences' sensibilities decline when packaged entertainment consistently dominates the performance circuit. It also marginalises many 'uncompromising artists who seek to create thoughtful, honest and moving music without smokescreens of show or fanfare', as the khayal singer Priya Purushothaman described them.[12] When some of them teach in order to earn an income, the mainstream, in a perverse reversal of cause and effect, denigrates them as mere pedagogues. Some musicians reluctantly acquire academic credentials such as a PhD in order to become eligible for salaried jobs in institutions, which diverts their energy from music and accounts for the uneven quality of these dissertations.

Undeniably, throughout khayal's history, at least some excellent musicians failed to receive opportunities commensurate with their abilities. Additionally, khayal singers who also sang devotional or film music inevitably became more popular than those who did not. But in the previous era, almost all those who did get the bulk of concert opportunities were artistically sincere. Moreover, those who did not become as well-known nevertheless commanded respect. From the previous era, many examples spring to mind of contemporary pairs whose careers went in different directions: Kesarbai Kerkar, famous and highly paid, versus Mogubai Kurdikar, less known and not widely heard; similarly, Bhimsen Joshi, a celebrity, versus Basavraj Rajguru, far from a household name; and Mallikarjun Mansur, who eventually received a Padma Vibhushan but himself penetrated the concert circuit late in life, versus Gajananbuwa, whom many listeners still do not know about.

⁓

In the new ecosystem, the more complex styles are at a disadvantage because they are probably more demanding on lay listeners. Of the six most widespread styles, promoters tend, perhaps subconsciously, to privilege the Kirana, Patiala and Rampur-Sahaswan styles over the Agra, Gwalior and Jaipur gharanas. As described earlier, styles in the first, heterodox group lean towards a note-based, linear ascending and free-flowing model of elaboration while those in the second, traditional group veer towards a phrase-based, composition-directed and avartan-linked paradigm, with some deviations. Ironically, styles that grew out of non-elite groups now have the upper hand. Those who have not heard much of Hindustani music seem to be able to follow the movement of a note-driven elaboration more easily than a phrase-driven one, for which they have to absorb a string of notes in one shot. This may be less true of those who have some listening behind them because they may be able to recognise certain phrases, especially from common raags, the way they catch familiar tunes. But in general, phrases are like idioms in human language, which are not the straightforward sum of their parts. Just as someone needs immersion in a language to understand its idioms, a listener requires a fairly deep engagement with a raag to fully follow a phrase-driven elaboration of it in real time. In addition, linear ascending elaborations are probably easier to follow than composition-driven ones, which do not follow a predictable path. Finally, free-flowing improvisations may be easier on the ear of lay listeners than those more tightly linked to the rhythmic cycle.

Overall, styles in the second group generate an aural texture that some might describe as being 'busier' than those in the first. Relative to popular music, they are even more stylised. This is what many lay listeners say about Carnatic music as well. Styles in the second group also have a larger repertoire of raags that include compound and complex raags, and they use a greater variety of taals. People should not read a value judgement into these distinctions because complexity and breadth are not inherently superior. Simplicity all the way to minimalism can be powerful, while musicians with relatively small repertoires can stand out for their depth and originality. Nevertheless, by marginalising complex styles, the ecosystem makes it more difficult for their adherents to practise their art.

Despite these obstacles, some exciting developments are taking place in these traditional styles behind the scenes. For example, since 2015, many fine women performers have emerged at the forefront of the Agra gharana, which, like dhrupad, has traditionally been pigeonholed as a male domain because the style calls for rendering the vigorous nom-tom aalaap and for gaining a high level of mastery over rhythm. I remember how excited I was in my teens to hear Lalith Rao, a rare woman from the Agra tradition, rendering the nom-tom. Unfortunately, just when she was set to establish herself as a leading khayal singer, she developed voice problems and receded from the concert stage. But a new generation has arisen, such as her own student, Bharathi Prathap, as well as Pournima Dhumale and Priya Purushothaman. Two of Guruji's senior students, Ketaki Chaitanya and Sugandha Sainath, are also fine performers in the Agra mould as are some of Shubhada Paradkar's female students.[13]

The future appears perilous also for some small gharanas, such as the Mumbai-centred Bhendi Bazaar and Kunwar Shyam styles, which have rich repertoires of compositions and have made original contributions to the khayal genre. When All India Radio penetrated almost all households, people had access to the sounds of all gharanas and a multitude of raags, taals and compositions. But in the new era, organisers inevitably gravitate towards styles that they believe are more likely to appeal to a mass audience.

※

Among the arts, the performing traditions resist commodification because, unlike paintings, they are perishables without exchange value. To earn quick profits from the performing arts, private promoters will inevitably come under pressure to package them for mass consumption. Yet in the long run, pandering to an assumed lowest common denominator might be bad even for business. 'Promoters of Indian classical music frequently say that the genre is too complex for the average concert-goer and needs to be watered down into "digestible capsules" for it to be appreciated,' Arnab wrote.[14] 'However, such suggestions also seek to remove the key ingredient that keeps any art form relevant to society—sincere intent.'

Why should society worry about what happens to Indian art music? The one-word answer is: civilisation. An enlightened society makes a concerted and fierce effort to protect what is valuable in its culture from the untrammelled writ of market forces. Most markets do not embody the perfect competition envisioned in economic textbooks, and their outcomes in many spheres have been detrimental to human development. The social benefits from activities like classical music, fundamental science research, literature and the visual arts are not tangible and may not have a direct monetary value. Rather, they can subtly and deeply nurture a society's humanistic ethos, its compassion and tolerance, its rationality and scientific temper, its well-being and quiet confidence. For India, khayal is special in many ways, possessing a tradition of artistic excellence going back centuries. Generations of musicians have invested their minds and souls in this music. It is, in short, one of the Indian sub-continent's great inventions.

If khayal is to survive in its full glory, it needs to be pulled back from the brink. Art music probably always had a precarious existence, but the market's apparently unstoppable propulsion presents a challenge of a different order of magnitude, compounded by the fact that this force is an 'invisible hand', as Adam Smith, the eighteenth-century Scottish moral philosopher, famously described it. There may be some truth to Pablo Picasso's adage that 'the people who make art their business are mostly imposters'. But enlightened state or non-profit institutions could have tempered, if not neutralised, the market's weaknesses. In Mumbai, one non-profit institution, flush with resources and founded precisely with a mandate to support and preserve Indian art forms could have played this vital role. But around the turn of the millennium, it began moving away from its founding priorities.

◈ Backwaters: 1943–57

BLEARY-EYED, ARUN SPLASHED WATER ON HIS FACE, BRUSHED his teeth and climbed down to the music room on the ground floor. It was about 5:30 a.m. and his father was already tuning the tanpura.

'Tea,' his father said, pointing to a couple of steaming steel tumblers on the floor. Arun sat opposite his father and gingerly picked up a tumbler.

'Sing the Sa,' his father said a few minutes later, handing the tanpura to Arun.

'Sa …,' Arun sang, suppressing a yawn.

'Sit up straight,' his father said.

Arun pulled his spine up and pushed his shoulders back. He began strumming the tanpura, laid lengthwise across his lap. He had just turned six and looked tiny in relation to the instrument.

'*Pag ghungaroo* (Anklets on my feet),' his father said, lifting the round cloths covering the tops of the tabla and dagga.

Arun started singing the composition in raag Malkauns, his father joining in on the tabla with Teentaal. His father let Arun sing the composition a few times without interrupting him. He then told him to sharpen some notes, pause at specific points, emphasise particular syllables. He made Arun sing it several times. He knew that correcting the child too much at one go would demoralise him. Arun needed time to absorb the refinements.

Arun's father had begun daily lessons with his eldest son a year earlier, in the mornings and evenings. For the first few months, Arun had been indifferent, mechanically going through the motions. His father had given him no choice and there was no court of appeal. His father had begun by teaching bhajans because they were part of daily life in many Hindu households and were easier for a beginner to sing than khayal compositions. After a while, he introduced natya geets, which like bhajans, had catchy beats because they were aimed at mass audiences. After a few months, his father began slipping in raag-based compositions, making sure that Arun sang them fluently before introducing the raag's notes and basic phrases.

That day, after about an hour, his father gave him a break. Arun heard the comforting clatter of his mother working in the kitchen, which was adjacent to the music room. He darted to the first floor. His younger brother, Shrikant, five years old, was up. He had begun learning a few months earlier, but was allowed to come down later.

'Let's go down,' Arun said.

His father began singing *Mama atma gamala ha* (My soul yearns for this), a natya geet based on raag Bihag. He discovered early on that his eldest son could pick up melodies astonishingly quickly. The class went on for another hour. Shrikant just listened, a luxury that Arun had not enjoyed. His father, a lawyer, ended the lesson at about 7:30 a.m. in order to receive clients in the foyer and let Arun get ready for school, which he had recently started attending.

On the way out, Arun peered into two cloth hammocks hanging side by side in a corner of the room. Lying inside were his eighteen-month-old twin brothers, Prakash and Subhash. He liked to stroke their cheeks to make them gurgle. In less than an hour, bathed and dressed, Arun returned downstairs for his breakfast. He saw Krishna, who was in charge of his family's tract of land outside town, entering the kitchen with a basket of vegetables and leaving with the family cow, which stood in the backyard, out to graze. Arun was always fascinated by how the animal gently went around him and his brothers when they happened to be sitting or crawling on the floor. When it was time, Arun left home and began walking to school, less than a kilometre away.

Arun was seven-and-a-half years old when his sister Usha, two years older, passed away. A shroud of silence descended on the Kashalkar home. Arun's father indefinitely suspended music lessons. All Arun knew was that Usha had been running a high fever for two days, but the family doctor had been unable to bring it under control. Grief-stricken, his mother went about her arduous day with blank eyes. A distant relative came to help her, but only for a few days, so she had to resume her household duties while mourning her first child. She cooked, cleaned, washed clothes in the Khuni river nearby and looked after her two-month-old infant, Vikas, the latest addition to the family. Arun's stepsister, Sulochana, older than Usha by six years, took over some of their mother's tasks. She was the daughter of their father's first wife, who had died of a brain haemorrhage ten months after giving birth to Sulochana.

With his father cancelling music lessons, Arun felt sad all the time. He had loved his sister. True, they had occasionally quarrelled, the bickering mainly taking the form of a tug-of-war with a lantern that they had shared after sunset while writing on their slates. But that shared activity had also fostered a special closeness. In the immediate aftermath of her death, Arun discovered the art of silent singing. Unable to sleep one night and to avoid disturbing his brothers, he tried to reproduce in his mind the tune of *Chameli phuli champa* (Jasmine flowers and frangipani), a composition in raag

Hamir that he had heard Rajabhau, a blind musician from a nearby village, sing a few days earlier. Rajabhau played the harmonium for devotional singing at the largest local temple, the Gopalkrishna Mandir, and often dropped in at the Kashalkar home. After a week, Arun began to wonder when life would go back to normal.

⁂

Clackety-clack. It's flying. Eeeeee. Your turn. Oh baba.

Arun heard the carefree squeals of boys playing viti dandu from his home's music room, where he was having his evening lesson with his father. He felt a twinge of longing for the normal life of a nine-year-old. For the previous four years, he had spent almost all his mornings and evenings learning music. He had felt less lonely when, one by one, his three younger brothers had joined him and a few children in town had started attending the evening classes, but he sometimes yearned for the pleasure of unsupervised play. The only physical activity that he had time for was an occasional swim in the river. But before his yearning could make itself at home, he was jolted by the sound of the tabla. Shrirambuwa had started playing. He and Balajibuwa were attached to the Gopalkrishna Mandir and regularly came over to Arun's home to provide accompaniment to his father's students. Shrirambuwa and Balajibuwa were kirtankars, those who performed the kirtan, which combined storytelling, singing and philosophical exposition largely using religious and mythological characters. In that pre-television era, the kirtan was hugely popular in the Marathi-speaking regions. The two men had undergone formal training in khayal and dhrupad because the kirtan used raag-based music. When Arun's father, who was largely self-taught, had a question about raag grammar, he asked them and other kirtankars who passed through town.

Shrirambuwa started singing a dhrupad composition in Yaman, *Parabrahma parameshwar* (Supreme truth, supreme God), set to the twelve-beat Chautaal. Arun was immediately charmed by it and forgot about viti dandu. For him, compositions were like new toys.

As Shrirambuwa began singing the second verse, Arun decided that the composition's appeal lay in its slow but sure-footed pace, evoking an elephant's regal gait, and its long meends, which reminded him of the sinuous movements of the animal's trunk.

⌘

One morning, Arun waited apprehensively for his father to begin his music lesson. For almost a week, his father had been trying to teach him *Aaye na baalam* (My lover has not come). The problem was not that Arun disliked the thumri. It was that he liked it too well. Arun had heard the Patiala gharana maestro Bade Ghulam Ali Khan rendering it on the radio several times. When his father started singing the composition, Arun desultorily repeated the first line.

'How are you singing?' his father asked him, frowning.

Arun said nothing. His younger brothers—Shrikant, the twins Prakash and Subhash, and even Vikas, not yet four years old—all looked apprehensively at Arun. He again sang the line, faltering. His father told him to repeat it. Arun continued to sing tentatively.

'Why are you not singing this properly?' his father asked, sounding puzzled and upset at the same time.

Shrikant, too, was perplexed. He admired his elder brother's grahan shakti, his ability to quickly grasp melodies and retain them. Arun picked up even the idiosyncrasies of various singers. Why was he struggling with this thumri? Arun knew why. The perspicacious eleven-year-old could tell that his father was not singing the composition with the accent and lilt that were so alluring in Bade Ghulam Ali's rendition. Arun felt that his father may have picked up the accents of bhajans, natya sangeet and classical compositions, but not of thumris. Yet the question of telling his father this or imitating Bade Ghulam Ali Khan did not arise because both responses would have been considered to be rank insubordination. Yet despite having a premonition of the consequences of not cooperating, Arun, with his precocious sense of aesthetics, could not bring himself to imitate his father.

After a few more futile attempts to get Arun to fall in line, his father grew quiet.

'Come up with me,' he said in a flat tone.

His father came down alone and ended the lesson early. Anxious, Shrikant ran upstairs to discover that their father had locked Arun up in their bedroom. His elder brother was crying softly but Shrikant did not dare to let him out. Ever since their school had shut for the summer a few days earlier, the house had been filled with the boys' chatter and music. That day, a tense silence prevailed. Their mother looked distressed. She did not switch the radio on again at noon, after the morning broadcast had ended, to listen to Hindi film songs and bhav geet, sentimental Marathi songs, which aired in that session.

When their father returned home for lunch, she immediately went up to him.

'I am going to let him out,' she said with uncharacteristic firmness. 'He has not eaten all day.'

Arun was fast asleep when his mother went to fetch him. When he came down, he was so hungry that he forgot the spanking. His father was mostly gentle and soft-spoken, but it was no secret that he was hugely invested in the musical education of his eldest son, who had shown unusual ability and maturity early on. This was not the first time that his father had punished him, but that day he had gone much further. Paradoxically, Arun felt proud that his father was singling him out for attention even while being aware that his passion could tip over into fury.

※

Arun's father may have been projecting his own unrealised ambitions in music onto his first son. Born in 1906, Nagesh Dattatreya Kashalkar grew up in Satara, the epicentre of an extraordinary musical efflorescence. At the turn of the twentieth century, a musical revolution was sweeping through southern Maharashtra as the khayal genre caught the imagination of its people. Southern

Maharashtra had a large concentration of princely states, such as Aundh, Kolhapur, Miraj and Sangli, whose rulers nurtured art and music, from the mid-nineteenth century to the mid-twentieth century, attracting talent from all over the subcontinent. In the last decade of the nineteenth century, Alladiya Khan, for instance, moved from North India to Kolhapur, to become a musician at the court of its ruler, Shahu Maharaj. Marathi-speaking singers such as Balakrishnabuwa Ichalkaranjikar found employment in such courts on returning home from Gwalior, where they had gone to learn khayal. Balakrishnabuwa became one of khayal's main propagators in Maharashtra, training numerous students, such as Antubuwa, Neelkanthbuwa Jangam, V.D. Paluskar and Yashwantbuwa Mirashi, who further spread the genre.[15]

As khayal took root in Maharashtra, the sangeet natak, or Marathi musical, also burst on to the scene. This theatrical form combined prose with poetry set to raag-based compositions sung by actors. These songs served a dramatic function, of moving the narrative forward and describing characters' emotions. The songs were inspired by a range of contemporary forms: devotional genres such as the kirtan, folk genres such as the lavani and ovi, as well as raags from both the Hindustani and Carnatic music traditions.[16] The musical quickly became one of the mainstays of popular entertainment in Maharashtra, remaining so until the rise of cinema about half a century later. The musicals' semi-classical songs, or natya geet, were a crucial part of the attraction, becoming so popular that singers, including classical vocalists, began performing them independently. Marathi drama companies hired khayal singers to compose music, train their actors and, sometimes, act. Performances in musicals often included improvisation in the form of aalaap and taans, sometimes approaching levels seen in full-blown khayal performances.[17] Over time, music came to dominate many of these plays to the extent that it diluted their dramatic content.[18] In the first half of the twentieth century, along with the pioneering activism of Bhatkhande and Paluskar to democratise khayal, the rise of these musicals contributed to popularising the genre among a larger swathe of society. Khayal and natya sangeet mutually reinforced each other, leading to a virtuous cycle of expanding audiences.[19]

In primary school, Nagesh learnt singing for three years from Keshavbuwa Matange, trained in the Gwalior tradition, and took in as many Marathi musicals as he could. On finishing high school, Nagesh went to Fergusson College in Pune, the heart of the music world. Along with studying English, mathematics and Sanskrit and participating in debates and literary events, Nagesh attended many concerts every week. After getting his degree, he moved to the Nagpur area, in contemporary Maharashtra's eastern region, working first as a school teacher and then in the accountant general's office. Subsequently, he got a law degree, and in 1933, reasoning that an entrant into the field might get a foothold more easily in the underserved hinterland, he moved to Pandharkowda, south of Nagpur, in Yavatmal district, where the number of land disputes was rising.

In Pandharkowda, while building his practice, he deepened his musical knowledge by reading books, listening to radio programmes and talking to any musicians he met. But for a decade, Bhausaheb, as locals began calling him, did not have time to teach anyone, including his first two children, Sulochana and Usha. Once he had established his practice, he began teaching music. Gradually, this became as important to him as arguing cases.

❧

In Arun's childhood, Pandharkowda had about ten thousand inhabitants, consisting of a variety of Hindu castes and linguistic groups as well as several Muslim families. Besides a majority of Marathi speakers, it had Marwaris, who were traders with roots in Rajasthan, and native Telugu speakers who had migrated from Andhra Pradesh, which bordered Yavatmal district in the southeast. Pandharkowda buzzed with modest economic activities. It had carpenters, doctors, farmers, goldsmiths, lawyers, moneylenders, priests, shopkeepers, school teachers and tailors. Many of the town's residents, including the Kashalkars, owned land in the surrounding countryside, which those engaged in non-agricultural professions tilled on the side, growing crops such as cotton, jowar and toor dal as well as vegetables. The town's diverse residents by and large lived harmoniously together, although Muslims had their own neighbourhood and Dalits lived on the edge of town in a separate quarter. The Kashalkars, who were among a dozen brahmin families in town, lived in a simple two-storey brick house, in a mixed Hindu neighbourhood.

Yavatmal and neighbouring districts were not as economically developed as the state's leading cultural and intellectual centres of Bombay, Kolhapur and Pune, in western Maharashtra. But the east did feel ripples from developments in the west. Yavatmal also belonged to another sphere of influence, one radiating from Gwalior. Pandharkowda, for instance, is about as far east of Mumbai as it is to the south of Gwalior. Many musicians visited the town between the Ganesh festival in August–September and the end of harvesting the following year in March. In between, there was Navaratri and a three-day urs, a carnival commemorating Sufi saints. Whenever Arun's father learnt that a musician was touring that region, he circulated an appeal to the town's well-off residents requesting them to contribute money so that he could invite the artist or troupe. As the harvest season picked up from October, locals flush with money obliged, not just to please Arun's father, but also because they wanted entertainment. Musicians came readily because knew they had a hospitable and knowledgeable host in Arun's father. Visitors included rising young musicians, such as the singer and composer Ganga Prasad Pathak, the tabla player Shanta Prasad and the singer Jagdish Prasad; a music troupe founded by the brothers Motiram and Jyotiram Prasad; and singer-actors from Marathi musicals. The urs brought in many good qawwals, such as Ismail Azad and Jani Babu.

For Arun, the excitement around the annual festivals compensated for the near-militaristic training schedule that his father had instituted for him. During one Ganesh festival, when Arun heard two young girls from South India singing bhajans, he realised that he wasn't the only youngster immersed in music.

Early one morning, about two weeks after his twelfth birthday, Arun set out for Nagpur with his father and Shrikant. Arun's mother was nursing her sixth son, Ulhas, born just a week earlier. On the bus ride, Arun kept track of the time on his father's watch, which had a gold-plated strap and for which he had a childish fascination. His father had submitted Arun's name for an open music competition, one without any age or gender restrictions. The contest was being organised by the government of Madhya Pradesh, in Nagpur, then the state capital. By then, Arun had been performing in Pandharkowda and towns nearby for five years, mostly at social or religious events, for solicitous adults. But Arun's father felt that his son was ready for a larger stage. Some locals were sceptical. They conceded that Bhausaheb had trained his son well enough to sing in their hick town, but were indignant that he thought he could catapult Arun to a state-wide competition. About a week before the event, Arun had been upset when he had heard stray words like 'presumptuous' and 'empty-handed' when his parents had spoken to each other in low tones.

The competition took place a few days before Republic Day in Morris College. Arun counted about fifteen participants. When his turn came, naive and enthusiastic, he was unfazed that he was by far the youngest competitor and was being accompanied on the tabla by an unknown adult. He had practised raag Todi, his favourite at the time, in which he rendered the slow composition *Ab more Ram* (Oh my Ram), in Ektaal, followed by the fast composition *Allah jaane* (The lord knows), set to Teentaal. Todi is full of complex tensions, which makes it hard to sing accurately. The treatment of Pa, for instance, is particularly challenging. The singer must initially dance around the note in such a way that it makes its absence strongly felt, like a phantom limb, and must take the audience by surprise when finally landing on it.

In Nagpur, Arun, Shrikant and their father stayed at a relative's home. The city's small and tightly knit music community knew that Arun's father, a well-known figure in the region, was visiting with his two sons. Having a broader outlook than those in Pandharkowda, people were excited that such a young boy was taking part in this prestigious event. They lined up performances for him in the evenings. On the eve of Republic Day, as Arun was setting out for a performance, his father unclasped his watch and handed it to him. Arun looked puzzled.

'You got the first prize,' said his father, who had received word from the competition's organisers.

The next evening, the Kashalkars arrived at about 5 p.m. at one of Nagpur's largest grounds. As the prize winner, Arun had to sing, and he chose raag Multani. He returned on a high to Pandharkowda, where those who had scoffed at him realised that they had been wrong.

―

Within a month, Arun's father took him to another competition in Amravati, eastern Maharashtra's cultural capital. This competition was part of a week-long music festival featuring leading musicians of the day. These included Amir Khan, Bade Ghulam Ali Khan, Khadim Hussain Khan, Kumar Gandharva and Mallikarjun Mansur and top instrumentalists such as sitar players Abdul Halim Jaffer Khan and Ravi Shankar, sarod player Ali Akbar Khan, tabla player Alla Rakha Khan and shehnai player Bismillah Khan. Arun was attending a festival showcasing so many stalwarts for the first time. He sat through one recital after another as though in a dream, almost forgetting to show up for his event. He made it just in time and again sang Todi. On the tabla was the young Gopal Wadegaonkar, whom he had befriended in Nagpur. Boosted by the Republic Day prize and a familiar tabla player his own age, he was even more at ease than in Nagpur. He again won the first prize, glowing when he received the trophy from Abdul Halim Jaffer Khan, whose rendition of Komal Rishabh Asavari on the radio had earlier deeply moved him. For Arun's father, it was another vindication of his appraisal of his eldest son.

On a mid-morning during the summer vacation, Arun, who had just entered his teens, took some money from his mother and headed out with Shrikant tagging along. They went to the post office to send off a parcel of books to the United States Information Service library in Mumbai. Their father regularly borrowed books from there as well as from the British Council's library, on a variety of subjects, including education, philosophy and art. The libraries sent him the books via registered post and he returned them the same way. The United States Information Service's library had even mailed him its entire catalogue. That morning, the books that Arun had to post were on Montessori education, his father's latest topic of interest. Arun, who could just about read English, had leafed through one of them, but had given up after failing to make sense of the sentences, with their profusion of incomprehensible words like 'adolescent' and 'pedagogy'.

After dispatching the parcel, the brothers went to a watchmaker's shop to buy Miramax batteries for their National Ecko radio, which their father had bought five years earlier. Arun remembered how excited he had been the day it had arrived. In that era, the radio had a prominent presence in most homes, representing a link to the outside world. Many people developed an emotional relationship to it. One of the Kashalkars' neighbours had even garlanded his radio after hearing Hirabai Barodekar's singing emanating from it for the first time.

Before returning home, the boys dropped in at the home of Shankarrao Phatak, a lawyer who lived down the street and subscribed to *The Indian Listener*, a weekly magazine published by the All India Radio. The magazine published the broadcaster's programme for different cities, and carried profiles of musicians and articles about a range of subjects. The brothers wanted to find out who was performing that week in the National Programme of Music, which B.V. Keskar, the country's information and broadcasting minister, had launched four years earlier, in 1952. Shankarrao regularly gave Arun older editions of the magazine, from which he cut out musicians' photos and pasted them in a scrapbook. He marked the photos of musicians he had heard and waited eagerly to hear the others on the radio so that he could check them off too.

The radio in the Kashalkars' home was always switched on during the day, tuned to the All India Radio station, and outside its broadcasting hours, to Radio Ceylon, which broadcast Indian film music, a genre that Keskar had banned on All India Radio along with cricket commentaries. The radio formed a comforting aural backdrop to life in the home and marked the time of day. On Saturday night at 9.30 p.m., when the National Programme aired, the entire Kashalkar family sat around their radio in the music room with the seriousness of listeners at a mehfil. The ritual was one of the high points of Arun's week.

One Monday morning, Arun woke up and sat slumped on his mattress. Why had his father not woken him up for his music lesson? As he yawned and stretched, it dawned on him. The Diwali vacation had begun! That in itself was cause for a minor celebration. But he was even more elated that the Akashvani Radio Sangeet Sammelan, a week-long radio festival of classical music, had started the previous day. Over the week, the broadcaster's stations all over the country would air the festival's programme. In North, West and East India, the programme would overwhelmingly consist of Hindustani music, and in South India, Carnatic music. Keskar had begun this festival two years earlier, in 1954, to coincide with Diwali week.

The previous morning, bathed and breakfasted, Arun and his brothers had huddled around the radio. Arun had got goosebumps on hearing the first notes of Bhairav that B.R. Khaladkar had played on the shehnai.[20] After this, Hafiz Ahmed Khan sang Alhaiya Bilawal and Chand Khan sang Asawari. After a short interval, Kishori Amonkar opened with Khat, followed by Radhika Mohan Maitra, who played Bilaskhani Todi on the sarod. The session ended with a duet by the sisters Hirabai Barodekar and Saraswati Rane, who rendered Shuddh Sarang. Throughout the session, Ulhas, a few months shy of his second birthday, had mostly dozed on a mattress nearby. For some time, after being fed, he had sat on Arun's lap, preternaturally calm and alert. He had been listening to classical music literally from his cradle.

The night session had begun with Ishtiaq Ahmed Khan playing Kedar on the sarod, followed by Abid Hussain Khan singing Khambavati. After the interval, the dhrupadiya duo Nasir Aminuddin and Nasir Moinuddin Dagar had sung Malkauns, followed by Rasoolan Bai, who had presented a thumri and tappa, accompanied by Alla Rakha on the tabla. Arun's younger brothers had fallen asleep one by one, but he had stayed up till the very end and, overwhelmed by the music he had heard, had been unable to fall asleep for a long time.

That morning, Arun felt sorry that one day of the festival was already over, experiencing the wistful feeling that the end of an event's beginning heralds the beginning of its end.

Arun's father had suspended music lessons that week so that his sons could stay up through the night sessions. Arun spent the day ticking off photos of musicians in his scrapbook, helping his mother with minor tasks and playing with his brothers. The week went by in a delirious daze of music, scrumptious Diwali treats and lazy afternoons. The Kashalkars' simple house sparkled with lanterns, oil lamps and, thanks to the messianic Keskar, Hindustani music's leading lights.

Under Keskar's stewardship, the festival had grown every year. That year, 1956, it had fifty Hindustani musicians, up from thirty-four the previous year. Just the number of vocalists totalled thirty-three, with khayal singers accounting for the overwhelming majority, at twenty-nine, and two dhrupadiyas and two thumri singers filling the remaining four spots. Instrumentalists, including two percussionists playing solo recitals, numbered seventeen. The programme thus reflected two trends: the dominance of vocal music and, within that, of khayal. Otherwise, the programme was remarkably thoughtful and balanced. It had a mixture of mature performers, young musicians and promising talent, and a range of gharanas and raags. It featured a variety of instruments: been, flute, jaltarang, sarod, shehnai, sitar, vichitra veena and violin. It had solo percussion recitals, of both the pakhawaj and the tabla. It featured a performance by the All India Radio orchestra, Vadya Vrinda, conducted by Ravi Shankar.

The vocalists and string instrumentalists belonged to a variety of gharanas. The list is worth reproducing because it reveals the quantity, quality and diversity of what was on offer. Among vocalists, the veterans included Altaf Hussain Khan (Khurja), Anant Manohar Joshi (Gwalior), Krishnarao Shankar Pandit (Gwalior), Rahimuddin Dagar (dhrupad), Vilayat Hussain Khan (Agra) and Vinayakrao Patwardhan (Gwalior)—all born in the last decade of the nineteenth century, except Altaf Hussain Khan, born even earlier, in 1864, and Anant Manohar Joshi, born in 1881. Those in the prime of their careers included Chidanand Nagarkar (Agra), Gajananbuwa Joshi (Gwalior with Jaipur and Agra), Gangubai Hangal (Kirana), Hafiz Ahmed Khan (Rampur-Sahaswan), Hirabai Barodekar (Kirana), Khadim Hussain Khan (Agra), K.G. Ginde and S.C.R. Bhat in a duet (Agra) and Nissar Hussain Khan (Rampur-Sahaswan), all born in the first two decades of the twentieth century. Young musicians, born after 1920, included Bhimsen Joshi (Kirana), the Dagar brothers (dhrupad), Kishori Amonkar (Jaipur), Malabika Roy (Kirana), Manik Verma (Agra and Kirana) and Ram Marathe (Agra, Gwalior, Jaipur).

Another notable feature was the absence of the harmonium as accompaniment, the result of an earlier ban by John Fouldes, a British musicologist that All India Radio had employed in the 1930s. In its place was the sarangi, the traditional accompanying instrument. When the festival's last performer, Nisar Hussain Khan, finished his concluding item, a tarana, a form that exploded into colour in his hands, Arun braced for silence and darkness. He knew that he would have to summon every last drop of motivation the next day to finish homework that he had avoided the whole week in order to give his mind the rare chance to wander as it wanted.

~

As Arun finished singing, he saw tears rolling down a woman's cheeks. Afterwards, other women surrounded him, silently putting their hands on his head to bless him. He had sung *Paradhin ahe jagati* (Man is a slave to destiny), from the *Geet Ramayan*, a collection of fifty-six Marathi songs chronologically narrating the story of the titular Sanskrit epic. Written by G.D. Madgulkar and composed and sung by Sudhir Phadke using Hindustani raags and taals, the songs were a landmark in the history of Marathi light music. A year earlier, in April 1955, All India Radio had begun airing one new song from the collection several times each week. Arun liked singing *Paradhin*, but its lyrics were lugubrious. 'If suffering is what God intends for you, no one is to blame,' the song begins, going on to say that 'man is merely a slave to destiny, no one is to blame.'

Arun had been singing this song for more than a year, and each time he did so, he got more engrossed in the rendition. He had not seen much of the world or experienced emotional pain, but testifying to the power of poetry and music, he always felt the sorrow of which the song spoke. His voice, yet to break even though he was nearing fourteen, was still sweet and high-pitched, quivering delicately at the appropriate moments. The fifty-odd guests had no doubt heard the song many times on the radio and were primed to react emotionally, but hearing a young boy expressing its solemn philosophical ideas moved them to tears.

Arun had sung copious amounts of light and devotional music, but the broadcast of *Geet Ramayan* created a fresh demand for sentimental fare. He began travelling to other towns in Yavatmal to perform. At a Sharada Utsav function in Wani, about fifty kilometres from Pandharkowda, he presented *Sangu kashi ga manachi vyatha hi* (How am I to tell you of my heart's sorrows?), a melancholic bhav geet. Arun infused so much feeling into his singing that he received a trophy. Another time, after he presented Hindi film songs in Yavatmal, a Hindi-speaking Englishman in the audience named Mr Graf invited Arun and his father home to tea, allowing the teenager, who could play the harmonium, to try out his upright piano.

In early 1958, before Arun's board exam at the end of high school, both he and his father sat for the Sangeet Visharad exam, equivalent to a bachelor's in music, in Yavatmal. His father realised that Arun had outgrown him and needed professional guidance. It was just as well that Pandharkowda did not have a college. Arun would have to leave home.

◆ Sport

TO BECOME A COMPETENT KHAYAL SINGER, ONE NEEDS YEARS, if not decades, of training and practice. But anyone with an interest in it can become a listener. Those who are daunted by the genre could start off thinking of khayal as a sport. Most people cannot become Olympic athletes, but they can surely enjoy watching them in action. Like almost all sports, khayal singing uses muscles and has rules. The writer and musician Amit Chaudhuri says that 'music is more akin to sport than to writing', implying that both music and sport call for developing one's muscle memory.[21] For unlike writers, athletes and khayal singers do not have the luxury of being able to revise their work before presenting it to the public.

Analogies with rugby, chess and tennis each illuminate a different facet of khayal: its athleticism, intellectualism and spontaneity. Just as rugby might appear like an unruly scramble of people to those in the dark about its rules, khayal might come across like a jumble of sounds to the uninitiated. A listener will thus find it useful to become acquainted with khayal's basic rules. Second, like chess, khayal has a cerebral dimension. Just as chess has complex winning strategies that have evolved over time from a small set of rules and moves, so does khayal. A listener wishing to appreciate khayal at a deeper level will benefit by going beyond the rules and becoming familiar with the equivalent of its winning strategies.

Finally, like playing singles tennis, khayal singing is a spontaneous, solo activity. Just as a singles tennis player, alone on the court, must choose a shot in a split second, based on years of training and playing experience, without consulting a coach during breaks in a match, khayal singers must produce music alone on stage, on the spur of the moment, based on their instincts, developed over years of training and performing experience.

One can push this analogy only so far. Yet even the points of divergence can be illuminating. In sports, except in gymnastics and similar activities, aesthetics do not count, as Roger Federer fans like me often bemoan. Athletes play to win and some to smash records, while khayal singers, at least those with sincere intent and artistic ambition, perform to create something beautiful and original.[22] A khayal performance has no scoreboard, no umpires or real-time commentary.[23] Each listener perceives and appreciates a performance in a very personal manner.

'Every moment in my improvisation is a reflex action. For years, I have honed the skill of instantly weaving together different ideas and impressions that I have imbibed through training, practice and listening. As I sing, new ideas keep emerging, some of which surprise or even thrill me. I am in effect saying to the audience: this is my khayal—my thought, my imagination.' —AK

8

◇ **Counterweights**

ON A HOT EVENING IN MAY 2016, I MADE MY WAY TO THE Godrej Dance Theatre at the National Centre for Performing Arts, or NCPA, Mumbai's best-endowed arts centre, where Guruji was singing for the first time. The Centre's eight-acre campus is located by the sea in Nariman Point, a business district in South Mumbai. A large crowd had gathered in the courtyard outside the theatre. Several people wove in and out looking for spare tickets. Minutes before the concert was to begin, a sign went up: 'House Full. Thank you.'[1] I had not attended a sold-out Hindustani music concert at this venue for several years. I was particularly surprised because it was a weekday, Thursday, at the height of summer, when many people are away on vacation. About ten of Guruji's students managed to coax the NCPA staff to allow them to sit in the wings, but an equal number of people without tickets were stranded outside. Music aficionados had apparently taken note of Guruji's re-emergence. Inside, the atmosphere was charged. The theatre's about two hundred seats and low ceiling made for an intimate ambience. At the end, the audience gave Guruji a standing ovation.

This concert had come about because I had phoned Suvarnalata Rao, the head of the NCPA's Indian music section, hoping to get her views for my profile on Guruji. In contrast with the connoisseurs who had turned up for the Secret Masters Sessions concert, she said, sounding embarrassed, that she did not know much about him. A couple of weeks later, she called me to ask for Guruji's phone number.

'I want to invite him to perform,' she said.

'In which auditorium?' I asked her.

'The Godrej Dance Theatre,' she said.

It is one of the smaller auditoriums in the Centre's complex.

'We don't get a good response for our Hindustani music concerts,' she quickly added. 'If the attendance is good, we can later present him at a larger venue.'

Although the concert was sold out, Guruji never heard from her again.

~

Rao may have been partly hamstrung by fundamental changes that had swept through the NCPA at the turn of the millennium under the leadership of K.N. Suntook. He had made Western classical music the NCPA's primary focus, departing in an unprecedented manner from the institution's founding focus on preserving and promoting Indian performing arts. This shift had evoked anguish from a wide cross-section of performing artists, collaborators, employees and members of the arts-loving public, who contended that many Indian performing arts were resource-starved and had far less funding than Western ones, which were amply supported in many countries. One would have imagined that a non-profit organisation that calls itself 'India's premier performing arts institution',[2] would focus on the country's traditions, they said.

At the outset, it is important to say that despite this change, the NCPA, given its huge resources, did continue to play a role in the city's cultural life. One must also clarify that people's concerns about its changed priorities did not stem from jingoism, parochialism or nativism. On the contrary, art lovers welcomed the NCPA's move to include genres from across the world. Further, they acknowledged that all institutions were likely to an extent to reflect the interests of those at the helm. It is also true that the NCPA's immediate catchment area of South Mumbai has during Suntook's tenure seen a demographic shift: a section of the traditional audience for Hindustani music, namely the middle-class Marathi-speaking intelligentsia, has been moving out to localities further north because of economic and urban policy changes. Finally, people recognised that all programming involved making choices, which could be contested from one angle or the other.

What upset people was the huge imbalance, which was evident from Suntook's own statements, the organisation's messaging and its allocation of funds, attention and energy. Suntook, an executive at the Tata Group, founded Bisleri, one of India's first mineral water companies. In 2000, he became the NCPA's vice-chairman. He took over as the chairman in 2008, a year after his predecessor, Jamshed Bhabha, passed away. Bhabha had founded the NCPA in 1966 'to promote and safeguard India's performing arts tradition' because 'he keenly felt the lacuna of a pioneering institution' in this sphere, according to the NCPA's website.[3] Bhabha raised funds for his dream from the philanthropic arms of various business groups, led by the Tatas.[4] Bhabha then convinced the state government to reclaim eight acres from the sea for the campus, procuring funds from the Dorabji Tata Trust and other corporate donors.[5] In 1965, in a letter to the Dorabji Tata Trust, Bhabha wrote: 'In India, more perhaps than in any other country, music and related arts constituted a most important part of the country's 5,000-year-old cultural and spiritual legacy.'[6] Bhabha further wrote, 'Music accompanied an Indian from the cradle to the grave; from birth to death.'[7] This is exactly what the playwright, actor and public intellectual Girish Karnad later said about Indian culture: 'If you don't know music, you cannot understand it.'[8] The state government leased the eight acres that it owned to the NCPA at a token annual fee of Re 1, which is what the institution has continued to pay.[9]

The NCPA is registered under both the Societies Registration Act 1860 and the Bombay Public Trusts Act 1950 (later renamed the Maharashtra Public Trusts Act 1950). Under the first law, the primary aim set out in the NCPA's memorandum of association, or MoA, was 'to establish a centre for the classical, traditional and contemporary arts and sciences of performance and communication.'[10] But both laws allow entities registered under them to change their founding aims by following specified procedures. The MoA under the first law was last amended in 2006.[11] In that MoA, the relevant clause was amended to say that one of the society's main aims was 'to give widest possible platform to and to encourage, promote and preserve in every way possible, the arts, classical, traditional and contemporary, in all its aspects and ramifications'. Under the second law, the MoA was amended in 2008 to include the same clause.[12]

Until 2000, under successive leaders, namely V.K. Narayanan Menon, P.L. Deshpande and Vijaya Mehta, the NCPA adhered to its founding aims. They were all, as the veteran journalist Anil Dharker noted in an article, 'products of, and deeply steeped in, Indian culture'.[13] Under Suntook, this changed.

After becoming chairman, Suntook invited journalists to a meeting where he told us that he had set up the Symphony Orchestra of India, or SOI, in 2006 to prove that India could produce 'world-class music'. I remember gently interjecting, 'But Mr. Suntook, we already have world-class music.' He went on to say that China had created not one, but numerous good orchestras. A former consultant to the NCPA, whom I will call consultant A, told me that Suntook had scant knowledge of India's musical heritage.[14] Given the NCPA's prominence in Mumbai, most people who spoke to me did not wish to be named. 'People have tried telling him that unlike China, we have several well-developed, rich traditions of classical music,' said consultant A. 'We should be nurturing those. Western music does not need India to survive.'

'Suntook's attitude to Indian art forms as a whole is contemptuous,' said Deepa Gahlot, who headed the theatre and film division from 2010 to 2017. 'He said, Indians don't know theatre. For him, theatre was only British theatre.' Because Suntook was busy with the orchestra, Gahlot said that initially she had enjoyed a measure of autonomy and had started several theatre and film festivals. However, the winds of change could already be felt. In 2011, the NCPA spent Rs 50 lakh on screening equipment to stream productions of the National Theatre in London.[15] Yet in the same year, the NCPA made it enormously difficult for the city's theatre groups to stage plays at its premises by overnight substantially increasing the rent it charged for its five theatres.[16] For example, for the Experimental Theatre, a black box greatly valued by the city's theatre groups, the NCPA raised the rent to Rs 35,000 on weekdays and Rs 40,000 on weekends—from Rs 6,500, plus a surcharge of Rs 2,700 or half of box office revenue.[17] Since then, the rents have increased further, Gahlot told me. Moreover, after Gahlot quit, the NCPA hired a Briton, Bruce Guthrie, in her place. Despite my repeated requests, the NCPA's public relations division did not grant me an interview with Suntook.

On the NCPA's website, the SOI had a tab all to itself, while *all* other art forms fell under a single tab titled 'Genres'. Apart from the orchestra, the website had a separate link for the organisation's Western classical music activities, while Indian classical music was clubbed under the generic category of 'Indian music', which included genres such as semi-classical, devotional and folk music. An incident in 2012 also revealed the NCPA's priorities. That year, Laura Battle, a journalist for the London-based *Financial Times*, came to Mumbai to write an article on Indian classical music in the city. Since Battle wanted to speak to someone at the NCPA, Devina took her to meet Suntook, with the help of Arvind Parikh, who had been associated for decades with the organisation's Indian music activities. At the meeting, which Parikh attended, Battle asked Suntook about the institution's vision for promoting Indian classical music, but he kept talking about Western classical music. 'It was embarrassing,' Devina recalled. 'Laura had to keep reminding Suntook several times that she was writing a feature on Indian classical music in Mumbai. At one point, he lost interest and abruptly ended the conversation. In the end, Laura only cursorily mentioned the NCPA in her article.[18] That was telling.'

Then in 2013, Suntook said that he wanted to make the NCPA 'a global brand', which many art lovers pointed out was a fundamentally different goal from Bhabha's aim to 'promote and safeguard India's performing arts tradition'.[19] Even from a marketing viewpoint, Suntook's critics said that it made more sense for someone looking to make the NCPA a global brand to focus on the country's unique selling proposition, namely its performing art forms, in which it was already world class.

Reflecting its new agenda, the NCPA has been spending the bulk of its funds on Western classical music. Consultant A said that the amount that the institution spent on this genre every year was a closely guarded secret, but estimated that it ran into crores of rupees. Arvind Parikh estimated that eighty per cent of the organisation's funds went to that single category.[20] I could not verify this because Albert Almeida, a consultant to the chairman's office, declined my request to see the NCPA's annual accounts for the three pre-pandemic years.[21] He merely told me that the institution's main sources of funds were the Tata Trusts, corporate sponsors and donors, and these were supplemented by interest income, membership fees and proceeds from ticket sales.[22] He said that the NCPA, although a public charitable trust, did not fall under the purview of the Right to Information Act, or RTI Act, 2005, and did not have an information officer.[23]

But the conclusions of a full bench of the Bombay High Court suggest that his contention is debatable. In 2024, while hearing a case on the applicability of the RTI Act to public trusts, the court clarified that any institution that received 'substantial government funding or land concessions' would be considered a 'public authority' and would therefore be subject to disclosure requirements under the RTI Act,[24] if the requested information did not fall under exemptions listed under this law. The NCPA's annual accounts did not seem to tick any of the exemptions mentioned in this section.[25] Separately, according to advice published online by an accounting firm, 'If [a] trust's annual income or the receipts generated by the trust's property has exceeded the amount of one crore rupees, then it is... essential for the trust to publish the accounts in the newspaper.'[26] If the NCPA does fall in this category, then, according to this opinion, it has to make its accounts public.

Even without the accounts, however, one can gauge the organisation's scale of spending on Western classical music. Just the orchestra, with its many foreign members, including the music director, and its regular international tours, requires a massive outlay of funds. 'The Orchestra's core group of musicians is resident at the NCPA all year round and forms the SOI Chamber Orchestra, performing a regular series of concerts through the year at the NCPA and at other venues around Mumbai and India,' the institution's website says. 'Additional players are recruited from a talented pool of professionals from around the world.' Further, every year from 2006 to 2025, the NCPA has had about twenty Western music instructors teaching under its aegis.[27]

The organisation spent Rs 6 crore to bring two operas to its campus for three nights, a newspaper article published in 2013 quoted a person close to the institution as saying.[28] A former employee, whom I will call employee A,[29] and two others closely associated with the NCPA said that it regularly flew in people from abroad to maintain an organ. Another consultant, who worked closely with Suntook, whom I'll call consultant B,[30] said that the institution had bought timpani, or kettledrums, for lakhs of rupees and had spent around Rs 25 lakh on orchestra members' costumes for one season. I could not verify these facts with Suntook. 'There is a caste system within the NCPA,' consultant B, however, went on to say. 'You can see it and feel it. Even the peons and canteen boys know it. The orchestra just has to say, I want something, and it will get it. The Indian music division has to keep asking.' Yet another consultant to the NCPA, whom I will call consultant C,[31] said that the institution gave Western classical musicians from the former

Soviet republics five-star accommodation, a car and driver, but booked top Indian performers in three-star hotels. 'This disparity irked me,' consultant C said. Only after this consultant repeatedly pointed out this discrimination to Suntook did some top Indian performers begin getting five-star accommodation.

The NCPA may have got sponsors for the orchestra and other Western classical music events, but this raised the question of why the institution had not invested the same effort in raising money for Indian performing arts, which require a far smaller outlay and are already teeming with world-class practitioners, these consultants and others said. The NCPA would have got audiences if it had promoted the Indian performing arts with the same vigour it devoted to Western classical music, and showcased their excellence, they also said. As for the orchestra, after all the resources poured into it, what was its quality by global standards, several people asked. Could the orchestra even be termed 'Indian'? In 2013, the orchestra had eighty-five members from Kazakhstan and ten Indians.[32] In 2025, it had between ninety and one hundred and ten members, the number varying depending on the programme, and fifteen Indians, only a slight increase.[33] The foreign musicians were Kazakh, Russian, Spanish, British and Dutch.[34]

⁂

Various stakeholders rued the missed opportunity for sustaining Indian art forms. 'I told Mr. Suntook that the NCPA was sitting on public land,' a person who had worked with the organisation, whom I will call employee B, told me.[35] 'I told him that it was a national centre, but was not catering to a wide swathe of the arts-loving public.' Anmol Vellani, a theatre director, teacher and founder of the Bengaluru-based India Foundation for the Arts, echoed this view. He had given the NCPA grants when he had been the Ford Foundation's programme officer for education and culture for a decade until 1995, and had subsequently followed the institution's trajectory. 'The government has given the NCPA extremely valuable land at a concessionary rate, presumably because it thought the organisation would serve the interests of art, artists and the public in India, and more specifically in Mumbai, not just a narrow set of people. By charging such high rents for its venues, how is the NCPA supporting the performing arts ecosystem of India and Mumbai?'

Members of the NCPA's governing council, especially representatives of the state government, should be asking these fundamental questions, consultant A said. The government's representatives are Maharashtra's chief secretary, the principal secretary in charge of revenue and the cultural secretary.[36] 'Perhaps the NCPA is not a huge priority for the Tata Trust, but why are at least the government members not playing a more active role?' consultant A asked.

By the standards of Indian performing arts, the NCPA has massive sums at its disposal.[37] In 2013, its annual budget was Rs 30 crore, and it was poised to get a windfall from the sale of Jamshed Bhabha's family bungalow, which he had bequeathed to the arts organisation. By then, his art and artefacts had already been auctioned for Rs 27 crore, while the bungalow was later sold for Rs 372 crore.[38] Yet in 2013, even as the NCPA was set to get the proceeds from the sale of the bungalow, Suntook seemed to suggest to a reporter that he did not have enough funds. The article spoke of the organisation's 'financial woes' and how 'Suntook and his team manage to make ends meet'.[39] Many people asked the obvious question. 'If the funds are scarce, why was an astronomical sum spent on rebuilding the Jamshed Bhabha Theatre, which was destroyed in a fire in 1998? If the funds are low, then why host western performances that drain the funds?' a newspaper article asked.[40]

As a concrete comparison, the NCPA paid Guruji less than Rs 50,000 for his maiden concert, an amount that included fees for his accompanists and students providing vocal support.[41] I use Guruji as an example only because I was privy to what he was paid.

But two other excellent Hindustani vocalists who had performed in the same venue told me that they, too, got amounts in this range. With the money it had, the NCPA could also have recruited some of the country's best Indian classical music gurus from its backyard, at a fraction of what it was probably paying its foreign Western music instructors.

Under such a regime, the Indian music division faced constraints. In a long interview with me in her office, Rao told me that she had no second-in-command and no succession plan.[42] She ran education programmes and organised events with the help of a small staff. The division's education initiatives, funded by corporate social responsibility, or CSR, money included giving annual scholarships to young musicians, paying several gurus to teach a couple of students each for free[43] and conducting lessons in schools for underprivileged children. These were valuable activities, but the money involved again showed the imbalance within the institution. For instance, in 2025, the scholarships, being given for about a decade to roughly ten students a year, consisted of Rs 10,000 a month per person, a fraction of what is needed to free youngsters from having to earn an income in order to focus solely on music.

When it came to events, consisting of performances and workshops, several insiders told me that the Indian music division was under constant pressure from the marketing department. Take its annual *Bandish* festival, one of its flagship events, begun in 2010 and funded by CSR money. The festival not only repeatedly presented the same few musicians, but also began including film music, something that even Durga Jasraj's *Jalsa* TV series did not do. 'Speak to the marketing section,' Rao said, when I suggested to her that CSR funds were meant to liberate an organisation from the market-driven mainstream.

Over and above its challenges within the NCPA, the Indian music division needs renewal, people said. In particular, it needs to become more diverse and engage with various gurus and their student communities, starting with those in Mumbai, they said. Rao had three advisors for classical music: besides Arvind Parikh, born in 1927, they were Neelima Kilachand, born in 1944, and Mala Ramadorai, born in 1952.[44] They were gracious individuals who had contributed to the field for many years, but they also belonged to South Mumbai's super-elite and had been associated with the NCPA for a long time. Rao, born in 1954, was Parikh's student.

People also pointed to the NCPA's opening of a branch of Shrutinandan, the Kolkata-headquartered music school run by Patiala gharana singer Ajoy Chakrabarty, in April 2022.[45] In principle, the NCPA hiring Indian musicians to teach is a good idea, but handing this job to one musician is not, they said. This decision further entrenched the already prominent influence in the Indian music division's activities that insiders told me Chakrabarty had long enjoyed. 'There is an informal arrangement with Shrutinandan to supply students for the NCPA's young performers' series,' said a person closely associated with the institution who did not wish to be named. Critics said the NCPA had made itself vulnerable to accusations of institutional capture by a powerful actor and of ushering in a monoculture in an art form full of musicians from diverse traditions, both in the Mumbai-Pune region and in Kolkata, Chakrabarty's home turf. 'To truly represent a country as populous and diverse as India, a national organisation should do some deep searching of the arts landscape,' said consultant C.

Perhaps because of her skeletal staff, Rao told me that she did not have time to attend guru purnimas, the annual performances of students of various gurus that are great talent-spotting opportunities. As a result, her division has ended up taking a top-down approach, even though an earlier experiment along these lines did not achieve much, Arvind Parikh, who had coordinated the effort, himself told me. He had set up the All India Musicians Group consisting of six well-known musicians each from the Hindustani and Carnatic streams.[46] The group had met about three or four times, and each meeting had cost about Rs 5 lakh, because the musicians took business-class flights and, initially, stayed in five-star hotels, till the ITC stepped in and offered them free rooms, Parikh said. The NCPA paid for these meetings, but little came out of them, he said.

'To have a chance of performing at the NCPA, most musicians have to constantly approach the organisers or get others to do it on their behalf,' said Kishor Merchant, a leading archivist and a former organiser who had presented a variety of excellent musicians. 'The NCPA should be going to where the listeners are and expanding the audience base by imaginatively promoting Indian classical music as aspirational. Small organisations are doing a much better job than the NCPA in showcasing the diversity and new talent in Hindustani music.'

The NCPA attracts scrutiny because expectations from a premier non-profit organisation are higher than from private firms and because its decisions have a ripple effect. 'The fact that powerful organisations like the NCPA have by and large thrown their weight behind a set of celebrity musicians in their high-profile festivals sends a message to the entire ecosystem and especially to prospective sponsors,' Devina said. 'It makes life really difficult for smaller and indie organisers who want to present lesser-known artists and offer them decent fees because sponsors recognise only brand names. Instead, the NCPA could have given visibility and legitimacy to a host of diverse and worthy musicians, helped build a listeners' base and become a driving force for the city's Indian classical music ecosystem. But it seems to revel in its exclusivity, with a conscious distancing from the city's varied cultural life. It probably did not feel the need to try fresh approaches because its scale and resources brought it easy accolades and insulated it from questioning or criticism by the public.' Consultant A said, 'In this day and age, the Indian music division does not have a digital strategy and has not harnessed the power of social media.'

To usher in more diversity in its curation, the NCPA could have a rotating panel of expert advisers from across the country, art lovers said. This is how academic journals, for instance, work. Furthermore, a resource-rich non-profit organisation has the wherewithal to take a long-term view, they said. 'A premier arts organisation should not programme only those shows that will sell,' said consultant C. 'That is a disservice to the art forms and turns them into popularity contests. A curator should pick what is good for the art forms in the long term. Audiences will come. If there is consistently high-quality programming, they will begin to trust the organisation.'

In March 2023, the Nita Mukesh Ambani Cultural Centre, a massive and sprawling structure, opened in the Bandra-Kurla Complex, a coveted business district in north-central Mumbai that is a counterweight to Nariman Point in the south, where the NCPA is located. The moving force behind the new centre is Nita Ambani, the wife of Mukesh Ambani, the billionaire chairman and managing director of Reliance Industries, one of India's largest conglomerates. Nita Ambani, who had learnt bharatanatyam for several years as a youngster, said in her vision statement that the centre was 'an ode to the nation' and had a 'commitment to preserve and promote Indian arts'. Set up by the Reliance Foundation, the conglomerate's philanthropic arm, the centre has theatres of three sizes: a 2,000-seater, a 250-seater and a 125-seater. It also has a massive visual arts gallery and an open-air square. Some commentators found the complex ostentatious and a tad soulless.[47] But early reports also revealed the centre's virtues. It has a few small theatres for art forms and performers who might not initially attract large audiences. Further, two performing artists told me that the backstage staff were efficient and supportive and the green room infrastructure was of a high quality. The centre did give a platform to some fine performers. But for its big Indian classical music events, it often presented the same mainstream names and packaged fare, evoking a sense of déjà vu. The centre's founding statement is laudable, but so was the NCPA's initial vision.

◆ Travels: 1958–64

ON A CHILLY OCTOBER EVENING IN NEW DELHI, ARUN THREW himself into raag Puriya Kalyan. In the audience were hundreds of students who had gathered for the 1958 Inter-University Youth Festival, a quintessential Nehruvian event showcasing the country's cultural diversity and fostering national integration. Arun had been chosen to represent Nagpur University, to which his college was affiliated. A few months earlier, Arun had moved to Yavatmal from Pandharkowda, at the age of fifteen, to do a one-year pre-university course followed by a bachelor's in music. His trip to the capital was his first foray outside Vidarbha. On the train journey, surrounded by Marathi-speakers, he had been his usual friendly self, but once the group arrived in the capital, he had turned uncharacteristically quiet. For the first time, he heard English being spoken all around him and became conscious of his lack of fluency in the language and of his small-town origins. 'I am going to learn English,' he promised himself.

Prime Minister Jawaharlal Nehru had himself inaugurated the festival, which had been started in 1954 'to offer students an opportunity [for] creative self-expression and [developing] a sense of Indian nationhood', according to the education ministry.[48] It usually took place before Diwali. That year the festival was held at the Talkatora Gardens, attracting nearly 1,700 students, who stayed in sturdy tents erected on the grounds.[49]

Once Arun got on stage, he lost his reserve and afterwards watched all the performances with interest, especially liking a tabla solo by a youngster called Shivkumar Sharma. Arun went on the festival's free Delhi tour, which included sites such as the Birla Mandir, Qutb Minar and Rashtrapati Bhavan, skipping the ticketed day-trip to the site of the Bhakra-Nangal dam, which was under construction. The high point was a visit to the prime minister's residence, where Nehru welcomed the youngsters. 'What a charismatic man,' Arun thought.

On the final day, Arun learnt that he had been disqualified because he had sung Puriya Kalyan instead of Yaman Kalyan, which is the raag he had informed the organisers he would sing. This mix-up was a sign that he had, after all, been a tad overwhelmed by the occasion.

Arun waited for his guru, D.V. Panke, to choose a raag. He had been learning from the Gwalior gharana singer for several months. Panke, who had trained under the stalwart Krishnarao Shankar Pandit in Gwalior, taught music and other subjects in a municipal school and held group classes at home after work. But after attending one of Arun's early performances, he offered to give the youngster solo lessons every morning.

're_____ re_____ Sa_____,' Panke sang that morning. 'Ah, we're going to do Bhairav,' Arun thought, going by the shade of the komal rishabh and the manner in which Panke was pulling it down from the shuddha gandhar above.

'Sa Ga ma Pa___,' Panke continued, offering more evidence for Bhairav. But right afterwards, he began going in another direction, falling down to the komal gandhar.

'ga ma ni-Dha Dha-Ni-Sa____,' he sang.

'Oh Bhairav Bahar,' thought Arun.

Bhairav Bahar is a jod, or compound, raag from the Gwalior gharana repertoire. Jod raags are perhaps most widely associated with the Jaipur gharana, because its founder Alladiya Khan resurrected many and created several new ones, but the Agra gharana also has many jods, because of family connections between the two styles. The Gwalior gharana is usually associated with canonical raags such as Yaman and Hamir, but it too has a clutch of jod raags, such as the Bahar series and compounds of Jogiya.

While elaborating a jod, a musician moves between its two raags through their shared notes. A performer might draw listeners into the web of one raag and, when they least expect it, suddenly but elegantly move to the other. Arun had earlier tried to copy the tunes of many jod raags from radio renditions. As he learnt Bhairav Bahar from Panke, Arun realised that to gain full creative control over a raag, one had to learn it from the bottom-up from a good guru. 'There's a subtle but important difference between reproduction and production,' Arun thought.

Within months, Arun began giving Panke vocal support.

⁓

'Look who's here.'

Arun turned to his left. He had walked into the quadrangle in front of his college building early one morning in the second year of college. It was three years since he had arrived in Yavatmal as a waif-like fifteen-year-old. Now, lithe and tall, he had sprouted a light moustache and acquired a deeper voice.

'You sang very well,' a girl said, smiling. She was Arun's classmate and was with two other girls.

'What?' he asked, stopping, but becoming self-conscious when a group of boys nearby turned around.

'The other evening,' she said.

'Oh that,' he replied. 'You liked it?'

The girl was referring to a bhav geet competition, whose organisers had invited Arun to the prize distribution ceremony to demonstrate how songs of this genre should be rendered. Arun had chosen *Raat ardhi chaand ardha* (A half-moon at midnight), a song from the 1954 Marathi film *Maharani Yesubai* (Queen Yesubai). The prolific G.D. Madgulkar had written the lyrics and Sudhir Phadke had composed the music and sung it in a duet with Lata Mangeshkar. It was a love song.

Arun was accustomed to strangers in Yavatmal complimenting him. Soon after arriving in town, he had begun performing almost every week in and around town at events organised by music schools, cultural organisations and local governments. He had earned the nickname 'khansaheb' because of his open-throated singing and exuberance. The local representative of the Congress party in the Bombay state legislature, Babasaheb Gharfalkar, was a fan of his. Lately, Arun had begun receiving attention from girls in his college. Many bhav geets and khayal compositions that he sang spoke about romantic love, longing and desire. He liked the attention, but also felt disoriented.

In Pandharkowda, the segregation of the sexes had been stark. When a female classmate of Arun's would come over to his home after school to learn from his father, instead of walking back together, they would choose different sides of the road. Yavatmal was slightly better, especially in music circles, where girls and boys had more occasions to make small talk. But Arun had earlier got a taste of society's narrow-mindedness. In his first year in Yavatmal, someone had carried tales to his mother.

'What is this I hear?' she had asked him on one of his trips home. 'You are roaming about town on your cycle at odd hours.'

Arun had indeed bought himself a bicycle to travel to his college, to the various schools where he was teaching music and to the homes of children to whom he was giving private music lessons.

'I am teaching to pay for my college fees and other expenses,' he told his mother, his voice trembling with suppressed anger. 'I bought a cycle because it is cheaper and faster than taking a horse tonga. You should tell people to mind their own business.'

'Okay, okay,' she then said, putting her arm around him.

Arun was polite to the girls who showed an interest in him, but did not encourage them. He smiled at this girl, too, but walked on.

———

Arun was in the living room when the poet rushed in from the bedroom waving a piece of paper. Arun knew that he was going to be the first to hear a newly minted poem. The poet recited a few lines,

> No one had seen such fragility, ever.
> We had never even glanced at her.
> So did we fear her fragility that we were sure
> The burden of our gaze she could not endure.[50]

This was not the first time that V.V. Patankar, or Bhausaheb Patankar, a lawyer, Sanskrit scholar and well-known poet, had bestowed this honour on him. Arun had become Patankar's paying guest in his second year, after a year of living with his uncle. In Patankar's huge house, Arun and a violinist friend shared a room. Patankar was among the first to adapt the Urdu ghazal to Marathi. But unlike in Urdu ghazals, where the lover's devotion to his beloved is often abject, Patankar's romantics are not wretched. He attracted huge crowds to his public poetry readings.

He became a father-figure to Arun. But unlike the understated Bhausaheb Kashalkar, this Bhausaheb was gregarious and colourful. He hunted game in the forests nearby, and before Arun arrived on the scene, had reared a tiger cub at home. He ate meat and drank beer. Arun was too much a product of his straitlaced upbringing to take to these novelties, but he warmed to the man's poetry. In a conservative and sexually repressed society, it became a medium, like music, into which he sublimated the inevitable longings of late adolescence and early adulthood. Patankar was also fluent in English, and from him Arun voraciously absorbed the language.

By Arun's third year, he began sharing a room with Shrikant, who had moved to Yavatmal for college. His college classes done by noon, Arun sat down to do riyaaz after lunch. Often, only when it turned dark did he realise how long he had been singing. Free of his father's structure, Arun began establishing his own relationship with music. From childhood, he had sung out of compulsion, then habit, then for adulation and eventually, because he was good at it, for a feeling of achievement. Now, he sang because he wanted to soak in the music.

His other musical talents also blossomed. He discovered that he had a flair for teaching music. His favourite stint was at a Montessori school, where he saw in action some of the principles that his father had been researching. Impressed by Arun's talent and maturity, the school's music-loving principal and other teachers fussed over him like mother hens. He also took to composing, setting to music a dozen songs in a Marathi play staged at the school and getting a fast composition of his in raag Nayaki Kanada set to Ektaal published in *Sangeet Kala Vihar*, a magazine brought out by the Gandharva Mahavidyalaya.

Despite being far away from Maharashtra's cultural hubs, Yavatmal had a lively enough musical scene to give Arun consistent exposure to great singers of the day. Television had arrived in India in 1959, but its widespread penetration into homes lay many years into the future. People still looked to the radio and live shows for entertainment. The town's annual Ganesh festival attracted heavyweights such as Mogubai Kurdikar and Bhimsen Joshi. It was in Yavatmal that Arun became crazy about the Kirana singer's music. Marathi musical hits regularly came to town. Arun himself founded and ran a music circle for a year with the help of his friends, raising money from local music lovers and patrons.

On a warm morning, Arun finished singing raag Ahir Bhairav for his final recital at the end of college. The external examiner was Sumati Mutatkar. She was in her forties and had trained with the Agra gharana's Vilayat Hussain Khan in Delhi. It was April 1962.

'What do you plan to do after this?' she asked Arun, when he touched her feet.

'I don't yet have a plan,' he replied. 'All I know is that I want to become a musician.'

'Would you like to move to Delhi to learn from Vilayat Hussain Khansaheb?' she asked. 'I can arrange it.'

'Yes!' he replied. 'But I can come only after six months.'

In his single-minded preparation for the music recital, Arun had failed the Sanskrit exam, one of his subjects besides music. He had not even bought the relevant books, deciding to retake the exam later in the year. He explained this to Sumati-tai.

'Can I get in touch with you then?' he asked.

'Of course,' she said, writing down her address in his notebook.

A week later, Arun dropped in to see Patankar, who, as usual, brought out a poem that he was working on. He read out the opening lines:

> O how you have let me down!
> Tell me, Death, when have I ever let you down?[51]

The next week, Arun heard the news on the radio: Vilayat Hussain Khan had passed away. It was May 1962. Arun had neither the luxury nor temperament to brood. He studied for his Sanskrit re-exam, got his degree and returned to Pandharkowda, where he began applying for jobs. In mid-1963, he received an offer to work as a librarian in the tapes division of All India Radio in Nagpur. He packed his bags for a second time.

In Nagpur, Arun knew whom he would learn from—Rajabhau Kogje, who had also been trained in the Gwalior gharana, by V.D. Paluskar's students. Rajabhau had later gone to Varanasi to learn thumri from Rasoolanbai. Rajabhau's voice was sweet and malleable, capable of expressing fine modulations of the kind demanded more frequently from thumri singing than khayal. Like Panke had done with jod raags, Rajabhau opened up the world of the thumri to Arun. Rajabhau's enunciation of words had an authentic lilt because he had spent a big portion of his childhood in the Hindi-speaking Central Provinces and Berar, which became Madhya Pradesh, and had spent time in Varanasi. Listening to the way Rajabhau caressed even khayal lyrics, Arun saw how an aesthetic enunciation of words could enhance the music's overall effect.

At work, Arun struck up a friendship with the much older Ram Phatak, a composer who had set many devotional poems to music for Bhimsen Joshi. Nothing about the Kirana gharana singer was too insignificant for his two acolytes to analyse: his facial contortions, his hand gestures, his Kannada-accented Marathi. In January 1965, after Arun gave a well-received public concert as part of his Alankar exam, Phatak began urging him to move to Bombay. 'You want to make it as a singer, don't you?' he asked. 'The sooner you move, the better.' Arun was mulling over how to go about this when a couple of months later, Gajananbuwa Joshi visited the Nagpur radio station from Bombay and breezed through the tapes library. Arun's boss introduced him to Gajananbuwa. On the way out, the musician told Arun, 'Come to see me if you are ever in Bombay.'

Within a month, Arun landed an entry-level clerical position at a government office in Bombay. Soon afterwards, as his train pulled out of Nagpur, he felt a twinge of anxiety. He had so far enjoyed a smooth life, a pleasant, uncomplicated melody with hardly any off-key notes. Money had always been tight, but it had never mattered. Even if he'd had more material comfort, the broad contours of his life would have remained the same. Music absorbed his mind and heart and almost all his free time and energy. It mediated his social life, being the sole means through which he struck up friendships and encountered the larger world. Perhaps music would come through for him in Bombay too.

◆ Sound

IN HINDUSTANI MUSIC, A SAPTAK IS AN INTERVAL BETWEEN two notes in which the higher note has twice the frequency of the lower one. Such doubling, or halving, of a frequency yields a note that our ears regard as synonymous with the original one. This is similar to how we feel when a child sings a tune: we think that it is like an adult's tune in most ways except that it is in a 'higher' voice.

The name saptak, derived from the Sanskrit word for seven, reflects the fact that in Hindustani music, this interval is conceptually divided into seven different fundamental notes, as is the case in virtually all music systems around the world. The notes in a saptak do not include the one that is double in frequency to the first. That note is considered to be the *next* saptak's first note.

Western classical music theory defines the octave in the same way and conceptually has seven different notes, but its name is derived from the Latin word for eight. This is because the octave *does* include the note that has double the frequency of the first. This, in turn, is because Western music measures, compares and quantifies the *intervals* between notes, but this is not relevant to Hindustani musicians. What matters is that the saptak and octave count the same notes in different ways.

In Hindustani music, these seven fundamental notes are called shuddh notes. Using one common convention, they are written, in order of increasing frequency, as Sa, Re, Ga, ma, Pa, Dha, Ni. Observe that the first letter of one of these notes is written in lower case. These notes are also respectively called shadja, rishabh, gandhar, madhyam, pancham, dhaivat and nishad, each prefixed by the word 'shuddh'.

Five of these shuddh notes, namely Re, Ga, ma, Dha and Ni, have affiliated notes. Four of these affiliates are called komal, or soft, notes because they have lower pitches than their shuddha brethen. They are denoted re, ga, dha and ni, using lower case for the first letter, and are also called komal rishabh, komal gandhar and so on. The fifth affiliate, however, is called a teevra, or sharp, note because it has a higher pitch than its shuddha kin. It is denoted Ma, with an upper case for the first letter, and is also called teevra madhyam. The Sa and Pa have no affiliates.

In all, therefore, there are twelve notes—seven shuddh ones and five affiliates. In increasing order of frequency they are Sa, re, Re, ga, Ga, ma, Ma, pa, dha, Dha, ni, Ni.

~

The shadja, or tonic Sa, is the anchoring note. Its pitch, which can vary from singer to singer, determines the pitches of the remaining notes. The note that is one saptak below the shadja is called the kharaj and the note that is one saptak above it is called the taar shadja. The frequency of the pancham is always one-and-a-half times higher than that of the shadja. By default, all notation refers to the saptak from the shadja to the taar shadja, which is called the madhya, or middle, saptak. If a note has a dot below it, this means that it is in the mandra, or lower, saptak. If a note has a dot above it, this indicates that it is in the taar, or upper, saptak. The bulk of improvisation happens in the madhya saptak.

Every raag has to have a Sa. With a couple of exceptions,[52] all raags must also have a Pa, ma or Ma, but can have two of them or all three. Some raags use both affiliates of one note from Re, Ga, Dha and Ni, while a smaller number uses both affiliates of more than one of these notes.

~

'The notes of a raag are like seeds. When you carefully nurture them, they flower forth and emit the raag's fragrance. Each seed blossoms to a natural rhythm, which may be hidden but has nevertheless been working its magic.' —AK

9

◇ Society

A QUARTER OF THE WAY INTO THE TWENTY-FIRST CENTURY, Hindustani music has, as we have seen, been shaped by the rise of profit-seeking companies and the decline of both non-government and government entities as moderating influences on the market. This mainstream's infirmities come into relief because there is a point of comparison: the Carnatic music ecosystem. The southern system is admittedly far from perfect. T.M. Krishna, for example, has comprehensively analysed its shortcomings.[1] He has criticised it for not being inclusive, dominated as it is by Brahmin men, and for tolerating gender discrimination. He has also said that the standard concert format has deteriorated into formula, compositions are increasingly being treated as songs conveying literal meaning, not as artistic expressions of various raags, and consequently the role of improvisation is diminishing. The Carnatic ecosystem nevertheless appears to be much healthier than the Hindustani scene. In the south, the gap between artistic merit and popularity is much narrower, and there are fewer instances of fusion and popular music being packaged as classical fare. 'The environment in Carnatic music is much more evolved than the Hindustani one,' Banyan Tree's Babu said.

This is so partly because a large, well-endowed non-profit institution, the Madras Music Academy, acts as a moderating influence. Located in Chennai, Carnatic music's capital, it stands at the top of a pyramid of charitable organisations, called sabhas, that filter down to neighbourhoods and small towns. This model represents a more structured version of what existed in the Mumbai-Pune region until the 1990s. 'The sabha system works as a feeder system, allowing young talent to emerge through opportunities in this network, including small towns and cities,' T.M. Krishna told me. 'This is why Carnatic music has artists emerging in every generation who are of very high quality.' He added that the informality and modest size of many sabhas, although posing a challenge to their sustainability, keep corporatisation at bay.

On closer examination, one may be able to find flaws in the Academy's functioning, but some of its processes appear to be enlightened. For instance, it has a much fairer and more transparent system of curation than anything that I have encountered in Hindustani music. The Academy's chairman, N. Murali, told me that the institution followed an informal rule not to allow performing musicians on its executive committee of two dozen members, of which a dozen belong to the programming sub-committee. 'Otherwise, there will be a conflict of interest,' he said.

The bellwether institution kept its focus on merit when it awarded T.M. Krishna the Sangeetha Kalanidhi, Carnatic music's most prestigious title, in 2024, even though he had boycotted the December music season for about a decade, saying that it had become too commercialised and lacked inclusivity. This arts festival is the high point of the Carnatic music calendar. 'We gave him the award for his music,' Murali told me. 'In a country like India, people can have diverse views. And there may not have been enough diversity when the new ecosystem evolved.' Murali was referring to the turn of the twentieth century, when music lovers established the contemporary sabha system in Chennai and refashioned the art form for the proscenium stage, following the decline of traditional centres of patronage and performance, which were mainly royal courts and temples. In modern India, royal courts ceased to exist while temples lost their status as socio-economic centres. Brahmins were at the forefront of this revival, but their blind spots and biases also ended up shaping the ecosystem. 'You cannot [have] one community dominating,' Murali said. In this instance, the Academy showed a willingness to consider good-faith criticism and evolve.

※

What about other stakeholders in the Hindustani music world? Over the 1990s, state institutions seem to have lost their dynamism along with their agenda-setting power in the face of market forces. Despite exalting Indian culture, Hindutva organisations have done precious little for the nation's art music or its practitioners, including during the COVID-19 pandemic. On the contrary, an investigative report revealed the 'artistic and moral decay' in the culture department of the BJP-led Madhya Pradesh government.[2] In any case, state support for the arts is a double-edged sword. It can be valuable if overseen by enlightened and self-confident administrators willing to give artists total freedom. If not, state funding carries the danger of discouraging artists from criticising the government of the day, either through their art or as citizens.

Arts funding agencies can be a source of modest but valuable support. But many prioritise interdisciplinary work, art forms practised by marginalised sections and projects that address topics of contemporary interest and social relevance, such as caste, gender, climate change and urbanisation, all of which are, of course, entirely laudable goals. But khayal falls on the abstract end of musical genres, with the role of lyrics being particularly small compared with the musical dimensions. Therefore, it is not easy to tie this genre to a hot-button issue or make it immediately relevant to people's lives just for the sake of procuring funding. Nevertheless, in the toxic mix of Hindu supremacism and crony neoliberal capitalism that has gripped India in the new millennium, the genre has radical potential because it is a melting pot, reflects religious syncretism and forces performers and listeners to slow down. But how can the form's radical potential be explored when it has become so difficult merely to preserve it? Perhaps funders are not aware of khayal's precarious future.

Some arts funders might also be tempted to view the classical performing arts as stagnant. With respect to khayal, this view is misplaced. The fact that improvisation lies at its core and that the performing culture puts a high premium on exponents developing their unique styles makes it dynamic and vibrant. Khayal's history, as we have seen, has a strong strain of heterodoxy. But for people to fully appreciate this music's virtues, they need to engage with it in a sustained way.

As in other fields, good journalism could have played a role in holding power centres accountable, in the form of concert reviews and a robust coverage of the whole ecosystem. Unfortunately, the early 1990s saw not just a commodification of music, but also of sections of the media. Professional plain-speaking was never common in the Hindustani music world, but at least concerts were regularly reviewed. But all reviews, except of films, disappeared from the pages of *The Times of India*, the most profitable English daily, one that is still hugely influential in Mumbai. Later, the *Mumbai Mirror*, part of the same business group and founded in 2005, began filling a part of this vacuum by giving space to thoughtful writing about the arts, but concert reviews did not reappear.

When I began writing about music in Mumbai in 2015, I approached it the way a journalist covers any beat, whether politics or economics, paying attention to how those in powerful positions were using their privilege to serve the art form, its practitioners and listeners. But many stakeholders in the music field did not fully understand my role. Unhealthy cults of personality surrounded some musicians and impresarios. One organiser and one prominent patron each offered me money after I wrote about events that they were promoting. I had to explain to them that I was covering these performances based on my independent journalistic judgement and that I would be paid by the publications in which my articles appeared.

Knowledgeable listeners are thirsting for fearless and intelligent writing about performers, performances and the ecosystem. Alongside some fine articles about Hindustani music, especially in some of the new digital news websites, we also see uncritical writing that fails to ask questions of those in power, while heaping praise upon popular musicians even when they fail to display the sobriety and taste that the art form demands. Candid reviews about such performers' concerts or music appear sacrilegious. Again, in comparison, the coverage of Carnatic musicians seems to be more objective and informed, with *The Hindu* offering a consistent forum for this. The Carnatic world does not appear to have taboos about hard-hitting criticism, including of musicians who are among the most popular, powerful and well-connected.[3]

Social media has, to an extent, whittled down the power of intermediaries, whether organisers or critics. Musicians can now upload their renditions to various platforms. But widening the audience on these platforms still requires marketing. There is also the danger of eyeballs being equated with artistic worth, especially if the audience's knowledge has not deepened. Judging by online discussions, the average Carnatic music listener appears to be more knowledgeable than his or her Hindustani counterpart. Online music criticism might be a solution.

※

What about the ecosystem's two most important actors: musicians and listeners? Lay listeners need to develop healthy scepticism towards marketing hype. The more discerning they become, the more aligned popularity will become with artistic merit. 'We listeners have not given these stars anything except monotonous and mindless adoration,' Devina said. 'We have not engaged with them as artists or sought out other promising artists. We have not taken the trouble to invest in seriously understanding the art form. Over time, musicians who have already "arrived" have encountered no challenges from us. Perhaps the dominant, all-pervading entertainment imperative across India over the past three decades has also contributed to the declining quality of listening to this music.'

Fringe musicians, for their part, have doggedly tried to keep their traditions alive, but do not have the resources to take on the system. Mainstream musicians with artistic merit have also not taken a public stance against its power dynamics. Even in the healthier Carnatic milieu, T.M. Krishna is a rare bird. The only hope for Hindustani music lies in young committed musicians uniting to address the core problem: the paucity of knowledgeable listeners. For, as envisioned by the original fringe movement in Edinburgh, artists must play a prominent role in resisting the mainstream. Gharana loyalties and the geographical spread of Hindustani music practitioners do pose challenges for anyone hoping to build a wider movement. But that does not mean it cannot be done. A local annual initiative, the three-day Thane Unity Festival, organised by musicians in the sprawling city north of Mumbai, highlights the power of solidarity and the benefits to a community when its members put their self-interest aside and come together for a larger purpose. Begun in 2013, the festival in 2025 showcased about sixty musicians and daily attracted about four hundred listeners, according to Anant Joshi, a harmonium player who is one of the organisers. 'Many musicians had not even heard one another,' he said. By the 2010s, Thane probably boasted a greater concentration of musicians than Mumbai, he said.

Again, the south might hold some lessons. In the early 1980s, Carnatic music seemed to be in the doldrums. Many of its leading singers were ageing and few artists from the younger generation seemed like they would spark a similar devotion from existing audiences. Youngsters, although free of nostalgia, were not entering concert halls in significant numbers. After a period of wringing hands and lamenting the predominance of grey hairs in the audience, several young musicians decided in 1985 to band together to form the Youth Association for Classical Music. They began singing in public halls, often for free or for a pittance, attending each other's concerts and each tapping his or her network to bring in audiences for others. The young musicians fanned out in Chennai, going into schools and exposing students to Carnatic music. They roped in older, well-known musicians who believed in their cause. To their eternal credit, many senior musicians generously supported the movement, whose momentum lasted at least until the year 2000. Looking back, it would not be an exaggeration to say that this effort led to a revival of Carnatic music in Chennai. 'Hindustani music needs a revolution like the one that happened in Carnatic music twenty years ago,' Banyan Tree's Babu said without a trace of irony.

◈ Mountain: 1973–80

INSTEAD OF FEELING REFRESHED AFTER HIS LUNCH BREAK, Arun could barely keep his eyes open. He usually ate what Dhanashree had packed for him, but that day, he had stepped out for a bite with a colleague. Perhaps it was the excessive oil in the food that they had ordered. More likely, it was the uninspiring task that awaited him. He stared at the aptly named waste book lying open before him on the desk, in which he had to enter credits and debits. He looked around the large hall that housed the bills department on the ground floor of the State Bank of India branch at Horniman Circle, one of South Bombay's office districts. A huge rickety fan, coated with dust, rattled on the high ceiling, circulating more noise than air. He sometimes feared that it would come crashing down on his head. How many dreary days had he squandered in that hall, jotting down figures from vouchers that piled up on his desk! Days that he could have spent working on Patamanjari. This unusual and complex raag had been bedevilling him for weeks. It was a collage of excerpts from other raags, such as Bageshree, Dhanashree, Mand and Tilak Kamod. He was grappling with how to merge these pieces into a seamless sound that subsumed the constituent tunes. For someone who took his sharp intellect for granted, he was frustrated that he was taking so long to become fluent in this raag. But no matter how insistent Patamanjari's call, he had to concentrate on the insipid job at hand. At the end of the day, he had to tally the credit and debit columns. If the totals did not match, he had to put in extra hours checking the entries against the vouchers all over again. He forced his mind into a mechanical groove and reached for the slips of paper.

<hr>

Tick-tock, tick-tock. Arun wished that he could gesture to the clock as he did to the tabla player when he wanted to speed up the tempo while performing. A few times, he had been accompanied by a tabla player who would play games by speeding up at will, instead of fulfilling his duty to take cues from the main artist. Arun had always managed to quell such mutinies by digging his heels in, ignoring the tabla player's pranks and continuing to sing at the tempo that he desired, eventually forcing the errant percussionist to back down. But life was not a khayal performance, over whose pace and duration he had some control. When the clock struck five, Arun gathered his belongings and bolted out of his chair.

On most days, Arun walked with colleagues to Victoria Terminus, or VT, to catch a train to Dombivli. Dhanashree also worked in South Bombay, in Montex Glass Fibre Industries' accounting department, but neither could predict when the other would finish work, so they almost always separately made their way home. After getting back home, at about seven, Arun immediately freshened up and sat down to sing, while Dhanashree got busy making dinner. But that day, Arun caught a bus to the Opera House area, about five kilometres north of the business district. He would be returning home late for the first time since he had got married a few months earlier. Dhanashree would almost certainly wait to have dinner with him.

Arun got off at French Bridge, a local landmark, and walked to a cluster of buildings under it called Raghav Wadi. As he rang the bell of a flat on the first floor of one of the buildings, he felt eager but tired. A woman opened the door.

'Usha-tai!' Arun said.

'Come in,' she replied, smiling broadly. 'He is waiting for you.'

Babanrao's face brightened when Arun walked into the tiny living room. He was excited to be taking on his first student, recommended by no less a musician than Gajananbuwa. Babanrao had learnt first from the Jaipur singer Mogubai and then for decades from the Agra stalwart Khadim Hussain Khan. Babanrao had simultaneously got a degree in chemical engineering and had worked in the corporate sector. Recently, he had quit his job to start his own consultancy. Arun had come to him at the right time.

Babanrao lived in a joint family with his three brothers. They shared a living-cum-dining area, but each had a private studio, all carved out of the flat in which they grew up. Like a Matryoshka doll set, Babanrao's home was a salon within the cultural hotbed of Raghav Wadi, which itself was located in a lively arts precinct, the Gamdevi-Girgaum-Opera House area. The Haldankar household saw a steady traffic of musicians, painters, writers, connoisseurs and students of art and music. During the Ganesh festival, Babanrao and his brothers, following a practice begun by their father, the outstanding water colourist Sawlaram Haldankar, hosted a night of music performances, eagerly awaited by South Bombay's aficionados.

Babanrao was sitting on the floor in his quarters, playing a tanpura. Next to him sat a tabla and dagga. Arun touched his feet and sat down. Usha-tai brought him a glass of water.

'Let's start,' said Babanrao, aware that Arun had a long commute home.

~

Arun suddenly felt refreshed. Music unerringly did that to him. He remembered the goosebumps he had got on hearing Babanrao singing for the first time, a physical reaction that was different from but as memorable as his initial encounter with Gajananbuwa's music. Babanrao had sung Bahaduri Todi, a complex raag that was a favourite with Agra and Jaipur singers. Meant to be sung early in the morning, this deeply meditative raag has both rishabhs, which play off one another like in a benign sibling rivalry. Arun continued to take deep pleasure in both musicians' art, but he never again experienced the sensual intensity of those initial experiences. Like a first kiss, they divided innocence from the beginning of knowledge, and how can you un-know something?

Great khayal singers stand out for their mastery over at least one aspect of the art form. For Babanrao, that was the creativity and delicacy of his bol work. Gajananbuwa was keen that one of his students imbibe this from Babanrao and in Arun he found a pupil with an affinity for both rhythm and language, bol work's two pillars.

Babanrao handed the tanpura to Arun, started singing a composition in raag Shree and simultaneously played Jhaptaal on the dagga. He sang it several times.

Garib naẋwaz o Khwaja	O Khwaja, saviour of the poor,
Dukhiyan ke dukh door karo tum	Deliver us from sorrow.
Saẋjan garib darbar ko sevak	The abject Sajan, your supplicant
Aaya hoon sharan tehari	I have come to surrender to you.

This composition, created by Khadim Hussain Khan, Sajan Piya, is a prayer to the Sunni mystic Moinuddin Chishti, known as Khwaja Garib Nawaz. Chishti, who lived from the mid-twelfth to early thirteenth centuries, was a Persian preacher, scholar and philosopher who travelled to the region that is present-day India and settled in Ajmer in Rajasthan.[4] Chishti founded an eponymous sect of Sufism and was possibly the first Islamic mystic on the subcontinent to encourage his followers to use music along with prayers and meditation to commune with God.[5] Among those who followed this stream of Sufism were Baba Farid and Nizamuddin Auliya.[6] Chishti became hugely popular among both Hindus and Muslims.[7]

Well into the 2020s, thousands visit his shrine in Ajmer, Rajasthan, believing that he can solve their problems.

Arun was already a consummate performer, so Babanrao skipped the preliminaries of raag grammar and made him sing the composition several times so that he developed a feel for how to pronounce the words and group the phrases. After a while, Babanrao gave Arun his first bol improvisation exercise.

'Sing "garib nawaz" in the set way and create variations with "o khwaja",' he said.

Arun attempted a few avartans. Babanrao sang several more. They kept alternating for a while. Arun easily filled the avartans, but noticed how naturally Babanrao's bol flowed. Soon, Usha-tai came in carrying a tray with two plates and two cups. Arun looked at his watch, surprised that Babanrao and he had spun out variations on just two words for more than an hour. He eagerly took a bite from a roti stuffed with a half-boiled egg and sipped his tea.

Before leaving, Arun pulled an envelope out of his sling bag and handed it to Babanrao. The musician peered inside, carefully took a one-rupee note out from among several notes and returned the envelope to Arun, who stood up, touched Babanrao's feet and then his own heart.

When Arun arrived in Bombay, the city had the country's largest concentration of Agra gharana musicians, including many of the founder's descendants as well as their students and grand-students from outside the family. By around the mid-twentieth century, a four-bedroom flat on the third floor of a five-storey building called Ruby Mansion had become the de facto headquarters of the family of hereditary Agra gharana musicians. It was about a kilometre from where Babanrao lived. Half a dozen musicians from the Agra gharana and the closely affiliated Atrauli gharana, named after another town in Uttar Pradesh, lived in that four-bedroom flat. By that time, these two styles had merged because their members had inter-married in successive generations and taught one another.

The move to Bombay from Agra began in 1842 with Sher Khan, the nephew and student of Ghagge Khuda Baksh, the Agra gharana's founder. Sher Khan eventually returned to Agra, but his son, Natthan Khan put down roots in Bombay. In 1940, his son, Vilayat Hussain Khan, bought the flat in Ruby Mansion, using it as his base even when he worked in Mysore and Delhi. His wife's brother, Azmat Hussain Khan, soon moved in. Later, Alladiya Khan came to live there for a few years and taught Azmat Hussain, the son of his second cousin, another Atrauli link. Vilayat Hussain Khan also brought over his three nephews from Atrauli—Khadim Hussain, Anwar Hussain and Latafat Hussain, who had trained under other family musicians. Ruby Mansion hosted other musicians from the family whenever they visited Mumbai, such as Faiyaz Khan, a national star who was the great-grandson of Ghagge Khuda Baksh. The flat was a hive of music and activity. On religious occasions, the family invited Sufi pirs and qawwals from all over the country to sing and lead prayers. Well-known musicians such as the ghazal and thumri singer Begum Akhtar and sitarist Vilayat Khan attended these sessions.[8]

Many of these hereditary singers taught students outside the family, several of whom became prominent musicians, such as Babanrao, Jagannathbuwa, Lalith Rao and S.N. Ratanjankar. Because Ruby Mansion was teeming with people, these musicians usually travelled to their students' homes to teach, developing close ties with them and their families. Vilayat Hussain Khan was so fond of Jagannathbuwa that he wrote a composition expressing his love for his student, who reciprocated with a composition of his own for his guru. In the next generation, Khadim Hussain taught Lalith Rao with great dedication and became a father figure to Babanrao. 'You must treat Baban like your son,' Khadim Hussain's wife sternly had told her husband at the beginning of Babanrao's tutelage.

Arun had missed learning from two leading Agra gharana musicians: Vilayat Hussain Khan and Chidanand Nagarkar, who was S.N. Ratanjankar's pupil. He struck lucky the third time.

About a year into his training, Arun entered his guru's living room one evening to find a special visitor—Khadim Hussain Khan. Arun touched the musician's feet and sat down.

'Good you arrived before I left,' Khadimsaheb said, placing his right hand on Arun's head.

A wordless benediction. Babanrao looked pointedly at Arun, who had an inkling of what was coming.

'Come on, let's hear something,' Khadimsaheb said.

Babanrao lifted his chin towards Arun and then in Khan's direction. Arun knew what it meant.

'You'll do fine,' his guru was saying. 'Sing *Garib nawaz*. Guruji will be pleased.'

Did khayal singers become adept at such precise wordless communication because so much of their music lived between the lines, replete with subtleties so fine that they defied being spelt out? Such as knowing how long to linger at the many frequencies in between Shree's two long, defining glides, from re to Pa and Pa to re. Such as knowing that on the descending glide, one could occasionally offer a fleeting, and tantalising, glimpse of Ma by dwelling on the note for a few microseconds more than all the others along the way.

Arun said nothing for several seconds. He heard Usha-tai's tadka spluttering in the kitchen. Babanrao looked on expectantly. Then, before the silence became uncomfortable, Arun moved his head from side to side in a slight downward arc, producing the quintessential Indian nod. In the secret language between closely attuned guru and student, Arun's initial silence meant: 'It has been a long day. This is a bit intimidating.' The gesture that followed meant: 'But it is an honour to be asked by your guru.'

Arun tuned the tanpura, Babanrao the tabla. Arun sang a nom-tom aalaap in three speeds and moved on to *Garib nawaz* (Saviour of the poor), singing the composition twice before beginning a bol aalaap. Khadimsaheb nodded once in a while. About half-way into his rendition, Arun arrived at the sam with an elegant teehai, using the phrase 'garib nawaz', surprising himself and eliciting a spontaneous 'wah' from Khadimsaheb. Arun became more daring, increased the tabla speed, plunged into bol laykari and gamak taans, before landing on the final sam.

'Wah!' Khadimsaheb exclaimed.

Not for the first time Arun marvelled at how an audience of just one person could bring out the best in him, while an auditorium full of listeners could leave him cold or even dampen his mood, when they, for example, began clapping when he hit the taar shadja, instead of realising that this melodic climax could bloom only in the soil of silence. He had seen the same phenomenon in other performances: how, for instance, Gajananbuwa walking into the audience could supercharge a singer.

'Very good,' Khadimsaheb said, making his version of the same arc-like motion with the head. 'Baban, his taleem is proceeding well.'

There they were, three generations of singers—the oldest tracing his family and musical roots back to the gharana's founder. In the hazy distance, Arun could see the gharana's sanctum—with Faiyaz Khan, Vilayat Hussain Khan and Ata Hussain Khan.

Arun looked at the clock: ten to five. Ever since Prime Minister Indira Gandhi had imposed an Emergency a few months earlier, the bank had become strict about employees' work timings. They could not leave even a minute before their official end time. As the clock struck five, Arun signed a register and darted out of the office. He was in one of his most musically fertile phases.

As the bus traversed its route, he reflected on his training. Soon after beginning with Babanrao, he had resumed going to Gajananbuwa on weekends. He was seasoned enough to juggle the two styles. Each gharana had its own principles, but they were the same *kind* of principles. He had embarked on his Agra training with this important realisation. He saw that at the core of gharana ideology lay the unique relationship between melody and rhythm, which influenced every aspect of improvisation. Arun saw that the Agra gharana had a roughly one-to-one linkage between beats and syllables, which naturally influenced bol work. In Agra bol, the singer worked at different levels: a whole line, its constituent phrases, the words in the phrase and syllables in the word. For long stretches in the cycle, the singer emphasised almost every syllable and beat to create a strong lilt. In Gwalior bol, predominant in Gajananbuwa's singing, the singer worked with a whole line, moving up and down one or more octaves, using different speeds to fit repetitions of the line in a cycle and stressing beats only at intervals.

'Opera House, Opera House!' shouted the bus conductor.

Arun got off the bus, wondering which raag Babanrao would take up. After persisting with Shree for the first six months, Babanrao had moved on to other Agra gharana specialities such as Sar Nat, Barwa and the haunting Agre gharane ka Chandrakauns. For every composition in every raag, Arun practised relentlessly in order to fluently distribute the words across the rhythmic cycle in a balanced and aesthetic manner, and create a variety of patterns to approach the sam. Maybe that day Babanrao would go back to *Garib nawaz*, as he had periodically done, each time imposing a different restriction.

'Today, do aalaap only from shadja to pancham,' he had said one day.

'Today, we will do only bol aalaap, and that too, at a slower tempo than usual,' he had said another time.

A few times, Babanrao had returned to his first exercise, of asking Arun to improvise just on 'o khwaja'. As Arun walked up the stairs to Babanrao's flat, he realised that the two-word phrase had been the key that had opened the door to the Agra gharana's treasure trove. The Sufi saint had heard Arun's plea and had allowed him to enter.

One night, Arun returned home at 11 p.m. after his class with Babanrao. Surprisingly, his son Ashish, nearly four years old, was still awake. He came running to Arun.

'Baba, will you go to the office tomorrow?'

Ashish had asked him this every day in the past week.

'No!' Arun could finally exclaim, for the next day was a holiday.

Arun sensed that Ashish was missing him. After Ashish went to bed, Dhanashree and Arun ate dinner in silence. She had been simmering with discontent. She was a couple of months pregnant with their second child, but continued to work. She was tired a lot of the time and anxious about finding a carer for the newborn baby. Ashish's babysitter, who picked him up after school, had said she could not take in an infant. Arun knew that Dhanashree was also worried about their financial situation. Another child entailed more expenditure and more crowding in their tiny one-room-kitchen flat. But his salary had remained more or less stagnant, barring minor increases to keep up with inflation. He had kept a low profile at work, skipping all the bank exams that he would have had to pass to get promoted because a promotion would almost certainly have involved a transfer. This Arun was simply not prepared to countenance because it would have ended his training with Babanrao.

'So you won't prepare for these exams?' Dhanashree had asked him a few months earlier.

'No,' he had replied.

'We can't move to a bigger place then,' she had said.

He had remained silent. She was right. But he had come clean to her at the very beginning about his priorities. He had no interest in banking. Still, he acknowledged to himself that it was too much to expect her to have known exactly how that would play out. But with Babanrao, a whole new world was opening up, daily offering new insights. He could not, would not, give up his training. However challenging, he would keep his music going, aloof from the pressures of daily existence. The stark truth was that this strategy meant that his income and designation would more or less remain the same, while costs increased and his colleagues advanced. A stagnant standard of living was the price that his family would have to pay for his pursuit of music. He knew that spelling the scenario out in those terms would be unwise. Hopefully, the issue would blow over.

But beneath this practical question lay another explosive one: after all these sacrifices, what would his music eventually yield? Fame? Money? Happiness? Happiness for whom? For many years, this stick of dynamite lay buried under the demands of the couple's more pressing mundane material and logistical concerns as well as the genuine joy and pleasures of family life. As Arun went to bed past midnight, he knew that it was always in danger of combusting—under suitable conditions.

⁂

Arun had an overnight programme in Mulund over a weekend. Dhanashree decided to go along, leaving Ashish, then nearly five years old, with her mother. Arun sang Shivmat Bhairav, accompanied on the tabla by his childhood friend from Nagpur, Gopal Wadegaonkar. Shivmat Bhairav includes the komal gandhar and komal nishad, in addition to all the notes in its parent, the sombre Bhairav. Listeners caught their breath each time Arun rose from the komal rishabh, which Bhairav also had, to the komal gandhar, which it did not, before falling back to the komal rishab and hitting the Sa. It was a delicate twist that held much of Shivmat Bhairav's magic. The other quirk, though not as dramatic, was a similar uptick to the komal nishad, which Bhairav did not have, from komal dhaivat, which Bhairav had. Listeners exclaimed each time Arun landed on the sam.

Dhanashree knew that Arun had been a star performer of semi-classical music in Dombivli, but extrapolating from listeners' reactions and the bond that he shared with many older musicians, she was gaining an estimation of his worth as a khayal singer. She was also developing a taste for this abstract form.

'When we got married, my wife did not know the ABC of classical music,' Arun told people. 'But she is marching steadily towards Z.'

After the concert, the couple and Wadegaonkar took a train to Titwala town, north-east of Dombivli, to visit a well-known Ganesh mandir there, before returning home at dawn. The couple rarely went out together. Arun spent every free moment on music, viewing everything else as an interruption. In any case, the couple did not have any disposable income. That night, freed temporarily from her duties, Dhanashree felt relaxed and happy, cherishing this rare outing with her husband.

By the late 1970s, Dombivli had become a hub for the Kashalkars. Arun's parents had moved there after his father had wound up his law practice in Pandharkowda, Shrikant was working there, Prakash had moved there to study law and Ulhas had won a government scholarship to learn from Rambhau Marathe after topping his MA course in music in Nagpur. On weekends, the brothers often came over to Arun's home for music sessions, while Dhanashree rustled up snacks and meals in the small kitchen. It was everyday fare, made with care; the technique sound, the masalas freshly ground.

But Arun was becoming concerned about Ulhas's training because Rambhau Marathe was, as Arun himself had found out, extremely busy with his career in musical theatre. For a whole month, Ulhas had essentially had no class. Arun felt that Ulhas should go to Gajananbuwa. After Arun, Ulhas had been the one who had brought home all the music prizes.

'He has brilliant grasping power,' Arun told his guru.

'My health is not doing well,' Gajananbuwa replied. 'I won't be able to do justice to him.'

Ulhas then floated the idea of learning from Mallikarjun Mansur, the intense and intensely sweet-sounding Jaipur gharana singer whom he admired. Mansur lived in Dharwad in Karnataka, another fertile region for khayal located across Maharashtra's southern border.

'We don't know whether Mansur will take on a new student or how much time he will have to teach you,' Arun told Ulhas. 'You will have to move to Dharwad. Where will you live?'

Arun felt it was too risky. He again approached Gajananbuwa. He felt Ulhas should at least get his foot in the door.

'You don't have to take responsibility for his future,' Arun told his guru. 'Just teach him when you can and see how it goes.'

'Let me hear him first,' said Gajananbuwa.

Ulhas looked up to his eldest brother, admired his musical mind and trusted his judgement. He had seen how Arun, whom the brothers called Baba, or father, was well-entrenched in Mumbai's music scene, known and liked by many senior artists. Ulhas easily got through the first hurdle and began going to Gajananbuwa for a couple of hours a day.

'Baba has introduced me to a whole new world of gharanedar music,' Ulhas thought after a few months, quickly recognising Gajananbuwa's depth.

Seeing his student's evident capability and focus, Gajananbuwa began increasing his teaching hours, for which good guru is not energised by an outstanding and dedicated student? Like his eldest brother before him, the youngest Kashalkar began rapidly rising to his guru's expectations.

⁂

Sitting behind Babanrao, Arun saw many connoisseurs in the audience, including a descendant of the Gaekwads, the arts-loving Maratha rulers of the princely state of Baroda. Babanrao was performing at the Laxmi Vilas Palace, from where the Gaekwads had ruled. Faiyaz Khan had spent many years at their court, as had his nephew Ata Hussain Khan, inculcating in many of the city's listeners a taste for the Agra gharana. Babanrao sang Lalita Gauri and Shyam Kalyan, giving Arun ample air time. Arun saw how delicately Babanrao expressed the gharana's various forms, in a way that suited his voice, which was sweeter than traditional Agra singers. Perhaps because of his Jaipur training, Babanrao used more meends than the average Agra singer.

Arun accompanied his guru as often as possible. It was an important rite of passage. Babanrao was thrilled to be accompanied by Arun, who had become a part of the Haldankar household, laughing and joking with Babanrao's sons, nephews and nieces.

'No one has a voice like Arun,' Babanrao gushed to Usha-tai more than once. 'No one can sing taans like him. He is second only to Bhimsen Joshi.'

On an average, Agra gharana musicians tended to spend more time polishing their nom-tom aalaaps and bol work than taans.

'He's so handsome!' Usha-tai gushed back on one occasion. 'And jovial and open-hearted. I sometimes fear that people will exploit his transparent nature.'

By the end of 1980, Arun completed nearly eight years of training with Babanrao. Lalith Rao, Khadim Hussain's student, was amazed by how quickly Arun had internalised the Agra idiom, just as he had done with Gajananbuwa's style. But Arun also heard rumours that a couple of musicians were mocking him for still being a student even though they knew that he had been performing for years and that Gajananbuwa was the one who had sent him to Babanrao to broaden his horizons. An acquaintance of Arun's wondered aloud what would have happened had he not gone to Babanrao.

'You were in your early thirties,' the man said. 'You had everything going for you. You could have made it big. Instead of building your concert career, you are mostly giving support to Babanrao.'

'Nonsense,' Arun responded without a moment's hesitation, 'I have acquired so much knowledge.'

But the man had correctly recognised this turning point in Arun's life and the implicit choice he had made. It was a testament to the adage that character is destiny. For Arun had become so intoxicated with his new artistic discoveries under Babanrao that it did not occur to him to capitalise on his growing reputation and enviable contacts with senior musicians to boost his performing career. By delving deeper into rhythmic and lyrical improvisation, Arun had dramatically widened his musical vision. By working on bol improvisation, he had developed a feel for the cadences of Brajbhasha, the Hindi dialect most commonly used in khayal, evoking in him the urge to compose. By training in the Agra style, he could sing as though he were dancing.

◆ Rope

A KHAYAL SINGER CHOOSES A PITCH FOR THE SHADJA, OR tonic Sa, so that he or she can explore half a octave below it and one-and-a-half octaves above it. Once a singer chooses a particular pitch for the shadja, he or she keeps it constant throughout a concert and often sticks to it for years on end. Singers may change this pitch on a given day depending on the condition of their voice or at some point in their life alter it permanently because of age-related changes to their vocal folds.

In every performance, the tanpura sounds the all-important shadja. The standard tanpura has four strings, but some have five or six. The tanpura's strings, from left to right, in the order in which they are played are: usually the pancham, but for some raags, the madhyam or shuddh nishad; the shadja; another shadja; and the kharaj.

For all practical purposes, the pitches of the Sa and Pa remain constant across raags,[9] but each of the remaining ten notes corresponds not to one pitch but a small range of pitches. The Hindustani music octave therefore resembles less a ladder with a finite number of rungs and more a rope with infinitely many continuous points. For example, conceptually we say that the raags Bhairav and Todi have a komal rishabh, denoted 're'. But the frequency of this note differs in each raag. Further, even in the same raag, the frequencies might minutely vary from singer to singer.[10]

Notes are also embellished in a variety of ways, but this is difficult to fully capture in notation. If one had to pick one embellishment that creates Hindustani music's characteristic sound, it would probably be the meend, which is a continuous glide between two notes.[11] A meend can be of different intervals, including the whole octave. Just as a child reproduces the sounds of its mother tongue through listening and osmosis, so do students of Indian music learn to perceive and produce the correct pitches and embellishments. Many students invent their own shorthand additions to the basic notation to represent some of this information. Some people have also come up with detailed notation systems.[12] But most performing musicians would argue that even these do not capture all the information because so much of it is incredibly subtle. They would probably also contend that even the most detailed notation system is useful more as a reminder of the melody's broad outline and can be accurately interpreted only by someone who has already internalised all the nuances and distinctions via oral training.

'Not every adult learns to cook, but most people acquire a taste for certain foods and flavours, and develop some discrimination. A person might say, my mother cooks this dish well, my aunt makes that dish well. That is because the person has been eating this food since childhood. The atmosphere for an activity is very important. Being immersed in a particular ambience from a young age is a form of indirect learning.' —AK

IDEAS

The best people possess a feeling for beauty,
the courage to take risks, the discipline
to tell the truth, the capacity for sacrifice.
Ironically, their virtues make them vulnerable;
they are often wounded, sometimes destroyed.
— Ernest Hemingway

10

◇ Garden

HISSING RAIN POUNDED THE ROAD AS I GOT OFF AN AUTO-rickshaw outside Guruji's building. His door appeared shut through the curtain of water. Was class cancelled because of the downpour? When I got closer, I saw a sliver of an opening. Relieved, I gently pushed the door inwards. Guruji was sitting, as usual, on the floor against the wall at the far end. For many of his students, especially those of us who had discovered him late both in his and our lives, this was a reassuring sight, telling us that we could continue to drink from the fountain of his musical wisdom, take pleasure in the company of musically like-minded people, savour the snacks that Kaku rustled up, enjoy a sanctuary, for at least a few hours a week, from the petty and the mundane. A year later, when I looked at my notes from this period, they were charged with euphoria, the prose proudly purple.

This did not mean that, after nearly six months since my first visit, I was fumbling any less. But I was less embarrassed by the fact, comforted by Guruji's long-term perspective. 'It takes six months to a year to get even a basic idea of a new style and at least five years to start singing in that mould,' he said. 'Real progress is measured in years, not months. Keep coming regularly and practise as much as time allows.'

I tightened my belt and kept the faith. That morning, two students had already arrived and had begun singing the slow composition *Karim naam tero* (Generosity is your name) in raag Miyan Malhar, the core raag of the Malhar family of monsoon melodies. I was eager to see what Guruji would do with it because he made precise, delicate alterations to raags, which, when integrated, significantly intensified their flavour.

People kept walking in despite the heavy rain.

'Sa____ ᵐᵃRe_____ ᵐᵃRe_____ Pa___, ga___ ma_ Re___ Sa___,' sang one student, rendering two of Miyan Malhar's most distinctive phrases, the second being a descending vakra, or zig-zag, phrase. Before she could continue, Guruji intervened.

'Don't prolong the initial Re so much,' he said. 'If you do that, you get a whiff of Kamod.'

She shortened the Re and sang: 'Sa____ ᵐᵃRe_ ᵐᵃRe_ Pa___.'

The phrase got an extra zing.

'Sa____ ni____ Ḍha_ Ṇi____ Sa___,' she continued, descending into the lower octave from the shadja and then looping back to it with another zig-zag phrase, this time an ascending one, also typical of this raag. Guruji stopped her again.

'In the beginning, when you slide from Sa down to ṇi, you should reveal the Ṇi in between,' he said. 'But do it in passing. Don't stall there.'

'Sa_ **Ṇi** ni_ Ḍha_ Ṇi____ Sa___,' she sang.

Again, this alteration gave the phrase more zest. This instruction, however, did not have anything to do with her phrase treading on another raag's terrain. Rather, it was an important nuance that had probably been flattened after notation systems gained currency. Guruji often warned us about the perils of taking notation systems, such as the ones introduced by Bhatkhande and Paluskar, at face value in an art form that had gained its shape via oral transmission over generations. These examples in Miyan Malhar vividly illustrated how notation could omit key details, such as the precise length of notes in a phrase and the pitches between two notes in a glide that needed to be highlighted and the manner in which this needed to be done. 'Notation can be only a rough guide,' he said. 'You need to have learnt from a well-trained musician for a number of years to be able to read between the lines.'

I had also not heard Guruji uttering the words 'aaroh' and 'avroh', or ascending and descending scales of raags, except to criticise their utility. Many books used by music schools mentioned them, but he contended that they gave a stunted view of a raag. Instead, like Gajananbuwa, he spoke only of a raag's chalan. 'One can go up and down a raag in multiple ways,' he said several times. 'You have to internalise the chalan.'

⁂

Despite Guruji's rigorous approach to raag chalans, he was not a rigid grammarian. In the very first class that I had attended, for instance, in response to Bhavik's question, Guruji had justified using the Savani phrase Ga-ma-Pa ma-Pa___, Ga___ Sa___ in Bihagada. At that time, I had not paid attention to his explanation, but later, while listening to my recording of the lesson, I noted that Guruji had offered three reasons. The first was context: he said that this phrase usually appeared right after and before a different phrase in Bihagada than in Savani. One could therefore sing that phrase in Bihagada and still maintain its character. The second reason was aesthetics: he said that the phrase contained a repetition of a double note, namely ma-Pa ma-Pa, a motif that was typical of the Jaipur style, which had considerably influenced Bihagada's development. The third reason was precedent: he pointed out that the venerable Vilayat Hussain Khan had used that double-note phrase in Bihagada.

The class on Miyan Malhar went on. Some of us used the ascending zig-zag phrase to rise to the taar shadja like this: ma Pa ni___ Dha_ Ni___ Sa___. Once, however, Guruji used a straight phrase, ma Pa Dha Ni Sa_, pointing out both that we should sing this rapidly and employ it only after we had used the zig-zag phrase several times to firmly establish Miyan Malhar's ambience. 'This straight phrase is like a subsidiary spice in a recipe, one that you should throw in only after you have put in the main masalas that have created the dish's essential flavour,' he said.

A few weeks earlier, Guruji had given me a similar explanation when I had got around to asking him why he had sung Re Re Sa ni Pa ma Re Sa ni Sa in Darbari at the January concert, a descending phrase that has neither dha or ga, two of Darbari's signature notes. 'Darbari evolved from Sarang,' Guruji had said. 'Sarang does not have those two notes, but Darbari uses all of Sarang's notes. As a result, you can use Sarang's phrases while singing Darbari, but only after you have established Darbari clearly, like an artist who creates an abstract painting using all the secondary colours, but later decides to add smidgens of a primary colour.'

In Miyan Malhar, Guruji's insistence that we not overly lengthen the Re in the first key phrase and that we sing the straight ascending phrase at a fast pace highlighted another key aspect of his raag interpretations: their rhythmic dimension. He was strict about students maintaining a specific pace while singing each phrase and preserving the relative lengths of notes within a phrase. 'A phrase loses its impact if one does not sing it at the appropriate speed, while its structure disintegrates if the lengths of notes in relation to one another are not in the correct proportions,' he explained. 'But within a narrow band, one can modulate the speed of various phrases to convey emotion, just like in language. For example, you talk faster than usual when you want to communicate a sense of urgency. Not just phrases, but whole raags can be sung in a variety of speeds. But some lend themselves to a slower starting pace than others. Darbari can be elaborated at a leisurely pace, but Adana, its close kin, requires a faster tempo.'

The rain continued to hammer down. One student said that she had not learnt Miyan Malhar before.

'You've heard *Bole re papihara* (So the cuckoo sings), right?' Guruji asked, referring to a popular film song. 'It is based on Miyan Malhar.'

Guruji assumed that most of us in the morning class had a base for about four dozen raags from the standard canon because we had encountered them before in his class, had learnt them from an earlier teacher or had heard online or live renditions of them. He presumed that we were actively engaged with the music and could tap into our aural memories. He then guided us onwards from our different starting points. At the same time, he encouraged us to grasp through osmosis whatever we could from the top down, without analysing the melody. His own singing constantly provided this aerial or holistic view. 'Every raag has a tarz [tune],' he often said. 'Try to get a feel for that too, then your ear will tell you immediately when you stray from it. Go by the sound of it. Ultimately, a raag is to be enjoyed in its totality.'

Guruji thus approached the raag from two directions. He relentlessly elaborated its chalan so that we absorbed it from the ground up, the way teachers might use drills to teach adults learning a second language.[1] As students gained control over a raag, his suggestions became more subtle, and once students became fluent in a raag, his interventions moved to the realm of aesthetics. He also immersed us in a musical atmosphere similar to the one in which children instinctively learn their mother tongues. But he cautioned us that using genres besides khayal as models had limitations. Right after mentioning *Bole re papihara* to ease a student into Miyan Malhar, he warned us that semi-classical and popular music could be only a starting point. 'We have made a hash of Bageshree and Bhimpalas because natya geet based on these raags include all sorts of combinations and stall indiscriminately on various notes,' he said. 'It is fine to take such liberties in natya geet, but you should not carry these over into classical music.'

Rain continued to fall hard as Kaku came around as usual at half past eleven with tea and, that day, a snack of palak puris. Guruji set the electronic tabla to a sprightly tempo and we moved to his fast composition, *Aiso na baraso badarawa* (Clouds, don't unleash such heavy rain) set to the fourteen-beat Aadaa Chautaal. In the first verse, a woman hopes that it does not rain so hard that her beloved cannot come to her. In the second verse, the woman wishes that once her beloved arrives, it will start raining so heavily that he cannot leave. Guruji had borrowed this theme from Urdu poetry. The room reverberated with us singing as it poured outside.

My elation was often clouded by dread, of wilting in this demanding environment. I always eagerly set off from home, but as I walked the last few metres to Guruji's home, anxiety would begin to rear its head. It seemed like every other day another revelation of my ignorance awaited me. That day it was Aadaa Chautaal, which I had come across as a student only once before. I was familiar with a close cousin, the twelve-beat Ektaal, but I was presumptuous to think that I could easily make the transition. Eventually, as before, I took a deep breath and reminded myself that I was in it for the long haul.

Furthermore, after just six months, even while juggling other commitments, I had progressed. I was already more at ease with the sixteen-beat Tilwada, which, like Aadaa Chautaal, I had barely used before coming to Guruji. But Tilwada and the fourteen-beat Jhoomra were mainstays for slow compositions in Guruji's lineage, in contrast with Teentaal, which was popular with Jaipur singers like my previous guru. Guruji had set up several compositions so that their lyrics' syllables fell precisely on specific quarter beats in the two core taals. These included *Jiya maanat nahin* (Unyielding is my heart) in raag Yaman for Tilwada and *Kavan des gaye* (To which land has he gone?) in raag Multani for Jhoomra.

'Sing these compositions hundreds of times the way I have set them up,' he told us. 'You will get a good feel of these taals.'

A fear of taal is common among Hindustani music learners. But Guruji worked on students gaining control over various taals as relentlessly as he instilled his meticulous chalans of raags in us. For this reason, he had acquired the reputation of being a 'taal doctor'. With new students, he worked on the fundamental skill of picking up the mukhda at the correct moment towards the end of the avartan and landing accurately on the sam. The image of Guruji raising his hand at the taal's three-fourths mark and counting, one, two, three, four, to help some of us who were faltering to land on the sam correctly in Tilwada is permanently imprinted in my memory.

Just as he did with raags, he kept raising the bar when it came to our control over taals. Once we could land on the sam with ease, he told us to create a compelling aamad, or approach to the sam. 'How to conclude an avartan is of great concern,' he said. 'It has to have punch. You should be so much in control of the avartan that listeners can recognise that you are soon arriving on the sam and anticipate your arrival.' He asked even more advanced students to consciously harness rhythm over the whole avartan. 'You should establish the laya right from the start,' he said. 'When you improvise, you should sound as though you are singing the taal.'

To gain competence in singing at quicker tempos, a student could do no better than to learn his fast compositions. Like his raag expositions, they were finely etched, rhythmically catchy and varied. He had used a range of taals, tempos, rhythmic patterns and starting points within the avartan. They had a variety of gharana flavours—Agra, Gwalior, Jaipur. In sum, they were an excellent didactic resource. I thought of them as miniature varnams, the instructional compositions in Carnatic music that every student has to learn to sing in several speeds.

As a way to begin improvising within fast compositions, Guruji suggested that we practise singing a part of a fast composition's first line and then come up with various phrases in the space left over in the cycle. 'Initially, make several sequences beforehand and sing them by rote,' he said. 'Gradually start varying them as you sing. Eventually, you will be able to improvise fully and freely.'

Guruji worked on the quality of students' sur and their perception of laya *while* helping them gain control over raags and taals. Sur and laya did not lend themselves as much to explicit instruction, according to him. As students sang the chalans of various raags, he corrected their pitches when necessary, but said that becoming tuneful was a lifelong process. 'Students have to first be able to perceive the pitches,' he told me. 'This happens over time. The more they listen to good music, the faster this process will be. Equally, the quality of their sur depends upon how much and how intensely they practise. To produce outstanding sur, one has to do outstanding riyaaz!'

As students progressed, he honed their sense of laya, which went beyond gaining control over specific taals. One skill was the ability to sing a composition in a range of taals and quickly switch from one taal to another by appropriately adjusting the composition's lyrics—the way he had expected us to do in Nat Bihag. Another was the ability to estimate various tempos, from very slow to very fast, crucial for communicating the starting pace of a composition to the tabla player and knowing how much to speed up during various stages of improvisation. Yet another crucial skill was the ability to maintain a chosen speed without unknowingly decelerating or, more commonly, accelerating.

I was amazed by how Guruji juggled so many students of different capabilities and precisely gauged each one's level in various skills at any given time. I lost perspective on my own struggles once I had overcome them, wondering why I had taken so long to acquire this or that skill. I was equally gobsmacked by the colourful cast of characters who kept turning up in class. They included tabla and harmonium players who came by to accompany us for various lengths of time. Once, a flautist, a sarangi player and pakhawaj player overlapped for several classes. On the first day that the pakhawaj player came, Guruji took advantage of the fact that this percussion instrument is used in dhrupad to teach us a composition in that genre. Another time, a tabla player turned up with a sheaf of papers containing special compositions that his guru had learnt from the great Ahmed Jan Thirakwa. 'These need to be preserved,' he told Guruji, going on to explain some of their intricacies. 'They are priceless,' he said. I remember thinking how unfortunate it was that there seemed to be no institution in Mumbai that could take charge of such treasures.

But on some days, Guruji's living room was packed so tight that there was no wiggle room. Was there an upper limit to the class size, I wondered. Surely, some students found such a huge class intimidating? 'A student can learn a lot just by listening to others and to the guru teaching and correcting others,' Guruji replied, when I later asked him about this. 'The advanced students push up the levels of others.'

∽

When Guruji retired from his bank job in 1994, teaching music became his main source of income, his pension being negligible. But I never saw him asking anyone for fees or requesting anyone to increase the amount, if only to keep up with inflation. I merely saw people handing over envelopes at the end or beginning of each month. He gave full or partial fee waivers to many people who said they could not afford to pay. He kept no record of payments. 'Those who want to pay will pay,' he told me. 'Those who think it right to increase the fee will do so. I am not going to ask anyone for anything. My gurus never charged me.'

Shaking her head, Kaku told me that he had always been like this. Down the line, I felt that a uniform fee with a sliding scale of generous financial concessions for those who needed them might have been better than leaving it to students to make what was a difficult decision. But I could not imagine Guruji supervising a formal system. He was among a clutch of dedicated musicians who taught from their homes far from the public gaze, primarily to pass on knowledge, not to make money. These gurus coexisted with more visible and out-and-out commercial music schools that charged hefty fees and knew how to get publicity.

Yet if one wants to become a performer, a version of the age-old seena-ba-seena taleem, or face-to-face instruction, is essential.

Students have to spend a certain number of hours with their gurus, like most of us did with Guruji. Fortunately, modern technology enables students to remain immersed in their gurus' music even afterwards. 'We had to absorb all that we could in the hours that we were with Gajananbuwa,' Guruji told us. 'Recordings are a big boon. But you cannot learn only from recordings. You need to learn from a guru for a number of years because you need someone to correct you.'

Given khayal's stylistic variety, the mode of training is specific to a guru. From the start, a guru imparts his or her style, a process falling between persuasion and brainwashing. Paradoxically, I initially resisted Guruji's indoctrination. I felt more comfortable singing in my old way, using the Jaipur gharana aakaar. I felt sorry that I had to give up a way of singing that I had grown to love, like a person who moves from a cosy home to a new one that she desires but nonetheless finds alien—a metaphor suggested by the very word gharana. At first, Guruji tolerated my wavering. But at one point, he made it clear that he did not appreciate it. I knew that I was skating on thin ice when, in several classes, he uncharacteristically did not respond after I had attempted singing and abruptly moved on to the next student. The jolt that I experienced was mild and brief, but it gave me a glimpse of a guru's power and the extent to which he could influence a student's emotional and intellectual well-being. Much later, I saw that within certain non-negotiable parameters, Guruji encouraged individualism, but initially, for many years, those who wished to make progress had to fully submit to his ministrations.

Guruji had built his pedagogy on the shoulders of his gurus, but, harnessing his analytical mind and gift for language, had added many features. He had adopted Gajananbuwa's highly effective method of drilling the chalans of various raags into students using sargam sequences, but with a few changes. Gajananbuwa's students closely followed their teacher's singing, while Guruji allowed us to take a kernel of an idea and run with it as long as we remained within the raag's ambit. In fact, he was often curious to see whether a student would come up with something new. Guruji's class sizes were, on average, much larger than Gajananbuwa's, with more than a dozen students often attending at any given time. Guruji also spoke much more than his taciturn guru, using metaphors and similes to get his points across.

In the first few months, I heard people talking about Guruji's teaching using a variety of metaphors. The way he handled so many students of varying ages, abilities and temperaments was like a performance, said his close friend, Vikas Karmalkar, or Karmalkar Kaka, as we called him. One student compared each of his lessons to a workshop, capturing the fact that, in his class, people learnt by doing, nudged along by an experienced guide. Yogesh, who had a science background, said Guruji's class was like a lab in which he worked on a number of experiments, fine-tuning them so that they yielded results. I began thinking of him as a gardener with a green thumb, gently tending to a variety of plant species, each with specific needs and at a different stage of growth, and of his class as a garden, full of life, yet serene. It was a pity that his pedagogical process had not been systematically captured through video recordings of his lessons, the way that Western classical conductor Benjamin Zander's master classes had been captured in the online series *Interpretations of Music: Lessons for Life*.

I regretted that I had joined the class just after what seems to have been its golden age. For fifteen years, from 2000 to 2015, almost every day in the morning and evening Guruji had taught those who went on to become his best students. There were about a dozen of them, including the six who had sung for the Swar Archana CD, namely Mandaar, Ravindra, Vishal, Mukul, Sugandha and Ketaki, as well as Omkar Dhumal, a shehnai player, who had helped produce the CD. Guruji's garden had then been lush with flowering plants.

Once I asked him, 'About a dozen of your students can perform, right?'

'Yes, and many more can come out of here,' he replied, gesturing to his living room's four walls.

He was not done nurturing seedlings in his garden.

◆ Cusp: 1981–85

ARUN AND DHANASHREE GOT READY TO SLEEP. AN OVERHEAD fan whirred and a clock ticked in their bedroom. Arun's parents were asleep in the only other bedroom and their sons had gone to bed on mattresses laid out on the living room floor. About two years earlier, Arun and Dhanashree had moved from their chawl room in Dombivli into a two-bedroom flat in Mulund East, just within Bombay's limits. As usual, that evening, soon after returning from work, Arun had washed up and wolfed down his dinner. As usual, afterwards, he had sat down to sing for about two hours in the living room, sitting on the floor with his back against the wall facing the main door. A tabla and harmonium player had come by to accompany him. About a dozen people had dropped in to listen to him. Belying his relaxed body language and the informal atmosphere, he sang with great involvement. Dhanashree had been busy in the kitchen. Ashish, nearly nine, and Adwait, four, had meandered in and out of the living room.

It was mid-1982, when a momentous event was playing out in the heart of Bombay. Earlier that year, Arun had seen the headlines in the newspapers. Led by the powerful union leader Datta Samant, about quarter of a million workers from numerous cotton mills that had helped make Bombay an industrial powerhouse had gone on an indefinite strike, demanding higher pay and better working conditions. Recently, one of Arun's train companions had said that he was anxious about the fate of his clerical job in Shrinivas Cotton Mills because no resolution to the industrial dispute seemed to be in sight. But like many middle-class families, the Kashalkars barely felt the strike's ripples. Arun harboured no curiosity about the labour unrest or its economic, political and social ramifications because it was not endangering his job and he did not have a jot of power to change the course of events. That night, he gave Dhanashree important news that did have a bearing on his life.

'I got a B-high grade in my radio audition,' Arun told her.

'Hmm,' Dhanashree replied, knowing that he could have auditioned more than a decade earlier.

Ignoring her feeble enthusiasm, Arun revealed another key bit of information.

'I learnt from a radio insider that one of the judges wanted to directly give me an A grade,' he said. 'Guess who it was?'

The radio had four grades, Top, A, B-high and B, but a first-time candidate usually received a B grade, occasionally a B-high, and in rare cases an A. Only Top- and A-grade artists got the flagship ninety-minute national programme of classical music, which aired every Saturday night, and only they could participate in the prestigious Akashvani Sangeet Sammelan, an annual festival of concerts across the country.

Dhanashree shook her head.

'Mallikarjun Mansur,' Arun replied, getting to the only bit of news that mattered to him.

The septuagenarian Jaipur gharana singer, Gajananbuwa's almost exact contemporary, did not feature in the core group of musicians whom the rhythm-oriented sub-cultures of khayal around Arun's gurus considered their touchstones. But he did command their admiration for his extraordinary purity of pitch, his scintillating treatment of the taar shadja, his fluency in various complex raags and the way he plunged into his renditions with a burning intensity from the start and kept turning the heat up. Dhanashree had an idea about Mansur's stature because she had heard Arun and Shrikant discussing Ulhas's desire to learn from him.

'Then why did you not get the A grade?' she asked.

Arun told her what he had learnt from two insiders. Barely a minute into Arun's audio recording of a slow composition in Miyan ki Todi, one of the judges, a Hindi speaker, had piped up.

'This singer is not pronouncing the words properly,' the man had said.

'That's not what we are here to evaluate,' another judge had said.

Mansur had remained silent. His pronunciation of Brajbhasha was not among the qualities he was admired for. As the recording had played on, he and other judges had intermittently emitted appreciative sounds. At the end, Mansur had spontaneously exclaimed, 'This Todi has meat! A grade!'

But the cavilling judge had dissented, possibly because he wanted to save face after his hasty criticism. The panel could consequently reach a consensus only of B-high.

But Dhanashree was reassured by Mansur's reaction, which she saw as more evidence that her husband had what it took to forge ahead. Arun's music had grown on her too. While cooking or doing other household chores, when she was not even intently listening to him sing, she would suddenly be moved. Also in his favour was the fact that he was, she sometimes shyly thought to herself, an attractive man.

Soon after Arun and Dhanashree moved to Mulund, musicians and music lovers began pouring into their home to accompany or listen to Arun, and sometimes, just to chat with him. Although their roughly 600-square-feet flat housed six people—their family of four and Arun's parents—it was a huge improvement from their one-room-kitchen in Dombivli. Mulund was also closer than Dombivli to downtown Bombay and their flat was at a walking distance from the railway station. This had cut Arun's nearly four-hour daily commute to less than three. Dhanashree, too, had a less demanding work schedule. She had gone part-time, working for a firm in Dombivli.

Mulund had a lively cultural life, with Marathi speakers being predominant in the Kashalkars' middle-class milieu. While living in

Dombivli, Arun had performed a few times in Mulund and knew local musicians, including the outstanding tabla player Sudhir Sansare, who had learnt from the legendary Farrukhabad gharana maestro Amir Hussain Khan. 'Listen as much as you can to Sansare,' Gajananbuwa had told Arun on learning that his student was moving to Mulund. Another local musician was the fine harmonium player Vishwanath Pendharkar, who had trained under Madhukar Pednekar, who all those years ago had suddenly doubled his speed while Arun had been singing taans. Many other high-level amateur tabla and harmonium players with day jobs also lived in the locality. Arun knew two prolific local music teachers: Shirish-tai Joshi, who had learnt from Master Navrang, a student of the Bhendi Bazaar gharana's Aman Ali Khan, and Vinayak Kunte, who had learnt from the Agra gharana's Anwar Hussain Khan, Khadim Hussain Khan's brother.

The Kashalkar flat had quickly become an adda, with Dhanashree pampering visitors with her Marathi-style milky tea and snacks. Ashish had begun going to a good English-medium school and Adwait to a babysitter nearby. A few months after the family had shifted, Arun's parents, who had been living with Shrikant, moved in. As the eldest son, Arun felt good that he finally had space to accommodate his parents.

Arun had Dhanashree to thank for the move. About five years before the move, his bank had announced that it was setting up a housing colony in Mulund and would sell its flats to employees at a subsidised rate and allow them to pay in instalments. But Arun had not wanted to take the interest-free loan that the bank was offering to employees to pay the initial sum to book the flat, because, having never been in debt, he was gripped by a fear of the unknown. But Dhanashree, who possessed a better survival instinct and business sense, realised that this was a once-in-a-lifetime opportunity. If she could help it, she would not raise her sons in a chawl. As Arun later colourfully put it to his friends, while graciously acknowledging his short-sightedness, Dhanashree and he had 'got into some juicy arguments'—until he had relented.

※

After several hours of disturbed sleep, Arun sat up on his bed at about four in the morning. Dhanashree stirred. He decided to get up and do his daily morning pooja a couple of hours earlier than usual. That would calm him. He went to the wash basin in the foyer, splashed water on his face, brushed his teeth and went into the kitchen. In the dark, he sat in front of a shrine in the corner. Instead of saying his usual prayers, he involuntarily began singing.

Tu vidhaataa tu hi daataa   You are the maker, you alone the giver.

He sang the line several times, realising that its tune was in Bairagi, a raag consisting of the five notes Sa re ma Pa ni, a raag linked to the more expansive Bhairav, which has seven notes, Sa re Ga ma Pa dha Ni. Both raags create a meditative atmosphere reflecting the still beauty of dawn, when the rising sun inspires in one an awe for the universe. Bairagi is sparer because it lacks a gandhar and dhaivat. Instead of these bright notes, it uses the tender komal nishad instead of Bhairav's more forceful shuddh nishad. Bairagi maintains throughout an austere and hushed ambience of prayer.

Arun sang a second line in the same raag.

Tu hi karta tu hi trata   You alone are the nurturer,
                                              you alone the protector.

He sang both lines several times, quickly realising that the appropriate taal was the seven-beat Roopak and that the sam should fall on the syllable 'dhaa' of 'vidhaata'. The other lines rapidly followed. In the past, he had come up with a tune or a phrase and had built out the rest of the composition over time, from within a few hours to a few weeks. Each composition had a different arc of coming into being. Arun often kept refining the first version.

He sometimes slightly altered the words or polished the tune. Occasionally, he even switched raags, like from Bilaskhani Todi to Bhairavi for *Bharanana det* (He doesn't allow me to fetch water) in Teentaal, or changed taals, like from Ektaal to Aadaa Chautaal for *Aiso na baraso badarawa* in Miyan Malhar. That morning was perhaps the first time that the lyrics, raag and taal had emerged at the same time like a three-stranded braid. He sat before his kitchen shrine in a trance.

He kept singing the composition, chiselling it in every iteration. A rose light suffused the room. As he entered Bairagi's deepest realms, his singing became more and more intense. Arun was a believer, but not in a specific god. Rather, he had faith in the abstract notion of a divine force, which he recognised from a young age was common to all religions. He was neither ritualistic nor interested in religious mythology or philosophy. Whenever he did dip into the *Dnyaneshwari*, the thirteenth-century commentary on the Bhagavad Gita that experts believed was the oldest surviving text in Marathi, it was more for its poetry than its philosophy. Because of Arun's upbringing, the few rituals he did follow, such as his morning pooja, came from the Hindu tradition. But he viewed his pooja as a form of meditation, not a means to salvation.

He believed that humans could hope for salvation only through their actions, not by conducting rituals. His first guru in ethics, as in music, had been his father, for whom the dominant religion was vidya, or knowledge, and who, following Mahatma Gandhi, regarded work as worship, a maxim that Arun had seen put up on a wall in his school classroom. Deep down, Arun knew that the Bairagi composition had been the fruit of his subconscious having watered the seed of an idea for weeks. Yet when the song emerged from his lips, he could not help feeling the hand of a mystical force. Facing the pooja niche in the wall, he did not see that Dhanashree was standing at the kitchen door, her eyes moist.

Arun looked radiant on stage. In his twenties, he had been good-looking in a soft, understated way. By forty, when a man is considered to be in his prime, he had acquired a more virile mien, enhanced no doubt by the fact that he was at a stage in his life when everything was on the upswing. When he happened to dress well, like on that day, he could look dashing. But, to Dhanashree's chagrin, he usually paid little attention to sartorial matters, as if signalling his disdain for outward appearances. Arun played a few phrases on the harmonium and looked up before beginning to sing his concert's concluding piece, a ghazal written by Jigar Moradabadi.

Ishq e la mehdood jab tak rehnooma hota nahin	Unless one is guided by infinite love,
Zindagi se zindagi ka haq ada hota nahin	One cannot fulfill the promise of life.

The ghazal appealed to Arun's romantic idealism. The concert, titled 'Ghazalanche gulshan' (A Bouquet of Ghazals), was one of two programmes that had been conceived by Vidyadhar Gokhale, a well-known writer of Marathi musicals who was also a poet, journalist and orator. For the other ghazal programme, titled *Preyasi te parameshwar* (From lover to God), Gokhale had chosen ghazals in which the devotee views God as a lover, a popular sentiment in the Indian sub-continent's poetic traditions. In all, Arun had set about fifteen ghazals to music, using raags as the base melodies.

Gokhale had first noticed Arun in a production of the Marathi musical *Panditraj Jagannath*, for which the playwright had written the script and song lyrics. He had subsequently kept track of Arun's musical career. For the ghazal programme, the pair toured on weekends and bank holidays, when Arun was off work. A few days earlier, they had performed at a Ganesh Utsav in Bombay. That day, too, the event was part of the same ten-day festival, in Deep Nagar, which had developed around a government-owned thermal power station nearly five hundred kilometres north-east of

Bombay. Before Arun sang each ghazal, Gokhale introduced it and expounded on the lyrics' philosophy. For Moradabadi's ghazal, Arun had chosen Shankara, a raag that, according to myth, was among Shiva's favourites. After Arun finished singing it and Gokhale gave a concluding commentary, people crowded around the stage.

'You were excellent,' an elderly man told Arun. 'You brought out so many shades of emotion, just the way you did when you were a young boy.'

'Oh?' Arun asked, puzzled.

'I am an engineer in the thermal plant here, but I am originally from Balharshah,' the man replied, referring to a town in Maharashtra's Chandrapur district, just east of Arun's native district, Yavatmal. 'You had visited my hometown when you were a boy to present the *Geet Ramayan*. I liked your singing so much that I even got a tape of it from the organisers.'

Arun enjoyed the novelty of composing music for lyrics in Urdu. For most of the ghazals, he used the six-beat Dadra taal. From childhood, Arun had listened to this genre, developing a special liking for renditions by Amanat Ali Khan, Begum Akhtar, Ghulam Ali, Hussain Baksh Gullo, Mehdi Hassan, Nirmala Devi and Shubha Gurtu, most of whom he had heard live. He had often sung ghazals at the end of classical music recitals, and knew he had a flair for semi-classical genres. His first radio broadcast had, in fact, been dedicated to natya sangeet. But after this collaboration with Gokhale, Arun decided to restrict such engagements because he did not want to unwittingly drift away from khayal. At the end, Gokhale paid Arun, saying, 'You kept performing with me, but did not once ask me how much I would pay. This is why I took such a shine to you. You were focused entirely on art.'

When Arun told Dhanashree what Gokhale had told him, she rolled her eyes.

Arun walked faster than usual from the railway station to his flat. At home, Gajananbuwa was sitting against the wall, in Arun's usual place, singing Shahana Kanada, with Sudhir Sansare on the tabla. A few days earlier, Gajananbuwa had told Arun that he was coming to stay with him for a week, arriving that morning after Arun had left for work. Several listeners had already gathered. A right royal mehfil was under way. Cries of appreciation met Gajananbuwa's landing on each sam of the popular composition in the ten-beat Jhaptaal.

More aaye kunwar kanhaiyee^x	Krishna, my prince, has arrived,
Chandra ki jyot malina bhayee	Putting the moon's light in the shade.

After freshening up, Arun came back out and sat down near his guru. Gajananbuwa continued to sing several avartans and began giving Arun turns to sing. Following his guru's lead, Arun began singing in pure aakaar. When Gajananbuwa switched to doing bol, Arun followed suit.

'Theek ahe!' Gajananbuwa exclaimed a couple of times.

Arun's time with Babanrao had both deepened his perception of laya and widened his bol repertoire. After a while, Gajananbuwa increased the tempo and moved to taans. Fully warmed up, Arun built up quickly to the super-fast taans that he had imbibed from Rambhau, whose blistering speed gave familiar patterns a new texture.

'Achcha!' Gajananbuwa exclaimed again.

Standing in the doorway, watching her husband and his guru, Dhanashree glimpsed for a few moments the ecstasy that this music could engender in its practitioners. After Shahana Kanada, Gajananbuwa began Sampoorna Malkauns. The session ended at about 11 p.m. After dinner, Gajananbuwa retired to the room used earlier by Arun's parents, who had by then moved out to live with one of his other brothers. Arun fell into a sweet slumber.

At about 4 a.m., Arun felt someone gently shaking his arm. He heard Gajananbuwa's voice.

'Chalo,' his guru was saying. Let's go.

Arun sat up with a start, disoriented for a moment before realising that he was not dreaming. He got out of bed, brushed his teeth and went to his guru's room. Gajananbuwa began singing a composition in Lalit Pancham, which combines elements of raag Shuddha Dhaivat Lalit with raag Pancham. Arun had not received taleem in this compound raag, but he had a good grasp of its constituents. He focused on absorbing phrases from each raag that his guru was bringing into play and how he was moving between the two raags. Gajananbuwa sang along these lines:

Ṇi re Ga ma____ (Lalit),
Ga ma Ma ma Ga_ (Lalit),
Ni Dha Pa ma____ (Pancham),
Ga re Ma Ga re Sa____ (Lalit),
ma Dha Ṡa____ (Pancham).

Before presenting this raag in public, Arun knew that he would have to practise layering the phrases in a variety of ways to see which combinations created an impact. Because he did so much bol work, he would have to practise elegantly melding the composition's lyrics with the raag's phrases. With any new raag, intellectually grasping it was only half the challenge. Arun knew it took time for the voice to express its many nuances. 'Raag gale pe chadhna chaahiye,' musicians often said. The raag had to settle into one's throat. Arun wanted to say something original about every raag—by experimenting with the spaces between notes, close by and far apart, spaces in which so much could happen; with the length of various notes relative to one another, which one could vary within bounds; and with the combination of embellishments that suited the raag. He could never say how long he would need to do this. It could happen in weeks or take several years. Patamanjari had, after all, resisted his advances for years.

Gajananbuwa moved to Dhuliya Malhar, another new raag for Arun, and then on to other familiar raags, until the rest of the house began stirring. Dhanashree brought them chai. The session continued until Arun had to get ready for work.

The next evening, more listeners dropped in because news of Gajananbuwa's visit had spread. Again, early the following morning, Gajananbuwa woke Arun up for another session. Gajananbuwa had caught up on his sleep in the afternoon, Dhanashree told her husband. Arun wondered how he was going to hold up that week if this was going to be the schedule. By then, he had moved from the bank's bills department to the foreign exchange section. The work was as mechanical as before, but the amounts involved were larger. He had to be alert to avoid making careless errors. Among other tasks, he had to calculate what the bank had to deduct from various importers' accounts, after converting the foreign currency into rupees and deducting the bank's commission. The job entailed doing simple arithmetic, a combination of addition, subtraction, multiplication and division, but the work was all the more enervating for being conceptually trivial. After the second pre-dawn taleem session, Arun dozed off on the train ride to work. As the train approached VT, Arun woke up

'Not well?' asked Dilip Kolhatkar, a friend of Arun's from his Dombivli days who was among his regular train companions.

Almost every day, Arun caught the same train in Mulund that Dilip boarded in Dombivli. Dilip was a theatre director with a day job in Bank of Baroda. Soon after arriving in Bombay, Arun had acted and sung in an experimental but critically well-received musical directed by Dilip called *Akhyan* (Story), with several acts, each representing a distinct style or phase in the history of Marathi theatre. Dilip's father was a violin player who had learnt from Gajananbuwa. Arun told Dilip about the musician's visit and invited him to drop in that week.

On Gajananbuwa's last night, after everyone had left, he told Arun to sing one of his own compositions. Arun chose *Laagi aas* (I have a yearning) in Yaman, set to Teentaal. Gajananbuwa listened impassively. 'You now understand music,' he then surprised Arun by saying.

The melody was not complicated, but Arun had used phrases that were off the beaten track but ones that Gajananbuwa had dinned into his students. Arun had also strung phrases together in unusual ways. Just the first line *Laagi aas milan ki tore* (I yearn to meet you), contained many alluring features. First, the Re went up to Ma instead of the more common Ga, and mirroring this jump, the Ma then rose to Ni instead of the more standard Dha, and finally, the Pa dropped directly to Re, rather than taking the more common route via Ma. The composition used a pleasing variety of lengths for the vowels.

Gajananbuwa's short response was the highest praise that Arun had received from his guru. Gajananbuwa mostly reacted in monosyllables, spontaneously praising his students for singing a good avartan, like he had done with Arun's improvisations in Shahana Kanada. But he also laughed when they arrived clumsily at the sam. Gajananbuwa had praised Arun using a full sentence only once before, after Arun had sung Chhayanat, before a much older vocalist's performance. A man who had missed the event had asked Gajananbuwa how he had liked the renditions. 'Arun sang nicely,' Gajananbuwa had replied.

Gajananbuwa spoke more eloquently through his actions. Arun noticed how every year that he had sung at the Aundh festival, Gajananbuwa had made sure that he was in the audience, even though as the organiser he had many responsibilities. Each year, Arun had requested his guru to not come. 'Your presence makes me nervous,' Arun would say. But within five minutes of Arun starting his rendition, Gajananbuwa would turn up and sit in the front row. He never said anything afterwards, but would be back the following year.

Arun knew he would feel a vacuum at home after Gajananbuwa left. Over a week, his guru had scorched a patch of Mulund. Arun had got through the days on several cups of chai and the exhilaration induced by his guru's presence and singing. After Gajananbuwa left, Arun thought, 'The fire of my guru's music has purified my house.'

⁓

After moving to Mulund, Arun had continued to occasionally drop in on Gajananbuwa's classes, including when he taught his granddaughter Apoorva, who was then a skittish school-going girl wearing frilly frocks. But it had been a long time since Arun had enjoyed daily contact with his guru. Like a drug, the sessions at his home had spurred Arun into heightened awareness. Unlike a drug, the effect was lasting. About two decades after he had come under Gajananbuwa's spell, Arun felt his relationship with khayal rapidly becoming more intimate, on the brink of a discovery.

Arun could see the common foundation of Gajananbuwa's style and those of other Gwalior gharana stalwarts. He began probing how each of their styles diverged from this shared base. Having relentlessly listened to great singers on the radio and in concerts since he was five, Arun retained vivid impressions of their music. Growing up, he had been adept at copying many of them. But imitating well-known vocalists without high-quality taleem was different from a well-trained musician judiciously taking on and adapting elements from other singers' styles.

The oldest Gwalior gharana singers whom Arun had heard belonged roughly to the tradition's third generation, born in the second half of the nineteenth century. Arun had over the years subconsciously made mental notes about their music. Antubuwa generously used gamaks, some reminiscent of Rahimat Khan, for whom Antubuwa had played the tanpura for a couple of years. Krishnarao Shankar Pandit incorporated a heavy dose of tappa movements. Ramkrishnabuwa Vaze was a master of rhythm, had a huge repertoire of raags and compositions and came up with twists to the standard gait of raags that almost always intensified their essence. 'He was peerless among his contemporaries,' Arun often told people.

In the next generation, Arun particularly respected Sharadchandra Arolkar, who had learnt from Krishnarao Shankar Pandit and his uncle Eknath Pandit. Arolkarbuwa developed a style that was intricate and had a good measure of ghasits, or long meends, perhaps because he had also learnt in Gwalior from another Krishnarao, whose last name was Mulye and who played the been, on which this melodic movement is frequently produced. Arun identified with Arolkarbuwa's intellectualism, which was evident in the way that he, like Vazebuwa, came up with unusual patterns in raags, even in a much-rendered one like Yaman. When Arun had been a bachelor, he had visited Arolkarbuwa, who lived in Bombay, to pay his respects. In contrast, Arolkar's contemporary, D.V. Paluskar, had a less ornate style. Arun surmised that Paluskar must have restricted heavy embellishments in his expression in order to project his honeyed voice. A singer had to play to his strengths. Paluskar died in his thirties, so his style would have almost certainly evolved. Arun also appreciated the solidity of Gwalior singers such as B.R. Deodhar, Lakshmanrao Bodas, Shankarrao Bodas and Vinayakbuwa Patwardhan, who reflected their gharana's principles but ultimately focused more on propagating music than on performing. Arun constantly drew from his mind's rich and expanding storehouse of musical impressions to integrate what he liked into the composite framework that he had acquired through his training.

Arun, however, concluded that the novelty in each musician's style was modest relative to the gharana's contribution, which represented the collective ideas of generations of musicians. When one trained with a musician from a leading gharana, one's style automatically embodied this multi-generational wisdom. Beyond reflecting their gharana's core principles, musicians obviously had a variety of voice qualities, used melodic embellishments in different proportions and emphasised rhythm to varying degrees. But Arun knew that a musician had to attain a high level of maturity before he or she could hope to usher in a true paradigm shift. He believed that such a shift, rather than transgressing a gharana's principles, because that would mean forgoing a wealth of knowledge and refinement, should transcend them.

Arun was in no hurry. All he wanted to do was to keep singing and thinking. He had arranged his life so that he could do both in the comfort of his home. If he continued to receive offers to perform in public, all the better.

―

Dhanashree felt Arun had his priorities upside down. She felt that he ought to focus on pushing his concert career to the next level, because while he continued to get invitations to perform, they came largely from his old stomping grounds of Dombivli and Thane. Arun had finished his blue-chip musical training, many senior musicians knew him, he had a steady if modest income, their two sons were doing well, they had a flat in Bombay. Yet again, like a canny entrepreneur, she recognised an opportunity and knew that timing was crucial. She sensed that Arun, then in his early forties, was on the cusp of entering a bigger arena. He was again at a crossroads, but only he could choose the direction. She found it hard to get him alone or when he was not tired. Finally, one night she fired her opening salvo. Their exchange went along the following lines:

'You should be performing in more places.'

'Perhaps,' Arun said softly, hoping that agreeing with her would end the conversation.

'The time is ripe for you to push ahead.'

'I don't even know what to do.'

'So you will allow all those years of training to go waste?'

'How am I wasting my training?' Arun asked, a slight shrillness creeping into his voice. 'I am singing every day. I am composing. I am thinking about music all the time.'

'You should be singing in bigger, better venues. You know so many senior musicians. You have contacts.'

'How preposterous,' Arun said, his tone falling to a cold whisper. 'You are suggesting that I canvass for concerts. I have not once seen Gajananbuwa or Babanrao doing that.'

This was his trump card—the precedent of his great gurus. She remained silent for a while. The way he blithely dug his heels in infuriated her. 'The world is changing,' she said hotly, pulling a higher card in the trump suit. She thought she had found a new line of argument.

'But I am not,' he said quietly, laying down the ace.

◆ Language

THE RAAG FORM CAN BE COMPARED IN SOME RESPECTS to human language.[2] Like human language, which allows people to produce and understand 'novel sentences of essentially unlimited complexity',[3] the raag form allows people to generate and perceive an infinite number and variety of melodies from a finite base. Many raags are likely to have evolved from devotional music and folk tunes. These tunes probably had some finite variations. In a slow process, the tune and its variations may have become abstracted into a set of rules defining the extent of variation, thus giving birth to a raag. Later, some raags came into being through a process called moorchhana, which involves shifting the scale of an existing raag.[4] A few may have also been inspired by versions of the Persian dastgah form.[5]

A raag's notes can be viewed as a language's vocabulary and a raag's rules for combining notes into phrases as a language's rules of grammar. Each raag also has a cadence, consisting of stress patterns and a tempo, the way a language does. Moreover, all raags share some underlying principles. Not any collection of notes and phrases can become a raag. Some basic requirements are that all raags must have a Sa and almost all raags must have a Pa, ma or Ma. One influential school of linguistics posits something similar for human language. Noam Chomsky, the father of modern linguistics, argues that human languages, despite their amazing diversity, share underlying principles or constraints that he calls 'universal grammar'.[6]

But the raag form differs from human language in a key respect. A raag may evoke moods but does not convey meaning in the sense of communicating specific information or referring to an external reality.[7] Because a raag does not convey meaning in a literal way, even lay listeners can begin enjoying it as pure sound.

> *'When you render a raag, you simultaneously paint on canvases of different sizes. The largest is the whole rendition. Then there is each avartan. Further, there are sections of the avartan. Then there is each moment. You might express something unexpected in a flash that has an immediate effect while adding to the whole picture. Later, you might consciously again use what was initially spontaneous.' —AK*

11

◇ Movie

ON A RARE DRY MONSOON DAY IN EARLY JULY, YOGESH AND I stood chatting by the road outside Guruji's house when his phone rang.

'Even five minutes more is going to be difficult,' I heard him saying in Marathi to the caller. 'I would help you if I could, but the schedule is packed.'

The caller, evidently a student, was asking for more time to sing at our annual Guru Purnima programme. Yogesh politely declined the request, his voice not betraying the slight irritation that I caught from his flicker of an eye-roll.

As he had done for several years, Yogesh was spearheading the organisation of the event, a yearly ritual in the Hindustani music world when students sing for their gurus, who give a short concluding recital. This event takes place on or after the actual Guru Purnima day, which, according to the Hindu calendar, occurs every year on a full-moon day in the month of Ashadh, coinciding with a period from June to August in the Roman calendar. The occasion celebrates the contributions of spiritual and performing arts teachers, those who traditionally taught students in their homes and became quasi-parental figures. By convention, students fund, plan and execute the music programme, consulting the guru about policy matters, such as, crucially, the line-up and the time allocated to each performer. That year, in our community, close to thirty students had to be accommodated over a day.

About a week after my conversation with Yogesh, a bunch of us walked together to the train station after class. The discussion turned to the Guru Purnima event.

'I plan to sing Bhoop,' said one young student.

'Have you booked the raag?' another youngster asked him. 'If you haven't, do it quickly. Yogesh will want to avoid repeating raags.'

'How much time have you been given?' asked a third student.

'I don't know yet,' the young student replied.

'But then how will you practise?' the third student persisted.

'Whatever it is, I am sure it won't be more than twenty minutes,' the first student replied.

'Twenty minutes!' exclaimed the third student, who seemed to think that it was too much, even as an outer limit.

The time allotted to students at the Guru Purnima function was like real estate in Mumbai, a scarce, prized and contested commodity. The time a student got reflected her or his position in the gurukul's pecking order. Every extra minute could boost a person's standing. No one had the temerity to bargain with Guruji so Yogesh was left to field people's requests. As for me, I had requested Guruji to excuse me from singing until I completed my two-year trial period.

※

On Guru Purnima day in mid-July, we went to class and presented Guruji with modest gifts: flowers, a notebook, a packet of dry fruit. He held class as usual, except that Kaku, instead of giving us just a chai break, had prepared a spread. Former students and well-wishers dropped in through the morning. From that day onwards, excitement about the following month's music programme began mounting. For students, it was the year's high point, serving as a stimulus for focused practice and giving them a vital performing opportunity in a demanding but supportive environment. Students who had moved to other cities sometimes returned to take part, because performing at this annual event was considered a seva, a service to be rendered as a sign of gratitude to the guru. Tabla and harmonium players associated with the guru came over to accompany students for free or for a nominal fee.

For gurus, this event was an opportunity to gauge students' progress over the year. Guruji, of course, heard us every week and had a rough idea of our abilities, but the class offered only glimpses. People told me that the programme always threw up surprises, in the form of students who took a backseat in class but practised hard and rose to the occasion, and more rarely, pushy personalities who ended up belying expectations. The typical audience at these events included students' families and friends, as well as the guru's admirers and supporters, including other musicians. The function offered them a unique listening experience.

When the morning came, brimming with excitement, I climbed up to the second floor of the Chitpavan Brahman Sangh hall, a few streets away from Guruji's home. I was still new enough to this world to find the casual existence of this upper-caste organisation jarring. The hall, I had gathered, was a regular venue for our Guru Purnima event. Simple but cosy, it could comfortably accommodate about eighty listeners. When I walked in, a young student was singing Ahir Bhairav. A lit brass lamp stood on a small table on one side of the stage, alongside garlanded framed photos of Gajananbuwa and Babanrao. The hall was half full. People were sitting on dhurries laid out on the floor and, at the back, on plastic chairs, which were ubiquitous at fringe music events. Three or four people from the organising team were coordinating with the caterers in an annexe, where food and snacks were to be served over the course of the day: breakfast, lunch and tea. Guruji was sitting on a large cushion on the floor in the middle, along with Karmalkar Kaka.

A few days earlier, Yogesh had sent the much-guarded schedule out to everyone. It had three sessions: post-breakfast, post-lunch and post-tea. Within each session, the order reflected increasing capability. The evening session was special because Guruji would conclude it. Along with this, Yogesh had tried, as far as possible, to preserve the time convention of raags. Juggling all these parameters along with managing people's egos and sensitivities must have been taxing. The seasoned organiser that he was, Yogesh pulled it off with aplomb.

I was looking forward to listening to everyone without the stress of having to perform myself. I huddled with other first-timers. We revelled in the music and the bonhomie, clapping vigorously for the performers. People kept trickling in through the morning. I tried to encourage a few youngsters who were singing for the first time.

'I am really nervous,' said a student in his early twenties. 'I am singing a nom-tom aalaap for the first time.'

'The very fact that you are attempting it is commendable,' I replied. 'Guruji knows how you sing. He hears you in class every week. So relax.'

I said this even while thinking that sustaining a rendition for even fifteen minutes with live accompaniment was altogether a different proposition from attempting a few rough-and-ready avartans in class. On this occasion, errors of raag, taal, sur and laya would stand out, while in class, they were acceptable, even expected. But since I was not sticking my neck out, I could blithely proffer facile advice to others. Such were the minor pleasures of this event. Among the major pleasures was being able to binge on a smorgasbord of raags.

By tea-time, the hall was jam-packed and crackling with anticipation for the final session. Mukul ended the student line-up by singing Pancham. I saw strands of Guruji's style running through most students' renditions. I heard the taut intertwining of melody and rhythm. I noticed that even junior students who presented standalone fast compositions improvised, by way of a short aalaap and a few rounds of sargams—the result of Guruji empowering students to take steps to improvise early on so that the process began to feel less intimidating.

·❦·

It was dark outside when Guruji's turn came. All of us moved forward, sitting packed around the stage. He sang Agre gharane ka Chandrakauns, serving up all the flavours characteristic of his music. When a singer pierces the bull's eye of the unusual rishabh microtone—which falls between the average komal and shuddh rishabhs—in the slow descending phrase 'ma_ ga_ re_ Sa___', it can give listeners goosebumps. Guruji began with the slow composition, *Begi aavana* (Come soon), composed by Mehboob Khan, the raag's creator, and followed it with the hauntingly beautiful *Teekhe nain* (Intense eyes), composed by Khadim Hussain Khan, who wrote under the pen name Sajan Piya. It goes as follows:

Teekhe naina tore bhauen ka̽maan	Intense eyes, bow-shaped brows,
Savari soorat mohani moorat.	Dark of face, enchanting of form.
ˣMora mukut tore seesa beerajat	A peacock crown on your head.
Murali bajaavat sajan aavat	My lover comes playing the flute,
Jhoomat jhoomat.	Swaying, swaying.

This composition melts the heart, melodically and lyrically. I was struck by how sensuously and sensitively a Muslim musician had depicted the Hindu god Krishna.

~

After the echoes of the last note had faded, I reluctantly headed home. The high from a day-long immersion in such honest and powerful music, in the company of other passionate listeners with cultivated tastes, lingered for a couple of days. The intimate setting with people who were receptive and knowledgeable had encouraged performers to create music that, though not always perfectly polished, was genuine, for they had no need to impress the uninitiated, only to give their best for the guru. The music sounded coherent because the leitmotif of the guru-musician's style ran through the renditions, delightfully refracted through each individual's voice as well as her or his ability, taste, personality and other traits that made the person unique. I already began looking forward to the next year's edition.

After the first class following the event, I walked with Kartik, a thirty-something software engineer who had begun learning a few months before me, to the railway station. 'Man, what is the level of this place!' Kartik, who had earlier learnt the Carnatic violin and Western classical piano, exclaimed. 'Incredible. One student after another, technically perfect—catching the sam, getting the raag grammar right, improvising. At different levels, they all have control over the form. All of them know what to do.'

In the following weeks, when I looked back on the Guru Purnima programme, I saw that it had provided a snapshot of Guruji's artistic vision and his contribution to preserving this music. The programme had showcased a large number of his students and the reassuring image of a ladder of progress that any learner could climb if he or she made the effort. It was also a note to myself.

⁂

About two months later, I entered a spare flat on a Sunday morning and heard a young woman singing Jaunpuri. The vitality of the music was almost tangible. This time, it was Babanarao's Guru Purnima event, in his flat in a high-rise building in Lokhandwala, a hip Mumbai suburb that is a magnet for people working in the television industry. A native of Mumbai, Babanrao, then in his late-eighties, had moved to Pune several years earlier. But he had taught so many students in Mumbai that he had one Guru Purnima event here too. For the rest of the morning, about thirty of us sat on the floor and soaked up the high-quality renditions.

For lunch, we headed out to one of Mumbai's longest shopping streets below to grab a bite. The switch from an understated savouring of pristine music in a spartan flat to the loud celebration of unbridled consumerism was quintessentially Mumbai. The afternoon session resumed and the intensity increased as the more mature students took their turns. Here, Guruji himself was a student, the senior-most, who concluded the line-up with Shahana Kanada. Then came Babanrao, whom I hadn't heard before. Slightly built and erudite-looking, he betrayed no signs of infirmity. At his age, he could not sustain notes for a long time, but his voice was clear and tuneful as he sang a deep Darbari and a powerful dhamar and tarana in Maru Bihag. Here was yet another musician woefully neglected by the mainstream when he was in his prime.

From then on, I knew what I had to do to hear some of the best Hindustani music: I had to go Guru Purnima-hopping. These functions were meant for the guru's student community and well-wishers, but genuine music lovers were usually welcome. By then, I was plugged into the grapevine. These events were an important institution in the fringe culture, resembling over the years a movie capturing the evolution of students in a gurukul. As I made my way home after Babanrao's performance, I looked forward to the next reel of the movie, or to be au courant, the next episode of the web series.

◆ Fire: 1986–95

IN THE YEAR 1987, THE USSR'S MIKHAIL GORBACHEV AND THE USA's Ronald Reagan signed a treaty that heralded the end of the Cold War. In the Middle East, Palestinian youth rose in protest against Israeli occupation in a movement called the intifada, or uprising. In India, the playback singer Kishore Kumar passed away, Sunil Gavaskar became the first batsman to cross the 10,000-run mark and the landmark Hindi film *Mr India* released to both commercial success and critical acclaim. It was the year India marked its fortieth anniversary of independence. These were some of the headlines that Arun may have cursorily read in the newspaper. But as the year came to an end, sitting in his designated place at home, with his back to the wall facing the front door, in his typical pose, the right leg with the knee up and the left one crossed under it, he recalled the headlines of his own life that year. All three involved his gurus.

Gajananbuwa had passed away in June, after being ill for several months. Arun knew where to turn in his time of grief—to a reluctant and complicated lover he had assiduously courted for years. After finally yielding to him, the lover had proved as reliable as the morning sun in assuaging his emotional pain. A few months after Gajananbuwa's death, when a group of listeners came over on Sunday morning for the usual mehfil, Arun released his paean to his guru. He had set the composition in Miyan ki Todi, because it evoked a reverential ambience with a hint of melancholy, and in Roopak taal, in a medium tempo that was neither sedate nor sprightly, because the composition was both an elegy and a tribute.

x	
Gunan gaaoon tumro gunan	Of your virtues I sing, virtues that
Guniyan ke guna saagar	Even for the virtuous are like the sea.
Guniyan ke guna saagar	The seven notes, raag and taal
Tu hi samaayo	You do embody.
x	
Tu Gajanan Anant	You, Gajanan and Anant
Guna tero hai apaar	Of virtues unending,
Aayo Rasadas sharan	Rasadas seeks your protection
Keeje kirpaa aaj	And today asks for your blessing.

The words 'Gajanan' and 'Anant' in the second verse's first line referred both to Ganesha and Vishnu, Hindu gods, and to Gajananbuwa and Anantbuwa, Arun's musical deities. 'Rasadas' was Arun's pen name. Both verses ended in an identical taan that was shaped like an upside-down tick mark, first rising from the middle of the central octave to the upper shadja and then tumbling down from there all the way to the base shadja. They gave the verses an energetic ending, an artistic device that Arun used in a few other compositions as well. The audience sat silently, absorbing the echoes after Arun had finished.

After a few weeks, Arun unveiled another composition at an event celebrating his father's sahasrachandra darshan, the appearance of one thousand full moons in the sky, a traditional milestone corresponding to nearly eighty-one years. At the festivities, Arun, as the eldest son, sang last, after Ulhas, Subhash and Vikas, ending his performance with an encomium to his first guru. It was in raag Ahir Bhairav set to Ektaal.

x	
Sab mil aavo aaj	Everyone, let's gather today
Rasadas gaavo bajaavo	Rasadas, sing and strum
Deho mubarakabad	Give your congratulations.

x	
Naad ko gun bakhaano	Praise the virtues of sound
Raag taal sung sajaavo	Beautify it with raag and taal.
Aaavo saath saptasuran	Come along you seven notes
Sa Ga ma Pa Dha ni re Sa	Sa Ga ma Pa Dha ni re Sa.

Arun had set the mukhuda, *Sab mil* ... in dugun, or double the base speed, sprinkling this laya throughout the composition to create variety. Every once in a while, Arun had allowed vowels to flow over several beats, adding a Gwalior flavour to an Agra base. Like the paean to Gajananbuwa, this composition included double meanings. In the second verse, the word naad, or sound, was also the Marathi acronym for Arun's father's initials—Na for Nagesh and D for Dattatreya. The seven notes in the last line stood for the saptak as well as him and his six siblings: the ni, a feminine suffix, represented his sister, and the remaining notes Arun and his five brothers. When Arun went to touch his father's feet, he touched his eldest son's head.

'Chaan,' his mother said. Lovely.

Usha-tai came out of the kitchen to find Arun sitting alone in the other room. Babanrao had stepped out to the joint family's living room.

'It went so well,' she told Arun. 'The food was excellent. The hall was overflowing. I saw so many youngsters. I was surprised that so many people had turned up to listen to khayal. You helped highlight Babanrao's music.'

Arun did not know what to say. Organising did not come naturally to him, but he had taken great pleasure in spearheading the celebration of his guru's sixtieth birthday at the Maharashtra Seva Sangh, a large venue in Mulund, the third big event in his life that year. About five hundred people had gathered, including many musicians, such as Bhai Gaitonde and D.K. Datar, as well as luminaries from other artistic fields, such as the celebrated poet Mangesh Padgaonkar, Babanrao's childhood friend, and Vidyadhar Gokhale.

Arun may have taken his guru's greatness for granted, but Usha-tai's gratitude suggested that Babanrao had not received the public recognition commensurate with his calibre. For a moment, Arun saw the situation from a wife's perspective. But in the very next moment, he drew ammunition from it for his next argument with Dhanashree. Even if he could muster the enthusiasm, how could he push himself ahead of his guru, whose musical depth had recently been on ample display? He was embarrassed by the thought. How would Usha-tai feel, Arun would ask Dhanashree, like a champion debater deploying the principle of pathos, appealing to human beings' emotions and sympathetic imagination to win the argument, as opposed to the two other strategies in the trinity of classical rhetorical devices, of logos, or reason, and ethos, or ethics, which he routinely deployed.

Could it have been that Arun, like many students in the guru-shishya tradition, was grappling with the age-old challenge of emerging from his guru's shadow? Throughout his training, Arun had maintained a degree of artistic autonomy, partly because when he arrived in Mumbai he was far from a blank slate. From childhood, he knew what he liked and what he did not care for in a singer's music, views that impressed and annoyed his father in equal measure. Although not an outright rebel, after leaving home at just fifteen, he became discerning about received wisdom. Arun had never imitated his gurus' application of voice, a tendency seen in some students and admirers of other influential musicians. Gajananbuwa's voice was powerful and Babanrao's was mobile. Arun's was both. He knew that he had to preserve and develop both attributes. As for music, Arun knew that he had been definitively moulded by Gajananbuwa, but with his passing away an era had definitely ended, while Babanrao, by the time he turned sixty, had begun treating Arun, fifteen years younger, more like a colleague. Self-effacing to a fault, Babanrao never held back from praising his student. He had long admired Arun's voice and virtuosity. Recently, he had begun commending Arun's renditions and compositions.

'For Khem Kalyan and Pancham, listen to Arun,' he told people.

On hearing Arun sing his composition in Patamanjari, a raag he had wrestled with for years, Babanrao said, 'I never imagined that anyone could create such a fine composition in this raag.'

Like many Agra gharana maestros, Babanrao himself was an excellent composer, who used the pen name Rasapiya—a lover of flavour. Arun had played on this name while choosing his own signature, Rasadas—an acolyte of flavour. But in his mid-forties, if Arun did not wish to actively promote himself, it was not because he was languishing in his gurus' shadows. He did not do it because it did not come naturally to him. It was out of character.

As he struck the shadja, Arun felt his anger rising. His first instinct was to breathe deeply in a bid to control his feelings. After a few seconds, he hit upon another idea. Rather than trying to stanch his emotions, he would try to channel them into his rendition. A performer's emotional state inevitably influenced the delivery. The question was whether a khayal singer, given the form's many technical demands, could consciously harness his or her feelings to colour the performance. Naturally, when Arun was relaxed and happy, he could sing more freely than usual. What about the effect of negative emotions such as anger, fear and grief? When Arun was sad, his body, including his voice, became limp. As for fear, he had not felt performing anxiety even as a child, and now only occasionally did he feel a mild initial nervousness when he knew one of his gurus was in the audience. But he imagined that fear, too, would have stymied his voice and impeded the flow of his ideas. Anger appeared to be a different beast.

That day, he was singing at the first anniversary concert in memory of Gajananbuwa. Arun decided to sing *Garib nawaz* in Shree because he was performing in his old student milieu after a long time and wanted to present music that reflected his stylistic evolution following his stint with Babanrao. By then, Arun had come to terms with Gajananbuwa's passing away. What he still had to overcome was his indignation over comments that had recently wound their way to him from someone in Gajananbuwa's circle. Their gist was that he had harmed his music by training in the Agra style. Arun was furious because everyone in that student community knew that Gajanabuwa was the one who had sent him to learn from Babanrao.

'I will show them the Agra gharana's power,' Arun thought, glowering at the audience.

The response to his psychological experiment came from listeners.

'That was amazing,' Madhu told Arun as he got off the stage. Then, turning to the audience, Madhu jokingly added, 'No one should sing after this.'

※

Arun straightened his spine. He was sitting in his usual spot in the hall while Ashish practised in the bedroom. For a moment, Arun forgot that his son was the one playing the tabla.

'He's becoming fluent,' Arun thought to himself.

Ashish had finished high school and had begun studying engineering at a good college in the city. He had been learning tabla from Sudhir Sansare for about five years. Arun, unlike his father, was too easy-going and engrossed in his own art to corral his sons for music lessons. But he encouraged whatever interests they organically developed while growing up in a house filled with music and teeming with musicians. Ashish had begun learning to play the tabla at the age of six. When he entered his teens, he became fascinated with the sitar after hearing Ravi Shankar playing at an event in Moscow that was broadcast on television. After a few weeks, Ashish had come home from school to find a sitar at home. Arun had requested Babasaheb, a string instrument maker from Miraj who was a frequent visitor to the Kashalkar home, to have the sitar made for his son. Miraj, in South Maharashtra, was a hub for string instrument makers. Arun had then also arranged for Ashish to take lessons from a sitar player who was his friend.

'He did not even wait to see whether my interest sustained or not before buying me an instrument,' Ashish told his friends. 'But after I began learning, he let go. He made it clear in many ways that he was very pleased that I was interested in music, but he did not load me with any expectations.'

While in high school, Ashish also learnt bharatanatyam for a couple of years from a lady who was his father's student.

'I want to teach, but I have no place where I can hold classes,' the lady once lamented to Arun.

'Why don't you start teaching in my home?' Arun asked her in the following class.

This the lady promptly did, joining the colourful cast of characters that enlivened the Kashalkar home. Ashish attended the lessons that she gave twice a week in the bedroom that he shared with his younger brother, until she moved out of Mulund two years later.

When it came to his sons' academics, Arun adopted a stance of benign neglect. He had a rough idea that his sons were doing well in school and left it to Dhanashree to get into the weeds. When Ashish was about twelve, the principal summoned Arun to school.

'Your son was reading a comic book in class,' the principal said cuttingly.

'You have called me all the way just for this?' Arun replied, incredulous. 'You should not involve parents in such trivial matters. You should deal with this yourself.'

Around that time, Ashish had in fact begun taking his schoolwork seriously and was topping his class. Adwait was also a bright student, but more fun-loving and outgoing than his serious elder brother. The two boys managed to study amidst the perpetual musical ferment in the Kashalkar household. The concept of privacy, especially for children, was yet to penetrate middle-class Indian homes, but the Kashalkars' flat was a virtual open house. Arun gave all the credit to Dhanashree for his sons' academic progress.

'Are you sure you have studied enough?' she asked them before each exam. When their results came, she almost always said, 'Try to do better the next time.'

Arun rarely praised his sons to their faces. But that day, when Ashish came out of the bedroom after practising, he said, 'That was all right!'

In his late forties, Arun entered a fecund phase of composing. He went from idea to final version more quickly than before, the melody, rhythm and lyrics often emerging simultaneously, like they had with the composition in Bairagi that had come to him before dawn. He drew inspiration from a wide variety of sources and gave every composition a few special features. For one composition, he got the idea for the song-text from something as pedestrian as the hoarding of an advertisement for investing in a bank fixed deposit. The advertisement told people that their money lost value every moment that they kept it idle. He turned the idea into a composition in Tilak Kamod set to Teentaal. Its first line went as follows:

Pal pal beetata saga̍ro din	Moment by moment
	does the whole day pass.

In this composition, he used the komal nishad once, in the second verse, although the note is not part of the raag. He applied a similar twist to a composition in Tilang, *Na roko mori baat* (Don't block my way), in which he included the shuddh rishabh, not part of the raag, in a few phrases in the upper octave. 'One can judiciously break the rules, but only after thoroughly understanding the raag's territory and that of neighbouring ones,' Arun explained to knowledgeable listeners who sometimes asked him about these transgressions. He often cited the example of Antubuwa's attractive composition *Chalo ri mayee* (Let's go, friend) in raag Shree, whose very first line contains such a kink: it substitutes dha for Pa in the raag's core phrase re Ma **Pa** Ni Sa, yielding re Ma **dha** Ni Sa.

'These unusual notes are like beauty spots,' Arun liked to say.

Arun often told listeners that, inspired by his love for poetry, he had given the character represented by Rasadas, his pen name, a variety of roles. In the Tilak Kamod composition, Rasadas appears as a student being addressed by a wise elder; in the Tilang composition, as the female protagonist's confidant; in the paean to Gajananbuwa, as a worshipper; and in the one dedicated to his father, as a close associate of the person singing the song.

Overhearing Arun talk to visitors about features of his compositions, Dhanashree sometimes felt her irritation rising. Why was her husband wasting time composing? What were the returns on this investment? Mostly, she muttered to herself. But one time she blurted out what was on her mind.

'Why are you spending time on this?' she asked Arun.

'Because it's a creative urge,' he replied calmly, confounding his wife.

⁓

Dhanashree was still coming to terms with the fact that Arun had once and for all firmly shut the door on taking bank exams, a prerequisite to rising in his organisation's hierarchy. After moving to Mulund, she had revived the idea that Arun should take them because they had begun living in a colony full of people working in the same organisation, many of whose new cars represented visible proof of their upward mobility, while Arun's salary only sluggishly inched up. In the end, to placate Dhanashree, Arun had for about a month taken a half-hearted stab at studying for an exam relevant to the foreign exchange department, where he worked. He found that he had zero motivation to memorise various components of the Reserve Bank of India's foreign exchange reserves and to come to grips with the distinction between a country's current and capital accounts. He became quicker to anger out of frustration that this undertaking was colonising the mental space and leisure that he wanted for music.

Ironically, as an employee in the foreign exchange section of the country's largest bank, Arun was working close to the epicentre of precisely the economic crisis in 1991 that had significantly contributed to pushing the Indian government into initiating a series of policies that gradually brought unprecedented prosperity to members of the middle and upper classes. That year, the central bank had found its foreign exchange reserves depleting rapidly so that at one point it could not pay for even a month's worth of imports. To tide over this emergency, the government had taken a loan from the International Monetary Fund. Soon afterwards, the government began opening various sectors to private products, services and investment, both Indian and foreign. These changes dramatically increased the incomes of the middle class and, consequently, their purchasing power. The new economic policies also expanded the variety of consumer goods that became available for them to buy.

Yet Arun, under the sway of a demanding mistress, barely registered the momentousness of these developments, except when Dhanashree periodically brought them to his notice. She was following the economic action around her and had a better sense of how the neighbourhood's Joshis and Jayaramans were advancing. But Arun promptly relegated her observations to the periphery of his consciousness because he had scant interest in pondering over the phenomenon of the new consumerist class, much less in riding its wave.

~

For several months, Arun had been turning over an idea in his head that would, at least initially, detach him even more from the consumerist boom. One evening, he broached the subject with Dhanashree crabwise. Their conversation went something like this:

'Our boys are doing well and will soon be independent,' he told her.

'Yes,' she replied.

'We have paid off the loan for this flat.'

'I know,' Dhanashree replied, confused.

Arun remained silent. How would she react?

'I have several students,' he said.

This was true. By then, he was teaching dozens of people.

'So?' Dhanashree asked.

'I am fifty now,' he said.

Where was he going with this?

'What do you want to say?'

'I have enough years of service in the bank,' he said.

She waited.

'I am eligible to take voluntary retirement,' he finally said with trepidation. 'If I retire early, I can focus on music. I can teach even more students.'

Three years earlier, in 1990, Dhanashree had quit her job altogether. She had just begun a small clothes business, but Arun's salary was the only steady income. Yet for some time, she had sensed his restlessness and was not surprised by his suggestion.

'If you want to quit, you should get a PhD in music,' she replied. 'It might open up other opportunities.'

She knew Arun would continue to charge paltry sums as fees from his students. Their sons were not yet working. Arun was touched by her immediate support for what was a radical move for a middle-class family with meagre savings.

※

Arun stood in front of the mirror examining his forehead. Just below his hairline, his brown skin had light-pink flecks from one end to another, not visible from afar but noticeable at talking distance. Similar small patches had begun appearing on some of his fingers. The first doctor whom he had visited had told him that it was leucoderma. Arun later learnt that this was merely a fancy word for a loss of pigmentation, not a description of its cause. Physically, he felt no discomfort but was disturbed by the visual effect. As Dhanashree well knew, he did not pay attention to how he dressed. But the onset of an aberration like this would make most people anxious. Did conventionally good-looking people especially feel the loss of the subtle social capital that they have become habituated to accumulating on account of their pulchritude, whether while buying groceries, talking to the boss or singing on stage?

'This is worrying,' he told Dhanashree. 'I wonder how much it will spread.'

'The doctor said it is not contagious,' she replied. 'We'll consult more doctors.'

Stoic and practical, she took this adversity, too, in her stride.

※

Arun walked out of Ruby Mansion feeling pumped up after meeting Vilayat Hussain Khan's son, Yaqub. Arun had decided to do his PhD research on the aesthetics of the Agra maestro's compositions and improvisations. Yaqub had offered to sing a few of them. Arun had been particularly charmed by his rendition of *Tero dhyaan dharat* (I think of you) in raag Dhanashree. Always on the lookout for attractive elements in other people's music, Arun zoomed in on the way Yaqub had concluded a key phrase, Ga-ma-Re-Sa, with a khatka on Re, giving it a kick from below. Ga-ma-Re-Sa appeared in other raags too, each with a specific accent. In Dhanashree, the ma usually included a hint of Ga at the end, but the Re remained plain. From Yaqub, Arun had got a variation in which the ma remained plain and the Re got dressed up.

The PhD gave Arun the opportunity to make a long-pending pilgrimage to the Agra gharana's headquarters in South Mumbai. Arun had embarked on his dissertation after quitting his job a few months earlier. For all these years, Vilayat Hussain Khan had been like a phantom guru to Arun. Several years earlier, Arun had been travelling by train in a nearly empty compartment when he heard Vilayat Hussain Khan's Hem Kalyan emanating from his portable radio. He was immediately hooked by the aalaap. When the vocalist began singing Sadarang's composition *Daiya ri* (Oh my), Arun softly joined in, soon realising that he was echoing the Agra doyen's rendition down to the minutest inflection. Even students of the same guru often subtly alter the default tunes of compositions, influenced by the capabilities of their voices, their implicit aesthetics and crucially, tempo they choose. In that recording, Vilayat Hussain Khan was evidently singing in a tempo very close to the one that Gajananbuwa had used to teach Arun, which explained the surreal synchronisation. 'For a few seconds, I thought that I had learnt in person from the ustad,' Arun later told his students. 'It was a fantastic feeling. I again saw how powerful our seena-ba-seena taleem is in taking tradition forward.'

Almost certainly, Arun would have eventually got around to delving deeper into Vilayat Hussain Khan's music, but the PhD precipitated the process. Arun already knew many of his compositions, having learnt them from Gajananbuwa and later, Babanrao. Arun noticed that Vilayat Hussain mainly combined the base tempo with dugun, or a double speed, only rarely incorporating tigun and chargun, triple and quadruple speeds. He loved the way Vilayat Hussain improvised in units of four beats and multiples of them. Arun saw that this disciplined creativity through the avartan paved the way for an arrival on the sam that was as smooth as silk.

'His singing reflected a pure love for raag, taal, sur, laya and bol, expressed at the highest level, totally precise and well-proportioned,' Arun wrote in his notes. 'His compositions had the same elegant restraint. He surrendered so fully to the fundamental elements of khayal that he had no room for extraneous drama. He called minimal attention to himself, the singer, thus exemplifying the maxim that a khayaliya should be just an instrument for his art. His music exuded both sahaj bhav [a feeling of ease], and bhakti bhav [surrender to a higher force].'

For all these reasons, Vilayat Hussain Khan commanded huge respect among musicians. Arun had heard about recitals at which the Agra vocalist had held musicians spellbound, eliciting exclamations from them after every avartan. In music lore, these gatherings came to be known as Vilayat Hussian Khan's 'wah-wah mehfils'. During his study, Arun fell madly in love with *Baalam ho* (O my beloved), in Paraj Kalingada. The Agra maestro had created both the raag and the composition. Arun knew that intertwining Paraj and Kalingada while keeping their identities distinct required a high level of skill because the two raags were closely related. The phrase Ga-ma-Ga appears in both and acts as the link. The raags, however, have one big point of divergence: Paraj is one of those minority raags whose resting place is the taar shadja, while Kalingada's is the shadja. This lends the compound raag a compelling up-down tension, like this:

Ma dha Sa____ re Ni Sa____ Dha Sa Ni____ Pa dha Pa____
  Ga ma Ga____ (Paraj),
ma Ga Re Sa ___ Ga ma Pa dha Pa _ Ga ma Ga re Ga _ (Kalingada),
Ma dha Sa____ (Paraj).

Arun liked to compare the effect of this raag to a woman wearing bangles of two closely related colours on her wrist, like blue and green or red and pink. When one sees the bangles from up close the individual pigments stand out, but from afar they appear like a single in-between shade.

Arun's study of Vilayat Hussain Khan's music organically led him to analysing other Agra gharana musicians, beginning with the scintillating Faiyaz Khan. Rhythmic control was only one of his virtues. If Vilayat Hussain Khan's music was understated, Faiyaz Khan's was exuberant, even though both rested on the same fundamental principles. 'Faiyaz Khan exuded a playfulness and aesthetic effervescence,' Arun told his students. 'He had a feeling for what appealed to listeners yet never indulged in gimmicks and was thus able to raise the audience's tastes. He was free-minded but rooted in his vidya.'

Arun drew from Faiyaz Khan's romantic touch in bol work. He saw how the Agra singer relegated rhythm to the back burner every now and then to focus on expressing the words, now tenderly, now passionately, like a thumri singer. For these traits, Arun particularly admired Faiyaz Khan's renditions of *Phulawan ki gend* (Balls of flowers) in Jaunpuri, *Tarapata hoon* (I am agitated) in Lalit, *Un sanga laagi akhiyan* (I locked eyes with him) in Ramkali, and the thumri *Bajuband khul khul jaye* (My armlet is loosening) in Bhairavi. Arun studied Faiyaz Khan's pukar and explored its expressive potential. 'The intonation of your pukar when you address God should be distinctly different from when you call your beloved,' Arun told his students. 'You can harness lyrics to enhance your bol improvisation, but you should not make your voice overly dramatic or emotional because this will detract from khayal's aesthetic. Khayal's main aim is not to interpret lyrical meaning but to explore the raag.'

Arun went deeper into bol work. He had to mesh words with music in a way that was aesthetic. He paid attention to sounds in the language, working on softening the enunciation of stop consonants such as k, kh, g, gh, p, ph, b, bh to make his bol work sound smooth. He became hyper-discerning about compositions. He wanted to use those that not only allowed the raag's essence to bloom and had punchy mukhdas, but were suitable for bol. 'The language in some compositions might be impressive,' Arun told his students.

'But compositions are not meant to be recited. They must serve the needs of music.'

For his PhD degree, besides doing a thesis, Arun had to be prepared to present a hundred raags, including several rare and complex ones. In several, such as Hindol Bahar and Basant Mukhari, he could not find compositions that he felt exhibited the qualities that he was looking for, so he created ones himself.

He analysed the music of other Agra maestros. He had naturally inherited aspects of Khadim Hussain's style via Babanrao. But he particularly admired the dhrupad touches in Khadim Hussain's nom-tom aalaap, his deep gamaks, and his renditions of dhamar compositions. Arun listened closely to Sharafat Hussain Khan, who had trained under three masters, Faiyaz Khan, Ata Hussain Khan and Vilayat Hussain Khan, and had inherited several inflections from his ancestors belonging to the Atrauli and Rangile styles, which were eventually subsumed under the label of the Agra gharana. Arun admired how Sharafat Hussain's sur never faltered even while singing the gharana's characteristic triple-note taan patterns at a blistering speed.

Arun developed an even greater awe for the Agra style's depth and breadth—the nom-tom aalaap derived from dhrupad, the huge potential of bol work, including a version of the soft bol banaav used in thumri, and the creative use of rhythm. He understood why many of its practitioners considered it the sampoorna gayaki, the complete style.

―

Ajay Risbud, a high-school student, sat in the audience listening to Arun singing, his voice bordering on ferocious.

'Guruji has begun in fourth gear,' he whispered to his friend.

It was a private concert at the home of Arun's friend Ashok Sahasrabuddhe. About fifty people had crowded into the living room, including about a dozen of Arun's students. It was raining outside, but the room was also drenched—in Arun's Miyan Malhar.

After a brief interval, he sang a Khem Kalyan that Ajay's friend said he would never forget.

Ajay thought Arun could not surpass his renditions at the Sahasrabuddhe home, but soon afterwards, on the occasion of Kojagiri Purnima, Arun sang Malkauns at his own home with even greater intensity, presenting two of his creations, a slow one, *Karim rahim* (Generous and merciful), one of only a handful of his slow compositions, and his fast composition *Maang bharo* (Put vermillion in my hair parting), accompanied by Sansare.

Having quit his job, Arun felt deliriously free, like a tiger let out of the nine-to-five cage. He released his pent-up energy into every mehfil. By then, he had a style that stood out as distinct. Students were flocking to him. Ajay showed considerable promise, and an older student, Smita Wagh, was already giving him excellent vocal support. A variety of tabla and harmonium players came to accompany Arun and his students in class. He performed regularly at home, at baithaks and occasionally outside Mumbai, with accompanists of a high calibre, such as tabla players Bhai Gaitonde, Omkar Gulvady, Sudhir Sansare, Vibhav Nageshkar and Yogesh Samsi, and harmonium players Govindrao Patwardhan, Tulsidas Borkar and Vishwanath Pendharkar.

Many people from Arun's circle thought that at this stage he ought to be blazing concert venues around the country. But he was less sanguine about his prospects. He sensed how the Hindustani music ecosystem, along with the rest of the economy, was transforming in ways that were alien to him. He had glimpsed this change while running a music organisation for a few years with the help of his students, using seed money that Babanrao had donated. Arun had done it for several years, inviting Bhimsen Joshi, Kishori Amonkar and others who were already well known. But he saw how difficult it was to raise money from sponsors for other excellent musicians who were not celebrities, and was in the process of winding down the organisation's activities.

◆ City

THE RAAG FORM CAN BE COMPARED TO A CITY'S STREET network.[1] Its important phrases are like its arterial roads, raag renditions are like journeys across the network, and compositions are like different entry points into a city.[2] The idea of a raag as a landscape diverges emphatically from the linear view found in many books and academic approaches, in which the raag is viewed as just an aaroh and avroh, the ascending and descending scales respectively. In many people's minds, this pair of scales virtually defines the raag. But they are more like the two halves of a city's ring road.[3] People who use just the ring road will move around only along a city's periphery, missing its dense network of streets. So too will those who travel only along the raag's aaroh and avroh miss its many possibilities.

Another idea found in academic approaches to music is that of the vadi-samvadi, which singles out two notes in every raag as being the most important and second-most important ones. Like the aaroh-avroh concept, it oversimplifies a complex situation. First, many pairs of notes in a raag are important, not just one. These are pairs that have swar samvaad, or are in consonance with one another. Second, unlike the vadi and samvadi notes, the consonance between notes in such pairs is not necessarily hierarchical. While improvising, one can give these pairs equal importance and move from one to another. In raag Yaman, for example, a singer might work for some time with the pair Ma-Ni and move on to Ga-Dha.

The converse of swar samvad is that one cannot pair any two notes in a raag. The rules for which notes can be paired and which cannot are implicit in the raag's chalan. As students mature, they can more explicitly employ swar samvad in their improvisations.

'The important notes in a raag at which singers halt or through which they frequently traverse are like a city's important localities that inhabitants pass through often, such as Churchgate or Dadar in Mumbai. Also, the number of such junctions and their importance vary depending upon the route, its length and one's stage in the journey.' —AK

12

◇ Carnival

AS THE MONSOON RECEDED, EXCITEMENT ABOUT ANOTHER annual ritual started building up, relieving the oppressive stillness of October. It was time to go to Aundh for the annual music festival. I had heard many students talk about their trips there. 'That year in Aundh …,' they reminisced, narrating anecdotes, describing the ambience and going into raptures about certain performances. Since arriving in Mumbai in the mid-1960s, Guruji had gone there almost every year.

Successive generations of Antubuwa's family had steered the festival with the help of their student communities and other well-wishers. Since 2012, when Guruji became secretary of the trust running the festival, each year he and a group of students had travelled to Aundh a few days before the event to help with the arrangements. In 2015, the festival's seventy-fifth anniversary, a particularly large contingent, of about thirty students, had gone. From the photos, I could tell that the visit had been very special. Guruji had sung Darbari, followed by Agre gharane ka Chandrakauns, whose recordings I later heard on YouTube. But Yogesh told me that one of Guruji's best Darbaris had emerged on the festival's sidelines, engineered by his wily students. 'We were all relaxing in the temple,' Yogesh recalled. 'Guruji was lying down, but was only half asleep. A bunch of us began singing Darbari, deliberately introducing errors in the phrasing. It worked. Guruji could not take it. He got up and joined us. Soon, he was the only one singing. What a Darbari that was!'

Yogesh had recorded it, but when he got back home, he could not get the audio file to open. For the rest of us who were not there, that rendition acquired a mythical status, one that was, because of its elusiveness, even higher than a much-praised Pancham that Guruji had sung at the main festival in 1990, of which there *was* a high-quality online recording. For many students, these impromptu sessions before the festival were as much of an attraction as the official line-up.

That year, I was slated to travel to Aundh in Yogesh's car, along with Guruji. It was a roughly seven-hour journey. I did not then know that a spot in a car carrying Guruji was, like the Guru Purnima time slots, a precious commodity, in this case, an actual bit of real estate. Only much later did Yogesh tell me that each year students had scrambled to travel in the vehicle ferrying Guruji. Kaku usually followed a few days later, just in time for the festival. Freed from the domestic straitjacket on these rides, Guruji apparently turned mildly boisterous, cracking even more jokes than usual, of which some, when the troupe was all male, bordered on the risqué. The double entendres were usually in Marathi, but, depending on the trigger, occasionally in English, the principle being that no opportunity for a repartee should be wasted. One year, after the long car ride from Mumbai to Aundh, the tabla player Praveen Karkare asked Guruji if he wanted a mild massage, to which he answered, 'What I really want is a wild massage.' Yogesh told me about a student who was initially given a spot in Guruji's car but eventually had to be shifted to another vehicle. 'He dropped out altogether, saying that half the fun had vanished,' Yogesh told me. 'Guruji can be great company.'

The enthusiasm for Aundh was, however, a niche phenomenon. Far from the din and dazzle of the metropolitan centres, the festival was unknown to the vast majority of listeners. In this respect, it was similar to the Sawai Gandharva festival in Kundgol village in Karnataka's Dharwad district, another region with a rich musical heritage. That festival, too, was an all-night affair in a rural setting, very different from the high-profile festival with the same name held in Pune.[1]

For many musicians, performing in Aundh held huge sentimental value. Before leaving for the festival, I spoke to several artists who had performed there. Rajshekhar Mansur, a Jaipur gharana vocalist and son of Mallikarjun Mansur, sang there for the first time in the early 1990s. He was to take the stage at 4 a.m., so he reconciled himself to singing for a handful of sleepy listeners. But when he walked on to the stage, he was surprised to see rows and rows of white-capped, dhoti-clad villagers sitting on the floor, wide awake. 'I sang Lacchasakh and Shivmat Bhairav,' Rajshekhar Anna told me from Bangalore, referring to two offbeat raags. 'But they were listening attentively at that unearthly hour. It was an audience that wanted genuine music, of the older kind, not a tamasha. If Indian music is going to live, it is probably going to do so in these little-known centres.'

Yogesh Samsi, a leading tabla player from Mumbai, had a similar experience. 'Artists go there to pay their respects and absorb an energy that has been generated over decades,' he said. 'There is no commercial angle. I have witnessed performances there by great artists that would never happen anywhere else. Listeners there are hardcore music lovers. Even though it is a rural area, they have been exposed to intense, traditional classical music. Many of them even know the Gwalior and Agra gharana khayals being sung. They are not like urban audiences, who keep clapping for everything. You get proper daad and appreciation from the heart.'[2]

Before I had put even one foot into the car to occupy what I did not yet know was a coveted seat, Aundh had become, in my mind, a mythical land where, at least for a few days, music flowed like milk and honey.

I set off early one morning with Guruji, Yogesh and Prasad Kulkarni, the founder of Sanskar Prakashan, which was dedicated to publishing books related to Hindustani music and had brought out Guruji's book of compositions. That year, Prasad and Yogesh were heading the festival's organising committee in place of Gajananbuwa's granddaughters, Apoorva and Pallavi, who had taken over the task from their father but were away in the US on a concert tour. The car ride proved to be tame, my presence preventing the banter among my three male co-travellers from turning raucous. Instead, I suggested that we listen to Gajananbuwa's recordings, Yogesh's early anecdote about having done this making this one of my minor ambitions. What could be a better prelude to the festival?

On the way, there were established pit stops. We halted at Mukul's home in Pune for mid-morning chai. For lunch, we stopped at a bhojanalaya, a homely restaurant where the profusion of spices in the dishes told me that we had crossed into southern Maharashtra. We got to Satara town at tea time, resting for a while at the home of the Katdares, who ran a thriving masala business. Katdare Kaka, a shy but sprightly man, had been supplying provisions to the festival for several years. We were to transport some of his stock, and he was to bring the rest, including private orders from organisers and volunteers. I put in an order for methkoot, lasoon chutney and goda masala, typical spice mixtures of Maharashtra.

At Aundh's entrance we were greeted by a huge billboard carrying the festival's schedule and photos of several artists. We got off outside the temple complex where the organising committee and volunteers set up base each year. Across the complex, beyond a narrow lane, stood the big concert hall, the Aundh Kala Mandir. Anyone seated on the dais in the hall had a straight line of vision to the idol in the temple's sanctum, housing the shrine of Antubuwa's spiritual guru, Shivanand Swami.

Over the next two days, Yogesh, Prasad and their team of volunteers got down to the serious business of organising, while I did some sightseeing. During the day, I visited the Yamai Devi temple on a hill, which afforded sweeping views of the countryside, and a museum nearby housing the impressive and eclectic art collection of the princely state's last ruler. I visited the former palace, in whose grand hall Antubuwa had performed. I walked through the town, which, like many others in India, was a higgledy-piggledy spread of buildings and poor roads. But it was not as densely built up and it abutted green fields, which freshened the air and soothed the eyes.

The fun began with Rambhau's mini-recital in the temple green room, with Antubuwa peering down from a portrait above. The following evening, in the same green room, a regular visitor from Pune had played the sitar. Finally, on the night before the festival, by which time many more people had arrived, Guruji sang Hem Kalyan in the temple. It was one of the first raags that he had presented at Aundh as a young student of Gajananbuwa's, in the presence of several stalwarts, many of whose black-and-white photos lined the temple walls. 'We are listening,' they seemed to be saying.

The morning after Rambhau's green room recital, I waylaid him to find out more about his life.[3] After breakfast, as volunteers briskly went about their tasks, the two of us sat down in the temple for a leisurely conversation. Rambhau was born in 1930, in Aundh, into the Gadshi caste. Although low in the caste hierarchy, the Gadshis were associated with music. Their menfolk traditionally played the shehnai for ritual occasions, from marriages to daily ceremonies in temples. Rambhau's father followed his community's occupation, playing the shehnai almost daily at the Yamai Devi temple's aarti. The tunes of the devotional songs that he played were based on classical raags. Rambhau's father also regularly played at the court of the local ruler, where he got to know and accompanied Antubuwa, thus getting exposed to high-quality khayal. But Rambhau's father was paid only a modest sum for his playing, barely enough to support his huge family of nine children. He also spent money on alcohol and did not send Rambhau to school.

Rambhau had to begin working even before the age of ten to contribute to the family income. He largely herded cattle for others, earning a daily wage, he said, of not more than one rupee. The only experience that he had of receiving anything resembling formal instruction was in music, and even that was indirect. Till he was twenty-one years old, Rambhau bathed every morning in a lake opposite Antubuwa's home. On the way there and back, he would hear Antubuwa teaching Gajananbuwa, and in later years, Gajananbuwa teaching his children. Rambhau often lingered outside their home. 'Every day, I would look forward to listening to Gajananbuwa's resonant voice,' Rambhau told me.

Rambhau was thirteen years old when Antubuwa started the festival. He roped in Rambhau's uncle to help with the organisation. The following year, Rambhau began getting involved, and that year, his son, Sunil was doing the heavy lifting. Rambhau had attended the festival almost every year, listening to some of the best classical musicians of their time, imbibing their sounds and artistic values. 'The festival is the high point of Rambhau's year,' said his grandson, who joined our conversation midway.

By his teens, Rambhau had taught himself to read and write and in his early twenties left Aundh to work as a peon in a government office in a nearby town. There, he joined bhajan groups. Then, in 1958, he moved to Kolhapur, a major cultural centre, for three years, which proved to be a turning point. He attended a bhajan group at the city's famous Mahalaxmi temple every weekday evening. In addition, he sang at a weekly bhajan group run by Shankarrao Sarnaik, who ran a drama troupe that employed great classical singers such as Alladiya Khan and Rajab Ali Khan. Rambhau developed a good rapport with Shankarrao and travelled with his troupe to other towns and villages to sing during religious festivals. Some of these sessions went on till 4 a.m., after which Rambhau had just enough time to return to Kolhapur, get ready and set off for work.

That Rambhau was welcomed without ado into the bhajan circle run by Sarnaik underlined the inclusive nature of this devotional music culture, rooted as it was in the regional bhakti movement, the Varkari sampradaya, or tradition. The movement was pioneered in Maharashtra in the late thirteenth century by the mystic Dnyaneshwar. He preached that the path to God was through bhakti, or devotion, and that it had no room for caste distinctions. His defining work, the eponymous *Dnyaneshwari*, a commentary on the Bhagavad Gita, became the foundational text of the state's bhakti ideology.

As with bhakti movements in other parts of the Indian subcontinent, adherents of the Varkari tradition too came mostly from the countryside and spanned the caste hierarchy, from upper-caste landlords to lower-caste farm labourers. Within the state, South-west Maharashtra, where both Aundh and Kolhapur are located, became a thriving hub of the Varkari movement as Dnyaneshwar's influence radiated out from his birthplace of Alandi nearby. 'My voice rapidly improved because I was singing so much more,' Rambhau recalled. 'I got to hear excellent bhajans and befriended other singers. I began understanding raagdari.'

Rambhau befriended a couple of Shankarrao's students and plied them with questions about the raags on which various bhajans were based. Slowly, he went from singing devotional songs based on raags to improvising in those raags—that crucial phase of metamorphosis when a singer becomes a musician, remarkable for someone who hardly had any training. 'He imbibed most of what he knows about classical music subconsciously, like a child learns its mother tongue,' Guruji later told me. 'Rambhau may not be a full-blown concert performer but he has definitely gained command over certain aspects of classical singing. He can render aalaaps and chhota khayals. He understands rhythm well. He was very devoted to Gajananbuwa and has mastered most of his compositions, even in uncommon raags such as Raisa Kanada.'

Yet Rambhau's experience highlighted the importance of sustained training under a good guru. Without that, he never had an outside chance of becoming a khayal performer. His life showed that caste and class were powerful barriers to accessing knowledge.

The day of the festival dawned with the ringing of temple bells.[4] The programme began after priests performed a pooja to the temple deity. The morning was sunny and pleasant; Aundh's elevation several hundred metres above sea level took the edge off western India's post-monsoon heat. Volunteers moved around purposefully, rustling in their silk sarees and kurtas. That year's line-up was characteristically dominated by vocal music, but included, as was the tradition, a couple of instrumental recitals, including a tabla solo recital, and a kathak performance. The post-sunset kathak and tabla performances attracted a full house, as they did every year. For me, one of the highlights was listening to Babanrao, then eighty-nine, for a second time. He sang a vigorous Shyam Kalyan, followed by a powerful Ram Gauri, an Agra gharana speciality. But that day at Aundh was, sadly, also the last time I heard him; he passed away a month later.

The hall of more than two hundred listeners responded with 'wah-wahs' and other appreciative interjections. More than half the listeners were from villages and small towns around Aundh and further away in south-western Maharashtra and northern Karnataka. Others in the audience included musicians, music students and aficionados from big towns and cities. Many were regulars, carrying memories of great performances they had heard. 'The ambience is wonderful,' said Dattatray Kadam, a farmer in his fifties who had attended the festival for the previous eight years. 'I listen to classical music on the radio and TV, but a live performance has a different feel. It's too bad that this happens only once a year.'

Like Rajshekhar Mansur, sitarist Anupama Bhagwat, in her early forties, who had come from Bangalore, was amazed to see a full hall past midnight during her recital. 'One has to give one's best here, to honour Antubuwa and Gajananbuwa, and for the large number of serious listeners,' she said.

At dawn the next day, it was Guruji's turn. About a dozen of us crowded into the temple green room as Guruji warmed up with Vishal, whose alter ego, Mukul, was missing that year because of a family commitment. As the festival's host, Guruji had been up all night, welcoming musicians. Instead of using the comfortable rooms at the government guest house nearby, he had chosen to sleep in the communal rooms and use the public bathrooms nearby. Despite his lean frame, Guruji had a sturdy constitution and could rough it out. But the demands of the festival seemed to have taken their toll. He looked wan and tired. On stage, he took a deep breath and started raag Bhairav. When he began the nom-tom aalaap, the sun began sprinkling its golden dust into the hall. As he sang, his fatigue seemed to evaporate. He was fully warmed up when he began the slow composition and was soon twirling the lyrics and indulging in high jinks with the taal. He concluded with Bhairavi, finding new pathways in a raag that he must have sung thousands of times, making Vishal repeatedly shake his head in wonder.

On the way back, I got another coveted spot—in Vishal's car, carrying Babanrao and Usha-tai. The three of them went up to Pune, where I got off and took the first bus to Mumbai that came along. It was a rattling state transport bus carrying many farmers, travelling with huge gunny sacks of rice and dal. I had no idea what they knew about classical music, but I felt a new bond with them, a sense of us being kindred souls.

◈ Susegado: 1996–97

A BREEZE BLEW ACROSS THE TEMPLE COURTYARD. THE SUN had set and a dim light illuminated a wooden stage. On one side of the stage sat a tabla and dagga, on the other a harmonium. In the middle, a tanpura lay horizontally on its back, looking forlorn. About a hundred people sat or stood around talking in the courtyard. Most were locals who lived within a forty-kilometre radius of the temple, but the crowd included several prominent people from Goa's cultural world who had come from all over the small state. Many people looked tired and impatient.

'Where has she disappeared?' a man asked his companion.

'Is she going to return at all?' the companion replied.

'Should we leave?' asked a third man.

Momentarily, a short, stout elderly man walked up to the stage, raised his hand and requested the audience to quieten down.

'While we wait for her to return, I have requested Pandit Arun Kashalkar to sing for us,' said the man, the writer Madhav Pandit.

People looked quizzically at one another, but those who had been standing found spots on the floor and the chatter slowly subsided. All eyes fell on the tall, well-built man with salt-and-pepper hair who had climbed on to the stage. His beard covered much of his face, leaving visible his eyes and brown forehead with some pink specks. He was wearing a long-sleeved kurta over pants. The tabla and harmonium players took their places. Most people sat expressionless.

Arun knew that the crowd was listless. He struck the shadja, his voice booming as it ricocheted off the temple pillars. The murmurs subsided. Arun began a nom-tom aalaap in Sar Nat, sending its syllables undulating across the open space. By the time he began the fastest nom-tom segment, many listeners were keeping the beat. Taut and pulsating, this singing was different from the flowing and lissom music that they had heard earlier in the evening. After the nom-tom, Arun began a slow composition, *Saajan ghar aa* (My love, come home), as the tabla player joined in with a leisurely Teentaal. Arun gradually moved from a slow to medium tempo to create a tapestry of Sar Nat using the threads of the composition's lyrics. The audience listened almost motionless, as if held in place by the music's magnetic pull. Finally, Arun moved to Khadim Hussain's gem of a fast composition, *Manoji tum mano* (Say yes, oh do), doing delicate bol work and concluding with virtuosic taans. As listeners applauded, Arun walked off the stage and made his way to the rows of chairs for special guests, set to one side of the courtyard. There, he was startled to see Kishori Amonkar. She had sung before Arun and called an interval, but had not returned for nearly an hour. That's when Madhav Pandit had requested Arun to placate the restive audience. When had she returned?

Then in her mid-sixties, Kishori-tai was in her second, experimental phase and at the height of her popularity. Having established herself as a superb exponent of a pristine Jaipur style, she had begun probing the boundaries of raag grammar. The temple was one of many in Goa dedicated to Ravalnath, a ferocious form of lord Shiva whom locals believed protected his devotees from natural disasters. The temple was located in South Goa's Valkini-Bhati village, adjacent to Kurdi, from which Amonkar's mother, Mogubai, took her last name, Kurdikar.

The programme had begun at about 5 p.m. Several Goan musicians had performed before Kishori-tai. The doyenne had then opened with raag Savani, singing the composition *He Mahadev* (*Oh Mahadev*), set to Jhaptaal. She had rendered this Jaipur raag in the traditional manner, creating an intoxicating effect with her aakaar and curved offbeat two-note patterns. She had followed this with raag Tilak Kamod, singing the composition *Sur sangata* (Consonance of notes), set to Rupak. After this, she had excused herself, saying that she needed a brief interval.

'She came back just as you began singing,' Vikas, Arun's friend from Mumbai, whispered to him. 'She was listening intently.'

After Arun finished, Kishori-tai went back on stage and tuned her tanpura for her second act.

'Arun sang so well,' she said. 'What raag can I possibly sing now? I will present some light music.'

As night fell, she began a bhajan, *Ghat ghat me panchi bolta* (A bird sings in every cloud), and ended with an abhang that she had composed in raag Bhairavi, *Bolava Vithhal* (Call out to Vitthal). When listeners finally began making their way home, it was nearly midnight.

The next morning, Arun had just about sat down at his desk in his office at the state-run Kala Academy in Panaji when a peon walked in and handed him a copy of *Gomantak*, a local Marathi newspaper. The man pointed to an article on an inside page. It carried the headline 'Kishori Amonkar's and Arun Kashalkar's singing delights Valkini-Bhati'. 'Listeners were spellbound by Amonkar's and Kashalkar's music ... Dr Kashalkar's music thrilled the audience, which responded with thunderous applause,' the article said.[5]

What an irony. Arun was not even supposed to have been part of the line-up. He had gone there in his capacity as the director of the Kala Academy's music and dance department, a post that he had recently taken up, in mid-1997. The Academy often lent its instruments to various events, and the head of the music and dance department had to escort them.

After getting his PhD degree, Arun had applied for the job, which Babanrao had earlier held for six years. Dhanashree would join him once he had settled down. Their sons were independent: Ashish had a job and Adwait was finishing his degree in catering and hotel management in Bangalore. Arun had arranged for Suresh Degwekar, a student of Ram Marathe who lived in central Mumbai, to travel a couple of times a week to Mulund to teach his students. Arun liked the Kala Academy's imaginative building complex, designed by the eminent architect and urban planner Charles Correa, and the campus's setting by the sea. As soon as he arrived at the Academy, Arun reported to the relevant official to pick up the keys to his flat.

'Your flat will be ready in about two weeks,' the official told him. 'You can stay in the guest house until then.'

Arun fought off the urge to point out that he had informed the Academy well in advance exactly when he would be arriving.

'He is not even bothering to apologise,' Arun thought.

At the guest house, the floor of his room was caked in dust; it had obviously not been swept in weeks. The walls were peeling. The uncovered mattress on the single cot was stained. But the official continued to act as if all this was normal.

'Someone will bring you pillows and sheets,' he said to Arun, handing him the key and leaving.

At night, to Arun's utter disbelief, he heard a couple of mice scurrying about. After a few hours of restless sleep, Arun woke up early in the morning only to find out that the Academy's small canteen had not yet opened. It functioned only during office hours, and even then, served only beverages and rudimentary snacks. For the next few days, Arun fended for himself for all his meals. He then called Prachla Amonkar—no relation of Kishori-tai's—a singer in Panaji then in her early thirties. She had trained under Alka Deo Marulkar, a fine multi-gharana singer, and Babanrao. Prachla immediately invited Arun to stay with her and her husband in their three-bedroom flat until he got his own accommodation.

Two weeks came and went, but Arun did not hear from the Academy. The favourable newspaper review of his performance at the temple had obviously made no dent on those in charge, if they had noticed it at all. Arun knew that the chief minister, Pratapsingh Rane, as the Academy's ex-officio chairman, had the authority to allot him a flat overnight. Did he even know what was happening at the Academy? In the same guest house where Arun had got a grubby room, bureaucrats received politicians and other bigwigs in a spotless well-furnished chamber. Not Arun, but the bureaucrat to whom he reported, got the perk of a vehicle and driver.

A few weeks after taking charge, Arun requested an employee in his office to make several photocopies of his doctoral thesis to distribute to students.

'Why do you need this?' the employee asked.

'To hand them out to students.'

'Why so many?'

'There are many students in the department.'

The employee grudgingly took the thesis. Arun would have done the job himself but the protocol was to give such tasks to a designated photocopier. In the end, Arun found little enthusiasm among his students. Arun felt that he might be able to attract more motivated students if could teach in the evenings and on weekends. He knew from his experience in Mumbai that many people who were interested in music had to go to college or office during the day.

'I am willing to stay back and put in more hours,' he told the relevant official.

The Academy declined his request, saying that it would then have to ask another employee to stay back to lock the premises after him. Apparently, the head of the music and dance department could not be entrusted with this task, just like he could not be trusted to photocopy his own thesis. Arun was probably taking his job a little too seriously for the Academy. He had noticed that of the roughly ten teachers in his department, those who had come from outside Goa tended to be more sincere about their work. In this small state, most local musicians had links to politicians and bureaucrats, giving some of them a vicarious sense of power.

'There's a Goan sitar player in my department who behaves as though he is not accountable to anyone just because he teaches the chief minister's wife,' Arun told Dhanashree over the phone.

One day, Arun's friend in Mumbai called him to find out how he was doing.

'I won't take up too much of your time,' the friend said after they had chatted for a few minutes, 'because you must be very busy making preparations for the festival.'

He was referring to a forthcoming performing arts festival in Goa.

'I have nothing to do with it,' Arun replied.

'Really?' the friend asked. 'But the Kala Academy is organising it.'

It was one of several music festivals that the Academy was responsible for organising each year, but the head of the music and dance department was not on the programme committee. Arun learnt that the bureaucrats had always taken the decisions, employing an event manager to run the festivals on the ground. None of the officials whom Arun asked about this practice thought it was odd to leave the in-house expert out of the loop.

Arun was not the only department head who felt sidelined. Prasad Vanarse, a dynamic director and actor in his late twenties, headed the Academy's repertory group and was responsible for directing and producing plays. The previous year, Vanarse had staged a successful play that had toured the state and had been heartily appreciated by audiences. For his next project, he had submitted a proposal to dramatise the work of a beloved Goan poet, Balkrishna Borkar, known as Bakibaab, who wrote both in Konkani and Marathi.

'The authorities rejected my proposal without giving me an explanation,' Vanarse told Arun.

'That sounds familiar,' Arun replied.

'I am not renewing my contract for the next year,' Vanarse said.

Vanarse was soon to get married and did not yet have another job lined up.

'I know that this job comes with a regular salary and accommodation,' he told Arun. 'But I have reached the end of my tether.'

About two months after joining the Academy, when Arun finally got a flat, he almost felt sorry. He had settled nicely in Prachla's home, where he had a room to himself. Prachla, too, felt bad when he moved out. During the week, à la Gajananbuwa, he woke her up at five in the morning to sing until he left for work. She particularly enjoyed his lessons on Agra specialities such as Barwa, Jhinjhoti, Khem Kalyan and Sar Nat.

'He is lost in his music,' she thought. 'Musicians like him are true seekers.'

She liked his jolly personality too. He chatted with her and her husband late into the night. On weekends, they hired a car and visited the Kadamba Mahadev Temple, Bondla Wildlife Sanctuary, Molem

Wildlife Sanctuary and other places. When Prachla's three-year-old daughter got tired of walking, Arun hoisted her on his shoulders.

Once in his own flat, Arun wanted to get into a regular schedule of singing.

'I'll do what I can within the restrictions at the Academy,' he thought. 'Since they don't want me to teach after office hours, I'll have a lot of time to sing, compose and think.'

He told the administrative office that he would like to borrow one of his department's dozen or so tanpuras to practise in his flat for the duration of his tenure.

'It's against the rules,' an official told him.

'Why?' Arun asked, incredulous. 'I am the one who has to permit others to take instruments out of the department for events outside campus.'

'But you can't take a tanpura out,' the official insisted.

'So I cannot permit myself?' Arun asked.

'No,' the official said, missing the sarcasm.

'Most of the tanpuras are lying unused,' Arun said.

'It's against the rules,' the official repeated.

'I will pay a deposit,' Arun said.

'There is no provision for this.'

Arun knew that the department paid someone every year to refurbish the tanpuras. The instruments would have been in better shape had someone regularly used them. But Arun gave up. The Academy had ample resources, but Arun realised that it saw the promotion of arts as a burdensome diversion.

'Goa is beautiful, the campus is lovely,' he told Dhanashree over the phone. 'But the Academy is a like a government office that has forgotten why it exists.'

※

One evening, Arun sat down in his flat to sing Savani, playing a tanpura that he had brought back from Mumbai even though it had been cumbersome. He was returning to Savani after a while, spurred by Kishori-tai's rendition at the temple. The Jaipur idiom was now entrenched in his style. Over the years, Arun had imbibed ideas from many of its stalwarts, such as Lakshmibai Jadhav, Anandbuwa Limaye, Kesarbai Kerkar, Mallikarjun Mansur, Mogubai Kurdikar, Nivruttibuwa Sarnaik and Padmavati Shaligram. He particularly liked Mogubai's tender aakaar and her bol improvisation's tisra patterns, in which she sang three notes over four beats. For off-beat patterns, he admired Kesarbai, but above all Nivruttibuwa, whose music he had been analysing for years.

In Mumbai, Arun had enjoyed some enlightening sessions with Nivruttibuwa's student, Vinayak Ganpule, who had often dropped in to his classes in Mulund. Arun had got him to sing rare Jaipur raags such as Dagori and Malav. A couple of years earlier, at an acquaintance's home, Arun had heard a cassette with a recording of Nivruttibuwa's lesson on Savani. Arun had paid close attention and extracted deeper principles from the patterns, which he used as a template for other raags. He used Nivruttibuwa-style off-beat patterns in some of his compositions, such as *Malaniyan* (Garlands) in Kedar and *Banara mora re* (My groom) in Raisa Kanada. Some listeners had begun asking Arun whether he had trained with Nivruttibuwa. In Goa, Arun had time to expand these Jaipur designs in several raags.

In contrast with the most common taan designs, which consist of blocks of even numbers of notes, Nivruttibuwa fluently created patterns with several odd-numbered clusters. Even-numbered patterns are easier than odd-numbered ones to embed in Teental, which has sixteen beats and whose four sections have four beats each. Odd-numbered patterns create a tantalising off-beat texture because odd clusters end either just before or after the taal's main divisions, creating an impression that the melody is playing hide-and-seek with the taal throughout the avartan. Arun knew that for singers to spontaneously and aesthetically spin these odd-numbered patterns out without sounding like they had learnt them by rote, they would have to invest in specialised practise. For many years, he had been trying out such combinations. That day, instead of a common even-numbered pattern in Savani such as Ga-Ga Ga-Re-Sa-Sa (six notes broken up into two-four), Re-Sa-Sa Dha-Pa-Pa (six notes broken up into three-three), Ga-Ma-Pa-Pa Ga-Re-Sa-Sa (eight notes, broken up into four-four)—adding up to twenty, Arun came up with patterns such as Ga-Ga Re-Sa-Sa (five notes broken up into two-three), Re-Sa Dha-Pa-Pa (five notes broken up into two-three), Ga-Ga Ma-Pa-Pa (five notes broken up into two three) and Ga-Re-Sa-Sa (four, the concluding pattern)—adding up to nineteen. For the next few hours, losing track of time, he went deeper and deeper into this dense Jaipur jungle.

About four months into his stay, Arun received a phone call from the state's minister of culture, Sanjay Bandekar.

'I'd like you to sing at an event in Canacona,' the minister said, referring to his constituency. 'I'll accompany you on the harmonium.'

Goa had a tradition of producing fine harmonium players.

'Kishori-tai has told me all about you,' Bandekar told Arun after the programme. 'Please join me for dinner. Let your staff know.'

Arun reluctantly told those who had accompanied him from the Academy to find a place to eat on their own. Through those months, Arun got invited to perform at several baithaks, including one at Madhav Pandit's home in Madgaon, Goa's second-largest city, after Panaji. He sang at the home of Ram Pagé, who worked for the Reserve Bank of India and was a record collector and an amateur tabla player. Pagé had also moved to Goa, leaving his family behind in Mumbai. Over the weekend, the two of them visited temples all over the state.

'I'm having a great time,' Arun told Dhanashree. 'But outside the Academy.'

After Kishori-tai finished her recital, Arun went up to the stage and greeted her. She had sung on the penultimate day of the multi-day

Samrat Sangeet Sammelan, an annual festival in Ponda, about thirty kilometres south-east of Panaji, several months after the temple recital. Unlike the intimate temple programme, this was a large event, with hundreds of listeners filling a huge tent each night. As with the temple concert, Arun had not planned to be there that night. A few days earlier, he had called Kishori-tai to wish her well and excuse himself from attending her recital.

'I have to perform on the festival's last day,' he had said. 'I'd like to remain in Panaji the previous day and get some rest.'

'No, you must come,' Kishori-tai had replied. 'We musicians should listen to one another. I will reciprocate and come and listen to you.'

It was dark when Arun began his recital on the last day. He sang Puriya Dhanashree and Gaud Malhar, accompanied on the tabla by the young Yogesh Samsi. Afterwards, as several people came up to the stage to talk to Arun, he remembered that Kishori-tai had said that she would be there. Had she sat quietly in the audience the way she had at the temple? This time, Vikas was not there to be his eyes. Arun never found out. But the culture minister Bandekar, who had earlier invited Arun to perform, had definitely been there. That evening, someone informed Bandekar that Arun had resigned from the Academy. Arun knew that he could have continued in Goa, earning a salary from a minimally demanding job, performing and composing. But even before completing six months, he felt drained by the Academy's apathy.

The day after the concert, Bandekar phoned Arun, who was serving his notice period.

'Please take back your resignation,' Bandekar said.

'Why?' Arun asked. 'I have no reason to.'

'I'll come by your office tomorrow and take you to the chief minister,' Bandekar said. 'You can tell him in detail about your problems.'

At the meeting with the chief minister, Arun described the red tape and total lack of autonomy for creative heads.

'Give me two days' time,' the chief minister told Arun.

Just as the deadline of two weeks for getting his flat had come and gone, these two days went by.

'If the chief minister had been serious about taking action, he would have picked the phone up then and there and scheduled a meeting with me and the Academy's top bureaucrat,' Arun told Dhanashree.

'Come home,' she said.

◆ Time

INDIAN RAAG AND RAAG-BASED MUSIC USES THE CONCEPT OF the avartan, the rhythmic cycle that repeats throughout a performance, just as the day cycles through our lives. The difference is that the duration of the avartan is not fixed.

In khayal, as well as in thumri, the tabla player marks out the avartan by playing one of many taals, each having a certain number of beats. In dhrupad, the percussion instrument is invariably the pakhawaj. When khayal singers begin presenting a slow composition, they often use a series of claps and waves to communicate which taal they want the percussionist to play. This is because each taal is represented by a unique pattern of claps, called taalis (hence the name taal), interspersed with a few waves, called khalis.

A taal is further divided into sections, mostly consisting of two, three or four beats.[6] Taalis or khalis always fall on the first beat of these sections. The taal's first beat, the sam, is always a taali, except the seven-beat Roopak, whose first beat is a khali.

For instance, Teentaal has sixteen beats divided into four sections: 4-4-4-4, while Jhaptaal has ten beats divided into four sections: 2-3-2-3. In Teentaal, the first beats of the first, second and fourth sections are taalis and the first beat of the third section is a khali. The presence of one or more khalis in every taal is what creates a repeating or cyclical pattern. In Teentaal, for instance, this repeating pattern is taali, taali, khali, taali. If all four of the taal's sections had begun with a taali, one could not have ordered them as first, second, third and fourth. They would have simply been a linear sequence of taalis. One could think of the khali as the rough equivalent of the night, which is what separates one day from the other.

The way a taal is divided into sections and the manner in which the taalis and khalis are distributed create a characteristic rhythmic gait, called the chhand, which is similar to prosody in poetry.

In a slow composition, the tempo is leisurely, so the interval between two consecutive beats is long and therefore, the intervals between claps and waves even longer. In order to help performers follow the progression of the avartan, the tabla player offers more fine-grained information than just taalis and khalis in the form of a theka. A theka is a set expression of the taal's beats in specific tabla sounds. These sounds have names called tabla bols, or syllables. These bols are often onomatopoeic. For example, the bols for Teentaal's first four beats are dha-dhin-dhin-dha.

As a rough analogy, one could think of keeping time through claps and waves as the equivalent of a clock with a big dot for 12 and small dots for 3, 6 and 9, and the theka as a clock with all the numerals written out, as in 1, 2, 3, etc. The first kind of timekeeping has just a few signposts, of two different types, while the second kind has many more signposts, of a variety of types.

In fast speeds, seasoned singers can keep track of time even without the theka, using just the taali and khali pattern. Singers with an excellent rhythmic sense can do so even in slow tempos, by keeping track of the sub-divisions between beats. In that case, the tabla player stops being a timekeeper and can focus on adding an aesthetic layer to a singer's exposition. Each vocalist has his or her own preference for how spare or ornate the theka should be. Some singers like the theka to be pared down. Others might say to a tabla player, thoda bharke bajao—please fill the theka. The style of accompaniment is the result of a delicate negotiation and adjustment between the singer and the tabla player.

A taal can be played in a range of layas, or tempos. The time interval between a taal's beats determines this tempo. The time intervals in a taal are equal in theory, but vary slightly in practice.[7] When starting a rendition, if a singer uses a series of claps and waves to indicate the taal, then that will also convey the tempo. But if a singer simply names the taal, then he or she can convey the tempo to the tabla player by gently moving one hand in the air up and down, by nodding the head or reciting a few tabla syllables, all of which reveal the interval between beats. A musician can also simply start singing or playing an instrument at a particular tempo, with the tabla player following right afterwards. Seasoned tabla players may themselves develop a feel for the tempo that will suit a particular composition and begin with it of their own accord.

After setting the initial tempo, singers can increase the speed one or more times during a rendition either by gesturing to the tabla player or simply singing faster. The initial tempo and the degree of acceleration depends upon the singer's gharana and personal preference. Khayal employs a wide range of tempos—from very slow to super-fast, a range that is among the largest of any music form in the world.[8] A very slow tempo would be roughly eight seconds to a beat and a very fast one one-eighth of a second to a beat.[9]

Part of being a good and reliable accompanist involves maintaining the tempo determined by the vocalist. The tabla player should not inadvertently, much less deliberately, speed up or slow down, and must arrive on the sam along with the singer. But singers are the ones who are more likely to make rhythmic mistakes; professional tabla players simply adjust to such errors.

'When we begin a train journey to a known destination, we might become engrossed in reading a book, talking to a companion, listening to music or day-dreaming. A little before the train is due to arrive at our destination, we automatically become alert and get off at the right station. All the while our subconscious has indeed been keeping track of the passing stations.' —AK

13

◇ Colours

GURUJI SURVEYED THE AUDIENCE, STUDDED WITH EMINENT individuals such as the singer Raja Miya, archivist Kishor Merchant, publisher Ramdas Bhatkal, arts curator Aditya Ruia, film-maker Chaitanya Tamhane and painter Sudhir Patwardhan. First Edition Arts was presenting Guruji for a second time, in December 2016. The concert was a tribute to Babanrao, who had passed away a few weeks earlier, and was taking place at the GSA Foundation for Contemporary Culture, a new arts organisation, in the Lakshmi Mills Estate, a former textile manufacturing complex. 'I will begin with Shree, the first raag that I worked on with Babanrao,' Guruji told the audience. 'I will sing *Garib nawaz*, composed by Babanrao's guru, Khadim Hussain Khan.'

He plunged in, coming up for air almost a whole hour later. With every hearing, that rendition of Shree yields insights that had earlier eluded me. After that, he kept up the intensity with Malgunji, and after an interval, sang Barwa and Sampoorna Malkauns.[1] He went deep into these raags' territories within minutes and probed them for new spaces. His rhythmic play was robust and intricate. In those three hours, he put on display all the styles that he had mastered, singing Shree and Barwa largely in the Agra mould, Malgunji mainly in the Gwalior style and Sampoorna Malkauns in a Jaipur-heavy idiom that showed how he had, to translate a Tamil phrase, dissolved and drunk Nivruttibuwa's designs.

He deployed all the improvisational forms in his arsenal: the nom-tom aalaap; the full range of bol work, which included his elaborate middle-tempo section; patterned sargams bearing his stamp; and taans inspired by all three gharanas. At the end, I saw Kaku, normally phlegmatic, shaking her head, as if in disbelief. Stoked by the memory of Babanrao, Guruji had poured every ounce of his being into that evening's renditions. I thought of Guruji as being quietly confident, not given to preening, but that evening, his musical persona reminded me of a male peacock showing off its magnificent feathers, full of rainbow colours in swirling designs.

Over the next three years, until the COVID-19 pandemic struck in early 2020, Guruji's concert career got a modest boost, showing that a shift in values in even a corner of the ecosystem could make a difference. In this period, about a dozen of us regularly landed up at his concerts, crowding into the green room to listen to him warming up, usually with Mukul and Vishal. Sometimes, the green room rehearsal evolved into a mini-recital, a before-party. But there was no predicting what Guruji would sing later. On some occasions, there was simply no time or space for a rehearsal. As a result, all of us, but most pertinently Mukul and Vishal, were left in the dark. Sometimes, if Guruji introduced an offbeat raag in class a few weeks before a concert, Kartik alerted Mukul or Vishal.

'Guruji taught us Khat for the first time,' Kartik told Mukul a couple of weeks before one concert.[2] Khat is thought to be a variation of the word 'shat', meaning six, the number of raags whose phrases have been woven together in the raag.

'Oh! I have not got taleem in that raag,' Mukul replied, so Kartik sent him a recording of one of our lessons. At a concert soon afterwards, when Guruji began Khat, poker-faced Mukul let slip a smile.

Later that year, a few weeks before the Aundh festival, Guruji began teaching us raag Bhim, but Kartik forgot to inform Mukul and Vishal. About half an hour before it was Guruji's turn to take the stage at Aundh, Kartik suddenly remembered, ran and caught Vishal just as he was entering the green room carrying a tanpura. 'Bhim?' Vishal asked. 'I haven't learnt that from Guruji. Quickly, sing the basic phrases.' Standing outside the green room, Kartik pointed out forks in the road where Bhim branched away from its more common kin, Bhimpalas. Vishal had no time to tell Mukul. When Guruji began singing Bhim on stage, for a few seconds, Mukul looked like a deer caught in the headlights. But his jungle instincts finely honed, he quickly recovered and began picking up the basic phrases on the fly. 'Bhim was impressive,' Madhavi later told Guruji. 'And Nakul and Sahadev did their bit.'

We rang some false alarms. Before another concert, Guruji began teaching us Sindura, a fact that Kartik again conveyed to Mukul and Vishal. But Guruji did not go there. Sometimes, Guruji sang recently minted compositions of his in a concert, so Mukul and Vishal had to absorb them in real time. Whatever the circumstance, they usually appeared unfazed. Listeners were often as impressed by how the duo kept pace with Guruji as they were by Guruji himself.

The forums that invited Guruji in this period were removed from the heart of the mainstream, with its razzmatazz and visibility, because the big organisers were unmoved. But Guruji had made peace with his marginalisation. He neither sought nor rejected money, fame, power and recognition. He treated them like elements of the weather, whose vicissitudes he could not control and therefore would not take personally. But with the sudden increase in attention on him in the autumn of his life, I sensed that he was nervous about how well his voice would cooperate, especially before a large, amorphous audience. After four years of knowing him, I still did not know what the problem was. He told me that he had visited a few doctors but none had given him a definitive diagnosis. Chandra suggested to me that perhaps it was related to his ambitious integration of various styles. Guruji did not rule this out. Kaku and Vishal speculated that the issue was at least partly psychological. Guruji was exceptionally even-tempered, but I knew that he had felt let down and hurt by the way some people had treated him over the years. He had made a conscious effort not to allow this to dampen his joie de vivre, but perhaps it had taken a toll on his most vital organ.

Kaku welcomed the belated attention on her husband. For years, she had toiled, running the home, raising their sons and accepting a simple and stagnant lifestyle to support her husband's music, only to watch him languish on the sidelines. Unlike her husband, she could not as recompense derive fulfilment and solace from a deep involvement with the music itself. She continued to steadfastly support Guruji's musical activities, but was both frustrated and sad that he had neither made money nor received recognition. She was by far the more practical and worldly of the two. Once, at a concert, she nodded in the direction of a well-dressed young man and astutely remarked, 'Lagta hai, woh bade ghar ka ladka hai.' It looks like he's from a 'big house', a metonym for a wealthy background. I knew the man. She was right.

⁓

In these years, I observed the work of many individuals and non-profit organisations in Mumbai who, as Kishor Merchant pointed out, had for decades been tirelessly and silently working to keep the art form alive in diverse colours. They reflect what the scholar Tejaswini Niranjana calls 'musicophilia', which she contends became an important part of Mumbai's identity over the twentieth century.[3] 'Although it was not Hindustani music alone that shaped this musicophilia, it formed a hugely significant part of it,' she writes.[4] These organisations also reflect the religious and linguistic diversity that has characterised Hindustani music's history in Mumbai. These musicophiliacs were bound together by a shared language that Niranjana calls 'lingua musica'.[5] 'Coming from different religious, caste and linguistic backgrounds, the musicophiliacs learned to speak to each other through the lingua musica,' she writes.[6] By the twenty-first century, however, they had become a part of the de facto fringe culture, along with annual Guru Purnima programmes, intimate baithaks, neighbourhood concerts and festivals like the Aundh Sangeet Mahostav.

Among these energetic individuals was Mukund Athavale, a businessman in his sixties. A tabla player manqué, he had channelled his unfulfilled ambition into providing a platform for other percussionists. From 1994 to the onset of the COVID-19 pandemic in early 2020, he held a free tabla concert every month.[7] The solo repertoire for tabla is incredibly rich, consisting of a range of compositional forms such as the chakradar, gat, laggi, qaida, peshkar, rela, teehai and tukra. But most tabla players spend the bulk of their time accompanying other performers and lack opportunities to display their full solo artistry. Athavale helped fill that gap.

His monthly event quickly became a fixture on the calendars of tabla players. After each recital, their WhatsApp grapevine would begin crackling with post-mortems. The audience consisted mainly of percussionists because the solo tabla repertoire faced an even greater chicken-and-egg problem than vocal music. Lay people did not go to solo tabla concerts because they did not understand the genre and did not understand it because they did not attend such concerts. To break this impasse, Athavale hit upon a clever ploy. In 1998, he added a second act: a vocal recital. This indeed brought in a different profile of listeners and almost doubled the audience size. Over the years, in addition to giving a platform to scores of tabla players, Athavale presented about seventy-five singers.

In 2020, he wound down this activity to focus on another non-profit, the Abhijat Forum, which he co-founded with three others.[8] Since 2016, the Forum has been organising an annual three-day festival in various venues across the country. Athavale curated these festivals using a rough formula in which one third of the musicians were well-known, another third were somewhat known and the last third were unknown. The Forum raised funds mainly from individual donors and listeners. Athavale said getting corporate sponsors was difficult. 'Companies keep saying they want only big names,' he lamented. 'But how will new people become big names unless they get opportunities?'

D.R. Khadke was another silent contributor to the fringe. He began the Alladiya Khan Music Festival in Mumbai in 1978, after retiring from the police service and settling in the Chembur locality of Mumbai. In Chembur, he developed a deep connection with music by learning from Wamanrao Sadolikar, a student of Alladiya Khan's who lived nearby.[9] Like the Aundh Mahotsav, the multi-day festival that Khadke founded began presenting a variety of fine non-mainstream artists from all over the country. It was there that I heard the wonderful Shanno Khurana for the first time in 2016. The Rampur-Sahaswan singer was then eighty-eight, and she told me that she had sung in Mumbai only a couple of times before that.[10] The festival attracted a high-quality audience that included musicians. Khadke also held a monthly baithak featuring new talent. After he passed away in 2013, his son took over and has continued to hold both the festival and the baithaks.

~

The non-profit Swar Sadhana Samiti has exemplified low-key but steadfast commitment to Hindustani music for decades.[11] It was founded in 1961 by Keki Jejina, a sitar player, and his protégé, Aban Mistry, one of post-Independence India's first professional female tabla players, who went on to train under Amir Hussain Khan of the Farrukhabad gharana. Mistry passed the baton to a second generation of trustees, led by the dogged and efficient Rupa Sethna. For decades, the Samiti has unfailingly organised a monthly programme with a line-up of two or three musicians. In June 2025, the Samiti held its seven hundred and sixtieth such event. The organisation also holds an annual concert showcasing excellent musicians who have a scant or no presence on big stages. Equally valuable is its annual performing arts competition for different age groups. Over the years, I saw how Sethna and her team conducted these events with a rare combination of clockwork precision and warmth.

Jejina and Mistry were Parsis, a community known in the twenty-first century for its appreciation of Western classical music. Less appreciated is the fact that the Swar Sadhana Samiti originated in an age when a section of their community was intimately involved with Indian classical music. Some fine Parsi musicians include the khayal singers Firoz Dastur and Jal Balaporia and the sarod player Zarin Sharma née Daruwalla.[12] The Parsis' involvement with Hindustani music goes back to the second half of the nineteenth century, the heyday of Parsi theatre, which reflected an Indo-Persian cultural sensibility. In the late decades of that century, the Parsi Gayan Uttejak Mandali held regular concerts featuring both professionals and amateurs.[13]

The non-profit Suburban Music Circle is yet another example of long-term dedication to honest music and of Hindustani music's cultural heterogeneity. The Circle was begun in 1937 by a group of Chitrapur Saraswats, a tiny Konkani-speaking Hindu minority numbering about 28,000[14] people that has a disproportionately large presence in Hindustani music.[15] Half of its members live in Mumbai and its environs. Besides pulling their weight as avid organisers and listeners, the amchis, as they call themselves, have produced leading music critics in Mumbai, such as Mohan Nadkarni and Prakash Burde, and prominent musicians, such as flautists Devendra Murdeshwar, Naresh Kumta and Nityanand Haldipur; tabla players Omkar Gulvady, Sadanand Naimpally, H. Taranath Rao and Yogesh Samsi; sitar player Vinayak Chittar; and vocalists Chidanand Nagarkar, Dinkar Kaikini, Kausalya Manjeshwar and Lalith Rao.[16]

Till the turn of the millennium, the non-profits Dadar-Matunga Cultural Centre and Kala Bharati Karanataka Sangh played a major role. While no longer as influential, they continue to support good musicians. In recent years, Suranjan Trust and Vertical Notes, both based in Thane, north of Mumbai, have been presenting fine musicians. This is by no means an exhaustive list of such organisations.

⌘

Among more recent organisations, the G5A Foundation for Contemporary Culture, where Guruji's tribute concert to Babanrao took place, has potential. The foundation's arts centre, which opened in 2015, is part of a rapidly gentrifying working-class district in central Mumbai. Its founder, Anuradha Parikh, an architect and independent film-maker, envisioned the arts centre as 'a refuge for independent arts practice, which flourishes in spite of the mainstream', she told me. The foundation has been able to pursue this goal for dance, film, theatre and contemporary music, but Anuradha told me that she found it hard to get funding for non-mainstream Hindustani music performers. This was unfortunate because the G5A Warehouse's Black Box, which can seat a hundred and fifty people on average, is an excellent space for khayal performances because of its size, minimalist decor and fine acoustics.

Then there is First Edition Arts, which has diligently been mining the fringe since 2016. Founded two years before that, it started out by presenting the small pool of mainstream musicians with artistic integrity. After the rousing reception that it got to the Secret Masters Sessions recital featuring Guruji, it took a different direction, going on to present three more vocalists like him—Jayashree Patneker, Narayan Bodas and Sharad Sathe. The series did not come a year too soon because Bodas passed away in 2017 at the age of eighty-four while Sathe breathed his last in 2019 after crossing eighty-seven years. First Edition Arts soon won enormous goodwill among connoisseurs. They and many musicians whom it presented recommended other artists who deserved a platform, creating a snowballing momentum. 'It was a galvanising moment, one of those rare ecosystem moments,' Devina told me.

A hugely important part of the start-up's strategy was to invest in producing high-quality video recordings of its concerts with the aim of giving viewers as close an experience to the live concert as possible. Devina's husband, Pepe, is the force behind these videos. A lean man with spectacles and curly shoulder-length salt-and-pepper hair, he can be seen at many of the organisation's concerts wielding one of the several cameras. He is the one who also painstakingly edits most of the footage. The popularity of these videos began revealing that listeners all over the world were receptive to music with subtlety and depth. The videos also made business sense because they gave sponsors, not just musicians, global visibility. This fact, in turn, relieved First Edition Arts from the pressure of having to pack large venues and clutter stages with sponsors' logos. The company's record also showed that even for-profit firms could nurture the ecosystem if those setting the agenda had the necessary vision and values.

Nevertheless, getting marketers to open their purses for non-celebrities was getting increasingly difficult. Consequently, in 2021, Devina and Pepe founded a non-profit organisation called Kishima Arts Foundation, to document art music beyond the narrow confines of its visible expression in concerts, and thereby create a digital archive available to the public.[17] 'I want to be released of sponsors terrorising me to get "big" names and become viable in their eyes,' said Devina. 'The grip of the big and shiny is only tightening. Mainstream players will trot out the token alternative musician, but the set of performers whom they are constantly circulating is getting narrower and narrower.' At the same time, she wanted to keep First Edition Arts relevant. 'Indie organisers should not completely flee the field because then we only embolden the powerful,' she said.

If First Edition Arts resembled a lean, mean army unit, Mihir Thakore employed guerrilla tactics. He was a successful Ahmedabad-based lawyer and a longstanding music lover. Starting in June 2020, soon after the first COVID-19 lockdown, he began presenting a musician almost every week on his YouTube channel, keeping up the pace well into 2025. By April that year, he had ended up presenting more than two hundred different musicians. 'I am still getting new artists,' Thakore told me. Most of them were younger than fifty and had excellent training.

Thakore was able to maintain this blistering pace by asking musicians to record themselves performing, investing most of his energy in searching for and vetting potential performers from all over the country. He paid them all a fee from his own income. He essentially worked his way down from the top of pedagogical family trees of major styles, a rational and systematic method because, apart from rare prodigies, most people cannot become good performers without excellent training. This is not rocket science. 'More than three-fourths of the musicians I presented met my expectations,' Thakore said. In New Delhi, since 2018, an organisation called Upstairs has been attempting to offer an alternative to the mainstream by holding chamber concerts funded by the audience, thus eliminating intermediaries and their demand for the same celebrities.[18]

The fringe gave musicians valuable opportunities to perform, usually for small knowledgeable audiences, but could usually pay them only modest fees because sponsors, even when spending CSR funds, were tightfisted when it came to funding non-celebrities. As a result, over the years, I noticed that some fringe organisations and festivals had begun including celebrity musicians in their line-ups.

◈ Beauty: 1998–2000

THE EARLY MORNING AIR WAS COOL AND A PALE ORANGE light dappled the large music room that occupied the first floor of the house in Baroda belonging to Madhavi's parents. Yogesh switched on the electronic tanpura, slid the cloth covers off the tabla set and looked at Arun, who had travelled to Baroda for a lecture-demonstration the previous evening and had spent the night with Yogesh and Madhavi. It was early 1998.

'*Garaja ghata* (Thundering cloud)?' Yogesh asked. 'Megh. Jhaptaal.'

Arun nodded. Megh, a monsoon raag whose name means 'rain cloud', was not traditionally sung in the morning. In public concerts, Arun followed Hindustani music's time convention for raags, but was sceptical of its logic. Yogesh and Madhavi were Arun's admirers from Mulund. After marrying Yogesh a year earlier, Madhavi had moved from Baroda to Mulund and had begun learning from Arun. She had earlier learnt in Baroda from a student of the Gwalior vocalist Yashwantbuwa Joshi. Her father was an avid amateur sitarist. On learning that Yogesh played the tabla, Arun began calling him over to accompany him. Yogesh recorded many of these sessions, in which just the two of them had been present. 'So many of those renditions are gems,' Yogesh had thought. 'I don't know how Arun Kaka fires on all cylinders even when there are no listeners.'

That day, too, there was no audience. Even Madhavi was not around. Arun began singing as Yogesh set Jhaptaal galloping, its hoofs thumping dhi-na, dhi-dhi-na; ti-na, dhi-dhi-na. Arun gracefully hoisted the composition on to the taal's saddle. After a couple of sedate rounds, the rider stood up and began making slow lissom gestures. Horse and rider—taal and composition—went around the circular track of time several times, oblivious to the empty stands, the first lost in its rhythmic clip-clopping, the second in its agile dance. With each round, the rider's gestures changed. After many rounds, the horse began galloping faster and the rider dancing more vigorously, twirling and doing backflips. Many more rounds later, the horse accelerated once more and the rider became even more daring. About twenty minutes after the cantering had begun, horse and rider slowed down and came to a standstill.

'*Ata dhoom* (Now a bang),' Yogesh suggested. It was a fast composition in Ektaal in the same raag.

The horse resumed galloping a few notches faster from where it had left off, while the rider resumed dancing. After two dizzying minutes, the dancer-rider sat back down and brought the horse to a halt.

'Another gem,' thought Yogesh.[19]

For the first time, Yogesh saw worry lines on Arun's forehead.

'Adwait has had a serious accident,' Arun told Yogesh. 'I have to rush to Bangalore.'

It was May 1998. Adwait was at the end of his second year of a bachelor's course in hotel management. The previous day, about a week before his final exams, he had flown off his motorcycle trying to avoid a man crossing the road and had landed flat on his face. His friend, who was riding pillion, had got away with minor scratches, but blood had streamed down Adwait's face. They had rushed to a nearby hospital, where the doctor had told Adwait that he had dislocated his jaw and sustained hairline fractures on both cheekbones.

When Arun walked in to the hospital, along with Ashish, and saw his son's face bandaged up, he blanched. Adwait, however, felt half his pain receding on seeing his father and elder brother. Soon, the doctors informed Arun that the fractures would heal in a few months and that his son would recover his looks. But Adwait knew that he would not be able to do his final exams. He would have to move back to Mumbai for a year and take the exams the following year. He knew his parents had stretched themselves to pay his college fees. Now, they would have to pay for an extra year. But Arun said nothing to his son, either about his not wearing a helmet or about losing an academic year. On the contrary, when he was convinced that Adwait would be all right, he went back to being his old self, smiling and joking.

Adwait realised then that his father had rarely passed on his anxieties to his family. Day after day, almost without exception, his father had come home from work, washed up and begun his singing session, warmly welcoming all visitors. Adwait had never heard his father complaining about his arduous commute or his humdrum job, except by way of a joke. His father had never insisted that Ashish or he do this or that, whether it was their schoolwork, friends, or indeed, girlfriends. He had merely laughed when Adwait had showed him school report cards that put him in the middle of his class, unlike his elder brother, who almost always came first. Arun took as much pleasure in Adwait's fun-loving personality as his elder brother's earnest one. Only once, when Adwait had been head over heels in love with a girl from a Christian background had Arun come close to laying down a party line. 'You should try to marry someone from our religious background,' he had told his son. But he had treated even that girlfriend cordially, and as it turned out, Adwait's youthful infatuation had passed.

Arun had been easy-going about music too. Until the age of ten, Adwait had picked up vocal music by osmosis. Like Ashish, he had begun learning to play the tabla from Sansare. In the eleventh standard, when he had showed an interest in learning the sarod, Arun had immediately sent an old instrument that someone had given him to a craftsman to refurbish. Adwait also appreciated his father's decision to send them to English-medium schools, unlike some of his contemporaries. Adwait had noticed his father's special liking for the language. He had seen him frequently looking up dictionaries, mulling over words and phrases, their meanings and usage. While Adwait had sometimes felt that he might have benefited from more guidance from his father, he eventually grew to appreciate the fact that he had been able to experiment, make mistakes and grow in the absence of judgement. Dhanashree had made up for Arun's relaxed approach. She had sent Adwait to French classes in the next suburb, to a rigorous summer camp teaching archery, horseback riding and other sports, and to a retreat in the Himalayas.

From his hospital bed, Adwait looked at the bright side. He would convalesce at home, enjoy his father's music and his mother's food, and the extrovert that he was, mingle with the endless stream of visitors. He smiled, thinking how he found his friends' self-contained homes strange, even boring. He revelled in the hustle-bustle of his open house.

~

Arun sat in his usual place against the wall, mulling over a question that he had relentlessly been thinking about for years. It was about virgin real estate—within the avartan and in the overall rendition of a slow composition. His training had been in the traditional gharanas, which linked raag elaborations to the avartan. But he saw that the taal structure could be tapped even more systematically to enhance renditions of slow compositions and subsequent improvisations. He set up some slow compositions to match the taal down to one-fourths of every beat and began aesthetically meshing his improvisations with the taal. He also thought deeply about how to mix different layas within the avartan to create variety. These experiments began lending an intricate rhythmic texture to his singing, becoming one of his style's defining aspects.

He began thinking about the suvarna madhya laya, the golden medium tempo, one that was not too fast and not too slow. This is what many of his role models, including Gajananbuwa, used. Arun believed that this tempo was natural and universal. He had observed that people used it to sing folk and devotional music, and children tended to use it while clapping their hands. It also characterised the cadences of everyday human conversation. 'Are these phenomena related to the tempo of the human heartbeat?' he wondered. Arun thought of the tempos that were slower and faster than this golden medium as dramatised or stylised tempos, akin to the ones humans used when delivering formal speeches, which are often slower than daily conversation, and when arguing in debates, which are usually faster. Many khayal singers, and indeed, styles, tended to restrict themselves to these stylised tempos, moving directly from the slow to the fast. But Arun believed that the golden medium tempo's connection to human life held considerable potential for improvisation and made it appealing to listeners. This tempo, Arun further believed, was especially suitable for bol work because it used human language—the composition's lyrics—to explore the raag.

His innovations gathered pace, each fuelling another. For several years, Arun devoted himself to refining his medium-tempo bol work. He ensured that while improvising on a line, as far as possible he pronounced the words the way they were spoken. To maintain the linguistic integrity of every word, he did not elongate short vowels inside words if doing so distorted their sounds or meanings. Further, to preserve a whole line's syntax, he matched grammatical clauses with a raag's phrases. With years of riyaaz, he achieved fluency in this technique in the plethora of raags that he sang.

Within the spectrum of the medium tempo, Arun often increased the speed a couple of times in order to keep building momentum. By presenting an expanded medium-tempo bol segment, Arun could gradually and unobtrusively move from the slow-paced aalaap to fast taans, a transition that felt abrupt in renditions lacking this bridging segment. Over time, Arun kept polishing his bol work to the extent that it gradually acquired a unique flavour.

By then, Arun was also artistically mixing and matching designs from the three gharanas in which he had trained. Often, he began with Agra's lilting beat-by-beat progression, then presented Gwalior's quicksilver swing patterns and finally moved on to singing Jaipur's startling off-beat designs to create special effects. He added his own innovations to the mix. Enhancing commonly used linear sargam sequences, he created layered patterns that combined short sequences of notes into larger strings and those into even larger ones. He thus gave sargam sequences an internal structure, partially inspired by Carnatic music. He also explored patterns used by other singers, such as Abdul Karim Khan and Amir Khan.

Some sections of the Hindustani music world looked down on the use of sargams in a performance, viewing them solely as a pedagogical tool. Some musicians did suffer from an affliction that some critics called 'sargamitis', making excessive use of them and singing them mechanically as though they were doing vocal exercises rather than presenting art. But Arun saw that sargams, containing only monosyllabic units, lent a texture to the raag that was distinct from aakaar and bol, the other two vocal means of elaboration. Like aakaar, sargams had no meaning, so a singer had more flexibility in creating patterns. But sargams used the names of notes, so they offered glimpses into a raag's structure. He thought of aakar, bol and sargams as various brushes that a painter could use to create an array of effects on a canvas.

Arun delved into the aesthetics of the nom-tom aalaap, gently chiselling it to create his own idiom. He used a pleasing variety of inflections, such as delicate kan swars, which are touches of neighbouring notes, and meends of different lengths and textures, including the gend uchhal, meaning a ball springing upwards, a dramatic long meend that entails pushing off forcefully from a low note and vigorously hitting a much higher note, often traversing an octave or more. He also used gamaks of different speeds, including a slow one called the behlava. The nom-tom is not set in a taal cycle, but Arun built his improvisation on passages that ended in a manner that mimicked landings on the sam. He experimented with several combinations of nom-tom syllables, choosing mostly soft ones that meshed with the mellifluous tones of Brajbhasha. Like with his sargams, in addition to singing linear sequences, he created layered sequences consisting of smaller units. These units could, for instance, be two-three or three-five pairs, such as ri-re, ri-re-na and ri-re-na, ri-re-re-na-nom.

Arun did not expect most listeners to notice the minutiae of his many enhancements and innovations. He wanted them only to enjoy their overall effect when he marshalled them to create a fresh and dynamic soundscape.

News about Ulhas's career had trickled in over the previous five years. As the new millennium approached, the import of this news was clear: Arun's youngest brother had broken into the mainstream. One turning point had come in the early 1990s, when Ulhas, in his late thirties, had received an offer from the ITC Sangeet Research Academy in Kolkata to become one of its gurus. The Academy was founded in 1978 as a modern gurukul for Hindustani vocal music, aiming to combine the advantages of gharana-based seena-ba-seena taleem with the resources, stability, structure, opportunities and visibility of a well-funded institution. It paid a salary to its gurus and a stipend to the students, whom it selected through a highly competitive nationwide process. It gave both groups housing on a pleasant campus in Kolkata's Tollygunge area. Alongside teaching, its gurus could pursue their performing careers. The Academy opened with a roster of excellent vocal teachers, such as the Agra gharana's Latafat Hussain Khan, the Jaipur gharana's Nivruttibuwa Sarnaik, the Kirana gharana's Hirabai Barodekar and the Rampur-Sahaswan gharana's Nisar Hussain Khan. Ulhas belonged to the next generation.

This turning point had followed an earlier one, which came when Ulhas was in his early thirties and was working as a producer in the All India Radio's office in South Mumbai. He and his wife, Sanjeevani, who also worked at the radio station, lived outside the city, commuting nearly two hours each way to work. Ulhas soon knew that his job was taking a toll on his music, but needed the income because he had begun working only in his late twenties, after finishing his taleem with Gajananbuwa. On hearing that Ulhas soon was stuck in a nine-to-five job, well-wishers such as the writer P.L. Deshpande stepped in. Deshpande had followed the young man's career after noticing him shining as a teenager at statewide music competitions. On Deshpande's suggestion, an administrator at the radio station suggested that Ulhas go on long leave to focus on music. His wife's salary could support them both, frugal as their lifestyle was, the man told the couple. He told Ulhas to try this out and later decide whether he wanted to quit altogether.

'There's another issue to think about,' Arun told Ulhas. 'As a producer at the radio station, you will have to kowtow to other musicians. If you stay there for too long, you may find that when you do strike out on your own, some of them will continue treating you as a subordinate, not as an artist in your own right.'

⁓

For eight months, exhausting all his leave, Ulhas worked intensively on all that he had learnt from Gajananbuwa, churning musical ideas in his mind as much as singing. In the end, realising that he had benefited enormously from being able to single-mindedly focus on his music, he quit his job, deciding that he and his wife could manage on her income. He began performing whenever he got opportunities. Around that time, he began pairing up with Suresh Talwalkar, a tabla player who was part of Gajananbuwa's circle and was becoming an influential figure in Maharashtra's Hindustani music world. Arun had not hit it off with the erudite and enterprising tabla player, whom some contemporaries found self-aggrandising. Unlike Arun, who had kept Talwalkar at an arm's length, Ulhas got along with the older, go-getting tabla player.

Unlike Arun, who had emerged from his taleem while his two main gurus were still active, Ulhas entered the concert scene after Gajananbuwa, his principal guru, had passed away. Arun had instinctively recoiled from promoting himself in full view of his gurus, who themselves had not got the attention they deserved. In this respect, Ulhas had timing on his side. He began gradually making a name for himself in Maharashtra, the most important state for khayal. He then caught the attention of the Sangeet Research Academy's director, Vijay Kichlu. At the Academy, Ulhas made the most of the opportunity. Almost at once, he began training students. He used his free time to think about music, moulding Gajananbuwa's style to his voice and aesthetic sensibilities without sacrificing its depth. Influenced by styles popular in Kolkata, namely the Kirana and Patiala gharanas, Ulhas expanded the aalaap and began at a slower pace than usual when singing for the city's audiences. He made use of the Academy's rich archives to imbibe new raags and compositions. He rapidly expanded his audience through the Academy's nationwide concerts. By the end of the 1990s, he had won a reputation, at least among connoisseurs, as one of India's most compelling khayal performers and finest musical minds. He was also proving to be a highly effective guru.

Until the late-1990s, in many music circles in Mumbai, the word 'Kashalkar' was associated with Arun. By the end of the decade, it was increasingly being associated with 'Ulhas'. But Ulhas knew that his eldest brother had paved the way for him. In their childhood, Arun had led by example. 'When we were growing up, we heard Arun practising for hours every day,' Vikas, the second-youngest brother, who also became a performing musician, often told people. 'He has done more riyaaz than the rest of us put together.' As a child, Ulhas had been enchanted by Arun's renditions of thumris and natya geet. As an adult, Ulhas recognised that Arun had enabled his transformative taleem with Gajananbuwa. Eventually, after Arun had moved to Mulund, Vikas, too, had moved from eastern Maharashtra to Dombivli to learn from Gajananbuwa. Now, Ulhas, as a khayal musician, admired his eldest brother's robust voice, his command over rhythm, his fluency in three gharanas, his deep renditions of Agra gharana raags, his elegant nom-tom and his compositions. But while they retained love and respect for each other, their lives began to diverge.

'It's good that everything worked out for him,' Arun said to Dhanashree. 'But I have also been lucky. I found amazing gurus and I am engrossed in music. Our sons are flourishing. We have more than enough to eat and live on. We should not worry about what is not in our control. People like my gurus took music as a mission and did not make material calculations. Ultimately, music is meant to give you bliss.'

Bliss. Dhanashree's expectations from life did not include the idea associated with this word. Like most Indian women of her generation, from childhood she had been conditioned to believe that her main role was to help her husband and children realise *their* potential and ambitions. She perhaps felt the tedium of running the home less than many women because she had developed a genuine passion for cooking, one that she had passed on to Adwait. She looked at it as a way of expressing herself. Just as Arun regularly pulled out the stops at his home mehfils, Dhanashree cooked day after day with love and care as though for a feast.

'It gives me joy to feed others,' she often thought.

It ran in her family.

'My mother made even daal well,' she once told Arun. 'My elder sister, too, has a flair for cooking.'

She had also carved out an independent sphere for herself with her clothes business, developing a network of wholesalers selling textiles, sarees, leather goods and accessories such as bags and purses, across the city. Over the years, through trial and error, she had gone back only to those whose quality she found reliable. Like with food, she had a nose for her regular customers' sartorial tastes.

'How I would have loved to open a shop,' she thought.

She could only dream. Where was the capital? Where was the free time?

After all these years, Arun, was sitting in the same place, with his back against the wall. He seemed as content as before, lost in his music. But the spots on his body were spreading. She sensed that he felt less and less like venturing out for social occasions. She welled up with sadness on his behalf. Sometimes, she could not control her wistful thoughts from mutating into pangs of frustration. Her life and Arun's appeared to be stagnant even as people around her were surging ahead. Several years ago, her elder brother had quit his job at a car firm and started a business manufacturing and supplying components to a big auto firm. Her younger brother had his own auto parts business. They had become prosperous entrepreneurs.

Her neighbours, too, appeared to be thriving. Now, Ulhas was literally going places. To snap out of her mood, she usually thought of her sons. Bright, driven and dignified, they seemed set to take full advantage of the opportunities that the new economy had thrown up. At least they were moving forward.

Arun looked at a black-and-white photo of himself taken about a decade earlier in a studio. More than one person had told him that he looked like a film star in it.

'I have lost my looks,' he thought.

The beard that he had grown to cover the patches on his face could hide only so much. From the way strangers looked at him for just a few moments longer than was socially acceptable or quickly averted their eyes, he knew that the mottling was now immediately noticeable. He had visited a couple of more doctors, but their remedies had not worked.

Arun rarely articulated his thoughts. To most people, he appeared as jovial and focused on his music as before. But those close to him, like Dhanashree and Vikas, sensed a current of melancholy beneath his jolly demeanour. Vikas did not say a word about the skin condition, deciding that he would support his friend by spending as much time with him as he could. By then, along with Yogesh and Madhavi, Vikas and his wife, Neelima, had become Arun's staunchest supporters. Vikas, a businessman and collector of paintings, had met Arun more than three years earlier when he had taught music for several months at a school run by Vikas's father. 'I have never heard a male voice as sweet as Arun's,' Vikas had told Neelima. 'As someone who has been involved with education, I can also say that his approach to teaching is extraordinary.'

During a difficult time for Arun, Vikas took him on long walks in Mulund's gardens, where the two friends talked about the purpose of art and the meaning of life.

Arun cleared his throat to wake his voice up. It felt uncharacteristically sluggish.

'Come on, my red-blooded friend,' he told it. 'What's wrong?'

Fortunately, he was singing at home and his loyal listeners did not even notice that his voice was unsteady for the initial couple of minutes. But he was worried. His instrument had begun giving him trouble. He remembered a handful of occasions over the past decade on which it had acted up by wavering at the start. At times, he felt like he was dealing with a petulant child who was throwing tantrums. Only, he did not know what it was upset about. He had been especially rattled on one occasion. He had been recording for HMV, a leading music company, which had wanted to produce a cassette of his renditions. He had been accompanied to the music studio by two students. His friend, Bhai Gaitonde, had come along to play the tabla. Arun had been alarmed to find that his voice felt viscous, failing to move with the fluidity that he had taken for granted. After half an hour, he had told the executives that he could not produce his best that day and would like another session. After a few months, Arun had returned to the studio and this time, had sung easily. But for some reason that he never found out, the company never released the cassette. Arun had few expectations from the world. But he had been stung by this experience. Yes, he had a skin problem. Yes, his voice had begun occasionally giving him trouble. But there was his music. Did it not count?

In the years since then, he had gradually grown even more detached from the mainstream music world. He knew Dhanashree was disappointed. They were casualties of forces over which they had no control. He had kept investing in his music with an iron determination, but in the process had he placed unreasonable demands on his body? Was it not a fallacy to think of the mind and body as disconnected? Had his body first revealed its pain by stopping to make pigment? Even then, it had not endangered any of his vital organs, only leaching colour from the veneer of the body's outermost layer. Now, the body was rebelling again, through his voice. Yet again, even while revealing its distress, his body did not threaten his life.

To bear his body's burden without letting it singe his soul, he retreated into the shadows. But not for a moment from his art. He fell in love with it again with a renewed passion, almost as if he were channelling his ebbing physical beauty into his music, which became ever sweeter, more intricate and daring. But would he, who had wrought a vivacious khayal style and loved people, re-emerge into the light?

◆ Drama

KHAYAL HIGHLIGHTS THE PASSAGE OF AN AVARTAN AND the arrival on the sam in a special way. In a slow composition, a singer usually begins a new round of improvisation with each avartan.[20] An avartan in a slow composition has three acts. The first act begins slightly after the sam, when the singer begins a long stretch of improvisation. The second act begins about three-fourths into the cycle, when the singer renders an aamad, meaning approach in Urdu. The aamad signals that the avartan is ending through an increase in rhythmic density. In the third act, the vocalist sings the mukhda, which is an initial segment of a composition's first word or phrase, then lands dramatically on the sam, and completes that first word or phrase. Mukhda comes from the Sankrit word for face, its name capturing the fact that the segment sung before the sam is like the face of the whole first word or phrase. In the song-text,[21] one marks an 'x' above the syllable in a word corresponding to the sam, which normally coincides with an important note in the raag.

Some styles give special importance to creating drama before the sam and arriving on it precisely. For listeners, the build-up to and arrival on the sam can be a source of excitement and pleasure.

After the singer arrives on the climactic sam, the tension dissipates as the singer completes the mukhda. The singer then enters the next avartan's long first act and the whole process resumes.

~

The reiteration of the mukhda in every avartan, which signals that the climactic sam is soon coming, is a version of returning to the familiar that characterises many aspects of human life.[22] The way listeners might feel when the singer begins the mukhda resembles the way working people might feel every Friday night, which precedes the eagerly awaited weekend, or the excitement that children might experience on the night before their birthdays. In a khayal rendition, the repeated invocation of the mukhda can create a hypnotic effect.

Khayal singers like to say that they are 'filling' an avartan. Indeed, they dedicate their whole lives to filling empty avartans with original and beautiful improvisations, and compellingly linking each filled avartan to the next as they unfold a raag. From afar, the prospect of filling hours of empty avartans can appear forbidding. But lured by the intense gratification that rising to this challenge can bring, people willingly take it on. In thrall to the hypnotic cycle, these avartan-fillers belong to a community akin to a secret society.

~

'While shopping for fabric in a textile store, if we find even one small fibre sticking out of a swatch of cloth or even a minuscule part missing from a repeating pattern, we reject the item because its texture feels good neither to our hand nor eye. Similarly, when I sing, I try not to include stray matter or leave unintended gaps in my avartans because doing this will spoil the overall design and effect that I am aiming to create. Within the norms and rules of khayal, I try to fill each avartan as aesthetically as possible.' —AK

PATHS

> Only those who will risk going too far
> can possibly find out how far one can go.
> — T. S. Eliot

14

◇ Reception

THROUGH THE LATE MODEST REVIVAL OF GURUJI'S CAREER, I observed how listeners reacted to his music. Some could not get past his starting difficulties. The voice is the first point of connection for everyone, and for the lay listener, sometimes the only one. But the listening public was not a monolith. Among those whose responses surprised me was a young girl who came running up to Guruji after a concert and said, 'You sang really well.' Another was a dear friend who had been exposed mostly to Western music but who told Guruji following a concert that she had attended out of curiosity, 'That was magical.'

Carnatic music rasikas particularly seemed to get Guruji's music. Among them was Narayan Rangaraj, a professor of mechanical engineering at IIT Mumbai and a Carnatic singer. 'Gripping music …,' he wrote on rasikas.org about one of Guruji's recitals. 'He sang Komal Rishabh Asavari, something called Pancham, which was quite nice (just a little bit like Carnatic Music's Kannada, but not quite), Ramkali and then Jaunpuri. I had to leave before the concluding Bhairavi, reluctantly. He is adept in many gharanas, but sang what I believe is Agra gharana style today. I commend this gharana to all CM [Carnatic music] lovers, as it is quite a bit madhyama kalam [medium tempo], mostly in the middle octave and with a lot of words and strong rhythm and syllables articulated, and the tempo is something many will relate to … The man is just soaked in music and can and probably does sing all day and night and with raags very firmly etched in his mind. His voice is not pliable at slower speeds and he is quite hesitant in hitting the top sa at full volume for any length of time, at his age. It did not matter in the least!'

Similarly, *The Hindu's Friday Review* wrote about his concert at the Kalakshetra Foundation's campus in Chennai as part of the Svanubhava festival. 'His is a pristine and polished style of music,' wrote the reviewer. '[He] impressed [sic] with his full-throated voice in the nom tom alaap ... [using] every phrase to bring out its [raag Lachari Todi's] mood ... using ghamak [sic] and meend (glide) ... He followed this with a bada khayal, singing each line with an eye on powerful ornamentation of Lachari Todi that has two gandhars and two dhaivats. The soft glide from one gandhar to the next was a thing of beauty. He beautifully embellished the words "Ab tose na bolungi" with swaras.'[1]

Zarir Khariwala was another music lover who took to Guruji's music. Zarir had attended the Secret Masters Sessions recital, where I spotted him in the crowd that had climbed on to the stage. From then on, I saw him at many of Guruji's concerts. Among music lovers, Zarir belonged to a category of his own. For years, I had noticed him standing up at the end of Indian music recitals and, to everyone's amusement, shouting 'Bravo!'. This was rarely done in an Indian music concert, but Zarir always sounded so genuinely moved that the musicians found his burst of unconventional enthusiasm endearing. I got to know Zarir in the early 2010s when I found him sitting next to me at a performance by the khayal singer Venkatesh Kumar. Throughout the recital, Zarir took notes in a diary. At the end, after he had shouted his customary appreciation, I introduced myself to him and said that I admired his undiluted and transparent passion for music. Over the years, we became friends. The first time I visited his high-ceilinged flat in Mumbai's leafy Dadar Parsi colony, Zarir told me, 'The only people I love are musicians and people who love music.'

Zarir was a full-time connoisseur. When I met him, he was spending much of his time attending concerts and fighting a court case over some family property. His fervour for music extended to multiple genres: Carnatic, Hindustani and Western classical. In his living room, he had a cupboard full of notebooks with details about concerts that he had attended over decades and folders with programme leaflets, many of them autographed by musicians. He had got to know several of them well, including Western classical musicians who lived abroad and Carnatic singers who lived in Chennai. He was particularly close to one Hindustani musician: Kishori-tai. Watching Zarir interact with her for just a few minutes in the green room after one of her concerts, I knew at once that they were close. His mother had learnt from Mogubai, while Zarir had spent long hours with both of them. He was born a Parsi, but had a Hindu spiritual guru.

To say that he was a good storyteller does not do justice either to the content or style of his expositions. His tales unfolded in endlessly nested sub-narratives, vivid with detail and colour, interspersed with his own commentary and peppered with literary allusions, expressed in precise and evocative English, mixed, when apposite, with Gujarati, Hindi and Marathi, all delivered with a theatrical flourish. He had an astonishing memory for dialogue, reproducing verbatim what others had said in all these languages, occasionally going back to correct a word or two in order to get the phrasing absolutely right. Zarir told me that his phenomenal memory went back to his childhood, noticed and nurtured by his piano and drama teachers. He was as entertaining as insightful, but sometimes drifted so far from the original story that I had to rein him back. With his usual meticulousness Zarir relayed back to me a discussion that he'd had with Kishori-tai about Guruji soon after the Secret Masters Sessions concert.

'Hindustani shastriya sangeet madhe taalacha vajan tula havet tar go to Pandit Arun,' Kishori-tai told Zarir in the typical mixture of English and Marathi in which they conversed. If you want to understand the role of rhythm in Hindustani classical music, then go to Pandit Arun. She continued: 'He brings the aesthetics of taal into consciousness as no other vocalist does.'

'Haan, taal-pradhaan sangeetkaar aahe,' Zarir replied. He is a rhythm-oriented musician.

'Don't pigeonhole him,' Kishori-tai retorted. 'That would be a disservice.' Zarir's conversations with Kishori-tai appeared to often take the form of affectionate sparring. 'I love his music in its entirety,' she added. 'Kay full avaaz aahe. Kiti accurately sur lavtat ki bolu nako.' What a full voice. His sur is so accurate that I have no words for it.

⌘

Kishori-tai had obviously been among the tight circle of musicians and connoisseurs who had heard Guruji in the decades before his voice began troubling him. I tried to interview her myself, but before I could get an appointment, tragically, she passed away, in April 2017. I then began asking others from the same circle about Guruji's music in the years when he had been hidden to most other listeners.

Many of these musicians commented on how he had moulded the various gharanas in his composite style. 'I developed huge respect for Arun as a senior Gwalior gharana singer,' said the Jaipur gharana singer Arun Dravid, who was Kishori-tai's most senior disciple. 'I could see how much meditative thinking and listening he must have done in his lifetime.' In a profile of Guruji, Arnab Chakrabarty also wrote about his Gwalior base: 'Robust as [Arun] Kashalkar's voice is, there is a certain smoothness to his delivery that is undeniably a contribution of his early training in the Gwalior idiom, as is a big chunk of his repertoire.'[2] Sharad Sathe, the accomplished Gwalior gharana musician, told me, 'He has infused the Agra gayaki with a lot of sweetness. His gayaki is not just a mechanism, but has a lot of aesthetics.'[3] Vrinda Mundkur, who had taken me to see Aslam Khan, echoed Sathe, 'He does not blindly copy the Agra masters. His music is never aggressive or overbearing.' Arnab, in the same profile, wrote that '[Arun] Kashalkar switches effortlessly between the considerably disparate methods used by the Agra and Gwalior traditions of improvising bol taans ... Bol taan delivery methods are deeply embedded in gharana ideology and it takes a very evolved musical mind to switch styles in this area.' Arun Kulkarni, a senior student of Nivruttibuwa Sarnaik, told me, 'His Agra bol is so refined. He also imbibed the Jaipur style very well.'

Others spoke about Guruji's raag interpretations. 'He is a real authority on raags,' the veteran singer Alka Deo Marulkar told me. 'He has thought deeply about them. He is able to be creative and innovative while maintaining the discipline of the raag.' Pratima Tilak, a Jaipur singer, told me: 'He folds the raag so well into his nom-toms that sometimes you feel that he does not need to sing the bada khayal. I love his nom-tom aalaaps.' Zunain Khan, a sitar player, composer and the son of the sitar maestro Abdul Halim Jaffer Khan, told me, 'If you want to know the genuine form of a raag, you should ask Arun-ji. He has a comprehensive view of raags and is a very good reference. I call him whenever I have a doubt. I also love his gayaki.'

Some people highlighted specific raags. In early 1989, Bhimsen Joshi described Guruji's Shree to Chinmoy Khaladkar, a Supreme Court lawyer, connoisseur and harmonium player who had accompanied several leading vocalists. 'I asked Bhimsen-ji which artists in the next generation one should listen to,' recalled Khaladkar, who had then been in his teens. 'Bhimsen-ji went quiet for some time, and then said, "the Kashalkar brothers—the elder one".' Bhimsen-ji then handed the young Chinmoy a cassette and said, 'Someone recently gave me this. It has Arun's Shree. It is massive in conception and flawless in execution.'[4] On hearing Guruji's Sarnat, Babasaheb Purandare, the late historian and dramatist, told the music lover Nandan Wandre: 'We ... who wander the Sahyadri ranges ... have heard very beautiful things. But in this music, swar, laya and pronunciation are exceptionally unique, and took me far beyond the Narmada river. This music is calm and deeply soothing.

Pandit Arun Kashalkar's music is a great joy and extremely satisfying to the mind.'[5]

When it came to Guruji's use of rhythm, Kishori-tai had given her general view. Others described specific aspects of it. 'Arun Kaka perceives one-sixteenth of every beat, so his improvisations are very filigreed,' said Apoorva Gokhale, the Gwalior gharana singer. 'He takes a lot of risks while improvising, which makes his music spontaneous and unpredictable. He is one of those truly creative singers.' Arnab, in his profile, referred to Guruji's 'witty rhythmic play'. In a commemorative magazine, Mukul described Guruji's arrival at the sam as resembling 'a waterfall cascading from a great height, accelerating as it plunges towards a spot in a valley below that is visible from above, finding its mark with accuracy and force'.[6] Karmalkar Kaka referred to Guruji's style as 'dadagiri ka gana'—audacious singing.

'He was extremely talented,' said Lalith Rao, the Agra gharana singer. 'But he did not ride on that god-given talent. He used all the time he could get to work on his music. It is remarkable.'

❦

Guruji's sudden reappearance, however, also evoked a few hostile reactions that hinted at the pernicious politics that seems to vitiate some of our performing arts communities. In early 2016, I had contacted an influential individual who Guruji told me had attended a performance of his at a recent festival. I wanted to interview the person for the profile of Guruji that I was working on. 'I have never heard him singing,' the individual told me. I checked back with Guruji in case I had misconstrued what he had said. Guruji looked puzzled. 'He even spoke to me after my performance and we went to eat together,' he said. One of Guruji's students also told me that he had seen the individual in the audience and sent me a photo of the person sharing a meal with Guruji at the venue. For the same profile, I had also asked an ambitious singer in his thirties whether he had heard Guruji's music. 'Yes, but he could never sing fast taans,' he said. By then, I had listened to several of Guruji's older recordings, which showed that, if anything, he had overdone the fast taans. I was both confused and disturbed by their mendacity. Guruji didn't bat an eyelid. 'I have suffered and have learnt that only a few people do the right thing in this world,' he said. 'Society progresses because of them.' When it came to slights and vilification, he often said, 'Maro goli.' To hell with it. 'How else do you think I remained focused on my music all these years?'

Arnab got to the heart of Guruji's sangfroid. 'The monk-like detachment of Kashalkar's demeanour is, among other things, a consequence of the difficult hand life dealt this outstanding musician—a hand he has played with remarkable dignity and patience,' he wrote.[7] 'He expects little from society by way of worldly rewards or recognition for his services to music. This, in turn, allows him to make music on his own terms, unhindered by how it will be received by the market.' Guruji was, Arnab concluded, 'the Zen master of Hindustani music'.[8]

Guruji's increased visibility after nearly four decades also sparked a jejune parlour game: how did the eldest and youngest Kashalkar stack up against each other? Sundar Vishwanathan, a professor of computer science at IIT Bombay and a Carnatic music singer, simply called Guruji 'Mycroft', the name of Sherlock Holmes's mysterious elder brother. Some fans of Arthur Conan Doyle's wildly successful detective stories have argued that the reclusive Mycroft was even more intelligent than his famous younger brother, but decided to use his brains in private service, leaving his younger brother to help the public. Others contended that it was a tough contest between the two. Whatever the opinions of various individuals, all lovers of khayal should wonder at the fact that around the turn of the millennium two brothers from a remote hick town rose to become among the art form's most accomplished practitioners in the twenty-first century. What's more, another brother, Vikas-ji, also became a khayal singer and dedicated guru, while yet another brother, Subhash-ji, became a music professor and teacher.

The way I liked to think of it, Guruji had used his time away from the concert scene's hustle and bustle to think deeply about khayal's fundamentals, create a unique style, compose, nurture listeners and teach hundreds of people, from whom have emerged about a dozen fine singers, with many more in the making. Secret masters like him nourish the roots of the art form in a way that mainstream performers may not be in a position to do. But in art as in nature, these roots mostly cannot be seen. Ulhas-ji's contribution lies in the way that he has aesthetically personalised Gajananbuwa's gayaki by folding in a variety of meends and elongating the aalaap to produce a serene and chiselled sound. For decades, Ulhas-ji has uncompromisingly presented a khayal idiom in the commercialised Hindustani mainstream that might have otherwise been ghettoised as a connoisseur's delight. He, too, has trained more than a dozen fine singers.

Only once did I hear the two of them performing on the same stage. It was in 2017, when I had accompanied Guruji, Kaku, Mukul and Vishal to Pandharkowda, the brothers' birthplace, whose prominent elders were felicitating Guruji, Vikas-ji and Ulhas-ji. All of us arrived in town one evening. On seeing Guruji, Ulhas-ji, who came separately from Pune, at once touched his feet. At dinner in a dhaba near our hotel, while we waited for our order to arrive, Guruji put his arm around Ulhas-ji and told me, 'Did you know that he cooks well?', eliciting a shy smile from his youngest brother. The next morning, everyone congregated in Guruji's room, chatting, drinking chai and eating snacks that Kaku had brought along. Afterwards, the brothers took us on a tour of their hometown, showing us their old home, the court where their father had practised and the Gopalkrishna temple, where they had sung every year during the Ganesh festival. At around lunch time, the table player Suresh Talwalkar, who was going to accompany the Kashalkars later that evening, arrived. Soon, Ulhas-ji became preoccupied with his accompanist and friend, while the rest of us continued to wander around town.

In the evening, Ulhas-ji, Vikas-ji and Guruji performed to a packed hall, in that order. I heard the common thread in their music but also the differences. I decided to play my version of the parlour game. Ulhas-ji's music was like a swan, gliding across a blue lake dappled with sunlight, gently undulating its graceful and curvaceous neck, before taking flight and flapping its fringed wings in the air. Guruji's style resembled a gleaming black stallion, which begins ambling in a blazing green meadow, gradually starts trotting, speeds up to a canter and, before one knows it, is galloping across the landscape, its mane flying in the wind. The stallion or the swan? Music is not a zero-sum game. The stallion *and* the swan.

◆ Arun, Mandaar, Ravi: 2001–05

MANDAAR ENTERED THE GREEN ROOM ON THE OPENING night of the Shani Mandir music festival in Indore in the summer of 2001. Before taking his place in the audience, Mandaar went to the green room to quickly greet an acquaintance, Vivek Bansod, who was going to play the harmonium for a performer slated to sing later that night. Mandaar and Bansod both lived in Ujjain, fifty kilometres north of Indore. Mandaar had travelled to the festival to play the tanpura the following night for his musical hero, the singer Sanjeev Abhyankar, a student of the vocalist Jasraj.

Mandaar greeted Bansod and sat down in the green room. The performer was a tall, strapping man wearing an off-white kurta with red and blue embroidery running half-way down the front. His rectangular face was framed by a bushy beard. His forehead had a few pink splotches, but Mandaar found him imposing. He was tuning a tanpura.

'Pandit Arun Kashalkar,' Bansod said to Mandaar, who did a namaste. Turning to Arun, Bansod said, 'Mandaar learns khayal but sings light music well. He is a fan of Sanjeev Abhyankar's.'

'So you sing,' Arun said. 'Please play the tanpura for me while I warm up.'

Mandaar hesitantly took over the instrument.

'Sur lagao,' Arun said. Sing the shadja.

Mandaar was taken aback, but did not excuse himself. Unlike Jasraj and Abhyankar, who almost always travelled with an entourage, this singer had no hangers-on. Mandaar sang the shadja. Arun began singing raag Bhoop. After a few minutes, he said, 'Now you sing.'

Mandaar sang a simple phrase, 'Dha___ Dha___ Sa.'

'You have a good voice,' Arun said. 'Sit behind me on stage.'

'I am not dressed for the occasion,' Mandaar demurred, pointing to his jeans and T-shirt.

'Never mind,' Arun said. 'My voice sometimes takes a few minutes to warm up. You can help me out until it settles down.'

It was nearly 11 p.m. when Arun's turn came. The tabla player, Sangita Agnihotri, joined them on stage. She was then in her early thirties and nervous about accompanying Arun. But he put her at ease. 'Bhar ke bajao,' he told her. Embroider the theka. Arun began a nom-tom aalaap in Bhoop. Until then, Mandaar had heard only dhrupad singers present this form. For the first several minutes, Arun went at a leisurely place. A couple of times, he looked back, signalling that Mandaar should chime in. The youngster sang the simple Bhoop phrase Sa Re Ga___ using the nom-tom syllables ri and re, the way Arun had. In a while, Arun increased the pace, generating an overt, throbbing rhythm. Mandaar fell silent. The syllables flew off the stage like a flock of birds creating and recreating new patterns in the sky. After several minutes, Arun again accelerated, the nom-tom now sounding like thunder clapping. 'He said that he might be shaky in the first few minutes and might need my help, but I am the one who feels utterly helpless,' Mandaar thought.

Mandaar could see the who's who of Indore's classical music scene seated in the first few rows—the harmonium player and maker Bapurao Agnihotri, who was Bansod's guru; Shobha Choudhary, a student of the Agra-Gwalior singer C.R. Vyas; Deepak Garud, a tabla player who regularly accompanied Kumar Gandharva; the vocalist Kalpana Jokarkar; the violinist Kamal Kamble; and the Pawar Bandhu, a duo of dhrupad singers. They were all swaying from left to right.

※

After concluding the nom-tom-aalaap, Arun opened Bhoop's second chapter, the slow composition, starting again at a leisurely tempo as the tabla player started Tilwada. Arun sang the first verse twice and launched into a bol aalaap. Mandaar was lost almost at once because he did not know this taal, having used only Ektaal for slow compositions. He was further disoriented because the sam was arriving earlier than he expected: Arun had begun the slow composition with a faster tempo than the ati vilambit, or ultra-slow, speed that Mandaar normally used. Deciding to ignore the taal for the moment, Mandaar began trying to deconstruct the notes underlying Arun's bol improvisation. Singers that Mandaar followed focused on one note at a time, decorating it and moving through it in a variety of ways. Arun, however, appeared to be singing straight notes. 'This I can copy,' Mandaar thought.

The next time Arun looked back, Mandaar managed to repeat one phrase, but it sounded flat and he did not know what to sing next. As is its wont, the taal kept galloping ahead and Mandaar began stuttering. Arun quickly took the reins back and completed the avartan. Mandaar listened more closely, noticing that Arun was singing notes in clusters with stress points and subtle embellishments. Further, he was moving smoothly from one phrase to the next through the avartan and arriving at the sam so crisply that listeners jumped up in their seats. Chastened, Mandaar receded to holding key notes every now and then. 'Since I don't know what to sing, I am going to just enjoy the music,' he thought.

In a while, Arun increased the tempo, sang the second verse and began doing bol laykari. Mandaar had never heard a singer whose improvisations kept coming as if from an inexhaustible source and who had such a ferocious command over rhythm. Musicians in the first few rows were now virtually dancing in their seats. Arun then began reeling off finely etched patterns of sargams, of the kind Mandaar had not heard. The youngster had a gut feeling that this stormy night of revelation was going to be a turning point. Arun indicated to the tabla player to accelerate, moving into more familiar territory for Mandaar, that of taans. But he was left gaping by their variety.

Arun then opened the third chapter of Bhoop, singing two fast compositions: his own, *Jaa re bhanwraa jaa* (Go bee, go), and a traditional one, *Mora jhaanjh* (My cymbals). Here, he did more bol, of the soft and unhurried kind, and sang more sargams and taans. When he ended, it was past midnight.

☙

Mandaar had no time to think about what had gone by because Arun had plunged into raag Shahana Kanada, singing the medium-tempo composition *More aaye kunwar kanhaiyee* (Krishna, my prince, has arrived), in Jhaptaal, followed by his own sprightly fast composition *Kaare badaraa* (Dark clouds), in Teental. Arun then sang raag Sohini, presenting the alluring *Jiyaraa re* (Oh my heart) in Rupak, and ended his recital with Bhairavi, singing his own composition, *Kaahe kini mose barajori* (Why are you forcing me). Mandaar was amazed that Bhairavi could be rendered in a sweet yet muscular vein.

Afterwards, the musicians in the audience crowded around Arun. One was telling the singer, 'Where do you get to hear such music?'

Another man told Mandaar, 'You are lucky to have such a guru.'

'He's not my guru,' Mandaar replied. 'I met him just before the concert.

'In that case you should start learning from him,' the man replied.

After the crowd dispersed, Mandaar hesitantly asked Arun for his autograph and telephone number.

The next few days, Mandaar tried to analyse why Arun's music had blown him away. Above all, Mandaar concluded, the singer's renditions did full justice to the notion of improvisation, much exalted in theory but often diluted in practice. For while it is difficult for musicians to plan a whole raag elaboration, they can create a detailed outline. Mandaar himself routinely did so, rarely deviating from his script. But he knew enough to see that Arun had a pioneer's attitude of not knowing what he was going to find. This was why, Mandaar recognised, in a flash of insight, listening to the musician felt like an adventure.

'His entire body was humming with music,' Mandaar later told his family. 'I have never heard a singer who got wah-wahs at the end of every avartan. People were going crazy, as if they had never heard such music.'

The dulcet melodies of Jasraj and his students undoubtedly sounded lovely, but Arun's recital had shaken Mandaar to his core. He thought to himself: aisa bhi gaana hota hai. Music can be like this too.

Mandaar kept in touch with Arun, calling to wish him on festive occasions and to clarify his mounting questions about music. About a year after the first concert, Mandaar accompanied Arun again, at Indore's Madhav Sangeet Vidyalaya. This time, in the green room, Arun began singing Shree, giving Mandaar a crash tutorial when the youngster said he had not learnt the raag. But on stage, as Mandaar was trying to memorise Shree's phrases, Arun switched to Puriya Dhanashree, which the youngster had also not learnt. After feeling annoyed for a fleeting moment, Mandaar got into the spirit and tried to pick up the raag's key phrases as Arun sang, feeling like a student whom a mathematics teacher had deemed worthy of tossing a difficult problem. Arun then sang Yaman and Kedar, before ending again with Bhairavi, this time presenting *Banao batiyaa* (Spinning lies), in which a woman chastises her lover for making up tales about his whereabouts and tells him to go right back to where he has spent the night. Mandaar was amazed to see how different this Bhairavi was from the previous one. This time, Arun infused his rendition with a palpable eroticism. After the concert, Mandaar met Dhanashree, who had accompanied her husband, wearing an elegant silk sari and well-chosen gold jewellery.

The next morning, Arun and Dhanashree travelled to Ujjain, where Mandaar met them at the Mahakaleshwar Jyotirlinga temple, one of the several temples in which people believe Shiva once appeared as a fiery column of light.[9] After the visit, Mandaar escorted the couple to the home of Ravindra Parchure, a friend and singer who lived nearby. Mandaar and Ravi, as he was called, belonged to middle-class Marathi-speaking families who had migrated several generations earlier from Maharashtra to Madhya Pradesh, a region encompassing states such as Gwalior and Indore that had belonged to the Maratha confederacy. Mandaar's father was an accountant and his mother a homemaker, while Ravi's father was a lawyer and his mother a librarian. Mandaar was learning from the Gwalior gharana's Vishnu 'Bandu bhaiyya' Pitre, while Ravi was learning from Manohar Bhagwat, also from the same tradition, after having learnt from Appasaheb Phadke, a sitarist who had learnt from Bundu Khan, a renowned sarangi player. Both Mandaar and Ravi had a Sangeet Kovid, equivalent to an MA, were local stars, and had won prizes for their singing at national youth competitions.

Soon, Ravi brought out tea for everyone. The conversation turned to music and teaching. Ravi, who did not know anything about Arun, began breezily airing his opinions. 'The idea of the gharana is obsolete,' he said. 'Everyone sings in a mixture of styles. I, too, copy whatever I like from various singers, including women. If it's Malkauns, it's Ajoy Chakrabarty. If it's Shyam Kalyan, it's Veena Sahasrabuddhe. If it's Yaman, it's Rashid Khan.'

Until meeting Arun, Mandaar had listened mostly to Jasraj and his students, but he knew that Ravi could faithfully copy many contemporary singers, not just in short bursts but for whole renditions. Mandaar, who had begun to understand the importance of gharanedar taleem after getting to know Arun, looked apprehensively at the musician, who was listening expressionless to Ravi. Mandaar broke the awkward silence by suggesting that the group visit another tourist sight, the Chintaman Ganesh temple. Mandaar, Arun and Dhanashree waited outside, while Ravi put the tea dishes away.

'This friend of yours who is spouting nonsense, can he sing?' Arun asked Mandaar.

'Actually, he can sing very well,' Mandaar replied. 'He is three years older than me and showed me the way in music.'

Yet Mandaar felt that for once their roles had reversed. He had stumbled upon a whole new world of music before Ravi and had introduced his friend to one of its stalwarts, even if his friend was oblivious of it. Mandaar took Dhanashree on the back of his motorcycle, while Ravi took Arun on his scooter. Watching Arun, dressed in a simple cotton shirt and trousers and riding pillion on a two-wheeler, Mandaar thought to himself: Arun Kaka is behaving not like an accomplished artist who has parachuted into this town from the music hub of Mumbai, but like a family member, a common person, roaming around town like everyone else. Moved, at the temple, Mandaar told Arun, 'I want to learn from you.'

In the end, Ravi again led the way. While Mandaar stayed back in Ujjain to finish his undergraduate course in computer science, Ravi, having obtained a bachelor's in arts and a law degree by mid-2002, moved to Pune to do a master's in music at the Lalit Kala Kendra. Ravi's parents supported his musical ambitions. His father had trained in classical vocal music for many years before choosing financial security and becoming a lawyer. He merely advised Ravi to get a basic degree in a marketable subject as a backup. The Lalit Kala Kendra's master's in music was among the more enlightened of its kind because it admitted students with a first degree in any subject, not just music, selecting candidates via auditions, not their mark sheets. More important, it required students to train under a guru in the traditional way. Ravi approached several musicians in Pune, but none of them had time to take him on. Subsequently, the music department's head advised Ravi to approach Arun. Ravi recalled that he had met the musician in Ujjain, but still did not know much about him. He phoned Mandaar.

'Is he the same person whom you brought to my place a few months ago?' Ravi asked.

'Yes, he's the same person,' replied Mandaar, who had by then visited Arun in Mulund a few times.

'Is it worth commuting from Pune to Mumbai on weekends to learn from him?'

'Yes! Blindly follow what he says. I am crazy about his music.'

Ravi arrived in Mulund on a Saturday morning in the middle of a class brimming with students. After the class was over, Arun told Ravi to sing. The youngster sang *Mandir dekh dare Sudama* (Sudama is awestruck on seeing the palace), in raag Malkauns, in Teentaal, copying Ajoy Chakrabarty. Having never trained under a guru from the Patiala gharana, Ravi ended up exaggerating the singer's flourishes.

'Itne murkiyan kis khushi me le rahe ho?' Arun asked Ravi after he had finished. Why are you employing so many murkis?'

Ravi smiled sheepishly, but to his relief, Arun added, 'You can start coming to class.'

Dhanashree brought out their lunch plates with an array of piping hot dishes, the aroma of whose spices had already wafted into the living room and stoked Ravi's appetite. On the way back to Pune, Ravi thought, 'I understand why Mandaar fell in love with them.'

⚘

Ravi finished singing an avartan of *Jiyaa maanat naahin* (My heart can't bear this) for something like the thousandth time. After eight months under Arun, he was finally rendering this slow composition in Yaman precisely the way his guru had set it up in Tilwada. In the first months, Ravi had floundered. Like Mandaar, he was not familiar with Tilwada. He could not perceive the one-fourth beats in slow compositions, so he found it difficult to sing some syllables in their allotted quarter spots. Arun had then taught him to count the quarter beats using the lines dividing segments of four fingers, starting from the little finger.

A few months earlier, Ravi had moved base to Arun's home, commuting to Pune twice a week to attend classes. Dhanashree had felt that Arun and she could easily accommodate Ravi because Adwait had just left home do an MBA. But in the early months, Ravi had struggled. 'How am I going to imbibe this music?' he had thought. 'I have given many practical exams by copying musicians, but I just cannot copy Kaka. I am standing at the base of a steep mountain. I hope I have the persistence and stamina to make my way up.'

Ravi had come to Arun at a time when students and listeners were thronging to his home. After Arun had returned from Goa, news of his classes had spread in Mulund and its neighbouring areas. He was now teaching on all days except Sundays, when he gave a two-hour performance in the morning. His classes attracted between twenty and thirty students, with double the number of people squeezing into the small living room during the Sunday morning recitals. This initially allowed Ravi to take a backseat and listen to other students. Ravi noticed that among them, Ajay Risbud, then in his early twenties, and Smita Wagh, in her mid-forties, had imbibed many elements of Arun's style. Ajay had been learning for about a decade, while Smita-tai had begun about five years earlier. 'It's possible,' Ravi had thought to himself. 'One can start climbing this mountain.'

❦

After a year-and-a-half, Ravi had learnt to play the dagga by watching Arun do so in class, eventually even taking over from him. He knew that he still had to absorb many intricacies, but he no longer needed to constantly worry about rhythm. Ravi also developed a liking for the nom-tom aalaap. Noticing this, Arun told him, 'You should invest in practising this form and make it an integral part of your style.'

Ravi, by now, had gained a full appreciation for why one could not learn khayal outside the gharana framework. Ravi and Arun often laughed about how the youngster had foolishly boasted about his ability to sing a superficial patchwork of imitations. On one occasion, Arun told Ravi, 'Your suggestion was akin to putting all spices in all sabzis. If you do that, what will be left of the dish? This method kills the very idea of flavour.'

Ravi recalled how he had seen Gajananbuwa's photo in Arun's living room but had not known who he was. Now, as with most of Arun's students, Ravi looked upon Gajananbuwa as a touchstone. He progressed rapidly in all technical departments of his guru's style. He had many relatives in Mumbai, but rarely visited them, preferring to shadow Arun everywhere. Above all, Ravi waited eagerly each week for his guru's Sunday morning recital.

'The ambience is electrifying,' Ravi told his friends in Pune.

~

'Slow down,' said Arun to Ravi, who was doing his post-dinner practice, singing a nom-tom aalaap in Yaman. 'The initial fifteen minutes should have thehraav [repose]. You should not copy me. I sometimes speed up after starting because I am anxious about my voice. I never know how long I will need to steady it. You have no such problem.'

By then, Ravi had finished his master's degree, retaining a base in Pune but spending most of his time with Arun. He began giving his guru vocal support, which was often a dizzying experience. Once, at a memorial programme for Nivruttibuwa, Arun sang Shuddh Kalyan, deploying the full arsenal of complex taan patterns that he had imbibed from the late musician's repertoire. 'Kaka sang for just twenty minutes, but he was like a man possessed,' Ravi told his friends. 'I could not get a note in edgewise.'

As Ravi advanced, Arun kept pushing the frontier outwards.

'You have absorbed the structure,' he told Ravi. 'Now liberate yourself from it. Practise singing the same composition in faster or slower tempos. Experiment with spreading the composition out over two cycles. Practise singing it in other taals. In each instance, think about how to distribute the words over the cycle in such a way that the composition appears to have been set specifically in the chosen taal.'

Ravi began to understand the demands of true improvisation.

'Arun Kaka is teaching me his gayaki,' Ravi told his friends, who were curious about his makeover. 'But beyond that, he is showing me that khayal is a journey from the known to the unknown. To be spontaneous, you have to take risks. Yes, you may end up making a mistake or two. But if you sing only what you know, then you will begin to sound robotic. He has taught me that I have to think carefully about what will create an impact in each raag and each tempo. He has given me the tools to keep thinking.'

Ravi imbibed many life lessons too. Arun came across as eternally cheerful, but Ravi knew that he had faced many setbacks that might have embittered others. 'Whatever happens, whether you get concerts or not, keep doing music,' Arun told Ravi. 'Go deep into it. Aur khushi manao [Enjoy yourself]. Forget about what is not in your control.'

※

In the summer of 2004, after finishing his bachelor's degree in Ujjain, Mandaar went to Pune for a few weeks to see whether he could follow in Ravi's footsteps by enrolling in the same master's course, with Arun as his guru. But he quickly realised that he did not want to study music in an institution. Unlike Ravi, Mandaar could not count on his family's financial support because his father, the only earning member, had retired almost a decade earlier. He also disliked music theory, which was part of the coursework. Mandaar also saw Ravi struggling to get performing opportunities and earning only modest sums from teaching. In any case, Mandaar did not enjoy teaching. Meanwhile, many of his friends from the computer science course had got well-paying jobs or were going abroad to study. As for performing, Mandaar felt that he was trapped in no man's land because he had given up singing in his old way but could not sing in Arun's style.

Arun came clean to Mandaar that he would have to train intensively for at least five years to become reasonably fluent in the new style. Arun did not take any fees from Ravi and would surely have exempted Mandaar as well, but there would be other expenses. Finally, what would Mandaar do after five years? Possessing a hedonistic streak, Mandaar did not relish the prospect of leading the austere existence that he felt inevitably awaited him if he plunged full-time into classical music, especially of Arun's uncompromising kind. He was attracted by the corporate lifestyles being led by Ravi's elder brother in Pune, and Adwait, who had begun working in Mumbai after getting an MBA.

Mandaar decided to stay back in Ujjain to do an MBA, but to stop learning from Pitre and to visit Arun much more often and for longer periods. In this new phase, Mandaar was beset by a slew of fresh questions. Kaka is saying, bandish rato—keep singing the composition over and over again, but of what use was it? What did Kaka mean when he said, bandish ke dhang se gaao—improvise along the lines of the composition? Kaka was saying that the raag is not just about individual surs, but also about phrases. Can I sing in phrases and still take pleasure in sur, the pure sound of the note, like I used to while singing in my old style?

After a year, Mandaar saw the fog clearing. By simply singing a composition's basic tune hundreds of times, he began getting a good feel for Tilwada, for a raag's basic contours and for how a composition's lyrics were spread out over an avartan, the last an essential skill for doing bol work. For Mandaar, the 'open sesame' to Tilwada was Bhoop's *Yeri aaj*, the first composition that he had heard Arun singing. Mandaar also saw that one could certainly project sur while singing in phrases, but to do so required a huge amount of practice and assimilation. More fundamentally, he realised that in order to make progress, students could not waver; they had to have complete conviction that they wanted to sing in the guru's style.

◆ Quality

BESIDES RAAG AND TAAL, SUR AND LAYA ARE KEY CONCEPTS in khayal, as in all Indian art music. These words are used in two ways, one as an attribute and the other as a quality. The context usually makes it clear which of the two meanings is meant. Used as an attribute, sur refers to pitch. A female vocalist might say, 'My sur is A#'. But sur can also refer to tunefulness, a quality referring to the precision or degree of accuracy with which a singer produces notes. One might say that x or y singer has exquisite sur or is very sureela, or tuneful, which is a statement of quality. One can compare this quality to the precision with which a writer uses words or phrases, namely how close to the razor's edge of meaning an author is able to go.[10]

Used as an attribute, laya refers to tempo or speed. One might say that a singer has chosen a slow laya on a particular day. Digital tablas have counters displaying the beats per minute. But laya can also refer to a quality, which is a singer's rhythmic sense or how fine-grained his or her perception of time is. This can be felt throughout a rendition. One of its more easily perceivable manifestations is the precision with which a singer arrives at the sam. Another indication is how accurately a singer is able to determine the starting tempo and the subsequent accelerations, all of which must be conveyed to the percussionist. A singer with a highly developed sense of laya is said to be laydar, the rhythmic equivalent of sureela. One can compare this quality to how a writer paces a story, an equally subtle but crucial component of storytelling.

'A singer's gayaki determines the design and structure of raag, taal, sur and laya. The manner in which a well-trained singer renders the first Sa hints at the nature of his gayaki. Even more subtly, the way he pronounces that first Sa can reveal which raag he is going to sing. That initial Sa is like an actor's costume, which, when he enters the stage, becomes the first intimation of the character that he will develop further and portray using facial and body gestures, dialogue delivery and tone of voice.'—AK

15

◇ Cult

OUR TRAIN PULLED INTO ICHALKARANJI STATION ONE morning in March 2019. Guruji, Kaku and about thirty of us had set off the previous night from Mumbai on a three-day trip to South-west Maharashtra, where khayal had spread like wildfire in the late nineteenth century. Guruji's friend, Sharad Jambhekar, who was popular for his natya sangeet but was also an outstanding khayal vocalist, had come along. At the station, a fleet of waiting cars whisked us to our lodgings, arranged for by Harshad Kamble, a student who had grown up in the city. In Ichalkaranji, his family ran a thriving textile business, whose power looms spun cloth for a range of garments, from dhotis to jeans. His family's looms were part of a cluster of units in the city, known as the Manchester of Maharashtra. The region's musical culture had seeped into Harshad's family, which hosted regular mehfils. In Ichalkaranji, his uncle had learnt from the Agra gharana singer Kanebuwa, or D.V. Kane, who had also been one of Jambhekar Kaka's gurus.

Practically everyone linked to the city's cultural life knew that Guruji and Jambhekar Kaka were visiting, as did musicians in the surrounding region. Prominent business families had vied to help Harshad's family host Guruji and his entourage. The privilege, as they graciously made it out to be, went to a family who owned a construction business in addition to power looms. Outside their massive bungalow, a huge rangoli depicting a tanpura, harmonium and tabla welcomed us. A couple of women performed an aarti for Guruji and Kaku. We entered a long hallway, where women handed each of us a rose and sprinkled rose water on our heads. This grand reception set the tone for the sky-high hospitality that followed. Riding on Guruji's and Jambhekar Kaka's reputations, we enjoyed luxurious rooms, sumptuous food and personal attention.

After freshening up, we trooped eagerly to the Kambles' flat nearby for a round of student renditions. About half a dozen students, including Harshad, sang with aplomb in his family's living room, which was packed with listeners. I was to sing in the next session, in Kolhapur, where we were going next. But I began to consider backing out because for six months I had been suffering from extreme fatigue, but did not know the reason. I had pushed myself to go on this trip because I had instinctively felt that it would prove to be a once-in-a-lifetime experience.

In the evening, people streamed into the Kambles' large terrace. The sun had set, the air was cool. Guruji and Jambhekar Kaka were to perform. The audience included two musicians from the region, Sukhada Kane, from Kolhapur, and Hrishikesh Bodas, from Miraj. Sukhada-tai had learnt from the Jaipur gharana's Limayebuwa and Kamal Tambe, and from Kanebuwa, her father-in-law, who was also Bodas's guru.

After a short harmonium rendition by one of Guruji's students, Jambhekar Kaka took the stage. He sang a robust Shree and a lilting Nand. Finally, it was Guruji's turn. He reminded the audience that the region was a 'triveni sangam', a confluence of three musical rivers, the Gwalior, Agra and Jaipur gharanas, before beginning Darbari, an ocean that he plumbed deeper each time he entered it. He went on to render Agre gharane ka Chandrakauns, before ending with a Bhairavi under a sky sprinkled with stars.

The next morning, Guruji sat cross-legged in the middle of the dark stone floor of the Kopeshwar Temple's assembly hall. He glowed as ochre sunlight streamed in from the entrances on either side. The rest of us sat in concentric circles around him, in awed silence. We were the only ones in the hall of the temple, located in Khidrapur village near Ichalkaranji, on the banks of the river Krishna. Estimated to have been built in the twelfth century by successive rulers of the Chalukya dynasty, the temple, like Guruji and Jambhekar Kaka, was a hidden gem. Far from bustling urban hubs, the ornate temple, devoted to Shiva, exuded a rare serenity. Guruji began singing the first verse of one of his compositions in raag Todi. This one was set to the seven-beat Rupak.

Tero gun g̊aaoon	I will sing your praises,
Tu hi kartaar	You are the maker,
Jagat aadhaar	The world's benefactor.

The meditative melody reverberated through the hall, its stone walls and pillars making an excellent acoustic environment, reminding me of what Chandra, whom I had spoken to early on about Guruji, had said. We joined Guruji, creating an incantatory chorus. He then began improvising on the first verse and the rest of us trailed off.

'Sing one avartan each,' he then said. 'That way, everyone will have made an offering.'

An intimate mehfil, indistinguishable from a communal prayer, got under way. Earlier, we had stood in front of the temple's sanctum, containing the linga, and sung several of Guruji's compositions devoted to Shiva, in the raags Bahaduri Todi, Bhairav, Bhairavi and Yaman. The compositions' beauty and the energy of group chanting had moved not only us, but also the priest inside the sanctum and the handful of other worshippers. I thought of myself as an atheist, but felt the intangible thread of music linking us to a higher force.

After Khidrapur, we headed to Narsobawadi, a town with significance for those in Gajananbuwa's extended musical family. When Gajananbuwa was thirty, he had spent several months in this town on his way back to Mumbai from Mysore, where he had spent time with Faiyaz Khan. Gajananbuwa learnt that the Gwalior gharana singer Ramakrishnabuwa Vaze, then about seventy years old, was in Narsobawadi and went to meet him. For several days, the young vocalist, who deeply admired Vazebuwa, went over to his lodgings to sing for him. Finally, Vazebuwa offered to teach the young singer, doing so for four years until his death in 1945. Gajananbuwa later credited Vazebuwa with having taught him how to analyse the structure of raags. As Gajananbuwa's grand-students, we, therefore, owed aspects of our excellent training to that encounter.

In Narsobawadi, we headed to a temple dedicated to Narasimha Saraswati, a spiritual guru who lived in the early half of the fifteenth century and who the devout believe was an incarnation of Dattatreya. Located near the confluence of the Krishna and Panchganga rivers, this temple's exact age is hard to estimate. Its large compound was almost empty as we walked around soaking in the peaceful atmosphere. After these morning visits, we had lunch and set off to Kolhapur in another fleet of cars, taking along farewell gifts that the Kambles had presented us: kurta fabric from their looms.

In Kolhapur, we stayed at the family home of another student, Omkar Jambhekar (no relation of Jambhekar Kaka's), who wrote lyrics and composed light music. Omkar's grandfather lived in Mulund and had often accompanied Guruji on the tabla. Omkar and his family made us feel immediately welcome in a low-key manner, proving that hospitality can take myriad forms. In the evening, a home recital opened with Sukhada-tai. More than fifty of us—students, Omkar's extended family and their music-loving friends—crowded into the living room, sitting on every available free space, including a staircase at the back. In Kolhapar, too, Guruji's visit had created a buzz among the music community, yet again showing that he was well-known in a certain circuit. Sukhada-tai sang raag Gauri, her clear aakaars testifying to her Jaipur lineage and her rhythmic patterns to her Agra training. Most of us were hearing this fine singer for the first time.

Finally, Guruji began his renditions, of Sar Nat, followed by Paraj Kalingda. In this new locale, freed from our mundane duties, we savoured the music with a special fervour. We exclaimed at Guruji's rhythmic play and interjected with wah-wahs at his melodic flights of fancy. As time wore on, our cries became more vigorous in a bid to keep him going, even though we knew that he would have to stop.

Despite the parlous state of my health, I decided to go ahead and sing. My two-year trial period had ended a year earlier and I had decided to make a long-term commitment to learning from Guruji. I had made modest forays in his student forums thrice before. On the first two occasions, I had sung fast compositions and had done basic sargam improvisations. The third time, I had foolhardily decided to sing a slow composition even though I'd had little time to practise. I had thought of bailing out, when Guruji had called out my name. Too embarrassed to duck after that, I took my place. Instead of starting Bihag, which I had been thinking of singing, I impulsively announced Darbari because I had been obsessively listening to Guruji's rendition of it. My aalaap before the tabla kicked in was basic but without any glaring error. I then sang the slow composition, *Hazrat Turkman*, the one that he had presented at the first concert, and began the bol aalaap.

Back then, Tilwada felt like a jumpy creature that refused to sit still. It kept dodging me as I tried to go after it. I began missing the sam in every other cycle. In this community, beyond a year of training, occasionally going off-pitch while improvising was like a petty crime, but missing the sam was like a non-bailable offence. Guruji was sitting directly across the room from me. I had avoided his gaze for the most part, but once, when I looked up after missing the sam, I saw him laughing. Could it be that someone so gentle had a mean streak? Or was I such a comical sight? I had no time to dwell on the matter. His reaction galvanised me into heightened concentration as I began singing the fast composition, *More aangan* (My courtyard), which he had also sung at that first concert. I improvised using sargams, pegging the last avartan to the phrase in Sarang that Guruji had used but had intrigued me: Re Re Sa ni Pa ma Re Sa ni Sa. Mercifully, this time, I didn't miss a single sam and hoped this would partially redeem me.

In Kolhapur, when my turn came, I looked around the room to see who was there: my fellow students and a whole lot of unfamiliar faces. But no Guruji. As I waited for the tabla player to tune his instrument, from the corner of my eye, I saw Guruji and Kaku leaving the flat. I later learnt that they had received a last-minute invitation for tea from a person associated with the Gayan Samaj Deval Club, a prominent cultural organisation. I was both disappointed and relieved that Guruji would not be there. I told the tabla player which taals I would be using and he waited as I sang a nom-tom aalaap in raag Multani, giving this form a shot for the first time. I then moved to the slow composition *Kavan des gaye* (To which land has he gone?). After the first avartan, through my delirium, I thankfully realised that the tabla player was not playing the fourteen-beat Jhoomra that I needed, but, perhaps by habit, the more common twelve-beat Ektaal. I stopped, reminded him and we restarted.

In the vilambit section, I missed the sam a couple of times. By then, I had become more comfortable with Tilwada, but Jhoomra was a friskier beast. This fourteen-beat taal has a structure of 3-4-3-4. The last beats of all four sections correspond to the same tabla bol, namely 'ti-ra-ki-ta', which began feeling like banana peels. In order to not slip on the first three peels, one should have a good sense of the taal's total duration and be alert for the 'khali', the special beat at the start of the third section that opens the cycle's second half. Still, I did hear one or two appreciative noises from listeners. Merely taking a few steps in the direction of Guruji's gayaki gave heft to a rendition; it made the music sound taut and weighty.

For the first time, I had sung in an unfamiliar setting with a tabla player with whom I had not practised even once, in front of an audience that included many people I did not know. These were gifts that came unbidden when you learnt from a maestro who was a devoted guru and became part of the rich musical community around him. Guruji's training and my exposure to high-quality music had got me at this late stage in my life to a place out in the sea that I never thought I would reach. Like a tiny boat tied to a large ship, I got pulled along.

After the student presentations, we visited the famous Mahalaxmi temple, whose original structure is thought to have been built in the seventh century by the Chalukyas, with later rulers expanding and embellishing the edifice. Although impressive on the outside, it was much more crowded than the other two temples that we had visited, especially because we went during the evening aarti, one of the peak visiting hours. But we did get the goddess's blessings before returning to Mumbai.

Having local hosts had made all the difference to our trip. They had activated their music networks of performers, accompanists, organisers and listeners. On the train journey back, I was on the brink of collapsing from exhaustion, but insanely, my mind and body still had enough energy to register a feeling of exhilaration for having made this musical pilgrimage. I felt that I had, in my own small way, become part of a glorious tradition.

On a winter morning later that year, I walked into class to immediately be pulled into the swirling eddy of a new composition of Guruji's that about a dozen students were singing. More than three years into my training, I could still be blown away by the unpredictability of what awaited me in class. Not literally though. For by then, I had recovered from my weakness, a result of a severe vitamin deficiency. The composition that everyone was singing, in Todi, had a distinctly different mood from the contemplative one evoked by Guruji's four other compositions in the same raag, including the one that we had sung at the Kopeshwar temple. A tornado, this new melody began in the central octave's Ni, fell to Ma and rose to hit the Ṡa on the sam. It then pierced this barrier to caress the ṙe, before slowly descending all the way to the base Sa. From here, it rose again all the way to ṙe, then fell to the central dha, just below where it started. The second verse had the same looping pattern across the whole central octave. This trampoline movement created a mood of intense restlessness. Because the composition began and ended in mid-octave, it left in its wake an unresolved tension. In all these ways, the melody felicitously mirrored the lyrics, which opened with a woman wailing that she was losing her mind without her beloved. By the end, the woman wondered how she was going to pass her days and nights in this state of intense longing. The composition goes as follows:

Sajan bina a̅¹ bhayee mai bawari	I have gone crazy without my lover.
Parilo bhanakawa kaanan more	On my ears have fallen rumours
Unke aavan ki maayee	Of his return, oh wise confidante!
Jiyara jaṙat naina jharat	My heart burns, tears flow,
Rahi mein akelee birhan tarapat	Alone, tormented by separation.
Kaise kategi din ratiya Rasadas	Time hangs heavy, Rasadas.

This thrilling atmosphere partly relieved my eternal tension of having to keep afloat in the class's treacherous musical waters. For me, a part of the pleasure of learning from Guruji came from belonging to a community. By then, roughly four dozen of us were attending class with varying degrees of regularity, while another twenty who had learnt for many years remained in touch with the group. We were culturally quite homogeneous: we were all Hindus by background, overwhelmingly upper caste, mostly from middle- and upper middle-class backgrounds. Most students were native Marathi speakers. But we spanned a huge age range, which I found enriching: the oldest was past eighty and the youngest had just become a teenager. Like any bunch of people, we had diverse personalities as well as quirks and insecurities. Yes, there was a bit of competitive jostling, but we were also bound by a genuine sense of artistic solidarity. In some ways, we were even like a cult. Both 'culture' and 'cult' stem from the Latin root, 'cultus', which has a range of meanings, such as tilling, cultivation, training and adoration. In popular usage, 'culture' refers to a community's way of life and attitudes, while 'cult' indicates a system of beliefs that stand in opposition to mainstream culture, has devoted followers and usually, a charismatic founder. The word 'cult' can take on a negative connotation when used to describe a spurious religious sect whose founder often exploits followers. But in its neutral sense, the word accurately described the community around Guruji.

In the new millennium, not just khayal was being pushed from mainstream culture into a fringe cult. In 2009, the great American writer Philip Roth said that within the following twenty-five years, only a 'cultic' minority of enthusiasts would read novels because an increasing number of people were addicted to the computer, film and television screen.[2] 'To read a novel requires a certain amount of concentration, focus, devotion to the reading,' Roth said in an interview. 'If you read a novel in more than two weeks you don't read the novel really. So I think that that kind of concentration and focus and attentiveness is hard to come by—it's hard to find ... significant numbers of people who have those qualities.'[3]

I was therefore amazed by people's dedication in the twenty-first century to our cult's minority values. Many of them had sacrificed the relentless upward mobility pursued by many Indians from similar milieus. Apart from about a dozen excellent singers who had begun learning from Guruji well before my time, more than half a dozen very capable youngsters overlapped with me. They had their lives ahead of them, but I witnessed the sacrifices that two fine, older and well-educated singers in my cohort were making to pursue music.

Krishnna, who spelt his name with two n-s, was in his early forties when I started learning. He had an engineering degree from a reputable institution and an MBA from the Indian Institute of Management in Kozhikode. He had learnt Carnatic vocal music and the violin in Mumbai and then spent about fifteen years in Delhi learning Hindustani music from Robert Haryson of the Rampur-Sahaswan gharana while earning a living coaching students for MBA entrance exams. He saved on rent by living in a flat's servant quarters. In Delhi, just as Krishnna began getting opportunities to perform, he and his wife had to return to Mumbai in 2015 to be close to their parents. Soon afterwards, Krishnna heard Guruji at a concert and was so impressed that he decided to switch gharanas and learn from him. 'Only in my twelfth year with Haryson-ji did I learn to sing with repose,' Krishnna recalled. 'The Agra style is very different. It has the feel of a celebration. I struggled at first, but suddenly at one point, I began understanding the whole style all at once.'

Krishnna's financial situation was unpredictable because he had plunged full-time into music. His earnings from gigs accompanying Carnatic musicians and from teaching music were erratic. His wife was the one with the steady income from her job at a call centre. To save on rent, the couple lived with Krishnna's parents. 'Last week, I met a few former classmates from IIM,' Krishnna told me one day. 'They had all returned from places like London and Paris. Hearing about their lifestyles rattled me. I felt that I should not meet them, that in order to progress in music, I should remain in the bubble around Guruji.' He did not sound bitter; rather, he was laughing, as if to say, 'Isn't my predicament amusing?'

The other student was Ashish, in his late thirties. He had graduated from the Film and Television Institute of India in Pune, specialising in sound engineering. He went on to work in Bollywood films and serials streamed on OTT platforms. Ashish had a startlingly rich and sonorous voice and euphonious Brajbhasha accent. During his college years in Agra, he had learnt from Aqeel Ahmed Khan, the grandson of the Agra maestro Faiyaz Khan. Ashish later commuted to Gurugram over the weekends to learn from Sarathy Chatterjee, a student of the Banaras stalwarts Rajan and Sajan Mishra. Later, while studying in Pune, he learnt from Faiyaz Hussain Khan, a violinist who also sang ghazals. 'In North India, the focus is on vocalising notes to make them sound pleasing and expressing emotions through lyrics,' Ashish told me. 'In western India, the emphasis is on khayal's technical aspects. Only after coming to Guruji did I begin understanding raag structure and its role in making a rendition flavourful. I began understanding the importance of rhythm. Guruji's style is particularly hardcore. I would say that at least three-fourths of what I know about khayal has come from him.'

To make time for music, Ashish, who was single, selectively accepted film assignments even though he often got paid only months after he had finished working on a project. 'I could have had a much more comfortable life if I had taken on more work,' he said. 'I see others forging ahead financially, but they don't have music in their lives.'

◈ Arun, Vishal, Mukul: 2003–14

ONE LATE MORNING, VISHAL MOGHE WALKED TO ARUN'S flat from his aunt's home a few streets away. Vishal was visiting Mumbai from Gwalior, his hometown, in the summer of 2003, before the start of his final year of college, to look for a guru. The sky unleashed rain in pitiless strokes. Vishal gently pushed Arun's unlatched main door in to see, like hundreds of other visitors, the musician sitting on the floor across the room.

'Come in,' Arun said, pointing to his right. 'Want to clean up?'

Vishal shut his umbrella, washed up and came back out. No one else appeared to be at home.

'You told me on the phone that you had learnt to play the tabla for many years,' Arun said, pointing to his left. 'Play something.'

Arun turned on the electronic tanpura. Vishal sat down, unobtrusively taking in the pink patches on Arun's face, and began playing a peshkar.

'All right,' Arun said, smiling when Vishal was done, and gestured to a shelf on the left. 'Tune that tanpura and sing something.'

'He has an august presence,' Vishal thought as he gingerly brought out a tanpura resting vertically on a low shelf and laid the instrument lengthwise on the floor. He then sheepishly told Arun, 'I can play the tanpura, but I don't know how to tune it.'

Arun tuned it, handed it back to Vishal to play and began singing himself.

'ṇi_ Dha_ Ṇi_ Sa,' he sang, launching into a nom-tom aalaap in Miyan Malhar against the backdrop of rain hammering the earth. Like Mandaar and Ravi, Vishal had not heard a khayal singer rendering a nom-tom aalaap. He was awestruck. After Arun ended the aalaap, he asked Vishal, 'Do you know how to play Aadaa Chautaal?'

The youngster shook his head. Arun pulled the dagga towards himself and began singing, *Aiso na*. On the syllable 'na', which coincides with the sam, he began playing the theka. Dhin-traka-dhi-na went the first four beats. After singing the first verse, Arun began a bol aalaap. The avartans kept coming, one after another. 'I am standing under a powerful waterfall,' Vishal thought. 'He seems to be able to improvise endlessly.'

Arun sang the second verse a couple of times, increased the taal's speed and began doing bol laykari, followed by sargams and aakaar taans. 'I have never heard music with such energy and flow,' Vishal thought.

Throughout, Arun's face and body looked relaxed, as though he were shooting the breeze with an old friend.

'My search has ended,' Vishal thought. 'I *have* to learn from him.'

'You can join my class,' Arun said, as though reading Vishal's thoughts.

※

In Gwalior, Vishal had learnt to play the tabla for eight years, until the age of fifteen, by which time he could accompany local singers. But if they made taal-related mistakes, Vishal did not hesitate to point them out. 'You may be right,' his tabla guru, Ramachandra Telang, told his outspoken student. 'But they will stop calling you to accompany them. Maybe you are better off becoming a singer. Your tabla training has already given you an excellent command over rhythm. You also have a robust voice.'

Following Telang's advice, Vishal began taking vocal lessons from a music lecturer at the women's college where his mother taught philosophy. This teacher taught him the basic outlines of raags and some fast compositions, all from a book. About a year later, Vishal switched to learning from Jayant Khot, who had trained under Balasaheb Poonchwale, a reputable Gwalior gharana vocalist known for his tappa renditions. Khot, who taught at another college during the day, called Vishal over to his home in the evenings when he did his riyaaz. Khot inducted Vishal into singing slow compositions and taught him to sing simple aalaaps and taans. Khot found that, of all the students whom he had taught, Vishal stood out for his control over sur and taal, and for his grasping power. About two years later, Poonchwale himself offered to teach Vishal after hearing him sing at a temple. Poonchwale was then past eighty, but put Vishal through the paces for more than a year by making him sing each composition at least a hundred times until he felt his student could effortlessly reproduce every nuance. Poonchwale had been on the verge of starting Vishal on Gwalior-style improvisation when he was diagnosed with cancer and had to suspend classes.

Vishal, who had a year of college left, had first asked Ulhas whether he could apply to become his student at the Sangeet Research Academy in Kolkata, but the musician had said that he was full up for the next two years with eight students. Vishal had then decided that he would apply to the master's in music at the Lalit Kala Kendra in Pune. In anticipation, a year before the course began, he had travelled to Mumbai and Pune to look for a guru. His father, who ran a kitchenware business, and his academic mother took a lively interest in music of all kinds. They fully supported Vishal's musical journey and allowed him to find his own way.

In Mumbai, Vishal had wanted to take advantage of the lively concert scene, so a few days before visiting Arun, he had attended Ulhas's concert at the Dadar-Matunga Cultural Centre. In the intermission, Vishal had struck up a conversation with a gentleman sitting next to him.

'I had wanted to learn from Ulhas Kaka,' Vishal had told the man. 'But he does not have spots when I graduate next year.'

'Why don't you approach his elder brother, Arun Kaka?' the man had suggested. 'I happen to know him.'

Vishal had not known that Ulhas had an elder brother, let alone that he was a musician. 'What a coincidence,' Vishal thought, 'that this man was sitting next to me.' The following day, Vishal had called Arun, who told the youngster to come over. Vishal had then realised that Arun lived just a few streets away from his aunt. Another coincidence.

'Ma ga re Sa,' a student sang, concluding an improvisation sequence in raag Multani.

'Your final phrase did not have a full stop,' Arun said. 'Musical sentences need punctuation.'

He went on to sing: 'Ma ga re Sa **Ṇi Sa**___ ga Ma Pa ga _ Ma ga re Sa **Ṇi Sa**___.'

Vishal, who was playing the dagga, noticed that Arun had added the coda Ṇi-Sa___ to the student's final phrase and, to underline his point, had gone on to sing a second, longer phrase with the same coda. The student nodded. Arun rarely made students feel they were unworthy of being in his class, but Vishal, who had started lessons a few months earlier, felt that his guru was not ideal for beginners. Arun did not always explain how a student had erred, mostly just singing back the correct version. Students had to listen closely, figure out what they had done wrong and assimilate the correction. Vishal was commuting to Mulund a few days a week from Pune, where he had begun a master's degree. After a few months, when Vishal's friends asked him how his lessons with Arun were going, he uttered a familiar sentence, 'Everything about Guruji's gayaki is difficult. I am struggling.'

No matter how much talent or training students had, most of them found the first few months in Arun's class disorienting, partly because of his complex style and partly because he challenged students up from the level at which they had arrived. Vishal settled on a strategy that he felt would help him get the most out of class: he would just play the dagga and listen. This would relieve him of the stress of having to sing a few avartans, which would have diverted his attention from Arun's singing and from absorbing his guru's feedback to other students. In contrast with Ravi, who took meticulous notes and taped every class, Vishal did neither. He decided that riyaaz was the time when he would sing and check whether he could reproduce what he thought he had imbibed in class and to discover what remained hazy.

Mukul Kulkarni walked into Arun's cousin's flat in Pune to see Vishal sitting on the living room floor playing the dagga in front of the musician, who was singing raag Komal Rishabh Asavari. It was early 2007. For the past several years, Arun had been going to Pune once a week to teach a group of students. After Vishal had finished singing, Arun turned to Mukul.

'Sing,' he said.

Mukul attempted one round. The two youngsters took turns to improvise in this plaintive early morning raag, using the stately slow composition *Bir baamanuwa (My brother priest)*. Arun occasionally gave them tips and sang a bit after each of their turns. Mukul loved the way Arun had seamlessly pulled him into the lesson. After bringing this raag to a close, Arun said to Mukul, 'Sing Poorvi.'

Around a month earlier, Mukul, as a first-year student in the master's course that Vishal was completing, had performed Poorvi for his cohort and teachers. Afterwards, each student had to get a musician other than his or her guru to evaluate the rendition. Mukul's guru was Vikas, Arun's younger brother. 'If you want frank and meticulous feedback, send the recording to Arun Kaka,' a member of the department advised Mukul, who promptly did that.

'Your singing has some good features,' Arun later told Mukul on the phone. 'It reflects some good principles. Give yourself whatever marks you want. But come and meet me in Pune. I come there regularly.'

So there Mukul was, with the blessings of his guru, who told his student that he would benefit immensely from learning from his eldest brother. Mukul sang the first verse of a composition in Poorvi.

Diliya naˣgarawa jasa gaoon	Of Delhi's glory I will sing,
Taiso har pal chhin so hee mein paoon	To always be blessed.

Arun intervened. 'Har pal chhin,' he sang, but at a faster pace than the one Mukul had used. 'In every raag, some phrases are meant to be sung faster than others,' Arun said. 'In bol work, you can get additional hints about which speed to use from a phrase's sound and meaning. The phrase "har pal chhin" has only short vowels that should not be elongated. Also, its meaning suggests that it should be sung fast.'

Mukul sang the first verse again, speeding up this phrase, which means 'every instant and moment', surprised by how much this improved the delivery. He began improvising on the lyrics of the first verse. After a couple of avartans, Arun stopped him. 'Try to harness the theka to make your improvisation more impressive,' he said. 'Place some of the syllables bang on the beats.'

Mukul began another avartan, placing 'ga' from 'gaoon' on one beat and 'chh' from 'chhin' on another. Arun stopped him. 'Good. Now match a phrase with ti-ra-ki-ta,' he said, referring to the string of four tabla syllables that fill one beat and that appears twice in the sixteen-beat Tilwada: at positions two and ten.

In the next avartan, Mukul elongated the word 'so' into 'so-o-o-o' over four notes and meshed them with 'ti-ra-ki-ta'. Arun's eyes widened in the typical way when he appreciated a student's attempt. Mukul sang a couple of more avartans. Arun intervened. 'Of all possible patterns in Poorvi, you should choose from a subset suggested by the first verse,' Arun said, restating the principle of bandish-based singing. 'To be in a position to do this, you have to have a clear idea of the territory that the first verse occupies within Poorvi. To achieve this, practise singing it hundreds of times. Continue.'

Mukul sang. Arun intervened. 'The note on which you end your aamad should match the note on which the mukhda begins,' Arun said. 'The mukhda "diliya na ..." begins with the nishad, Ṇi, so you can end the aamad on Sa, which is adjacent to Ṇi, or even Ga, which has a consonance with Ṇi. But ending it on Pa will not sound as nice.'

Mukul sang a couple of more avartans, applying the principles of sur samvaad, or consonance between notes, that Arun had referred to. But Arun again stopped him. 'The standard phrase in Poorvi's descent is Ṛe Ni dha Pa, but this composition has the unusual descending phrase Ṛe Ni Ma,' Arun said. 'Build one passage of improvisation around this unique phrase and show me.'

'Yorkers blindsiding me in every other avartan,' Mukul thought.

So it went for the next hour. So it went for the next six months, during which Arun made Mukul improvise on the same composition in Poorvi in every lesson. Until coming to Arun, Mukul had, like so many students, mostly copied his gurus. Mukul saw that there was wisdom in imitation because it allowed students to imbibe some core facets of the guru's style, such as intonation, timing and stress points. But now Mukul had to constantly think on his feet. It was scary—and exhilarating.

⁂

Like Vishal, Mukul began learning music early, in Warananagar, a township in the Kolhapur metropolitan area that had developed around the Warana Dairy and Agro Industries. Like Vishal's family, Mukul's parents, who taught English at a local junior college, listened to music of all kinds—bhav geet, devotional music, natya sangeet and some classical fare. His mother, who had wanted to learn khayal in her youth but could not, got Mukul to learn it at the age of ten from a local guru, Nishikant Paramane, who had learnt from the Kirana gharana's Sadashivrao Jadhav.

After high school, Mukul studied mechanical engineering in Warana and began travelling every Saturday to Kolhapur to learn from Sukhada-tai Kane. On graduating in 2001, Mukul moved to Pune, enrolling in a computer programming course and continuing to learn music, from Vikas Kashalkar. A couple of years later, with his guru's permission, Mukul began learning intermittently from the Gwalior gharana's Sharad Sathe, who visited Pune from Mumbai three to four times a year. Sathe, who was president of the Dadar-Matunga Cultural Centre in Mumbai, had been impressed by Mukul during an audition for a scholarship that the organisation gave music students and offered to teach the youngster.

⁂

Vishal walked out of the green room carrying a tanpura behind Arun, who turned around and said, 'Darbari.'

'Tyachi mala azoon taleem milali nahi,' Vishal said. 'Mala yeit nahi.' I haven't yet had training in that raag. I can't sing it.

'Baghuya kay yeit aani kay yeit nahi.' Let us see what you can and cannot sing.

A variation of this exchange was a rite of passage for Arun's most promising students. After a year of training, Vishal had begun giving vocal support to his guru. Now, after three years, Vishal was, in his guru's eyes, worthy of being thrown without warning into the deep end, which, in this instance, was a concert at a venue in Dombivli known for its knowledgeable listeners.

During the nom-tom aalaap, whenever Arun turned back, Vishal latched on to the key phrase and echoed it. By the time Arun entered the heart of the slow composition, Vishal had quickly created a mental map of Darbari's main routes. Soon, he was fluidly taking unspoken cues from his guru. Arun had noticed early on that Vishal had a flair for rapidly integrating new musical ideas. On the way back to Mulund from Dombivli, Arun softly told his student, 'It's fine if you make a mistake. I will correct you. But don't ever say, "I can't sing that."'

'Let's hear something,' Arun told Mukul, who, after learning from the musician in Pune for two years, had begun a more intense phase of training by travelling to Mulund every weekend. This was his first class there.

Mukul sang the slow composition *Tyaj deoon praan* (I will sacrifice my life), in Miyan ki Todi.

'You have the content and are singing in the Gwalior style all right,' Arun told him. 'But you are not making an impact. Your real training starts now.'

Like an expert radiologist, Arun could X-ray a student's music and zero in on its strengths and weaknesses. Mukul took Arun's severe assessment in his stride. He was otherwise in a good place. He had got married in mid-2007 and a year later had become a father. The following year, he got his master's in music, topping the course. As the end of 2009 approached, he had a steady income from working as a web designer, while his wife worked at a state-owned company.

During the group lessons in Mulund, he played the dagga, like Ravi earlier had. Arun continued teaching him after everyone else left and during every other free moment. In addition to pushing

Mukul deeper into improvisation, Arun began working on his voice, which was sweet and resonant but needed more vajan, or weight. 'Practise singing in aakar,' Arun told him. 'Slow down and do long aalaaps.'

As if to compensate for Arun's increasing demands, Dhanashree plied Mukul with his favourite dishes. Every Monday morning, when it was time for Mukul to head back to Pune, he felt a pang of separation anxiety, as though he were, he told his elder brother, 'a young bride leaving her parent's home after a visit that always felt like it was too short'.

On a warm evening in Varanasi, Mukul felt nervous as Vishal and he took their places on either side of Arun on stage. Arun had been invited by the Kashi Sangeet Samaj to sing at a Gulab Bari mehfil in April 2010. Gulab Bari, which literally means a garden of roses, in this context refers to a centuries-old local tradition of communities celebrating the arrival of spring, after Holi, by inviting singers and dancers to perform, and afterwards, showering rose petals and sprinkling rose water on them. By then, Arun and his two students had become an impressive trio on stage, but Mukul was anxious that day because all three of them had arrived in town the previous night nursing sore throats. Arun had found it difficult even to talk.

On stage, Arun sang the first note, re____. 'Ah, Shree,' Mukul thought, the note's pitch and texture being a dead giveaway. Mukul and Vishal began alternately echoing Arun by moving locally around re, down to Sa back to re, up to Ga, down to re, down to Sa. Suddenly, without warning, Arun blasted off with Ma Pa Ni Ṡa ṙe____, bursting into the uppermost octave with one of Shree's most dramatic phrases and a voice that was unrecognisable from the previous day. Mukul widened his eyes and Vishal suppressed his laughter. Energised by the sudden resurrection of their guru's voice, his students found their own voices springing back to life. What followed was two-and-a-half hours of searing music. Mukul saw that the whole audience was agog, swaying. At the end, the organisers bestowed an award on Arun and showered the customary rose petals on all the musicians.

In these years, Mukul accompanied his guru to almost every performance. Arun may not have penetrated the mainstream, but he had his share of ardent admirers. He was popular in Gujarat, partly because Faiyaz Khan had spent several years at the Baroda court, inculcating in the region's music lovers a taste for the Agra gharana. Nandan Mehta, the founder of a prominent music organisation in Ahmedabad called Saptak, was a particularly big fan of Arun's. On these occasions, sitting on the tanpura behind Arun, Mukul observed how his guru was improvising. He noticed how Arun used the nom-tom aalaap to create a canvas of the raag before painting a finely etched picture on it guided by the composition, thus avoiding going over the same territory and illustrating the virtues of bandish-based elaboration. Mukul paid special attention to how his guru took a theme from one avartan and built on it in the next, how he created mirror-image designs across two halves of the octave, how once in a while he projected lyrical meaning. He saw how Arun made the most intricate khayal music so riveting that it caught the audience by the throat.

This was why even when Arun's voice did not fully cooperate, he could hook listeners. 'My god!' Mukul had thought when he had first witnessed this happening. 'This music is really of a different order.'

Being with Arun all the time, at home, while travelling, in the green room and on stage, Mukul absorbed his ideas about performing, thinking and living. Mukul soon began receiving compliments for his singing and for his voice, which had become weightier. 'Here is my guru, who can no longer take his sonorous voice for granted,' Mukul thought. 'Yet he is the one who has done the most to make my voice impressive.'

But Mukul had never heard Arun complaining about his voice, or for that matter, his skin condition or relative obscurity. Only once did he reveal that he was fully aware of his worth. 'It is only because of my voice problems that you are getting to learn from me,' he told

Mukul, who mentally filled in the rest of the sentence: because otherwise I would have been so much in demand that I would not have had the time to teach you. Some might have added: if the ecosystem had been responsive, for Arun's voice had been reliably robust for decades.

◈

Vishal and Arun strolled through Sambhaji Park in Mulund. It was after Diwali in 2010. Vishal, too, was in a good place. He was getting married in December to his college friend, Kshipra. She had also moved from Gwalior to Pune to do a master's in psychology. In Pune, the two youngsters had fallen in love. She was now teaching at Fergusson College. At first, her parents had not wanted her to marry a musician, but unlike Sayli, who had broken Arun's heart, Kshipra stood up to her parents. 'I like going out to work,' she told them. 'I will support Vishal if it comes to that.'

During their stroll, Arun and Vishal began talking about the merits of various gharanas. At one point, Arun began comparing the Gwalior and Agra gharanas. 'Gwalior-style bol can be impressive, but it is Agra that has deeply explored this form,' Arun said, going on to make more observations. Before wrapping up this topic, his eyes began twinkling.

'Since you are going to soon be married,' said Arun, who took special pleasure in teasing his insouciant student, 'you might want to think of the Gwalior gharana as foreplay and the Agra gharana as the climax.'

Vishal laughed as his ears turned pink.

◈

After passing the security check at Mumbai airport, Mukul phoned Arun. It was past 1 a.m., but both Dhanashree and he were awake, waiting for Mukul's call.

'I am on my way to the gate,' Mukul said.

'Great,' Arun said. 'All the best.'

It was July 2013. Mukul was on his way to London, his second trip abroad. The first time had been to Singapore, the previous year, when he had accompanied Arun for a concert. This time, Mukul had been invited to the UK by Ranjeet Sokhi, a professor of atmospheric physics and the chairperson of SAAZ Music, a non-profit organisation promoting Hindustani music. Sokhi's sitar teacher, Dharamvir Singh, had heard Mukul during a visit to Pune. Over a month, Mukul was to hold solo and group classes, lead workshops and perform in a few cities across the UK.

This trip went so well that he was invited back the following year. On returning from his second trip, in 2014, Mukul quit his job with a music portal because he had begun earning more from teaching. 'I never planned my musical career,' Mukul told his parents. 'One thing led to another. I am very grateful to all my gurus, but it was after going to Arun Kaka that I really began enjoying music. Gradually, I even began earning a living from it.'

◆ Weave

OF THE SIX WIDESPREAD GHARANAS, THE AGRA, GWALIOR and Jaipur take an avartan-linked approach to improvisation, whereas the Kirana, Patiala and Rampur-Sahaswan are more free-flowing. One could think of these six gharanas as falling on a horizontal line whose left end denotes the tightest link with the avartan and the maximum projection of rhythm, while the right end represents the loosest link with the avartan and the maximum projection of melody.[4] On such a line, the Agra gharana falls at the left end, while the Kirana gharana at the right end. To the right of the Agra gharana fall the Jaipur and Gwalior gharanas and to the left of the Kirana gharana fall the Patiala and Rampur-Sahaswan styles.[5] In other words, on that line, from left to right, the gharanas appear in this order: Agra, Jaipur, Gwalior, Rampur-Sahaswan, Patiala, Kirana.

What does a gharana's position on this line mean in musical terms? Let's look at the two ends. Agra gharana-style improvisation emphasises almost every beat in an avartan and includes considerable rhythmic play. To do this, the style on average uses a brisk tempo for slow compositions. By contrast, the Kirana style invests energy on the quality of sur and in showcasing virtuosity. Towards this goal, singers from this style tend to choose a sedate tempo, in which the intervals between beats are long.[6] This gives singers breathing room to focus on sur and sound. An Agra rendition appears playful and energetic, while a Kirana rendition comes across as languid and reposeful.

Within the first group of gharanas, there are more fine-grained differences in *how* each links melody to the avartan. The Jaipur gharana uses a lot of off-beat timing, indirectly recognising each beat. The feel of a Jaipur rendition has been evocatively called sarpa gati, or serpentine gait, capturing how melody weaves in and out of beats like a serpent's sinusoidal movement on the ground. Gwalior-style improvisation also involves rhythmic play but tends to emphasise the taal's sections, not every beat. The Jaipur style therefore falls between the Agra and Gwalior styles.[7] Like the Agra gharana, the Jaipur and Gwalior gharanas use a brisk pace for slow compositions.[8]

The Patiala style falls to the left of the Kirana and the Rampur-Sahaswan style further to the left of Patiala. The Gwalior and Rampur-Sahaswan styles, in other words, fall to the immediate left and right of the line's mid-point. This position reflects the styles' histories: the Rampur-Sahaswan was an offshoot of the Gwalior style.

A style's position on this spectrum inevitably influences the emphasis of its training. But it is important to realise that no musician is a pure representation of the model, because even though a singer might be rooted in one style, he or she imbibes influences from numerous sources. So Kirana singers may occasionally choose to speed up and link their improvisation to the taal in order to indulge in rhythmic play, while Agra gharana vocalists, in order to focus on sur and pure sound, can sing extended nom-tom aalaaps and mute the rhythmic dimension while improvising within a taal.

The horizontal line is like a colour spectrum between, say, blue to red. Which hue one likes is a matter of taste, which can be pluralistic and even change over time. How freely musicians are able to move along this stylistic range depends on each one's training, ability and taste.

'I have seen thick books about cocktails that describe different approaches to mixing drinks in order to cater to a variety of tastes. Similarly, a singer who has trained in more than one gharana might blend them while performing, each time in a different way. The singer thus creates a variety of gharana cocktails and by virtue of his training and experience is also best placed to be their first taster and approver.' —AK

16

◇ Boutique

'THEHRO,' GURUJI SAID, PEERING INTO HIS PHONE. WAIT.

He was teaching us raag Shree via Zoom, the ubiquitous video conferencing software that we had begun using in April 2020, following the first COVID-19 lockdown.

I had sung a standard ascending phrase: Ma Pa Ni_ Sa r̀e___.

'Don't elongate the Ni,' he said.

I sang the phrase again as he wanted: Ma Pa **Ni** Sa r̀e___.

It sounded so much better, like hundreds of times before, including in his memorable lessons on Miyan Malhar.

'Ni is not a holding note in Shree,' Guruji said. 'You should only pass through it, whether going up or down, and also not change direction from it. The same rules apply to the treatment of Ma.'

My error in Shree was more like an infelicity in usage than a flagrant grammatical mistake, but it had diluted the raag's flavour. Yet I had heard a rendition online that had stopped on Ma and Ni. Unlike in Carnatic music, in which a broad consensus on raag grammar prevails, in Hindustani music, traditional and heterodox gharanas diverge in some ways. Beyond that, even within the traditional gharanas, interpretations of some raags can vary slightly. Being steeped in all three traditional gharanas, Guruji had a panoramic view of the landscape of raags and meticulously staked out each one's territory. 'Raag grammar across gharanas should not vary by more than about ten per cent,' Guruji told us. 'But I will say this openly: many people today cannot sing even Bhoop properly.'

When we switched to online classes, we divided about fifty students into batches of five each and created a schedule that, in the face of persistent public health risks, we ended up following for the next two years. Guruji adapted remarkably quickly to the new technology, but habituated to a profusion of human contact, Kaku and he began to feel isolated in their flat. A couple of months into the lockdown, they moved to Bangalore to live with their elder son, Ashish. In Bangalore, Guruji did not let up. In class after class, he listened to us with a pair of large headphones, reminding me of an air traffic controller tracking various aircraft on a screen and intervening the moment anything appeared to be even slightly amiss.

In a subsequent lesson on Shree, for example, when I sang a nom-tom aalaap, Guruji swooped down like a hawk to correct an even more subtle but consequential infraction of mine. To explain how I erred, I need to get into some detail. But the explanation is short and reveals how invisible nooks and crannies in a raag also carry its lifeblood. I had sung another ascending phrase in Shree. When notated in its simplest form it is: re Ma Pa dha. To create a specific rhythm, as one must in a nom-tom aalaap, I had repeated each note thrice, thus: re re re, Ma Ma Ma, Pa Pa Pa, dha dha dha. In addition, I had tugged all these notes from the ones above. To capture this, the more detailed notation would be: ^{Ga}re ^{Ga}re ^{Ga}re, ^{dha}Ma ^{dha}Ma ^{dha}Ma, ^{dha}Pa ^{dha}Pa ^{dha}Pa, ^{Ni}dha ^{Ni}dha ^{Ni}dha. The superscripts represent the higher notes, or to be more accurate, note fragments, or kan swars, which I had grazed before singing the main notes. Despite being fragments, kan swars are very important and abound in khayal melodies. In a given raag, some may be essential, others optional. They can greatly enhance a raag's ambience. But while using kan swars, one should not violate a raag's chalan.

Guruji stopped me. 'Don't use the kan swar Ni with dha,' he said. 'Sing the dha straight.'

The dha-s had sounded slightly off even to me right after I had sung them, but only later did I figure out why. If I had sung ^{Ni}dha just once, it would have been fine, because the sequence Ni dha is allowed in Shree. But by singing ^{Ni}dha thrice, I had in effect twice introduced the opposite sequence dha Ni, as shown in boldface: ^{Ni}**dha** ^{Ni} **dha** ^{Ni}dha, even though both Ni-s were kan swars. The sequence dha Ni is not allowed in Shree, even if the Ni is just a kan swar.

This showed me that while students can internalise some aspects of a raag by repeatedly and closely listening to their gurus, registering finer details as they go along, they may also miss absorbing many nuances. Further, they may not be able to execute even those nuances that their ear registers. In other words, they may have a reasonably good mental image of a raag, but may still go wrong while singing. This happened with me all the time. I could tell when another student had strayed from raags that I had extensively heard, but I sometimes missed hearing my own transgressions. Moreover, even when I could hear myself going wrong, as with the nom-tom phrase in Shree, I could not always immediately determine the precise error.

Guruji's corrections and refinements therefore constituted an indispensable complement to learning by listening and osmosis. I understood again why Guruji kept saying that one could learn khayal only from a guru, not from recordings, and needless to say, not from notation. People with many years of high-quality training probably did have the wherewithal to interpret recordings of raags that they had not learnt from a guru. But even Guruji hesitated to do this. 'I have not had taleem in this raag,' he told a listener who requested him to sing Samant Sarang at one of his concerts. But he later told me: 'If I develop a strong liking for some raag that I have not learnt, I may try to imbibe it on my own.' This did happen. Guruji began exploring Viraat Bhairav, which he had not learnt from any of his gurus.

༄

Barely had we settled into our new online schedule when Yogesh's message about the Guru Purnima programme popped into our phones. COVID-19's first wave had not yet receded, so it was to be online. We had to send Yogesh recordings of ourselves singing. By then, Guruji had successfully bent me towards his khayal ideology. The previous year, I had sung Jaunpuri for the live Guru Purnima event. I had noticed that he was pleased because, even if my rendition may have lacked finesse, I had at least caught the spirit of the house style. For the online event, I decided to sing raag Dhanashree, the first raag that I had heard Guruji singing, choosing the classic slow composition. Its first verse goes as follows:

Thhe mhhaaro raajendra	My supreme king
Mohoyo mohoyo	Is infatuated, yes infatuated
Yeh dhheeli nathhawali	With a nubile courtesan.

Because the verse has an abundance of long vowels, it eminently lends itself to bol improvisation. But in one of our live classes, the verse's meaning had sparked some consternation. The verse refers to the nath utarayi ritual in the tawaif, or courtesan, community, during which a young woman's nose ring is removed when she is initiated into the profession, signifying to society that she has now fully entered her life and work as a courtesan.[1]

'Ishaan was asking me the meaning of this verse,' Kartik told Guruji, referring to a talented student then in his early teens. 'I don't think the lyrics are appropriate for his age.'

The rest of us laughed.

'Neither are many other compositions,' Guruji replied. 'What can we do?'

If khayal lyrics are rated like films, a significant number would attract an 'A' label. Many are also problematic in other ways, as participants in a seminar on sexual harassment in the arts had pointed out earlier that year.[2] A couple of panellists had flagged as troubling some khayal and thumri compositions describing the god Krishna teasing his lover by tugging at her dupatta, grabbing her water pot and blocking her way, despite her protests. The female narrator in these compositions often uses the word 'barajori', meaning coercion or force, to describe these encounters.

'Some lyrics could subtly normalise harassment,' I told Guruji, citing one of these examples.

'Uski na mein haan hai,' someone said. She means yes when she says no, implying that the exchange was harmless flirtation. The specific historical and cultural contexts in which these lyrics emerged must admittedly inform and moderate later interpretations. Judging them solely by contemporary mores and terminology would be anachronistic. But it is surely valid to critique the old-world values that underpin such lyrics and to argue that they embody regressive patriarchal norms, reflected, for instance, in the fact that the women depicted in most compositions appear to have very little agency. The men determine how and when they will interact with the female narrators, whose psychological states are tied to these actions. There was also the complex issue of consent. But I bit my tongue.

'Guruji, perhaps you should consider not using such lyrics any more in your compositions,' was all I said.

'That way I am not a social reformer,' he replied.

'You don't have to be,' I said.

Now, many months later, I sang the A-rated composition and sent off my recording.

※

The Guru Purnima programme opened with Omkar Dhumal playing Jaijaiwanti on the shehnai, the raag and the instrument together evoking a festive mood, not of the fun-and-games kind, but a majestic heralding of a grand event. The chat section started filling up with comments: 'pranams to Guruji and Kaku', 'good morning to all' and 'wah-wah Omkar'. About forty of us were to sing over twenty hours spread over two days, with breaks for lunch and tea. As the sessions unfolded, we soaked up the profusion of raags and appreciated one another in the chat section.

It was a wonder that we had summoned the energy and enthusiasm. It was a tense and difficult time. Those with jobs that could be moved online had continued working from home, sometimes keeping longer hours than before amid uncertainty about the economy and possible lay-offs. Those with children had to help transition them to online learning. Families were cooped up together at home 24 by 7, often in small spaces. The sudden rupture of the lockdown had splintered us into small batches. The online event represented a show of unity and strength. Whatever else happened, we seemed to be saying, the music would go on.

Impressive as it was, the event also felt unreal, because 'whatever else happened' was deeply troubling. The government had recognised the threat of COVID-19 only after cases had begun increasing. To compound this lapse, it hastily announced a lockdown, giving everyone just a few hours' notice, leaving thousands of daily-wage migrant labourers stranded overnight in cities without jobs and incomes.[3] Left to their own devices, many labourers crowded into trains and buses to get to their native towns and villages, increasing the risk of COVID-19 spreading.[4] Thousands who could not find places in overcrowded trains and buses began walking to their native places hundreds of kilometres away. The government did not release the number of casualties among labourers who undertook these arduous journeys home, but one estimate of deaths runs into the hundreds.[5] Top health ministry officials tried to communalise the pandemic, and the government used COVID-19 to go after dissenters.[6] Was the fact that we could allow these developments to cast not even a small shadow on the programme something to celebrate? Perhaps in this milieu, I was in a minority when it came to my views about the ruling dispensation's ethno-majoritarian ideology. But what about the humanitarian disaster?

After a few months of working on Shree in the Agra style, my online batch moved to Sampoorna Malkauns, a shining example of the Jaipur style, using its classic slow composition, whose verses go as follows:

x Baraja rahi waahoon yeri woh to Dheet langar chhail chikaro.	I forbid him. But my friend, he is Brash and naughty, yet handsome.
x Gyaana saras aiso natkhat Aalee ree woh to nand ke dularo.	Wise and charming, but mischievous. After all, friend, he is Nand's darling.

The raag adds the notes Re and Pa to the pan-gharana pentatonic raag Malkauns, which uses the notes Sa, ga, ma, dha, ni. This variant completes the octave, hence its label 'sampoorna'. It belongs to a cluster of allied raags: Agre gharane ka Chandrakauns, Gopika Basant, Jogkauns, Kaunsi Kanada and Pancham Malkauns. Not many musicians sing all these raags, but Guruji, being a gharana polymath, did, so we had to learn to keep them strictly apart from one another.

As with all raags in Guruji's traditions, Sampoorna Malkauns unfolded in a series of phrases. He showed us how the Jaipur gharana made extensive use of repetitions of two notes, such as the boldfaced ones in the following passage: **dha ni dha ni** dha ma___ ga **ma Pa ma Pa**___ ma ga Re___ **ga ma ga ma** ga Sa **ni Sa ni Sa**.

'When I was in college, I used to make fun of this gharana as the "ga-ma ga-ma, ma-pa ma-pa" gharana,' he said. 'I did not know better. Later, I realised that this basic motif opens the door to a whole universe of patterns.'

These two-note patterns and off-beat timing created by odd-numbered phrases give Jaipur renditions a unique texture. '*Baraja rahi* also has odd-numbered phrases,' Guruji said. 'A good composition reflects the gharana's ideology. But for such patterns to emerge spontaneously when you improvise you need to have practised hundreds of them. The calculations are tricky, so start with simple ones. It will take time before you can enter Nivruttibuwa's world of patterns, which is like the maze of lanes in Khotachiwadi.'

Guruji was referring to a quaint enclave in South Mumbai with narrow winding streets dotted by Portuguese-style bungalows, which lend it a distinctly different look and feel from the bustling city just metres away. Guruji loved metaphors, which he usually expressed in Marathi. Some of my favourites were:

'You should land on the sam like a lizard snapping up an insect.'

'Unspool a raag like you pull a string from a neatly wound ball of wool.'

'Sing taans like a squirrel running up and down a tree.'

He particularly liked metaphors from nature. He told us about how the iconoclastic dancer Isadora Duncan, whose autobiography he had read in a Marathi translation, had been inspired by the sea. He paraphrased her famous statement: 'My first idea of movement, of the dance, certainly came from the rhythm of the waves.'

Then came the Gwalior gharana, which, as the original khayal gharana, had moulded canonical raags such as Alhaiya Bilawal, Bhoop, Bihag, Deshkar and Hamir. 'Gwalior singers emphasise khand divisions,' Guruji said. 'They include a lot of phrases in double speed. Their improvisations also exhibit swings and have a downward, or avrohi, emphasis.'

Swings are sequences of notes that go up and down the octave, each upward sequence often hitting a higher note than the earlier one. An avrohi emphasis in improvisations means that a singer goes up to the taar shadja with a simple phrase and comes down forcefully with more complex patterns. 'It reminds me of an object falling because of gravity,' Guruji said. 'Coming down has a special power and feels natural. Throwing something up requires unnatural effort.'

Many Gwalior bandishes such as *Chameli phooli champa* in Hamir—whose rendition by a blind musician had charmed Guruji in his childhood—themselves have swings and a downward propulsion. As Guruji kept saying, a good bandish reflects the gharana's ideology. Because we had already worked on the Agra and Jaipur styles, we could see more clearly what set the Gwalior style apart. Guruji kept opening new windows for us, giving us views of arresting landscapes.

After focusing on each of the three streams represented in Guruji's style, we segued into lessons without gharana labels, mixing things up. Guruji began giving us more advanced feedback and suggestions. In one class, I attempted an Agra-style nom-tom aalaap in Alhaiya Bilawal.

'Speed it up a little,' he said.

I did so.

'Slow it down a bit.'

After some fine-tuning, I got the tempo that he wanted.

'You should practise new raags in this medium tempo,' he said. 'In this tempo, in every phrase, one can clearly perceive the length of notes in relation to one another. In a slower tempo, one needs control to maintain the correct proportions. In a fast tempo, one needs to practise a lot to remain in perfect sur while maintaining the raag's chalan. This is similar to a person who has recently learnt to bicycle. He will find it difficult to balance while riding it very slowly or very fast. He will be most comfortable while cycling at a medium pace.'

Guruji began insisting on greater precision in pitch. A pitch gains its identity within a tiny band of frequencies just as a colour does within a small band of hues. The more precise one makes the pitch within this range, the more powerful its effect. Careful and consistent listening to outstanding exemplars and to oneself while practising help in achieving this. 'Pitch is something you have to work on lifelong,' Guruji said. 'You can never take it for granted. It is like exercising, which you have to keep doing to remain fit. Rhythm is different. Once you imbibe it, it becomes your second nature. Also, you can practise rhythm anywhere, by tapping your foot for example.'

I saw what he meant. Perfecting pitch required the physical labour of reproduction in addition to the cognitive ability to perceive fine differences, while deepening one's rhythmic control was more an intellectual process.

'Establish the Sa,' Guruji said during this suite of lessons. 'Keep coming back and emphasising it. Create an environment of pure sound and play with rhythm within that. Faiyaz Khan did this all the time.' Another time, he said, 'The first time you hit Pa, consciously listen to the tanpura. See whether you are merging with it.'

Guruji invited us to send him recordings of our practice sessions and offered to give us feedback. A hugely committed guru combined with technology allowed us partly to replicate the conditions of a traditional gurukul, in which the student always practised in the teacher's presence.

Before we could say 'we're tired of Zooming', the next Guru Purnima programme was upon us. With new variants of the virus surfacing, most people felt that we should go online once again. I decided to sing Shree. By August 2021, Guruji and Kaku had returned to Mumbai. Before COVID-19's aggressive second wave had begun in March, Kaku had undergone an operation in Bangalore to remove her enlarged thymus, which doctors felt had contributed to her recent chest pains. This was one of the few occasions when I saw Guruji looking anxious. Then in April, he had got COVID-19. Both times, we had waited with trepidation. To our great relief, the resilient couple bounced back.

Again, the show went on, this time in the wake of the government's mismanagement of COVID-19's second wave, which claimed a dear friend of mine.[7] On the specified weekend, my sense of dread about what was happening in the country ebbed away as I feasted on the cornucopia of raag renditions. The following day was my birthday. I remembered how, on my first birthday in the gurukul, Guruji had got everyone to sing a composition in raag Bhairav at the end of the lesson. It was a class tradition. The composition goes as follows:

Shukar kĭta allah dargaah	We show gratitude at god's portal,
Tu saheb saanu	To the purveyor at the summit
Uttam janam deta	For this exemplary life.
Dhan dhan parava˘radigar	Praise be the lord
Jin aaye vande par	Who heeded our prayer
Manasa janam deta	And gave us this soul.

Five years later, wishes poured in for me on our WhatsApp group. The Guru Purnima had been a wonderful gift, delivered one day in advance.

―

I began thinking of Guruji as a one-man factory, churning out products unabated with his stamp on them. When it came to raag integrity and gharana-based discipline, Guruji's brand stood for uncompromising purity. Yet he did not produce standardised goods. Guruji's students could imbibe and express aspects of his style in different proportions, depending upon their previous training, voice qualities and tastes, and develop in different directions. The spectrum of outcomes was naturally most evident in his senior students. Ravi revealed a strong influence of the Agra gharana ideology, Mukul and Vishal revealed a Gwalior-Agra combination. Ketaki, Mandaar, Omkar and Sugandha normally reflected Guruji's composite style in toto. Madhavi was unique in her strong focus on the Jaipur idiom. Students could even incorporate a slow Kirana-style aalaap into the opening portion of Guruji's framework for canonical raags. At times, he himself did this. Guruji resembled a factory only in his productivity. Otherwise, he was like a high-end boutique creating bespoke goods.

◆ Arun, Sugandha, Ketaki: 2010–15

ARUN'S EYES SLOWLY CLOSED, HIS HEAD STARTED DROOPING and his playing became as soft as a whisper. 'Guruji, could you please play a little louder?' Sugandha Laturkar hesitantly asked him. 'I can't hear the taal.'

Arun, who had been keeping time on the dagga, jerked his eyes open and shook off his drowsiness. 'By now, Tilwada should be playing in your mind,' he replied. 'You should not need the tabla to keep time.'

Sugandha nodded meekly. About six months earlier, in May 2010, she had moved from Nagpur to learn from Arun. Like most students, she had until then learnt largely by trying to repeat what her gurus sang. She had learnt one raag for several weeks. She had used mainly aakaar, while here bol work was the norm. She did not have full control over Tilwada. It was a familiar litany of challenges. For the first few months, Arun had patiently helped her adjust to the new conditions.

'You keep singing,' he had told her in an early class. 'At the appropriate moment, I will pick up the mukhda and catch the sam for you. I am like an adult who holds the bicycle seat from the back when a child is learning to ride. At some point, the adult, sensing that the kid can balance, quietly lets go. Similarly, when I see that you are comfortable with Tilwada, I will stop singing the mukhda. You won't even notice. I call this "teaching from behind".'

As he had predicted, Sugandha began picking up the mukhda and arriving at Tilwada's sam on her own. She eased in more quickly than many students because, like Mukul, she had learnt from one of Arun's younger brothers, Subhash, in Nagpur. In her very first class with Arun, he had called his brother.

'You have trained Sugandha well,' Arun had told him.

Yet she realised that she still had many kinks in her expression, which Arun relentlessly pointed out. When she sang a couple of avartans in raag Des, he stopped her. 'Why are you using so many murkis?' he asked. 'You should not cheapen khayal by wantonly including them, even if they might appeal to the audience. You should selectively use them, in the appropriate contexts.'

Sugandha narrowed her eyes. 'You are wondering how to decide when and how to use them?' Arun asked rhetorically. 'Well, I will give you a clue, but only once, so listen carefully.'

Sugandha nodded. 'Think of the difference between how a kothhewali and a khandani woman dresses up and makes amorous advances,' Arun said, contrasting a courtesan with a married woman.

So far, this was the most colourful metaphor that Sugandha had heard Arun using to drive home a musical idea. As she progressed, he made higher-level demands. Another time, he stopped Sugandha after she had sung a slow composition's basic tune. 'You are sounding like a child reciting a nursery rhyme,' he said. 'You have to sing the composition as though you are having a casual conversation.'

His tone was uniformly gentle and he often gave feedback in a humorous vein, but his underlying message could be forceful. To get the most out of his teaching, Sugandha knew that she had to constantly think about his suggestions. 'You must listen to yourself when you do riyaaz,' he repeatedly said. 'Pay attention to what sounds good and retain it. Jettison what sounds boring or jarring.'

She happened to come to Arun at a time when the huge throng of students that crowded into his living room had, in a natural ebb and flow, receded. Between six and a dozen people came to the daily morning class. Mandaar, who had moved to Mumbai to work after finishing his MBA, came on weekends. Mukul and Vishal, who had moved back to Pune, also sometimes came on weekends. Ravi had moved to Singapore to work at the Temple of Fine Arts as a faculty member specialising in Hindustani vocal music, and visited a couple of times a year. Often, Arun called Sugandha for a second class, in the late afternoon. She knew that the attention she was getting from him was precious, but she was often seized by a fear of wilting under his expectations, like that morning, when he suggested that she should have developed such a fine perception of time that she should not have needed the tabla to mark the passage of an avartan.

Ketaki Shetye switched on her electronic tanpura and tabla. She was sitting in a tiny balcony facing a busy bridge going over railway tracks. She had shut the windows, but could still hear the sound of cars honking and trains clickety-clacking. From the room inside, she heard metallic, staccato voices from a television. She was living with a distantly related uncle who had retired from the police force, and his wife, a former nurse, in their one-room dwelling in a chawl next to Elphinstone Road railway station in Central Mumbai. Their only daughter had tragically passed away a few years earlier. Ketaki had moved in with them six months earlier, in July 2010, from Rajapur, her hometown in Maharashtra's coastal Ratnagiri district. She was learning from Arun and doing a master's in music at the University of Mumbai. Her aunt was strict, but Ketaki was grateful that she had a place to stay in Mumbai: she could not afford to pay rent from the Rs 3,000 that her father sent her every month.

When Ketaki had walked into Arun's class for the first time, she had been pleasantly surprised to see Sugandha, whom she had earlier met in Mumbai at a selection for a music scholarship. But like almost all students, Ketaki had been intimidated by the radical paradigm shift that Arun's teaching represented. Beneath the class's cosy and convivial atmosphere, Arun implicitly expected students looking to become professionals to quickly grasp the basics of his style. Yet Ketaki felt that she often sounded tentative, while Sugandha, four years older, appeared more self-assured. How was Ketaki to know of Sugandha's own anxieties? Sugandha had also perhaps gained more control than she herself realised.

Ketaki had enjoyed visiting Mumbai to take part in youth festivals, but now found that living in the city on a meagre budget, staying with her aunt on sufferance and making progress in Arun's class required pumping herself up with a daily dose of fortitude. On most days, she travelled up and down the long city to attend Arun's lessons and university classes, picking up meals on the go. However tired she was when she got back to the chawl in the evening, she sat down to practise. That day was no different. Ignoring the grating ambient noise, she sang the shadja and plunged into her riyaaz. Like Arun, she had come to this city to learn music and had found a great guru. She had to make the most of each day.

※

Sugandha began her training in music at the age of five by taking tabla lessons from her father, an avid percussionist and civil engineer who worked for the state-run power company in Chandrapur, in eastern Maharashtra. She also learnt to sing abhangs and bhajans from him and learnt to play the harmonium on her own. Her mother, who had briefly learnt to play the sitar, encouraged her musical pursuits. Sugandha began learning khayal singing at the age of ten, first from Rajeev Kaslikar and then his brother Vivek. Using the music school method, the Kaslikar brothers held group classes, teaching students a couple of fast compositions, a short aalaap and a few taans by making them repeat the tunes after them several times in class while they played the harmonium. They told students to practise these set tunes at home until they had them down pat. Students passed on their notes of aalaaps and taans, unchanged, to junior batches. In these years, Sugandha stood out for the ease with which she reproduced and memorised these passages, but she could not sing anything original.

When she was fifteen, her family moved to Nagpur, where she began solo classes with Subhash Kashalkar. He had trained with Prabhakar Khardnavis and Rajabhau Kogje in Nagpur and had recently returned to the city after retiring from his job teaching music at a college in the Andamans. Sugandha learnt from him for almost a decade—through high school and her bachelor's and master's courses in botany and biotechnology. She also picked up a master's in music. But the first year was touch and go. Her guru did not use the harmonium, which she had depended on until then to guide her singing, and wanted her to play the tanpura. He repeatedly pointed out inaccuracies in her pitch. He did not allow her to take notes, telling her to listen to him carefully instead and try to follow his singing. 'You have to first unlearn many things,' her guru told her early on.

Having passed several music exams and having stood out among her peers in Chandrapur, she felt deflated. She told her parents she wanted to quit. But they were unmoved and urged her to be patient. At some point, she faced the reality. 'I don't know anything,' she thought. 'All these years, I have been singing aalaaps and taans that I had mugged up like multiplication tables. I did not learn the logic.'

Over the next few years, she gained better control over both sur and laya, and began to understand the notion of a raag's chalan. She acquired the skill of attentive listening, which enabled her to at least faithfully repeat what her guru was singing. Subhash excoriated what he called 'meetha gaana', or sugary singing, and discouraged Sugandha from listening to such music. 'If that is what you want, then sing bhav geet,' he said. 'We'll come later to taans,' he also said, contending that these required more brute practice than an application of the mind.

A couple of months before finishing her master's course, Sugandha won a prize at a music competition in Nashik, about one hundred and sixty kilometres north of Mumbai, where Arun was the judge. Afterwards, the two brothers spoke and thought it would be good for Sugandha to move to Mumbai to learn from Arun.

Ketaki was seven when she won an annual competition organised by the Rajapur Nagar Vachanalaya, a library in her hometown, for singing *Keshava Madhava* (Keshava Madhava), a bhajan from a Marathi film that she had learnt and practised on her own. She had sung on stage for the first time, with tabla and harmonium accompaniment. 'She is naturally tuneful,' the harmonium player,

Shyamala Kulkarni, who taught music in the local high school and whose father was the respected poet and lyricist Kavi Sudanshu, told Ketaki's father. 'You should send her to learn from a classical music teacher.'

Ketaki's mother was a homemaker and her father ran a shop repairing TVs and radios, and farmed his own, modest-sized mango orchard. Neither had any training in music. What her father did have was an unusually progressive attitude towards his two daughters and their education. When Ketaki was three years old, he taught her swimming in the town's lake and river. Disregarding what the community might say about a girl in a swimsuit, he got her to wear one. After the harmonium player affirmed Ketaki's flair for singing, he decided to nurture that as well. 'Like everyone else your age, you have to go to school,' he told Ketaki. 'But how are you different? See how parents in Western countries invest in their children's talents.'

When Ketaki turned nine, he sent her to learn from Balakrishna Kelkar, a local singer. Over the next four years, she learnt the basics. All the while, she continued her swimming training, along with her younger sister. When Ketaki turned ten, her father sent her to a swim coach, who was also the local high school's mathematics teacher. But he could coach her and others only in the four monsoon months, when the local lake and river were full. Despite this limitation, Ketaki, specialising in freestyle, became the first girl to represent Rajapur in the state's western region competition. Her father put little pressure on his daughters over their schoolwork. 'Just try to get a first class,' he told them.

When Ketaki was fourteen, she came across a weekly column on Hindustani music in the *Tarun Bharat* Marathi newspaper written by a vocalist called Mugdha Bhat-Samant. 'I like her writing,' Ketaki told her father. Her father immediately contacted Mugdha-tai, who lived in Ratnagiri town, the district headquarters, about seventy kilometres away from Rajapur, and she agreed to teach Ketaki on weekends. By then, her father had realised that just four months of swimming practice every year was not enough for Ketaki to progress further and gradually wound down her training. Instead, every weekend, he took her on his motorcycle to Mugdha-tai's home, sitting through the nearly two-hour class before taking her back. Mugdha-tai had been in the first batch of students in the master's course in music at the Lalit Kala Academy in Pune, her hometown, and had trained under Vikas Kashalkar. Before starting her master's degree, she had learnt briefly from the vocalists Padma Talwalkar and Veena Sahasrabuddhe. Ketaki's father told her: 'Mugdha-tai is the one in Ratnagiri district who will show you the way.'

On Mugdha-tai's advice, Ketaki entered a prestigious inter-school competition of semi-classical and light singing in Pune. One singer from every district was selected, and Ketaki was chosen to represent Ratnagiri. She had just two weeks to learn a dozen songs in different genres—abhangs, bhav geet and natya sangeet—from which the judges could request a participant to sing any one of the twelve. Mugdha-tai hired an extra maid to look after her children and daily drilled Ketaki from six in the morning till ten at night. As the competition drew near, Ketaki found that her voice had gone hoarse. Mugdha-tai nevertheless urged her to take part. 'The experience will be good for you,' she said. 'You will hear what others sing and how they present the songs. You will get to know who the examiners are. The process is what is important, not winning.'

Ketaki had never been inside an air-conditioned auditorium like the competition venue. She did not get a prize, but as her guru had predicted, the experience was invaluable. Subsequently, she won prizes in many music competitions, both for semi-classical and classical music. For the eleventh and twelfth standards, she moved to Ratnagiri to study, living with Mugdha-tai. Ketaki followed a strict regimen set by her guru, and it did not include hanging out with her friends. For her college years, she moved to a paying-guest accommodation near her guru's home but continued to follow her teacher's schedule. As Ketaki had done with swimming, she soon began going to the state's zonal competitions for both classical and semi-classical music, easily progressing to state-level contests and inter-college youth festivals, frequently winning prizes.

In these years, Ketaki began listening to renditions of many well-known musicians in her guru's collection of cassettes and CDs. A year before Ketaki was to graduate, her guru told her that she should look for a teacher in Mumbai or Pune to learn from after graduating. Wishing to learn from a female singer, Ketaki first approached Ashwini Bhide Deshpande, whose recordings Ketaki had heard, but the singer said she did not have time to take on another student. Mugdha-tai and Ketaki discussed other possibilities, including musicians in Kolkata. At one point, Ketaki hesitantly asked her guru about Arun. She had been stunned by his performance in Ratnagiri, but did not want to sound presumptuous because he was the eldest brother of her guru's guru. She did not remember the raags that he had sung, but vividly recalled the effect of his music. The concert had taken place soon after she had begun learning from Mugdha-tai, in the hall of the Patita Pavan Temple complex, which V.D. Savarkar had had built for all Hindus. 'Arun Kaka's style is special,' Mugdha-tai had told Ketaki before the concert. 'You won't be able to listen to such music elsewhere.'

The hall, holding about a hundred people, was full. It was raining heavily. Ketaki watched as Arun, wearing a white kurta with purple embroidery, tuned one tanpura, while his student, Ravi, tuned another. Arun sang a long nom-tom aalaap before the slow composition. He was very animated. 'Outside, it's pouring, and inside it's raining music,' Ketaki thought. 'What is this amazing music? I wonder how he teaches it to students?'

Mugdha-tai phoned Arun, and Ketaki and her parents went to Mulund to meet him. Arun agreed to take Ketaki on, but told her, 'Don't let your master's course interfere with my classes.'

By the end of her first year in Mumbai, Sugandha was supporting herself financially by teaching singing at various music schools. She turned down lucrative corporate job offers and made the crucial decision to make a living from music. She began sharing a flat close to Arun's home with three other women. She found Arun's classes intense but lively. A tabla player came by and often a harmonium player too. She and other students went to concerts with Arun and analysed the music they had heard. She attended his performances. 'His music has a royal feel,' she told her parents. 'There's music that elicits applause, and there's his singing, which puts audiences in a trance so that they forget to clap.'

At his recitals, she saw how he declined to sing popular genres like natya sangeet and bhajans. 'I am ready to serve listeners pure ghee, but they want dalda,' he complained to his students. 'Don't plan your concerts according to the audience's tastes. Also, if you are given one hour, finish in fifty-five minutes. After you perform, never ask anyone, how was my singing? You will yourself know. Don't surrender your power.'

Sugandha also saw that he did not chase programmes and did his best to accommodate those who invited him, including by singing with any accompanist whom they chose or who was available. 'You play how you want,' Sugandha once heard him telling a much younger tabla player. 'I will manage.' Dhanashree later asked him, 'Why should you have to manage? You should be choosy about accompanists.' He merely smiled.

Sugandha felt bad when people asked her whether Arun was related to Ulhas. She felt the situation was upside down, that it was wrong that he had not got the recognition he deserved. But he did not seem to be bothered. 'His music is like his character,' she told her parents. 'He has had no godfather; he is entirely self-made. On stage, he sits like a king. He has lived all his life with an erect back. He will not bend. He doesn't care if he's not in the limelight.'

At the end of a year, Ketaki began teaching music and earning an income. She moved into the same flat as Sugandha, which drastically reduced her commute. After her first-year exams, which she topped, she had been forced to move out of her uncle's home because her aunt had wanted her to go back to her hometown for the summer break. The aunt had been willing to accommodate Ketaki as long as she was studying in a 'proper' institution, but felt that she had no reason to be 'hanging around' in Mumbai during the holidays. She did not know that, for Ketaki, the master's course was a sideshow and Arun's classes the main attraction.

It was just as well. As housemates, Sugandha and Ketaki benefited from listening to one another doing riyaaz. Their flatmates, who worked in various companies, enjoyed the duo's practice sessions, telling them that they were proud to know artists. Dhanashree took a shine to Ketaki, who felt the older woman related to the financial struggles of youngsters from small towns. Dhanashree gave Ketaki cookware and sometimes picked out an outfit from her home shop for her to wear at a concert.

After topping her second year as well, Ketaki began teaching at the respected Sharda Sangeet Vidyalaya, adding to her income from private lessons. She got used to Arun's carrot-and-stick approach.

'I find myself becoming repetitive when I sing an aalaap,' she told him one day.

'It doesn't matter,' he replied. 'What's wrong in repeating phrases? Keep singing them over and over again, and gradually variations will begin occurring to you.'

On the occasions when she failed to smoothly catch the sam, he was softly scathing.

'Your turn came after the others,' he said once. 'You shouldn't be messing up the mukhda.'

But mentally, she began owning Arun's style. 'The laya has to seep into you. You have to create a dancing feel,' she thought. 'How my tastes have changed!'

Into her third year of training, Sugandha felt that the peace that she had made with Arun's demands was beginning to fray. She hit a second wall of dilemmas, more advanced than before but just as disconcerting because she had begun performing in public. She wanted to be confident about what she was doing, yet was plagued by doubt. Although she had got an early exposure to rhythm through her father, she wrestled with aspects of Arun's vision of laya. She was often unsure whether she had picked the suitable tempo for a slow composition, which, as Arun emphasised, influenced the quality of the elaboration. She was never sure how effectively she was embedding the raag swaroop into the laykari—the linchpin of Arun's musical ideology. She was unsure whether she was compellingly combining different layas. She had not become as fluent in bol work as she wanted. Noticing how Arun moved imperceptibly from aalaap to laykari and then to taans, she found her own transitions wanting. As for taans, like Subhash, Arun did not give them too much importance. He demonstrated many patterns and left it to students to practise the sequences until they achieved clarity and fluency. He insisted, however, that students attain a high accuracy of pitch and adhere to the raag's chalan even at high speeds. 'Your taans should be as tuneful, resonant and powerful as Mogubai's and Kishori-tai's,' he often told Ketaki and Sugandha.

One day, in a state of panic, Sugandha thought, 'I have come to a great musician and guru, but I don't think that I am doing justice to his teaching. Overall, khayal singing has become way more complicated. Should I learn from someone else whose style is easier and who does more hand-holding?'

After a couple of months of feeling agitated, she turned to Mukul for advice. 'Yes, at every stage, Guruji wants students to think,' he told her on one of his weekend trips to Mulund. 'But look at it this way: because of this, even while resolutely transmitting his vision to students, Guruji leaves room for them to discover their own paths. His students are not carbon copies of him or one another.'

Over the next few months, practising with a cool mind, Sugandha found many aspects of Arun's music becoming clearer all at once. 'May be that's how one learns,' she thought. 'The mind gradually absorbs ideas but it takes time to integrate and implement them. Until this happens, one might feel that one is stagnating, but one has to be patient. I wish that I had not wasted time and energy bogged down in doubt.'

Three years after arriving in Mumbai, Sugandha got married and moved with her engineer husband to Navi Mumbai, across the harbour. His Tamil-speaking family initially had reservations about the match but came around. Six months later, Ketaki, too, got married to her college sweetheart, who moved to Mumbai to work as a chef at the Taj Land's End. They were from different castes, but both families supported the relationship. Ketaki's father was glad that his daughter had found a partner who fully supported her singing career.

In mid-2015, after five years in Mumbai, Sugandha returned to Nagpur when her husband got transferred there. She felt sorry to leave, but knew that Arun had given her enough matter to work on for years. 'Keep sending me recordings and I will give you feedback,' he said. Ketaki began receiving invitations to perform semi-classical music in Goa and Maharashtra and occasionally classical music. She got meagre performance fees, but valued the experience and exposure. She kept progressing in Arun's classes. She began thinking of Mumbai as home.

◆ Story

NOVELISTS HAVE TO MAKE MANY BASIC DECISIONS. THEY have to decide the point of view. They have to choose whether to tell the story in the first, second or third person. They have to decide whether to begin in medias res, in the middle of a critical situation, or lead up to a crisis. These basic choices influence the whole novel. Similarly, singers can adopt different approaches to musical storytelling. A couple of examples illustrate how fundamental choices create wider effects.

On occasion, a singer might skip the peppy fast composition and leave listeners with the meditative ambience created by the slow composition. The tempo that a musician chooses for a slow composition also influences the atmosphere, including the nature of listeners' anticipation for the sam. If the musician chooses a brisk tempo, then the avartan is correspondingly short, so the anticipation for the sam sets in fairly soon after the avartan begins. If the musician chooses a slow tempo, then the avartan is correspondingly long, so there might be a longer lull before this anticipation sets in.

Another example is the style that a singer trained in multiple gharanas emphasises in a particular rendition. Take the example of someone trained in the Agra and Gwalior gharanas. When veering towards the Gwalior mode, the musician moves rapidly up and down the octave over an avartan, constantly changing patterns, and finally surprises the listener when arriving on the sam. When choosing to hew to the Agra idiom, the musician persists with one design throughout an avartan, because of which the listener can predict the arrival at the sam, which offers a different kind of pleasure: one of recognition.[8]

'My gayaki is like a set of narrative principles for storytelling and the raags are like the different subjects about which one can narrate stories. I aim to tell gripping musical stories and to teach my students to do so too.' —AK

17

◇ Puzzle

'WRITE THIS DOWN,' GURUJI SAID ONE MORNING OVER ZOOM.

'Deem ta deem deem tana dre na,' he sang.

It was the first line of a tarana in raag Alhaiya Bilawal. As the class went on, I realised that the second verse was in Persian, as is the case with some tarana compositions.

'What do the words mean, Guruji?' I asked.

I was known to be fastidious about making sure that all the lyrics I learnt were grammatically correct and made sense, even if the words may have changed over generations of having been orally handed down. I was looking not for authenticity, but coherence. I acknowledged that in khayal the lyrics, spare as they were, were essentially a medium for the music, but I was pernickety like that. Guruji was mildly amused by my exertions and often tried to help me, although he might have legitimately wanted to say, 'First get proper control over the music, then worry about the lyrics.' Instead, he looked on indulgently as I scoured dictionaries—physical, online and human—and tried to make sense of the words.

'I have no idea,' Guruji replied this time.

❦

I looked up an online Persian-English dictionary in which one could enter Persian words in Roman script, but I did not make progress. I then emailed Muzaffar Alam, a historian specialising in the Mughal era at the University of Chicago, a great centre for South Asian studies and my alma mater. The Mughal dynasty, founded by

Babur, a warrior from Uzbekistan, ruled a large swathe of South Asia between the sixteenth and nineteenth centuries. Alam, who had recently published a book on the Sufis and the Mughals,[1] wrote back saying that he was not familiar with the tarana's lyrics, but that its metre resembled the one used in a long ghazal that may have been written by Mirza Ghalib, a celebrated poet active during the reign of Bahadur Shah Zafar II, the last Mughal emperor.

I sent this clue to Mohsen Mohammadi, a lecturer in ethnomusicology at the University of California, Los Angeles.[2] Mohammadi, who specialised in Iran's musical culture, wrote back with substantial information. He clarified that the long ghazal's author was not Ghalib, but the great Sufi poet Abdul Qadir Bedil, who lived during the reign of the sixth Mughal emperor, Aurangzeb. But the tarana verse, Mohammadi further clarified, came from an even older ghazal, written by Mohammad Jan Qudsi Mashhadi, a poet at the court of Aurangzeb's father, the fifth Mughal emperor, Shah Jahan.[3] Qudsi had migrated to the Indian subcontinent from the shrine city of Mashhad in Iran. It is possible that Qudsi's poetry had influenced Bedil. Mohammadi sent me Qudsi's entire ghazal in Nastaliq as well as the transliteration of the tarana verse in Roman script and its English translation.

Daaram dile amaa che dil	I have a heart, but what a heart!
Sud guneh hermaan dar baghal	With a hundred deprivations.
Chashme o khoon dar aasteen	Eyes dripping blood down the sleeves
Ashke o toofan dar baghal	And a storm of tears on the side.[4]

After I had nailed everything down, I announced the fruits of my detective work in class.

'Wah!' Guruji exclaimed. 'Maybe the ustads made a mistake.'

I knew Guruji deeply respected the ustads. 'We owe this music to them,' he often said.

Perhaps that is why he thought the mistake may have come from them. But the stereotype of the ill-educated or even illiterate ustad also had currency among at least some Hindu musicians. This view was perpetuated by Bhatkhande, despite the fact that he had learnt from Wazir Khan, the head musician at Rampur state, who was also a calligrapher, playwright and poet. 'He [Bhatkhande] is ... one of Indian music's most contentious, arrogant, polemical, contradictory, troubled, and troubling characters,' writes the historian Janaki Bakhle. '... All through his writings, there is ample evidence of elitism, prejudice, and borderline misogyny. In the pages that follow, a few of the most egregious examples of his contempt, his anti-Muslim prejudice, his Brahmanic elitism, and his privileging of theory over practice as it relates to music are offered without camouflage or disavowal.'[5] The work of another scholar, Max Katz, suggests that this prejudice lives on in institutions. Katz examined the 'fraught relationship' between the Bhatkhande Music Institute in Lucknow and the city's Muslim hereditary musicians, concluding that 'schools and colleges have participated with many other structures of civil society to gradually marginalize Muslims—in this case, hereditary musicians—from Indian public life.'[6]

Many scholars have, however, debunked Bhatkhande's sweeping assumptions about Muslim hereditary musicians. They include Ashok Ranade,[7] Dard Neuman, Katherine Butler Schofield and Max Katz himself.[8] Butler Schofield, the leading historian of khayal, says that her book *Music and Musicians in Late Mughal India: Stories of the Ephemeral, 1748-1858* at the very least 'showcases ... a vast, rich corpus of writings on Hindustani music c. 1660-1860 that has mostly been overlooked to date. ... Several of the most important and original late Mughal works turn out to have been written by the very hereditary musicians written off as "illiterate".'[9]

I decided to use the opportunity presented by the tarana's lyrics to add my two bits.

'We don't have any evidence for how and when these errors crept into the tarana's lyrics,' I said. 'It could very easily have been the Marathi-speaking musicians who misheard the words while learning from the ustads. After all, many ustads themselves probably knew

Urdu and even Persian. If we had to make an educated guess about who made the errors, it would be the Marathi-speaking musicians, wouldn't it?'

'Yes, that's very true,' Guruji replied, dousing my incipient belligerence.

Having scored a point, I ended my diatribe, but continued to ponder the irony that even if, for argument's sake, we assumed that an ustad had introduced errors, nothing prevented other singers from rectifying these mistakes. Ironically, among some aficionados who were native Hindi speakers, Marathi-speaking musicians, who account for a large proportion of contemporary vocalists, have acquired a reputation for giving short shrift to lyrics even in Brajbhasha, let alone in Persian. These Hindi speakers say that Marathi singers often mispronounce words and even mangle some of them so that they become unintelligible. For instance, many renditions of the tarana had garbled the Persian words in at least one place each: Guruji's, Ulhas-ji's, Apoorva Gokhale's and one on Swarganga.org, an online archive.[10]

Kannada-speaking khayal singers, such as Bhimsen Joshi and Mallikarjun Mansur, are thought to be even more guilty of such corruptions. For instance, people joked that Bhimsen Joshi enunciated the words of compositions so indistinctly that he may as well have recited the railway time table. Yet most people tend to view the Kannada singers' cavalier treatment of lyrics as an endearing idiosyncrasy rather than a serious flaw, because these musicians have the excuse that their mother tongue, like other South Indian languages, belong to the Dravidian linguistic group, while Brajbhasha and Marathi, as indeed Persian and even English, belong to the Indo-European linguistic family.

Other negative stereotypes about Muslim khayal singers are common in the Hindustani music community. In an environment in which the Sangh Parivar was replacing history with myth, devaluing scholarship and squashing debate, I felt it was important to evaluate these stereotypes. 'Since Hindustani music markets and sustains itself as being among India's classical arts and cultural traditions, it risks becoming colonised by Hindu nationalists who perpetuate a politics of othering and hate, especially of Muslims and Christians,' wrote Balamohan Shingade, an amateur singer.[11]

One common notion is that Muslim khayaliyas have selectively withheld knowledge from some students, such as teaching them the first verse but not the second. The 'secretive ustad' is a stock figure. This view also implies that the secrecy, if it existed, is linked to their religion. The first flaw in this generalisation is the large number of counterexamples. Even if some Muslim khayal singers did withhold knowledge, numerous others have proven to be extremely generous gurus, some of whom belong to the pedagogical lineages of the very Hindu musicians holding these views. Moreover, Muslim khayaliyas belonging to one hereditary lineage have often withheld knowledge from Muslim singers from other dynasties,[12] which offers more evidence that religion was not the reason for their secrecy.

But did they actually withhold knowledge? By many accounts, many hereditary musicians were indeed secretive about their art. What was the reason? One needs to examine and interpret the historical record, which is a delicate process requiring expertise, meticulousness and, above all, honesty. My understanding rests on the work of many scholars. Their research suggests that the secretive behaviour of hereditary musicians was partly a response to the highly competitive milieu of court patronage.[13] These musician families operated like Europe's medieval craft guilds, which fiercely guarded their trade secrets. Other factors may also have been at play. 'A deeper look ... reveals that ustads withheld their music for fear that it would be played in lowly places, consumed by ill-mannered audiences or taught to disloyal students ...,' writes the scholar Justin Scarimbolo. '[The] pride that prevented some ustads from playing to the masses reflected an elitism learned from their patrons and students among the gentry, many of whom were Hindu.'[14]

Those who link some musicians' secretive behaviour to their religion make the elementary error of confusing correlation with causation, because it is probably the case that those musicians who did behave secretly were all likely to have been Muslim. This is because, until the mid-nineteenth century, *almost all* khayal singers were Muslim. The few exceptions included a couple of Hindu dynasties with roots in Banaras.

For more than two centuries khayal singers were Muslims because the genre took shape in Sufi communities. Musicians from these communities and their followers were the main exponents of khayal until the mid-nineteenth century, when they began teaching people outside their families, including Hindus, in response to political developments that wiped out their main source of patronage. Because many branches of knowledge in this part of the world were passed down within families from one generation to the next, khayal, too, ended up remaining in the hands of Muslims for a long time. The core point is that this art form would not exist but for the contribution of Sufis and the support of Muslim rulers.

Similarly, it is important to acknowledge that many Muslim musicians also harboured stereotypes about Hindu singers. 'Muslim ustads ... normally regarded Hindu khayaliyas with a certain amount of contempt,' writes Amlan Das Gupta, while describing an occasion when the vocalist and polymath Bhaskarbuwa Bakhale reduced even sceptical Muslim ustads to tears with his rendition of raag Bahar.[15] It is difficult to say whether the ustads' contempt was for singers who were not from hereditary families, who happened to be Hindu, or whether their religious affiliation was the main reason. Perhaps the two are difficult to tease apart.

Another source of heartburn among some Hindu musicians has been the subject of conversion within their community. Many Muslim exponents of art music, in particular khayal and dhrupad, were indeed converts from Hinduism. Numerous kalawants, for example, were converts to Islam through their involvement with Sufis.[16] Why did they convert? One musician told me that they were 'converted by the sword', but there is little evidence for this. Hindu musicians could have had several other reasons to convert to Islam or adopt some of its customs: they received monetary inducements, they sensed that assimilating with the ruling class's culture would be advantageous to their careers, they genuinely resonated with the patron's religion or this transformation happened organically over time. Yet another reason could have been that unlike North Indian Hindus, Muslims allowed marriage between cousins, which was a good way for musicians to keep knowledge within families.[17]

Cultural assimilation to the ruling elite has existed in many social contexts throughout history, including within the rigid Hindu caste system. Social scientists have studied Hindu communities in which lower castes adopted cultural practices of upper castes, such as turning vegetarian and venerating cows. M.N. Srinivas, the eminent sociologist who pioneered this research, based on his ethnographic work among the Coorgs in Karnataka, called this process Sanskritisation.[18] Anthropologist Nicholas Dirks did path-breaking research focusing on the history of the Kallar caste of brigands in Pudukottai, Tamil Nadu, who became kings by seizing land and adopting royal rituals.[19] Such assimilation to the cultural hegemon may even be sub-conscious, driven by subtle economic and social incentives. In the late twentieth century, for example, the United States's economic power contributed to a large number of youngsters in India, especially in urban areas, speaking English, wearing jeans, eating hamburgers and watching Hollywood movies.

※

A further complication lies in the nature of religious assimilation, especially in the world of Hindustani music. The ground reality was often much more complex than straightforward conversion. Many male musicians born into Hindu families later adopted some Islamic customs or married Muslim women, but continued to maintain their previous religious identities, by, for example, creating compositions dedicated to Hindu deities. A well-known example of such a personality was Tansen, the celebrated dhrupad singer at Akbar's court. Another vocalist who drew from both religious cultures was Zaoor Baksh,[20] a khayal singer in my own pedagogical lineage. He was the grand-uncle of Azmat Hussain Khan, who taught my first vocal guru. Zaoor Baksh was a poet of some distinction, who used the pen name Mumkin for his Urdu poetry and the alias Ramdas, or servant of Ram, for his Hindi poetry and several khayal compositions. He knew Persian well and learnt Sanskrit from several scholars of the language whom he had befriended.

In an earlier era, it seemed possible to simultaneously inhabit Hindu and Islamic cultures. They were not mutually exclusive; identities were fluid. This flexibility in identities extended to other religions, such as Sikhism and Christianity, right into the early twentieth century. 'For large swathes of the [British] Indian Empire, devotion to multiple faiths was seen as no more contradictory than subscribing to both religion and science,' writes Sam Dalrymple.[21] 'Punjabi Hindu Khatris traditionally raised their eldest son as a Sikh, while in Kerala the Virgin Mary was sometimes worshipped as the sister of the goddess Bhagvati.' The equivalent today might be the composite culture of many Indians who speak both their mother tongue and English, consume the literature of both languages, dress in both native and Western clothes, eat food from both cuisines, or of Tamilians who have moved to Delhi and speak Hindi as fluently as their mother tongue. These individuals inhabit two, if not more, linguistic and cultural worlds without a sense of contradiction.

We cannot a priori assume which combination of factors was at work in specific cases. Only trained historians, not rabble-rousing politicians with vested interests but no expertise, are in a position to tell us what might have happened in each case, through a careful and scholarly examination of the available historical evidence—textual, linguistic and archaeological. The excellent book *Religious Interactions in Mughal India* has some essays that touch upon this subject.²² Because evidence from the past is often incomplete, bona fide historians qualify their conclusions with caveats, offer an array of possibilities and admit when they are making educated guesses.

※

I have heard musicians also dubbing as 'outsiders' the Muslim founders of Sufi sects and ruling dynasties who migrated to the area that became modern India, as well as their descendants. This is anachronistic. One, migration and cultural exchange was and continues to be a feature of human life. Two, in previous eras, borders were more porous than they are now. People roamed as far as they could and wanted to in order to conquer territory, to trade, to find work or to satisfy their wanderlust. Three, migration was not one way. For a millennium starting in 250 BCE, rulers, people and ideas from the Indian sub-continent travelled far and wide, as described by the historian William Dalrymple.²³ Among other things, this is why Cambodia came to be the site of the largest Hindu temple, as he points out.²⁴ Migration continued even after this period. In the seventeenth and eighteenth centuries, for example, large communities of Hindu and Jain merchants, including Punjabi Khatris and Marwaris, made their way to Iran, the Caspian region and even Tsarist Russia, as the historian Stephen Dale has documented.²⁵ Four, for anyone interested in progress, the touchstone for citizenship in modern India should be the country's constitution, which came into effect in 1950, not what happened centuries earlier.

Indeed, my mission to recover the Persian lyrics of the tarana verse opened a window into a complex and refined poetic tradition and its accomplished cast of characters, illustrating how migration and the intermingling of religious cultures and languages had enriched the music and poetry that many Indians admire today. The fate of khayal in Pakistan under the fundamentalist regime of Zia ul-Haq holds important lessons for India. In that period, the Pakistani state attempted to marginalise khayal because it was perceived as being too 'Hindu', as Yusuf Saeed showed in his eye-opening film *Khayal*

Darpan. But many musicians who either remained in the region that became Pakistan or moved there during Partition continued to keep the music alive on the margins, as the film also depicted. One of them was Nasiruddin Sami, who traces his origins to the branch of the Delhi gharana spawned by Tanras Khan. Sami's rendition of the composition *Lanka charho Ram* (Ram goes to Lanka), in raag Adana, at the Lahore Music Festival, which is available online, is a moving testament to khayal's staying power and religious syncretism.

Whether in India or across the border, in Pakistan, religious fundamentalists' drive to 'purify' culture threatens to stymie the voice and stifle our imagination.

⁓

Most khayal musicians and students whom I know are gracious, hospitable people, admirable for their steadfast commitment to their art in the face of huge challenges. But my assumption that khayal's interfaith heritage would have blunted the edge of the Islamophobia that I detected in some of them was misplaced. It was both a puzzle and a source of anguish for me because when it comes to khayal, they are the ones with whom I share the deepest bond. The late respected Marathi playwright Vijay Tendulkar has shed some light on this conundrum in his illuminating essay titled 'Muslims and I'.[26] In it, he has written about attitudes in his upper-caste middle-class Marathi-speaking milieu, one shared by many khayal singers. 'I still remember a common expression very frequently heard in casual conversations among white-collared adults: manoos ahes ka Musalman?' Tendulkar wrote. Are you a human being or a Muslim? 'This was seldom said seriously; the tone would be light; half jocular, even frivolous, casual … Our upbringing taught … us to shun any contact with Muslims.'

In the same essay, Tendulkar wrote that he was able to transcend his early influences when he encountered the wider world and befriended Muslims, such as the writer and social reformer Hamid Dalwai. Through these friendships, Tendulkar learnt about

Muslims' culture and attitudes. Yet he has pointed out that they, too, harboured prejudices about 'the other', namely Hindus. 'I am aware of the games politicians have played among both communities from time to time and the communal passions whipped up by them to suit their politics of self-interest based on hatred,' he wrote. 'But those games would not have succeeded to the extent they did if we Hindus and the Muslims had known each other better; if we had grown together from our childhood as one community rather than two separate worlds within one nation, within one city.'

Prejudice, as historian Gyanendra Pandey points out, literally means 'already known'.[27] In other words, it is an a priori belief, one that has not been tested against reality. Yet as Pandey further writes, such 'prejudice always appears in the guise of common sense'.[28]

My views, whether on politics, economics or the music ecosystem, stem from the same principles—that everyone in society should have the same rights, that decision-making should be democratic, that resources should be distributed fairly and that powerful individuals should be accountable to society. Just as taleem and sanskar are essential for a person to become a khayal singer, a certain kind of education and further acculturation through a free and independent media are necessary for people in a society to become active, thinking citizens in a democracy. In the absence of this, they are prone to becoming passive subjects vulnerable to propaganda. This education should include a nuanced treatment of the humanities and social sciences, as well as inculcate a scientific temper and critical thinking, all of which foster a healthy scepticism towards authority. By critical thinking, I mean the process of evaluating evidence, opinions and arguments and being able to analyse their robustness to arrive at well-reasoned conclusions. 'The critical spirit,' said Mario Vargas Llosa, a giant of Latin American literature, is 'the engine of progress.'

Education and research in the social sciences, including anthropology, economics, history, political science, psychology and sociology, can play an important role in democratic life because they lift the veil on facets of human behaviour that we take for granted, whether it is whom we marry, what we buy, whom we vote for or how power is distributed in a group. Young Hindustani musicians may benefit from engaging more frequently in good faith with views about art, politics and society that are at odds with what they believe and might at first even make them feel uncomfortable. Such experiences could enrich their music and attract new audiences in ways that might surprise them.

As for Guruji, he repeatedly told me that he was not interested in politics. Quietly but firmly, he did not allow any discussion about politics in class. 'I freely admit that I don't know much about politics and history,' he said. 'I am also open to being criticised. But I don't want to spend any time on these matters. I want to remain fully focused on music. All I can say is that both pandits and ustads are my gods. A musician's religion and caste don't matter one bit to me.'

I had been particularly heartened to see that he had been among just a handful of male musicians older than sixty who had lent their names to a petition that young Hindustani musicians had circulated in September 2020. In the petition, they had criticised their field's 'fear-driven culture of silence' around sexual harassment and had asked for a code of conduct.[29] The petition did not mention specific incidents, but was clearly a response to allegations around that time by several women that they had been sexually harassed when they had been students at the Dhrupad Sansthan in Madhya Pradesh, either by Akhilesh Gundecha, a pakhawaj player, or his brother, the dhrupad singer Ramakant Gundecha, who passed away in 2019, when the two musicians had been gurus at the institution.[30] Yet I wondered whether it was possible for anyone to be truly apolitical, for can one remain stationary on a moving train? But I had to accept it. I also occasionally sympathised with Guruji's desire to disengage from realpolitik. Despite being a journalist, I sometimes wanted to do it too.

❦

Amid mounting global crises that threatened the future of organised human society, khayal had become a refuge for me. Authoritarianism was on the rise, economic inequalities had become grotesque, a climate crisis and the danger of nuclear war loomed over the planet. When I had begun learning from Guruji, I had wondered whether deep down I was actually trying to escape this dystopic world. In the initial weeks, when I rode the train to his home, I would flinch at the sight of slums lining the railroad tracks. How could we as a society allow people to live like this? But soon, I would avert my eyes and try to get into another frame of mind, one that demanded that I put aside such concerns. As his class got under way, I entered another zone. Khayal, the quintessential slow music, helped me anchor my mind in the moment, teaching me daily to wait, showing me that with any deep and meaningful activity, progress comes gradually. 'When we listen to music,' said Alan W. Watts, 'we are not listening to the past, we are not listening to the future, we are listening to an expanded present.'[31] Khayal engendered stillness, and 'sitting still,' Pico Iyer said, was 'a way of falling in love with the world and everything in it.'[32]

Yet at some point, I also began to see in khayal a potential to resist the toxic majoritarianism gripping Indian politics and society, because the genre's very existence represents a rebuke to monochromatic visions of the nation. After all, the turning point in my relationship to this music had come when a Marathi-speaking Hindu musician had sung a composition honouring a thirteenth-century Sufi saint in Darbari, a raag brought into North Indian art music from the south in the sixteenth century by someone who had a fluid religious identity, i.e., Tansen. Like the tarana, the history associated with the composition, this time the back story of its protagonist, not its author, show how migration and diversity have enriched the Indian sub-continent. The composition goes as follows:

x Hazrat Turkman	His holiness Turkman
Jooke bala bala jaiye	May he live long!
Yeri maayee peer mero saacho	Oh mother, he's my true saint.
x Shams-ul Aarifeen	Sun of knowledge
Dukh daridra door karan	Who keeps pain and poverty at bay
Aur roshan do-oon jahaan	And illuminates the world.

Hazrat Turkman, who lived in the early thirteenth century, was probably one of the first Sufis to arrive in Delhi. Historians believe that his shrine is the city's oldest. Three centuries after Turkman's death, the Mughal emperor Shah Jahan built Shahjahanabad with fourteen gates, naming one gate after the pir because locals worshipped a shrine nearby that they believed was his grave.[33] Turkman Gate, the only one not named for the direction it faces, is also, 'the only one that still throbs to the daily rhythms of its neighbourhood'.[34] I thought how wonderful it would have been if Guruji could have sung the composition at an open-air concert next to this gate, khayal's rhythms merging with those of the locality.

◈ Arun, Omkar: 2012–15

OMKAR DHUMAL STEPPED OUT OF A RECORDING STUDIO gripped by an urgency to find a guru. It was mid-2012. In the studio, Omkar had played the shehnai for *Balam Pichkari* (Beloved squirter), a song in the Hindi film *Yeh Jawaani Hai Deewani* (This crazy youthfulness), for which the mononymous Pritam had composed the music. After the recording, Omkar, just shy of twenty years, had chatted with Arijit, a singer who was not lending his voice to the music but producing it. 'Your father has a great gayaki style,' Arijit said, referring to the way Omkar's father, Madhukar Dhumal, an accomplished shehnai player, was able to express nuances of vocal music on his wind instrument.

Omkar's father belonged to a family of hereditary shehnai players from Satara district, in western Maharashtra. After moving to Mumbai in his early teens, Omkar's father had established himself in advertising and films. Like many instrumentalists, to deepen his classical repertoire, he had sought out a vocalist for a guru, Laxman Prasad Jaipurwale of the Kunwar Shyam gharana, and later went on to learn from his student, Rajaram Shukla. In the recording studio, Omkar had felt pleased on hearing Arijit praise his father, but noticed that the singer had not said anything about his own playing. Of course, Omkar knew that his father was a veteran while he was just starting his career, but in the preceding weeks, Omkar had been anxious, predisposing him to read meanings into people's utterances and elisions that they may not have intended.

A year earlier, he had finished a diploma in sound engineering at the University of Mumbai and had begun taking on independent assignments instead of just supporting his father. Around this time, his father, who had recovered from a serious illness, had given Omkar important advice. 'From me, you have learnt how to play the shehnai, you've learnt the technique,' Omkar's father had said. 'You have also imbibed the music that I have learnt from my vocalist gurus. But don't rely only on that. You need to widen your perspective, whether it is via deepening the gayaki ang or something else. Go find a guru, the way I found my own gurus. Try to create your own style. Make your way in music on your own steam.'

Omkar, too, did not want to end up in his father's shadow, but how was he to go about finding a guru? He considered approaching singers popular in his circle. Reflecting the post-1990s trend of heterodox gharanas gaining popularity with the masses because of their relative accessibility, these singers belonged predominantly to the Kirana, Patiala and Rampur-Sahaswan styles as well as allied ones such as the Banaras and Mewati traditions. Omkar ruled out Rampur-Sahaswan's Rashid Khan and the Banaras style's Mishra brothers because they did not live in Mumbai. He sent feelers to Jasraj, of the Mewati style, who did live in Mumbai, but did not hear back. He then contemplated contacting the celebrated flautist Hariprasad Chaurasia, also a Mumbai resident, because he had ushered in several innovations: he had adapted the rhythmic jhala from the string instrument repertoire to the bamboo flute and had created a new fingering technique that allowed him to play raags such as Bhatiyar and Lalit, which were otherwise difficult to render on the flute. As a wind instrumentalist, Omkar also felt that he had a better chance of catching Chaurasia's attention. Yet he kept postponing getting in touch because, deep down, for reasons that he could not articulate to himself, he wanted to learn from a vocalist. As Omkar headed home from the recording studio in Oshiwara, a locality in north-western Mumbai that is a film music hub, he thought to himself: 'A whole year has passed since my father advised me to find a guru, but I still don't have one.'

Like a desperate student who, having begun preparing late for an exam, begins to concentrate on the relevant subject matter with sudden intensity, within a week Omkar recovered from his memory's netherworld a lead that his father had given him several months earlier.

⁂

'Play something for ten minutes,' Arun said.

Omkar brought his shehnai out of its case, fixed the bamboo reed at its mouth and played raag Gurjari Todi.

'All right,' Arun said afterwards. 'Your raag grammar needs refining and your taans need to be much clearer. But you can start coming. I hold class in the mornings.'

Several months earlier, Omkar's father had given him Arun's phone number. 'You could try Arun Kashalkar,' he had told Omkar. 'But know that he is a deep musician.'

Omkar had ignored the recommendation because he had not heard of the vocalist. His father did not pursue the matter because he wanted his son to show some initiative. But after the recording at Pritam's studio, Omkar, at his wit's end, had contacted Prasad Chavan, a cousin who played the tabla and was much more clued into the classical music scene than he was. 'As you know, I have been looking for a guru,' Omkar told Prasad. 'My father suggested Arun Kashalkar. Do you know anything about him?'

'Do I know?' Prasad replied, his eyes popping out. 'You should jump at the chance to learn from him. He is a treasure house of musical knowledge. There are many excellent musicians, but there is no one at his level. He's also a loving teacher, very down-to-earth. I know someone who has been his student for many years. I could ask him to talk to Arun Kaka.'

'Yes, go ahead,' Omkar said.

Omkar found only one scratchy clip of Arun's online, of him singing Yaman. Omkar had not come across any concerts featuring Arun, while he knew that his younger brother, Ulhas, regularly gave public performances. Feeling that signing up with the wrong guru could be fatal to his career, Omkar dilly-dallied, until Prasad called him. 'My friend says you haven't yet called Arun Kaka,' Prasad admonished Omkar. 'What are you waiting for? Just make an appointment. I will come with you.'

Jolted by the reprimand, Omkar phoned Arun, and there he was that morning, accompanied by Prasad. By then, Omkar had learnt that at an event in 1992, his father and Arun had performed one after another. But Omkar did not tell Arun that he was Madhukar Dhumal's son. 'I don't want to piggyback on my father's reputation,' Omkar thought.

As he brought out a coconut and garland from his bag to give the musician to formalise the start of his training, he thought: 'My instincts tell me that I am doing the right thing.' Having worked from a young age with a variety of individuals, Omkar had learnt to listen to his gut feelings. As Omkar tried to garland Arun, the musician pointed to a cupboard shelf on his left. 'Put it over that photo instead,' he said.

On the shelf was a shrine with an image of Swami Samarth, a spiritual leader from the Dattatreya tradition who lived in the second half of the nineteenth century, whom Omkar, too, revered. It was another sign.

Like almost every other student, Omkar spent the first six months in class in a state of utter confusion. His father's gurus had written everything down, right from a composition's lyrics and notation to outlines of a raag's aalaap and taans, notes which Omkar's father had later used to teach him. In the new class, for months, he merely listened to Arun as he sang compositions, the chalan of various raags, corrected others and intermittently performed. He listened to senior students, Mandaar, Sugandha and Ketaki. 'One's ear and concentration have to be very sharp,' Omkar thought. 'I have to be patient.'

Omkar took notes, decoded them at home and tried to play the phrases on his instrument. He listened again and again to his recordings of lessons. He began to perceive the magnitude of Arun's style. Omkar then asked himself a question that nagged many students who came to Arun: 'What was I doing for all these years?'

If Omkar shared many students' sense of loss at not having discovered Arun earlier, he was also among those who had the grit to stay the course and the foundational training to grasp the musician's ideas. Omkar's father, believing that playing the tabla was an important skill for any musician, one that he regretted not having acquired himself, had started his son off at the age of five with Madhav Daté, a student of the tabla maestro Nizamuddin Khan. Omkar learnt from Daté for six years. At the age of nine, again nudged by his father, he began learning to play the piano from Manik Patel, practising on his keyboard what she taught at her home. Omkar's father had felt that his son acquiring a basic knowledge of Western classical music would be an asset for working in films. Omkar learnt from Patel for four years. At the age of ten, he also began learning to play the shehnai from his father, although at that time he had no special liking for it, partly because he had heard his father say that some people accorded a low status to the instrument and looked down on its practitioners.

Around this time, came a thunderbolt: his father was diagnosed with cancer. As if sent by a particularly malevolent force, the illness hit his father where it most mattered: in the oral cavity. Omkar's mother was a housewife, while his only sibling, his younger sister, was studying. His father was essentially a freelancer. If he could not play, his income immediately dried up. The family could not afford medical treatment, so they cobbled together funds from several philanthropic organisations. The Dhumals went through a precarious few years during which Omkar's father underwent chemotherapy and two operations. The disease kept returning. The doctor finally suggested a third, more aggressive, operation that would entail excising a part of Omkar's father's left cheekbone. Omkar was devastated when he walked into the hospital for the first time after the operation: his father's left cheek was stitched up and he was strapped to a chair that was hooked up to a large machine.

During these years of turmoil, Omkar began practising the shehnai with a new sense of purpose. But could his father ever teach him again? Having lost parts of one cheekbone, he could not initially latch on to the reed. He gave Omkar verbal instructions, but his son realised that learning from a disabled artist was a huge challenge. Gradually, showing superhuman determination, his father found ways to compensate for the missing bone and began playing again. Incredibly, even before his stitches had fully healed, he was putting in two hours of riyaaz, half of his earlier quota, and even began accepting work. On these assignments, Omkar took over when his father found it too painful to continue playing.

Omkar was aware that he had begun rigorous riyaaz much later than most master instrumentalists, who start as early as four and five years of age. Fuelled by grief and a feeling that he had to make up for his late start, Omkar began astonishing his father with the speed of his progress.

―※―

About two years into his training with Arun, Omkar walked into class one day to discover that his guru was teaching Jogkauns. Omkar did not know the raag, but had by then become blasé about what he might encounter in class. That day, Arun asked him to stay back. 'My senior students have been recording themselves singing my compositions for a book and CD that we want to release,' he told Omkar. 'But these compositions need to be carefully edited to snip out unnecessary pauses, repetitions and the odd error. There will be about one hundred and fifty compositions, so it's a lot of work. You will have to listen to each composition numerous times. But I think you will also benefit enormously from editing them.'

After taking up the marathon task, Omkar began visiting Arun more often to discuss the edits. After the business was done, Arun began giving Omkar solo classes. This went on for months. As Arun had predicted, Omkar found his understanding accelerating. During the editing sessions, Omkar heard a recording of Arun's Pancham. 'This is almost unreal,' he thought. 'The sur, the laya, the power.'

Many months later, accompanied by a friend, Omkar was driving when he pressed his MP4 player intending to listen to jazz. But he made a wrong selection and instead heard the voice of a male khayal vocalist blasting out of the speaker. It was the Gwalior gharana's Yashwantbuwa Joshi singing a composition in raag Basant, set to Ektaal. The taal sounded as though it had been shot out of a cannon: dhin dhin dha trak ... 'What force, what rhythm, what a voice,' Omkar thought.

He and his friend looked at each other in stupefaction. 'One can get pumped up by this the way many people do while listening to electronic dance music,' Omkar told his friend.

He listened obsessively to this Basant and other renditions by Yashwantbuwa. This opened the floodgates. Omkar moved to singers in Arun's family tree, beginning with the fountainhead, Gajananbuwa. Arun rarely told students whom to listen to, but they got the implicit message from the musicians he mentioned in class as inspirations for particular melodic passages or rhythmic patterns that he had sung. Omkar went on to listen to Babanrao and Vilayat Hussain Khan. He began to see the varied origins of Arun's fused style. Omkar was still too intimidated to listen to Faiyaz Khan and Khadim Hussain Khan, deciding that he would get to them later. 'There's a bifurcation in Hindustani music between this avartan-wallah gaana with strict raag grammar and the other styles,' he thought, becoming aware that he had crossed over to the other side when he began to find it difficult to listen to raag renditions that were stylistically not in the first group.

Omkar found that he had to invent new ways of playing because the mechanisms that he had learnt until then were not adequate for Arun's style. As he began translating Arun's gayaki into the shehnai's language, his father, naturally, noticed his son expressing a new vision of music in a novel shehnai accent. Omkar's playing was beginning to reflect a greater influence of vocal music than his father's. Omkar suspected that his father felt proud but also a twinge of regret that his son was leaving his music behind. Omkar did not broach the topic. Why poke around in a sensitive spot?

Obviously, Arun, too, heard the new sound emerging from Omkar's shehnai. As a guru, he was pleased, but he also had some advice. 'Your playing has become too vocal-oriented,' he told Omkar. 'You should incorporate some purely instrumental techniques into your presentations. Every instrument has unique capabilities and can produce special sounds. You should also incorporate some aspects of Bismillah Khan's techniques into your playing, especially the ones he uses to play semi-classical forms like the kajri, chaiti and thumri.'

The youngster had himself begun realising the limits of replicating Arun's style on instruments because they could not express the beauty of bol work, which was such a big part of his guru's idiom. Omkar knew that he had to inject variety into his playing in other ways, eventually perhaps by incorporating some elements of Carnatic rhythm. Furthermore, Omkar knew that the shehnai, in its current form, had some limitations. A shehnai player produced various notes by closing one or more holes along the instrument's body. But in the lower octave, the shehnai had just one hole from which the player had to produce five notes, namely Sa, Ṇi, ṇi, Ḍha, ḍha, purely by varying the blowing technique and embouchure, which is the manner of applying the mouth to the mouthpiece. This limitation made playing some raags, such as Shree and Todi, challenging.

Omkar began ruing the fact that Indian instruments had not evolved over the centuries as much as Western instruments had. After starting to learn the alto saxophone from Luke Pereira in early 2015, Omkar began researching the history and evolution of Western instruments. Omkar had become intrigued by Western instruments as a child because his maternal grandfather had been a clarinet player in Mumbai who performed in a brass band and provided background music for abhangs and film songs. Omkar decided that he would himself study the process of making a shehnai and explore ways to enhance the instrument. As the year drew to a close, he also knew that he would continue going to Arun to keep drawing from his seemingly bottomless well of musical knowledge.

◆ Word

THE MAJORITY OF KHAYAL SONGS USE A HINDI DIALECT that most people call Brajbhasha, a language spoken in the Braj region in western Uttar Pradesh, where Lord Krishna is believed to have lived. But in reality, this dialect, is 'neither the classical Braj of [the sixteenth-century devotional poet] Surdas nor the modern dialect which is spoken in the region of Mathura,' writes Lalita du Perron, an expert on khayal and thumri lyrics.[35] In reality, khayal lyrics use an artificial language not spoken by any community but that incorporate lexical and grammatical elements from many Hindi dialects.[36] This blend reflects alterations made by the various communities who took to khayal as it spread over time to different parts of the country. For simplicity, however, I have referred to this language throughout just as Brajbhasha. Some compositions also use versions of Marwari and Punjabi, while some taranas have Persian lyrics.

Whatever the language, khayal's lyrics are primarily a vehicle for melody and rhythm. 'The linguistic component is not the principal feature of the khayal bandish: [its] musical importance lies in the way it integrates and concretizes the abstract theoretical notions on which Hindustani music is based,' writes Amlan Das Gupta.[37] Sheila Dhar says that 'the presentation of a khayal is not the rendering of a song, for here it is not the words that are set to music but almost a reverse process.'[38] This is why khayal lyrics use sounds that are 'suitable for singing', such as many open vowels and dental consonants, and not many conjoined consonants, says du Perron.[39] Dental consonants such as 'th' and 'n' are softer than conjoined ones such as 'kr' and 'gr'.

Khayal singers use the composition mainly to explore a raag within the parameters of a taal. This goal occupies the bulk of singers' training, practice and performance. Singers who use lyrics instead of aakaar to improvise, however, do try to preserve a sentence's grammatical structure and try to pronounce the words aesthetically to enhance the overall effect. For brief spells, these singers may also choose to foreground the meaning of some phrases or lines.

Most khayal lyrics focus on romantic love. Religious devotion and nature are other common themes. In the love songs, the singer is almost always a woman, often pining for a fickle lover or complaining about her mother-in-law and sister-in-law. Lord Krishna is a central figure in many songs. Many people believe that khayal compositions, comprising all of two to four lines, do not have much literary value. Du Perron, too, writes that khayal lyrics have 'no life as independent items of poetry outside of musical performance'.[40] But they nevertheless deserve to be viewed as a special kind of poetry, she says. The strength of the lyrics, she says, 'lies in their brevity and allusiveness: a [khayal composition] tells a story of a thousand words in four lines of poetry.'[41]

The language and subject matter of khayal compositions evoke a culture that resonates with many listeners. 'The picture a khayal song paints is already there in the pan-Indian collective consciousness; the song merely reminds the listener of this picture,' du Perron writes. 'The song works its magic by inspiring identification.'[42] Nevertheless, because a singer's central concern is to elaborate a raag, even those who don't understand the lyrics or do not pay attention to it can still derive a lot of enjoyment from a rendition.

At the same time, because khayal lyrics can subliminally exert their influence, some young khayal vocalists want to broaden their scope. Finding the standard subjects to be limiting, a few of them are composing bandishes that express sentiments relevant to their lives and that revolve around contemporary issues that they care about. For example, Radhika Joshi has addressed adoption and social discrimination,[43] Nishad Matange has touched upon environmental degradation and consumerism[44] and Achintya Prahlad has given the protagonist of one of his compositions a transgender identity.[45] Besides being modes of self-expression, these compositions are likely to resonate with young listeners, who are crucial to the future of the genre.

 These young singers have created mainly fast or medium-tempo compositions because these give lyrics more prominence than do slow compositions, in which the singer's focus is to establish the raag's ambience. In addition, after singing the slow composition's default tune, some styles move on to improvising in aakaar, which does away with the lyrics altogether. Styles that improvise using the lyrics stretch the appropriate vowels in order to fill the rhythmic cycle, a process that changes the way the words sound. In fast and medium tempos, the enunciation of lyrics is closer to how they are spoken.

❦

These young composers, however, continue to use Hindi dialects for their khayal compositions. Because khayal evolved using compositions in Brajbhasha and similar dialects, it is possible that the cadences of these languages themselves shaped the music. In other words, a part of khayal's *musical* identity may be rooted in this language group. Singing compositions in another language may alter the music itself. In Western music, there appears to be evidence that a composer's mother tongue influences his or her use both of rhythm and melody, in both vocal *and* instrumental music.[46] So if another language, say Marathi, had been used for khayal compositions from the start, it may have evolved into a different kind of music.[47] One can only wonder how different this would have been.

 Is it possible for an expert singer to compose in a language other than the traditional ones while preserving all of khayal's musical principles or altering them in ways that find wide acceptance? Some people have tried to compose in Marathi and there is even a jocular attempt in English. These have not caught on. For such experiments to find takers perhaps the poetry, the music and the musician all need to be of a very high calibre and hit a sweet spot.[48] Or perhaps the khayal we know and love can never stray very far from its linguistic roots.

&

'Sur, laya, raag, taal and bol are like spirits in the fairy tale of my rendition. As I unfurl my tale, I do not know which spirits or how many of them I am going to summon into the spotlight to influence the scene. In one scene, I may give sur the limelight by prolonging and intensifying notes. In another scene, I might give rhythm the centre stage. In yet another scene, I might give bol the lead role, by repeatedly singing a phrase in different ways to highlight its meaning.' —AK

18

◇ Voice

I FOLLOWED THE SOUND OF MUSIC TO A HUGE ROOM ON the ground floor of the Gandharva Mahavidyalaya's headquarters in Navi Mumbai, across the bay from the financial capital. Guruji was in full flow, singing raag Jaitashree. Mandaar and Mukul were giving him support and about twenty-five listeners were responding with brio. It was a particularly big before-party in a green room the size of a mini-hall. When someone called time for the actual concert, I was disappointed that Guruji had to stop singing.

It was January 2022. Guruji's concert was the first live recital that I attended after the COVID-19 lockdown went into effect nearly two years earlier. In this period, online concerts had kept the music going, but I realised how much I missed a live recital's warmth and vitality. In the main hall, Guruji began Jaitashree all over again, and after a few shaky minutes, he began probing the raag for unseen treasures and tripping with the tabla. Before I knew it, he had sung for nearly an hour. Demanding undivided attention, Guruji's music shrank the passage of time.

In the interval, I munched on crisp samosas and sipped steaming tea in an open courtyard outside the hall while catching up with my friends after an age. Following the interval, Guruji sang Sampoorna Malkauns, rendering the canonical *Baraj rahi* (I forbid you), followed by his own new sparkling fast composition, *Aayee shubha gadi* (The auspicious hour has arrived). It surely had. He rounded the evening out with Chandrakauns and Bhairavi. It was wonderful to see him in action again.

As I made my way home, I told myself that I would finally try to get to the bottom of his voice troubles. I had a friend, Nupur Nerurkar, who was an excellent laryngologist and voice surgeon with a clinic at the reputable Bombay Hospital in the city's downtown area. My voice, too, was becoming hoarse when I sang for prolonged periods in the upper octave. I would get Nupur to check my vocal folds too.

―⁂―

About a month after Guruji's concert in Navi Mumbai, I arrived at his flat at tea time to conduct an experiment that Nupur had suggested we carry out when we had visited her clinic a week earlier. Guruji switched on the tanpura on his iPad and sang an aalaap in Todi for about ten minutes, followed by his composition *Gunana gaavoon tumaro* (I sing of your virtues), while I recorded him on my mobile phone. This was the control recording. Soon, Kaku brought us a tray with a bowl of chivda, a cup of chai for me and a glass of whisky for Guruji. I sipped my chai and Guruji slowly consumed his drink, waiting for the alcohol to get into his blood stream. After an hour, I recorded him singing another aalaap in Todi and the same composition. Then and there, I emailed the two sets of recordings to Nupur's clinic.

At her clinic a week earlier, Nupur had done a laryngeal stroboscopy on Guruji and me. This involves passing a thin flexible wire emerging from a machine through a person's nose and down the throat until the loose end, which has a tiny camera, dangles in front of the larynx. She told us to make a series of sounds and to briefly sing. Video images of our vocal folds appeared in real time on the machine's screen, which Nupur was examining. She detected a gentle sulcus, or groove, on my right vocal fold, and two tiny varices, or burst blood vessels, on the left side. She said this meant that I was using my voice sub-optimally and, at times, singing beyond my range. She recommended that I start sessions with Anuradha Bantwal, a speech-language pathologist who worked with professional voice users.

As for Guruji, Nupur said that his vocal folds were fine, but told him that he had a mild vocal tremor, a neurological condition that can afflict the hands, neck or larynx. Nupur further said that as Guruji kept singing, his folds steadied, which reflected what happened at his concerts. Nupur said that the more relaxed he felt, the faster his voice would steady. This again matched his experience of barely having starting difficulties when he sang for small, knowledgeable audiences. She explained that the latest research showed that the brains of people with such tremors had lower-than-average levels of gamma-aminobutyric acid, or GABA, a neurotransmitter that played a role in controlling neuronal excitability. The only drug based on this molecule was still at the stage of clinical trials, she told Guruji. 'But alcohol also contains this molecule,' she said. 'After a drink or two, the voice can temporarily improve. We can first check whether you respond to the neurotransmitter so that I can decide whether to prescribe the drug, if and when it becomes available.' Nupur told him to experiment with singing before and after drinking a large peg, or 60 ml, of whisky.

That afternoon, when Guruji was doing just that, Karmalkar Kaka called him.

'What am I doing?' Guruji asked. 'I am enjoying a glass of whisky.'

'So early in the day!' Karmalkar Kaka must have exclaimed, for Guruji began laughing.

Karmalkar Kaka would have been taken aback to hear that Guruji was drinking at all. I had certainly never seen him do so before. Guruji had told me that he did occasionally drink, mostly at the behest of his younger son, Adwait, a bon vivant who sometimes pressed a glass of whisky or scotch into his father's hands on a special occasion. Kaku disapproved of it.

'I went to a voice doctor who is Sumana's friend,' Guruji explained to Karmalkar Kaka, telling him what Nupur had recommended, and how it came to be that he, for all practical purposes a teetotaller, was quaffing whisky down in the middle of an afternoon, from a glass that Kaku, of all people, had served him on a tray.

'I am drinking because the doctor ordered it,' Guruji said.

The experiment with alcohol slightly improved Guruji's voice, as judged both by him and a voice therapist in Nupur's clinic who reviewed the recordings. The voice therapist suggested that we repeat the experiment a few more times, but Guruji could not summon the enthusiasm. 'Let it be,' he said. Given his age, I understood.

For my own voice issue, I began sessions with Anuradha. She had begun her career focusing on children with hearing loss and autism, but over time became increasingly interested in working with professional voice users, particularly singers, because she herself was a longstanding student of khayal. Coincidentally, she had trained in the same gharanas that I had, in the same order. She had learnt from Padmavati Shaligram for several years and then for a brief period from Shruti Sadolikar, both from the Jaipur gharana, and was now learning from Raja Miya, an Agra gharana vocalist.

Anuradha introduced me to an aspect of music that had been missing in all my training stints: voice care and development. She began our first session by observing the way I used my voice in normal speech. 'If singers want their voices to serve them well, they must take care not only while singing, but also in every other instance of voice usage,' she said. She was also surprised to hear that I was often singing in class at pitches well above my natural one of A. Depending on our class composition on a given day, we used anything from A# to C#.

She then moved on to visually and aurally evaluating my singing technique. She said that I was tightening my neck, whose muscles, along with those in the tongue and jaw, are directly or indirectly attached to the laryngeal mechanism, which is used for singing. Tension in these linked muscles can impede this mechanism's smooth functioning and even become the source of vocal problems such as hoarseness, heaviness and pain after singing, a loss in pitch range, difficulties in making smooth pitch changes and trouble projecting the voice. In a dozen sessions spread out over a year, Anuradha took me through relaxation, strengthening and breathing drills as well as exercises to enhance resonance. At the end, I felt a much greater sense of vocal well-being and control. I was better able to detect incipient problems, sparked by overuse or illness, and to take remedial action, starting with resting my voice.

No system of musical training can prevent voice problems. Like any other body part, the vocal folds are susceptible to wear and tear. But a training routine can certainly be sensitive to the physiological effects of using the voice in different ways. After interviewing numerous singers, including Guruji, I saw that an evidence-based regimen for voice care, or fitness, had not been a part of their music training. Some people did tell me about drills that their teachers had suggested, such as singing in aakaar, doing kharaj riyaaz, in which one slowly descends the lower octave by holding each note for as long as possible, and om chanting, but only as optional add-ons.

Yet voice problems among classical singers appeared to be common. Many were approaching voice therapists only after experiencing these problems. Anuradha had treated several classical singers and students facing a range of issues, from mild to severe. I interviewed six of them, who spoke to me on the condition that I not name them or their gurus. They spanned several decades in age, from the late twenties to the early sixties. Four of them specialised in khayal, one in dhrupad and one in thumri. Five were female, one was male. Three of them were performing regularly in public. The other three were committed students. Most of them had trained under more than one guru. All these gurus were highly respected musicians, of which those specialising in khayal covered a wide spectrum of gharanas. A couple of gurus had recommended that their students do breathing exercises and the standard kharaj riyaaz, but none had a systematic voice fitness regimen rooted in science. The singers told me they knew others like them who had faced problems. They also told me that after undergoing therapy they had gained more control over their voices.

'Home remedies, popular quick fixes, exercises described on the internet or in books, exercises that helped someone else and remedies suggested by well-meaning lay people are all risky,' Anuradha said. 'An equally wrong strategy would be for a singer to borrow exercises that someone else might have learnt from another therapist. If we accept that a learner of khayal needs guidance from a well-trained guru to ensure that Bhoop does not begin to sound like Deshkar, for example, then why should vocalists find it difficult to accept that they should do voice drills only under professional supervision?'

~

We know of musicians from previous eras who had voice problems. Alladiya Khan was a prime example. Guruji told me that Gajananbuwa, too, was often worried about his voice, even though it appears uniformly robust in the online recordings. Some singers may have simply fallen by the wayside before coming into public view. We don't know what they did to tackle their voice troubles or ailments. The broader concept of voice fitness itself is largely absent in classical Indian music. One reason could be financial. In sports, fitness started gaining importance when the field began attracting huge amounts of money, which spurred research in sports physiology. Today, almost everyone aspiring to play a sport at a high level has a fitness trainer, if not an entire team, in addition to a coach for the sport's specific technical skills.

Another reason for this lacuna in khayal's tradition of training might lie in the genre's creative demands. The khayal singer's central goals are to become fluent in a number of raags, gain rhythmic control and acquire command over several improvisation forms. Seasoned listeners of khayal, too, look mainly for originality in a singer's raag elaborations, rhythmic play and style. As the music writer Oliver Craske explained, 'Where audiences in the west tend to prize the voice beautiful, the bel canto, what count in khayal are inventiveness and mastery of musical grammar. Some singers are blessed with an exquisite voice, but it is not a requirement.'[1] Craske quoted the musician and broadcaster Narayana Menon as saying that 'in India the voice is no more of an asset to a singer than, say, good handwriting to a poet.'[2] Guruji once said something similar to encourage a student who cried off from singing in class because she had a sore throat, 'Hum gaane ka kaam karte hain, gale ka nahin.' We do musical work, not of the throat.

By contrast, the internet teems with Western voice coaches demonstrating a profusion of vocal exercises. The reasons for this are probably the opposite of those that hold true for Indian classical music. Western classical genres are practised in more affluent countries, which have more resources to devote to studying voice fitness. Further, their singers largely interpret composed music, so the quality of the voice is a central concern. The exception is jazz, which does entail improvisation.

Despite these differences, surely khayal singers want to express their hard-won musical ideas in their optimal voices? But Guruji was sceptical about specialised voice training because he said he was yet to see a critical mass of scientific studies evaluating the effects of various voice exercises on Indian genres. 'The professional arena is also very competitive and doesn't encourage openness,' Anu said. 'Singers who have recovered do recommend their peers to professionals, but understandably hesitate to talk openly about their experience. We, as a society, seem to easily accept that a top sportsman who takes time off for an injury is as good as new after treatment, yet we unrealistically expect singers to always have trouble-free voices. I hope that, with time, not only singers, but also event organisers and audiences will accept a scientific approach to voice care and therapy.'

One musician, however, has gone public with his voice problems: the leading Carnatic singer Sanjay Subrahmanyan. In his 2024 autobiography, written with Krupa Ge, he described with searing honesty how he 'hated' his voice. 'I've felt that it's not up to the mark, that it has issues,' he writes. 'But I managed because of my superior ability to interpret the music.' In 2015, after he won the

Sangita Kalanidhi award, Carnatic music's top honour, he felt freer to confront the issue, he writes. He began reading up about voice training, especially Western methods. 'It helped me realise that there is a scientific approach...I hadn't even thought about these things before.' He eventually began working with a voice therapist who was familiar with Carnatic music. '[She] is helping me understand how I can use my voice in a scientific manner so that I can get rid of habits that can be injurious to its health,' he writes.

For professional singers to talk openly about their voice problems requires enormous courage. I asked Guruji why he was willing to do so. 'I hope my story will help others,' he said.

My sortie into the world of voice fitness led me to Samyukta Ranganathan, a New York-based Carnatic singer and teacher, a student of Hindustani music and a rare researcher in the virgin field of voice science applied to Indian classical music. Samyukta was working on a doctorate in this subject after getting a master's degree in it. Growing up in Chennai, she had trained for two decades with Bombay S. Ramachandran, an outstanding guru, who, incidentally, had also taught my father for a few years. Since 2017, Samyukta had been learning khayal in New York from Sanjoy Banerjee of the Kirana gharana. 'Most research articles that I have seen are based on a Western classical or contemporary music voice,' she told me over Zoom. 'From the over two hundred researchers at a voice conference in Estonia in 2023, only two of us were presenting work connected to Indian music. Further, whatever little research has been done on Indian classical vocal music is from a clinical, scientific perspective. We do not have research on how to apply those findings in the classroom to prevent problems. There is a massive gap.'

Eager to fill this lacuna, Samyukta tested a toolkit of techniques to address Carnatic singers' common complaints, such as the lack of vocal range, speed and agility. She said that she had received positive feedback from students, teachers and speech-language pathologists who had tested the techniques. 'We do have indigenous knowledge about the voice,' she said. 'By understanding the science, we can systematise and better communicate what we already know, and also evaluate what works and what doesn't. For instance, our oral tradition relies on imitation, but it may not be suitable for young learners to adopt their older gurus' vocal techniques along with their music. What I like is that in the West, people are thirsting to find out how they can use new knowledge to help their students.'

Psychological factors can also influence a singer's vocal health, Samyukta said. She had studied the relationship between students' voice issues and the lack of safety in their learning environments as well as the role of compassionate guru–shishya relationships in mitigating those negative impacts. Her findings were published in a peer-reviewed journal.[3] 'When a student walks into a space to receive knowledge from someone, it creates a power imbalance,' she said. 'From my study, authoritarianism and a demand for blind obedience seem to be common in the guru–shishya parampara. But it is crucial for gurus to realise that what they say can cause a student psychological distress, which at best, may lead to a poor learning experience, and at worst, may make the student's nervous system instinctively respond in a way that leads to voice issues and performance anxiety. But I did find examples of more egalitarian guru–shishya relationships, ones that prioritised compassion and trust. These need to be recognised and championed, and should become standard practice. Compassion improves the way someone's nervous system responds to a threat, and is therefore an antidote to students feeling shame when they make mistakes and descending into self-critical rumination.'

In the classroom, examples of threats include harsh criticism, the absence of positive feedback and the differential treatment of students. I had experienced the many virtues of the guru–shishya parampara, including its sheer efficiency in transmitting knowledge. I also saw its pitfalls, arising not only from the power imbalance intrinsic to any learning environment, but also because the transfer of knowledge often took place not in a neutral, professional space but at the guru's home, with no oversight or forums for students to complain if they faced problems.

※

Another external weakness of the informal gurukul is that a student looking for a teacher has no easy source of reliable information, including details about musicians' styles, teaching methods, fees, their efficacy and integrity. This was one reason that I learnt about Guruji so late. With respect to khayal, unfettered commodification and the consequent ghettoisation of many excellently trained musicians to the fringe has exacerbated this data scarcity. In other fields, an institution gains its reputation over time by word of mouth; through formal surveys, which, despite their shortcomings, provide a ballpark estimation; and from the quality and trajectories of its alumni.

Students looking for doctoral advisers, for instance, can tap the internet and the academic grapevine. In music, unless students are well-connected, they might not know whom to ask for advice and there is no guarantee that people will give them honest responses. Even after collecting background information, students take a huge leap of faith when they sign up with a guru. The whole process is hit or miss. Kartik's article about Guruji in the magazine we brought out for his seventy-fifth birthday revealed the role of chance. 'I presumed that Arun Kaka was just another music teacher in my locality,' Kartik wrote. 'Little did I realise that I had won the lottery of a lifetime.'

Not everyone gets lucky. Until a generation ago, a guru's pedagogical lineage guaranteed that he or she would transmit a coherent style. In the new millennium, this is perhaps no longer true. 'Many young musicians in the twenty-first century do not reflect the aesthetic values of any gharana tradition,' Arnab Chakrabarty told me. 'They have embraced whatever their guru embodies, or purports to embody, as their personal artistic ideology. But it is a toss of a coin whether students land up with decent gurus who know something or not. Once this embrace of a guru happens, it is hard to shake off, for better or worse.'

◆ Light: 2001–14

ARUN WENT UP ON STAGE, NOT TO SING, BUT TALK. PEOPLE had gathered in a huge hall in Mulund to celebrate his sixtieth birthday.

'I have met many good people in my life,' Arun said softly. 'I am what I am today because of all of them.'

Praveen Karkare blinked back tears. The tabla player, young enough to be Arun's son, had met the singer three years earlier under intimidating circumstances. Praveen was to accompany the vocalist Shubhada Paradkar at a morning concert. He had played with her before, but at the venue she told him that he would also have to accompany Arun, who was going to sing after her. Growing up in Dombivli, Praveen knew that Arun Kashalkar was highly respected and had heard him once, when the vocalist had lived up to his reputation. That morning, Praveen hoped that he would be able to rehearse with Arun in the green room, but there was no time. On stage, Praveen felt his jaws tightening. He heard Arun instructing him to play Jhoomra but did not even register the raag that the musician began singing.

'The pitch of my tabla is too high,' Praveen fretted to himself. 'I am playing the theka but not enjoying it.'

Afterwards, when the musicians sat down for lunch that the organisers had arranged, Praveen found himself sitting next to Arun.

'You play well,' the musician told Praveen, who gaped.

Two days later, Arun called Praveen.

'Your theka is good,' Arun said. 'If you want, you can come to my classes.'

Praveen was stunned. He had asked many lesser singers whether he could go over to accompany them when they practised or taught students, but none had shown any interest. Because Praveen's guru, Sadashiv Pawar, specialised in accompanying instrumentalists, some people had slotted him too in that category. Tabla players did have greater scope to exhibit their artistry when playing with instrumentalists because they got many solo interludes, but accompanying vocalists required skill of a more subdued sort. With a vocalist, a tabla player got virtually no solo time but had to remain in the background marking out avartans and supporting the singer's vision. But Praveen wanted this experience. Tabla players can learn how to accompany vocalists only by doing it. A safe way to begin is by accompanying musicians when they do riyaaz or teach students.

The very next day after Arun called, Praveen went over to his home. Over the following year, Praveen flowered in Arun's garden. Praveen saw the singer watering his house plants with his knowledge and nourishing them with his sunny temperament. But Praveen astutely glimpsed an occasional cloud of melancholy passing by. 'He must feel bad about his skin condition and capricious voice,' Praveen thought.

By then, Praveen knew how vicious the music world could be. He had spoken to Arun about it when he had accompanied the musician to hand in an article on music that a Marathi magazine had commissioned. On the way back, as they had walked on one of the bridges connecting the various platforms of Dadar station, Praveen had confided in Arun about the meanness and nepotism in his field. 'You have no control over how people behave,' Arun had replied. 'Try to ignore what others do and keep improving yourself. Compete only with yourself. After some time, you will see what happens.'

Over the next two years, Praveen felt the sky over Arun's garden darken less and less frequently. Now, as Arun spoke to his well-wishers on his sixtieth birthday, Praveen felt that the musician was glowing with an inner light.

For a couple of years till he turned sixty, Arun had decided not to sing outside his home. Now he began performing whenever people invited him. He often hit the ground running or quickly found his momentum. He got no official accolades, but over the years, appreciation came from quarters that he valued even more. Nivruttibuwa's students gave him the last slot at their guru's memorial concerts. Baba Azizuddin Khan, Alladiya Khan's grandson, on listening to Arun singing at the Kolhapur home of Vinod Digrajkar, one of Nivruttibuwa's students, exclaimed, 'Look, he's singing our music!' On listening to Arun's nom-tom aalaap in raag Miyan Malhar, the dhrupad singer Saifuddin Dagar told him, 'You'll put us dhrupadiyas out of business.' After attending one of Arun's concerts, the daughter of the Agra gharana singer Anjanibai Lolekar told him how much she liked his bol work.

On a few occasions, Arun got weighed down by his starting difficulties and sang indifferently. Once, he could not find his voice at all and called the concert off after ten minutes. But he kept going, taking one performance at a time. Throughout, he kept refining his style. As he turned seventy, his music was full of vitality and grace. His raag renditions were drenched in flavour, his rhythmic play flowing and intricate. Even as he worked around his voice problems, his music became sweeter and more elegant. Through the decade, he energetically composed and relentlessly taught, reinvigorated by excellent students who had reposed their faith in him. He had the pleasure of watching his sons, Ashish and Adwait, flourish. They distinguished themselves in their jobs, got married and had children. Arun travelled outside India, visiting Ashish in the US, when he was posted there, and Adwait, in Malaysia and then Singapore. Dhanashree, too, took pleasure in caring for her grandchildren. After Ravi began working at the Temple of Fine Arts in Singapore, Arun began visiting the city-state every year—performing, teaching and gaining a following there.

Arun continued writing Marathi poetry, reading some of his poems aloud in a literary circle in Mulund. By then, he had written nearly forty poems. Among his favourites was one called *Birth of the Ego*:

> You roused an innocent infant from its sleep,
> A charming name for it you did keep.
>
> Following tradition, you also gave it a paternal and family identity,
> Thereupon you awakened its ego, that too, with a ceremony.
>
> The ego began caressing itself for fun,
> Soon, it was growling at you, me and everyone.
>
> It fought with the boy next door,
> Roaring like never before:
> 'I am Arun Nagesh Kashalkar! Get that, or …'[4]

◆ Feeling

BARRING A COMPOSITION'S FEW LINES OF LYRICS, A RAAG rendition does not represent an outside reality. But like all music, it evokes an emotional and intellectual response in the listener. This response is hard to predict. Some people ascribe one rasa, or essence, to a raag. Rasa traditionally described the various emotional qualities that a performer or performance as a whole sets out to convey, such as eroticism, heroism, pathos. This concept originates from a theory of aesthetics that was delineated in the Sanskrit Natya Shastra, attributed to Bharata, who lived sometime between the first century BCE and third century CE. About a millennium later, the theory was further elaborated in other Sanskrit treatises written by Abhinavagupta, who lived in the tenth century CE. Rasa theory is substantial and has been influential in the Indian performing arts, especially dance and theatre. But it may not be as useful for describing raag music.

Each raag does create a particular mood, which we can call raag bhaav. But attributing one rasa to this mood appears to be sweeping because many other factors are involved in how a musician renders a raag and how a listener perceives it. The same raag can lead to a variety of effects depending upon the type of composition, its tune and tempo as well as the length of a rendition and the range of improvisation methods that a singer uses. A slow tempo creates a different effect from that of a fast one. A rendition with a long aalaap but a brief taan section will have a different feel from one with a short aalaap but a long taan section or one that focuses mostly on medium-paced rhythmic play. Even in a single rendition, the mood shifts from the aalaap to taans. Why, the mood changes even within a single avartan, with its characteristic rise and fall of intensity. One could therefore think of a raag rendition as a staging ground for continuously changing mood within the genre's parameters.[5]

How a listener responds to a rendition depends upon a slew of musical factors, such as his or her familiarity with the raag and understanding of rhythm as well as a host of non-musical parameters. If a person is familiar with a raag, its effect depends upon his or her previous impressions of it. The listener might also instinctively like certain raags, styles and voice qualities. As a result of all these variables, one would be hard put to be more specific than saying that a khayal rendition evokes a mental response in a listener that is both emotional and intellectual. One cannot predict the nature of this response.

'Let's say several friends decide to meet at a particular place at a certain time. To arrive on time, everyone has to plan properly. Each one has to calculate the travel time and leave home accordingly. Everyone needs to be disciplined in order to reach the meeting point on time. If all the friends arrive punctually, they experience a thrill— because it reflects everyone's commitment and sincerity.' —AK

19

◇ Flame

THE SWEET STRAINS OF RAAG BAGESHREE FILLED THE room. A student was singing a slow composition. 'Bahuguna kaam na aave …,' she began, going on to finish the line, '… jab lag karam nahin jaage.' Of what use will your many virtues be if you do not rigorously fulfil your duties?

This was our first physical lesson after two years of online classes. It was April 2022. Other students began arriving. We were all together again! At the same time, after two years of nestling comfortably in my online habitat of five students, I was now out in open terrain again, with its unpredictability and lack of cover. I had last learnt Bageshree as a teenager. I tried to absorb the composition's tune.

Among the many skills that Guruji's students developed was the ability to pick up musical material extempore, whether a new composition, raag or taal. People started out with different levels of competence in each area. One can notate a new composition and then follow the notation, but this is time-consuming. A faster method is to pick up its tune by ear, without worrying about what the notes are. In this case, the voice needs to begin producing the melody even before the brain has time to work out the notation. I noticed that those who had experience in learning film music could do this well because that was how they learnt various songs. But in order to improvise within a raag, one has to not merely reproduce a melody on the spot, but also break it down into notes. Students who had earlier trained as violinists or harmonium players could do both. For instance, Kartik, who had learnt to play the Carnatic violin, told me that, in order to follow a singer within split seconds, his hands began playing the music even before his brain could analyse the melody. But in addition, as he played, his mind heard the melody in the form of notes. Any serious student who learnt from Guruji for a sustained period eventually acquired both skills.

About three-fourths of the way into our lesson, a couple of students began singing a new fast composition of Guruji's that he had taught to their online batch. 'Khelana aaye hori brij me Nandalal,' they sang. Look, Nandalal has come to Brij to play Holi. The revelry had indeed begun.

⁂

'Mana laga tumi sana mo_, mana laga tumi sana mo_, mana laga tumi sana ...,' sang Swara, before landing effortlessly on the sam with the syllable 'mo' in the word 'mora', thus completing a teehai, a pattern repeated thrice. It was the first line of one of Guruji's fast compositions in raag Shree, in which a woman tells a man that she has fallen in love with him. The room erupted into applause. Swara smiled, bowing her head and bringing her hands together in a quick namaste. Cutting a diminutive figure on the stage, the ten-year-old had already wowed listeners with her fluent rendition of *Garib nawaz*, that iconic medium-paced composition that was a perennial favourite in our gurukul. After Swara finished her performance, messages began pinging on our students' WhatsApp group describing her rendition for the benefit of those who could not attend the event. One student posted a clip from Swara's rendition with the caption, 'Jaisa naam, waisa hi gaana.' Her music lives up to her name.

Swara performed as part of our 2022 Guru Purnima programme. For the first time, we held the event at the Gandharva Mahavidyalya, where Guruji had performed at the beginning of the year. We were able to use its large premises because Guruji had become its principal earlier that year. The line-up consisted of more than forty students. Ravi came all the way from Singapore. After two years of isolation, everyone's pent-up energy, the capacious venue, tailor-made for such an event, and the long list of performers combined to evoke a festive atmosphere reminiscent of a wedding. The premises had excellent infrastructure, including several large green rooms, clean bathrooms and a few air-conditioned suites. In this fringe culture, resources were so tight that such amenities appeared like luxuries.

Swara was one of two youngsters who became sensations at that year's event. The other was Ishaan, who presented Gaud Sarang, exhibiting a sense of ease and aesthetics belying his sixteen years. These youngsters clearly had talent and had benefited from Guruji's remarkable teaching method, but their precocity also showed that when it came to music, it helped to start early. 'In music, for many years, you are not required to apply your mind too much,' Guruji said, when I praised the youngsters' renditions. 'You have to keep learning from the guru, keep practising the way he directs, listen to his music, be immersed in it. You can improve rapidly. Children do this unquestioningly. They also have fewer preoccupations.'

Listening to such fresh music after what was essentially a two-year quarantine, I felt even more detached from the mainstream, which began to appear like a play, parts of it like a farce, written by an invisible hand and directed by handlers who ensured that the actors stuck to their scripts. If khayal survived, it would probably be in nooks like ours.

A couple of days before the event, I had a nightmare that I was supposed to sing raag Hamir at a student baithak, but blanked out just as I was about to start. I could not remember even the raag's chalan. Desperate, I spotted another student standing nearby and asked her to help me locate the page in my notebook where I had jotted down Hamir's key phrases. The audience was waiting impassively. Guruji was sitting in the front row, expressionless. But in a bizarre twist, I then recklessly switched to singing raag Nayaki Kanada, which I loved but had not practised. Fortunately, the dream then went blurry. I woke up before its denouement, with a catch in my throat. This was my first music nightmare, the equivalent of the scary exam dreams that had periodically haunted me even until a few years earlier. But there was so much positive energy at the Guru Purnima that, by the time my turn came to sing, I had forgotten all about the nightmare.

After the Guru Purnima, Guruji gently gave us feedback in class. 'When you sing in the uppermost octave, move back from the mike,' he told me. 'Otherwise, it sometimes sounds harsh.' I had sung Bihag. 'Practise the phrases Ga-ma-Pa-Ni and Ga-ma-Pa-Ni-Sa with various bols,' Guruji said. 'The pitches in those fast, ascending phrases need to be more accurate.' As he went around the room, it was evident that he had listened to our renditions with laser-sharp concentration. Later, I asked him what importance he gave to the Guru Purnima presentations. 'There is a vast difference between singing in class and on stage,' he replied. 'In class, students sing along the lines of the guru. In class, they practise. In class, they follow my ideas. On stage, they have to express independent musical thoughts. In class, they sing in a familiar setting. On stage, they reveal their courage and alertness, and more fundamentally, their urge to sing. I can gauge their progress as well as their strong and weak points.'

Yet again, I was touched that the gurukul, teeming as it was with excellent singers, had space for people like me. I later learnt that the Gandharva Mahavidyalaya had streamed performances during the morning session, when I had sung, on its Facebook page, because it had been V.D. Paluskar's birth anniversary that day. Fortunately, I had not known that they were doing this. In retrospect, I felt pleased, not because I felt my rendition was worthy of being publicised, but because it meant that I had become entangled in this world.

❦

On the contrary, Guruji had sharpened my discernment to such a level that I found it hard to tolerate my own singing. This came with the terrain: the horizon kept receding as one got closer to it. Guruji was routinely encouraging, but his classes could be bruising. One had to dust oneself up each time and carry on. He was no doubt being sincere when he said 'one lifetime is not enough to understand this music' and 'I am still learning', but the statements also expressed the dispiriting prognosis that permeated our khayal cult: no one could be good enough. On occasion, I felt a wave of resentment towards the music. Hah, this is why you are becoming obscure, I thought. Fortunately, this phase was always short-lived. On the other side emerged my old masochistic self, back to saying that the only way to continue was to focus on enjoying the journey. A dear friend of mine kept telling me that, at this stage in life, I should be learning music for swantaha sukhay, personal contentment. But was I feeling contented? Perhaps in a tortuous way. I was hooked by the promise of the joy that I thought I would feel by improvising fluently in Guruji's style. As Woody Allen said, 'one must have one's delusions to live.'[1] I told myself to be patient, remembering that Guruji counted progress in units of five years.

But even if wishes became horses, I wondered how many people, apart from members of my gurukul, would understand this khayal style and its depth. In the end, I concluded that I had nothing to lose and everything to gain. Guruji's style was like an adventure sport, full of athleticism and edge-of-the-seat excitement, without the risk of injury or death. I pressed on, keeping in mind Guruji's simple but potent advice: Karat raha. Keep practising.

One more Guru Purnima came and went. I made my offering, of raag Sampoorna Malkauns, and feasted on those of others. By then, I was fully hooked to the avartan. I got a high merely hearing Tilwada or Jhoomra on my iTabla app and began thinking of raags as friends. But outside, the world became increasingly dystopic, with neo-fascism rearing its head in many countries, public life further deteriorating in India, Israel's genocide of Palestinians being live-streamed and war raging in Sudan, Ukraine and elsewhere. I thought of the central question in Pico Iyer's book *The Half Known Life*: will human beings' yearning for paradise always be out of reach? After all, Iyer points out, conflict grips so many places that are associated with paradise, like Jerusalem, Kashmir, Sri Lanka, and indeed, Iran, whose culture gave us the very idea—'paradise' evolved from the Persian word 'paradaijah'. Or, as Iyer asks, is paradise ultimately a way of being and seeing, to be found amid the rough and tumble of life and within ourselves? He quotes the Persian polymath Omar Khayyam, 'Take care to create your own paradise, here and now on earth.'[2]

A year later, the reverberations of yet another Guru Purnima fiesta slowly faded. This time, in August 2024, it had been held at a music college in Pune and its students were welcome to attend. Several musicians in the city had also been invited. I had sung Malkauns, feeling slightly better equipped to take the intimidating circumstances in my stride. Because I was hooked. Because I wanted to keep going.

As Diwali approached, I had a dream. About a flame that burns forever.

> A dancing flame, with many hues,
> Its glow warming all who gather.
> Where rhythm, melody and words fuse
> Into a deep dream of wonder.
>
> In this hypnotic circle
> Bursts of laughter, gifts of insight
> Make an eternal festival
> Of sweetness and light.

◈ Tailwinds: 2015

ON RETURNING HOME FROM WORK ONE DAY, YOGESH opened his master bedroom to find one of Arun's students asleep on the double bed with the air-conditioner turned on. Yogesh withdrew and went into the kitchen, where his wife, Madhavi, was preparing tea. Yogesh pointed to the bedroom. 'Someone is sleeping in there,' he told her. Madhavi looked surprised and then smiled. It was mid-2015. For several months, on weekends, their living room had turned into a de facto recording studio. During the day, Arun's senior students and accompanists came by in groups to record the musician's compositions for the CD and book set. Mukul and Vishal often came on weekends. Madhavi kept whipping up chai and snacks for the visitors. Sometimes, other students came along to listen. The recording sessions took on the flavour of mini-mehfils. That day, a listener had decided to appropriate the bedroom for his nap. It was part of the fun. 'We are hosting a swar yagnya,' Yogesh told people. 'Every weekend, we have a musical havan in our living room. We are notching up a huge amount of punya.'

By the end of 2015, the yagnya had gone on for almost a year. The massive project, involving recording about one hundred and fifty compositions, had taken off in early 2014. Arun had divided the compositions among his senior vocal students, Mandaar, Ravi, Vishal, Mukul, Ketaki and Sugandha, as well as Apoorva, Gajananbuwa's granddaughter, who was close to him. Students recorded some compositions at their homes in different cities, some at the home of Arun's friend Vikas, some in Yogesh's flat, yet others in recording studios. By 2015, Arun had roped in Omkar to help edit the recordings.

If Arun had run a corporate-style set-up with generous funding and a clear chain of command, the project would have sailed smoothly. But he presided over an informal gurukul with a tight budget and many power centres, so the project acquired herculean proportions and had chaos baked into it. Arun did not lay down a strict format so some students included snatches of improvisation in their recordings while others did not. Arun wanted many compositions to be re-recorded to improve their quality, but also because he continued to refine some of them. He made up the protocol as he went along, like he did in his khayal renditions. He taught Mukul to sing one of his new compositions in raag Adana, *Kalana parata* (Peace eludes me), at a studio while the sound engineers were testing the microphones. 'Listen, this is the tune,' Arun told him. Being battle-hardened, Mukul hesitated only for a moment before plunging in.

Every now and then tempers frayed. People tore their hair at Arun's lack of planning, his indecision in the face of divergent suggestions from people stepping in to take charge, his last-minute changes. Through the fog of confusion, the mammoth job finally got done, and done well. What kept the project flying amid intermittent rough weather were the twin tailwinds of the profound love and respect that Arun's students had for their brilliant fakir of a guru.

◆ Spiral

LIKE THE AVARTAN, THE RENDITION OF A SLOW COMPOSITION has a narrative structure with several acts, in this case, four. This narrative structure is characterised by khayal's typical progression of tempo from slow to fast. This narrative structure varies slightly across gharanas, across musicians from the same gharana and across a single musician's renditions. The following rough guide is based on Arun Kashalkar's style because, as an amalgam of the three traditional gharanas, it encompasses a wide range of possibilities.

In the first act of elaborating a slow composition, khayaliyas sing the sthayi, or first verse, a couple of times and then begin improvising on it through an aalaap within the taal cycle. In an aalaap, singers prolong notes and liberally use glides to establish the raag's ambience. The avartans in this first act are not as busy and action-packed as what comes later. For the bulk of raags, whose home base is the shadja, or tonic Sa, improvisations have a downward, or avrohi, momentum. It is as if they are constantly pulled in the direction of home.

After a while, singers enter the second act, in which they begin working towards a figurative and literal high point: the taar shadja, the upper Sa. Singers who adopt a linear upward approach to raag elaboration, namely one that begins with lower notes and moves up the octave, do not normally even reveal the taar shadja until its turn arrives.[3] Singers who employ a non-linear approach might hit this note several times early in the aalaap, but even they will highlight it only after consciously deciding to do so at a later stage. In both cases, the improvisations now acquire an upward momentum, with the taar shadja acting like the magnet.

Singers gradually move towards this target by hovering in the region around it—on the notes below and sometimes even above it. They might then gently graze the taar shadja a few times, giving listeners tantalising glimpses of it. Then at some point, they will dramatically hit the note and prolong it. The more precisely singers render this note, the more powerful the effect. After this initial projection of the taar shadja, singers might choose to continue highlighting it by arriving at it in different ways and prolonging it each time. This whole process, called taar shadja bharna, filling or adorning the taar shadja, constitutes an important aesthetic challenge and draws considerable energy from singers. Often, singers fill the taar shadja as a prelude to rendering the composition's antara, or second verse, whose sam itself often coincides with this high note. But sometimes singers might do this only after singing the second verse.[4] Or they might do it both before and after singing this verse.

In these first and second acts, singers focus on establishing the ambience of the raag.

***

Just before entering the third act, singers often increase the tempo and continue improvising. Having established the raag's ambience, singers can reveal their originality and uniqueness in this act. They can showcase their creativity within the raag, their rhythmic prowess and their command over different improvisation techniques. These techniques include bol work, which uses the composition's words; sargams, which uses the names of notes; and medium-paced aakaar and bol taans. This act calls for specialised practice because of its rhythmic demands and because bol work is perhaps the most difficult of all improvisation forms. For this reason, in many singers' renditions, this act is either brief or absent altogether. But this act is well developed in the Agra gharana, which specialises in both rhythm and bol work. In Arun Kashalkar's style, it is particularly long, intricate and varied. One could say that it is the majestic high point of his elaboration on the slow composition.

After this, singers open the fourth and concluding act, often increasing the tempo once again. In this act, singers render fast taans, using both aakaar and bol. Taan singing is a sub-genre unto itself, consisting of many varieties, some of which are associated with specific gharanas. In this act, singers can speed the tempo up to the extent that they want. As the tempo increases and the taans become more rapid and complex, the fourth act heads towards a climax that concludes the elaboration of the slow composition. One can visually represent the characteristic increase in tempo and the density of musical matter over the course of an elaboration in the form of a conical spiral whose rings become smaller and thicker as they move upwards from the base. The rings represent avartans, which become shorter in duration as the tempo increases and become thicker with musical matter as the elaboration progresses.

> 'We tend to think of music only as melody. But without rhythm, melody cannot exist. Our heart beats to a rhythm. We coordinate our lives to nature's rhythms. To make our musical expression sound natural, we need to make our melody rhythmic. I would say that rhythm lies at the heart of my musical vision.' —AK

TRUTH

And, in the end, the love you take
is equal to the love you make.
— Paul McCartney

20

◆ Love

ARUN LOOKED AROUND THE HALL, FULL OF PEOPLE WHO loved him. He saw many musicians, including his dear guru, Babanrao. It was January 2016. People had gathered at the Dadar-Matunga Cultural Centre to celebrate the release of Arun's CD of compositions, Swar Archana. The seven singers on the CD were to each present a few compositions that day. Arun sorely missed the presence of the outstanding sitar player Abdul Halim Jaffer Khan, who was unwell. As a teenager, Arun had received a prize from Khan at a competition in eastern Maharashtra. Much later, in Mumbai, Khan had warmly appreciated Arun's compositions when he had sung several of them at the sitar maestro's home.

The curtains opened. Babanrao ceremoniously released *Swar Archana*, setting it off on its journey into the world. The book and CD set offered a window into Arun's musical contributions. Most obviously, it showcased his talent as a composer. It also highlighted his effectiveness as a guru. It further revealed his role in nurturing a community of discerning listeners, many of whom were present that day. Finally, the compositions exhibited Arun's unique style, one that some contended now warranted the label of a gharana. Among Arun's contemporaries, Kishori Amonkar had created a new khayal style by thoughtfully pushing the limits of traditional raag grammar. She had an aesthetic vision that was close in spirit to that of Kumar Gandharva, who went in the opposite direction, seeking the folk origins of raags and imbuing many raags with the rustic vigour of their progenitors. Both Amonkar and Gandharva pushed the boundaries of the classical idiom after having mastered it. By contrast, Arun was like Alladiya Khan, who, after experiencing voice issues, tapped virgin spaces within the classical ambit to create a new style, which came to be known as the Jaipur gharana. Arun's many innovations had already evolved into a distinctly new khayal sound. But by one definition, a new style merited the epithet of a gharana only if it was transmitted coherently for three generations. In other words, a style had to not only be original, but also go beyond experimentation to embody principles that could be taught. Arun's senior students were already performers and most were avid teachers. If, in turn, some of their students performed at a high level, then this prerequisite would be fulfilled.

Arun had an idea of where he stood. He knew that his musical quest had not intersected with worldly success, with its parameters of fame, money and power. He may have considered defining his success in terms of his legacy, such as his style, students and compositions. But legacy lived outside himself. He was more interested in the quality of a singer's relationship to his art. On this count, he was not held back by modesty. He knew one truth about his music. As he told people close to him: 'I fell in love with khayal and it fell head over heels in love with me.'

Dying embers can still start a fire.
— Western Han Dynasty

Notes

1.

◇ **Underground**

1. This chapter draws from the following article of mine—Sumana Ramanan, 'How a Maharashtrian cattle-grazer taught himself the intricacies of Hindustani music', *Scroll.in*, 29 March 2017: https://scroll.in/magazine/830162/how-a-maharashtrian-cattle-grazer-taught-himself-the-intricacies-of-hindustani-music.
2. The tanpura is also called the tanbura or tanbur.
3. See the section 'Sound' in Chapter 8 for basic details about the notation system in Hindustani music.
4. In order to avoid visual clutter, I have not used diacritics for English transliterations of words in Indian languages. Instead, I have used commonly accepted transliterations, even though they may not be phonetically consistent.
5. To save space and avoid repetition, I have dispensed with using titles such as pandit, ustad, vidushi and vidvan before musicians' names. This decision also relieves me of having to decide which musicians get titles and which ones do not.
6 'Underground Music', *Wikipedia*: https://en.wikipedia.org/wiki/Underground_music.

2.

◇ **Rabbit Hole**

1. I have used the English translation of this composition's title found in Nicholas Magriel with Lalita du Perron's *The Songs of Khayal—Book Two*. Unless otherwise stated, I have translated all other titles of khayal, dhrupad and thumri compositions with copious help from Ashish Verma.
2. Katherine Butler Schofield, *Music and Musicians in Late Mughal India: Histories of the Ephemeral, 1748-1858*, page 12.
3. For more details about the tarana, see Aneesh Pradhan, 'Tarana: How Indian classical music broke free from the confines of

language', *Scroll.in*, 6 September 2014: https://scroll.in/article/677935/tarana-how-indian-classical-music-broke-free-from-the-confines-of-language.
4. The following article is the profile I wrote—Sumana Ramanan, 'A Fine Balance', *The Caravan*, January 2015: https://caravanmagazine.in/reviews-and-essays/fine-balance.
5. Dard Neuman, a scholar of Hindustani music, contends that 'the secular politics of creativity found in Hindustani music presented other models to our political imaginaries than the choices provided by nation states'. See his online talk 'Heterodoxy, Hybridity, and the Politics of the Popular in Post-1857 Hindustani Music', *Manipal-Samvaad Centre for Indian Music*, 8 August 2021: https://www.youtube.com/watch?v=q6Qs5OJLq3c&t=9032s.

3.
◇ Fakir

1. Singing a composition, its tune, its basic, default or set tune all mean the same thing, namely rendering the composition's predetermined melody, which is distinct from variations resulting from improvisation.
2. In the Sufi and Bhakti traditions, the boat is a metaphor for a devotee's life. A devotee asks a higher force to help him or her cross the treacherous waters of the material world and reach a divine realm on the other side.

❖ Storm: 1970

3. Her name has been changed to protect her identity.
4. From Arun Kashalkar's unpublished poetry collection, translated from Marathi by Jerry Pinto.

◆ Alchemy

5. Many experts have justifiably found the labels 'classical' and 'semi-classical' to be problematic, preferring the term 'art' music for both. For one discussion about this, see T.M. Krishna, *A Southern Music: The Karnatik Story*, pages 30 to 34.

4.
◇ Verdict

1. Tragically, in 2018, a flood badly damaged this studio.
2. Some of these quotes appeared in the following profile of Arun-ji that I wrote—Sumana Ramanan, 'Mystery of the Maestro', *Mumbai Mirror*, 3 April 2016: https://mumbaimirror.indiatimes.com/others/sunday-read/mystery-of-the-maestro/articleshow/51664525.cms.
3. Robin Dunbar, 'How Your Brain Makes Friends': https://www.steelcase.com/research/articles/how-your-brain-makes-friends-with-robin-dunbar-transcript/; Robin Dunbar, 'The origins and function of musical performance', *Frontiers of Psychology*, 10 November 2023: https://www.frontiersin.org/journals/psychology/articles/10.3389/fpsyg.2023.1257390/full.
4. In future, tabla apps that use artificial intelligence may be able to follow singers in real time. The app Naadsadhana is a step in that direction, according to Paritosh Pandya, a computer scientist and music student whom I know. I, myself, have not used the app.
5. Peter Manuel, *Thumri in Historical and Stylistic Perspectives*, pages 148 to 151. Although this book is about thumri, the variation in intervals likely holds true for khayal as well. Praveen Karkare, a tabla player who plays extensively for khayal singers, also says that intervals minutely vary.

❖ Sea: 1965–68

6. Nicholas Magriel with Lalita du Perron, *The Songs of Khayal—Book One*, page 202.
7. Jon Barlow and Lakshmi Subramanian, 'Music and Society in North India: From the Mughals to the Mutiny', *Economic and Political Weekly*, 42, no. 19, 2007, page 1779.
8. Shanta Gokhale, *Playwright at the Centre: Marathi Drama from 1843 to the Present*, page 14.
9. For the information in this paragraph, I have drawn on the books *Hindustani Music in Colonial Bombay* by Aneesh Pradhan and *Musicophilia in Mumbai: Performing Subjects and the Metropolitan Unconscious* by Tejaswini Niranjana.
10. Govindrao Tembe, *My Pursuit of Music*, page 37.

11. Janaki Bakhle, *Two Men and Music: Nationalism and the Making of the Indian Classical Tradition,* page 138; Magriel with du Perron, *The Songs of Khayal—Book One,* page 29.
12. This transcription corresponds to a passage from a recording titled 'Darbari Kanada: Sargam' on the section of www.gajananbuwajoshi.com containing clips of Gajananbuwa's lessons on various raags: http://www.gajananbuwajoshi.com/guru_gajananbuwa_joshi#taleem. This and other recordings on the site offer a vivid glimpse into Gajananbuwa's teaching style.
13. This sequence is an approximation of what was actually sung, but illustrates the same principles.

5.
◈ Roots

1. Richard Widdess, 'The Emergence of Dhrupad', *Hindustani Music: Thirteenth to Twentieth Centuries,* edited by Joep Bor, Françoise 'Nalini' Delvoye, Jane Harvey, Emmie Te Nijenhuis, pages 124 and 126.
2. Ibid, page 126.
3. Ibid.
4. Ibid. Also Barlow and Subramanian, 'Music and Society in North India', *Economic and Political Weekly,* page 1779.
5. The generic meaning of kalawant is artist. It also has at least two other, specific usages. It is applied to hereditary soloists attached to the Mughal court and to the community of hereditary women performers from the Devadasi tradition, especially from Goa, who are also called naikins.
6. Katherine Butler Brown, 'The Origins and Early Development of Khayal', in *Hindustani Music: Thirteenth to Twentieth Centuries,* edited by Bor et al., page 160.
7. This is sometimes spelt 'chutkula', which in contemporary Hindi also means joke or witticism.
8. Emmie te Nijenhuis, 'Musical Forms in Medieval India', in *Hindustani Music,* edited by Bor et al., page 104; Madhu Trivedi, *The Emergence of the Hindustani Tradition: Music, Dance and Drama in North India, 13th to 19th,* page 107.
9. Butler Brown, 'The Origins and Early Development of Khayal', page 177.

10. Amlan Das Gupta, 'Reflections on the Early Khayal', *ResearchGate*, page 3: https://www.researchgate.net/publication/342916763_Reflections_on_the_Early_Khayal; also in *Poetics and Politics of Sufism and Bhakti in South Asia: Love, Loss and Liberation*, edited by Kavita Panjabi.
11. Butler Brown, 'The Origins and Early Development of Khayal', pages 174 to 178.
12. Ibid, pages 160 and 182.
13. Ibid, pages 170 and 171; Trivedi, *The Emergence of the Hindustani Tradition*, page 112.
14. Butler Brown, 'The Origins and Early Development of Khayal', page 162.
15. Ibid, pages 176, 180 and 181; Das Gupta, 'Reflections on the Early Khayal', page 6.
16. Butler Schofield, *Music and Musicians in Late Mughal India*, pages 11, 12 and 57. These pages provide information about the four communities described in this paragraph.
17. Barlow and Subramanian, 'Music and Society in North India', page 1792.
18. Daniel M. Neuman, *Studying India's Musicians: Four Decades of Selected Articles*, page 33.
19. Widdess, 'The Emergence of Dhrupad', page 129.
20. Neuman, *Studying India's Musicians*, page 33.
21. Men from another community called the mirasis also became accompanists. But Dard Neuman told me over email that the dhadhi and mirasi accompanists intermarried to become virtually indistinguishable. So I refer to them just as dhadhis.
22. Neuman, 'The social organization of a music tradition: Hereditary Specialists in North India' and 'Gharanas: The rise of musical "houses" in Delhi', in *Studying India's Musicians*; Adrian McNeil, 'Mirasis: Some Thoughts on Hereditary Musicians in Hindustani music', *Context—Journal of Music Research*, no. 32, 2007: https://researchmgt.monash.edu/ws/portalfiles/portal/240169136/32.McNeil.pdf.
23. Neuman, *Studying India's Musicians*, pages 39, 80 to 82, and 92.
24. Ibid, pages 93 and 94.
25. Neuman, *Studying India's Musicians*, pages 30 and 95.
26. Widdess, 'The Emergence of Dhrupad', page 133.
27. Neuman, *Studying India's Musicians*, pages 180 to 182.

28. Butler Schofield, 'The Origins and Early Development of Khayal', page 190.
29. Barlow and Subramanian, 'Music and Society in North India', page 1783; Trivedi, *The Emergence of the Hindustani Tradition*, page 114.
30. Barlow and Subramanian, 'Music and Society in North India', page 1779.
31. Butler Schofield, 'The Origins and Early Development of Khayal', page 189; Trivedi, *The Emergence of the Hindustani Tradition*, page 114.
32. Vilayat Hussain Khan, *Sangeetajnon ke Samsmaran*, page 53.
33. Widdess, 'The Emergence of Dhrupad', page 117.
34. Trivedi, *The Emergence of the Hindustani Tradition*, page 114.
35. Vilayat Hussain Khan, *Sangeetajnon ke Samsmaran*, page 53.
36. Ibid, page 52.
37. Ibid, page 53.
38. Magriel with du Perron, *The Songs of Khayal—Book One*, page 13.
39. Barlow and Subramanian, 'Music and Society in North India', page 1779.
40. Butler Schofield, 'Chief musicians to the Mughal emperors: The Delhi kalāwant birādarī, 17th to 19th centuries', Revised edition, 2015, page 5: https://shorturl.at/bc1Y9.
41. Barlow and Subramanian, 'Music and Society in North India', page 1779.
42. Ibid.
43. Ibid, page 1784; Das Gupta, 'Reflections on the Early Khayal', page 5.
44. Das Gupta, 'Reflections on the Early Khayal', page 5.
45. Joep Bor and Allyn Miner, 'Hindustani Music: A Historical Overview of the Modern Period', in *Hindustani Music*, edited by Bor et al., page 198.
46. Magriel with du Perron, *The Songs of Khayal—Book One*, page 28.
47. His name is sometimes rendered as Nathhan Khan.
48. Magriel with du Perron, *The Songs of Khayal—Book One*, pages 26 and 27.
49. The following summary of the history of thumri draws from Peter Manuel: 'Thumri, Ghazal and Modernity in Hindustani Music Culture', *Hindustani Music*, edited by Bor et al., pages 240 and 244, as well as Peter Manuel, *Thumri in Historical and Stylistic*

Perspectives, and Lalita du Perron, *Hindi Poetry in a Musical Genre: Thumri Lyrics*.

50. Vidya Rao, a thumri singer, editor and writer, pointed out to me that V.N. Bhatkhande had included some bandish ki thumris in his compilation of khayal compositions. One example, she said, was *Neer bharana kaise jaoon* (How am I go to fill [my pot with] water?), in raag Tilak Kamod, which was originally a bandish ki thumri.
51. This is evident from the music of the earliest proponents who were recorded, such as Krishnarao Shankar Pandit and Ramakrishnabuwa Vaze.
52. I have borrowed the term 'heterodox' from Dard Neuman, who used it in his online talk titled 'Heterodoxy, Hybridity, and the Politics of the Popular in Post-1857 Hindustani Music', *Manipal-Samvaad Centre for Indian Music*, 8 August 2021: https://www.youtube.com/watch?v=q6Qs5OJLq3c&t=9032s. The contents of the talk will be part of a forthcoming book. Amlan Das Gupta also uses the term 'heterodox' for styles that did not originate from dhrupad singers, in the following essay: 'Words for music perhaps: Reflections on the khayal bandish', in *Music and Modernity: North Indian Music in an Age of Mechanical Reproduction*, page 240.
53. Richard Widdess, 'Generative processes in Indian music theory', *Musica ex Machina Symposium*, 20 September 2024: https://www.youtube.com/watch?v=t1TW4aUSrYw.
54. I have derived these ideas from Dard Neuman's work, from Arun Kashalkar's observations and my own listening.
55. Neuman, *Studying India's Musicians*.
56. Neuman, 'Heterodoxy, Hybridity, and the Politics of the Popular in Post-1857 Hindustani Music'.
57. 'What happened to the...lineage of kalawants in the aftermath of 1857? It is true to say that the mists descend somewhat at this point,' writes Butler Schofield, in 'Chief musicians to the Mughal emperors', page 11.
58. Sangeet Samrat Khansahab Alladiya Khan, *My Life*, as told to his grandson, Azizuddin Khan, translated by Amlan Das Gupta and Urmila Bhirdikar, pages 49 and 70.
59. Ibid, pages 68 to 70.
60. Neuman, 'Heterodoxy, Hybridity, and the Politics of the Popular in Post-1857 Hindustani Music'.

61. For information on various gharanas, I have drawn from several articles, books and talks that I have cited in footnotes. I have also synthesised information from the following books: B.R. Deodhar, *Pillars of Hindustani Music*; Magriel with du Perron, *The Songs of Khayal—Book One*, pages 13 to 29; Kumar Prasad Mukherjee, *The Lost World of Hindustani Music*; and Wim Van Der Meer, *Hindustani Music in the 20th Century*, chapter 8. In some cases, I have also interviewed contemporary singers.
62. Neuman, *Studying India's Musicians*, page 76 has a chart that partly captures how Gwalior musicians were pedagogically related to other lineages.
63. Ramanlal Mehta, *Agra Gharana: Tradition, Musical Philosophy & Repertoire*, translated by Arijit Mahalanabis, page 16; N. Jayavanth Rao, *Sajan Piya: A Biography of Ustad Khadim Hussain Khan*, pages 11 and 14.
64. Mehta, *Agra Gharana*, page 20.
65. Das Gupta, 'Reflections on Early Khayal', page 6.
66. Sangeet Samrat Khansahab Alladiya Khan, *My Life*, pages 10 and 34.
67. Rao, *Sajan Piya*, page 39.
68 Das Gupta, 'Reflections on Early Khayal', page 6.
69. Magriel with du Perron, *The Songs of Khayal—Book One*, page 22.
70. Bhavik Mankad suggested to me this may have been the case.
71. Magriel with du Perron, *The Songs of Khayal—Book One*, page 25.
72. Wim van der Meer, *Hindustani Music in the 20th Century*, pages 176 and 177.
73. Neuman, *Studying India's Musicians*, page 84; Neuman, 'Heterodoxy, Hybridity, and the Politics of the Popular in Post-1857 Hindustani Music'.
74. Ibid.
75. Dard Neuman, 'Heterodoxy, Hybridity, and the Politics of the Popular in Post-1857 Hindustani Music'.
76. Butler Brown, 'The Origins and Early Development of Khayal', page 165.
77. Barlow and Subramanian, 'Music and Society in North India', page 1785.
78. Gokul Nag, Vishnupur Gharana, *Raga.hu*: http://raga.hu/en/vishnupur-gharana-2/.
79. Ibid.

80. Neuman, 'Heterodoxy, Hybridity, and the Politics of the Popular in Post-1857 Hindustani Music'.
81. Magriel with du Perron, *The Songs of Khayal—Book One*, page 23.
82. Jyoti Nair, 'A style as intriguing as its name', *The Hindu*, 4 January 2018: https://www.thehindu.com/entertainment/music/bhendi-bazaar-gharana/article22366824.ece.
83. 'Pt. Jasraj Speaks about Mewati Gharana of Indian Classical Music', *Strumm Spiritual*: https://www.youtube.com/watch?v=W3XTKAkRp8E; 'Mewati gharana', Wikipedia: https://en.wikipedia.org/wiki/Mewati_gharana.
84. Ram Chandrakaushika, 'The gharanas of India', *Saxonian Folkways*: https://saxonianfolkways.wordpress.com/tag/the-mewati-gharana/.
85. Rajan Parrikar, 'Jaipurwales—The Lost Link', *Music Archive by Rajan Parrikar*: https://www.parrikar.org/essays/jaipurwales/.
86. The website kunwarshyam.com did not have this information, as of 14 May 2025. Both Bhavdeep Jaipurwale the grandson of Lakshman Prasad Jaipurwale, who learnt from two of Lalji Maharaj's students, and Shyamrang Shukla, the son of Rajaram Shukla, who learnt from Lakshman Prasad Jaipurwale, told me they did not know whom Lalji Maharaj had trained with, attributing the lack of information to the fact that he was an inveterate recluse.
87. Interview with Bhavdeep Jaipurwale and Shyamrang Shukla, who are inheritors of this tradition.
88. Interview with Amit Chaudhuri, novelist and musician, who learnt from Govind Prasad Jaipurwale.
89. Ibid.
90. Interview with Shyamrang Shukla.
91. 'Major and minor gharanas of the Indian classical music: An Essay on Kotali', Ruchira Panda: https://www.ruchirapanda.com/major-minor-gharanas-kotali-gharana/.
92. See the pedagogical tree on vocalist Ruchira Panda's website: https://www.ruchirapanda.com/#gharana.
93. Bor and Miner, 'Hindustani Music: A Historical Overview of the Modern Period', page 214.
94. Interview with Amlan Das Gupta.
95. The Mewati gharana vocalist Jasraj makes a similar argument in this interview, 'Pt. Jasraj Speaks about Mewati Gharana of Indian

Classical Music', *Strumm Spiritual*: https://www.youtube.com/watch?v=W3XTKAkRp8E.

◆ Palace

96. This view is echoed by Magriel with du Perron, *The Songs of Khayal—Book One*, page 4, footnote 3.
97. McNeil, 'Mirasis', page 45.
98. I owe this metaphor to Kartik Prasad.

6.

◇ Fringe

1. All these renditions are available online on First Edition Arts' YouTube channel.
2. Butler Schofield, *Music and Musicians in Late Mughal India*, page 18.
3. Bor and Miner, 'Hindustani Music: A Historical Overview of the Modern Period', *Hindustani Music: Thirteenth to Twentieth Centuries*, edited Bor et al., page 202.
4. I wrote the following preview of one of Aslam Khan's concerts—Sumana Ramanan, 'State of Union', *Mumbai Mirror*, 15 August 2015: https://mumbaimirror.indiatimes.com/mumbai/other/a-state-of-union/articleshow/48486984.cms. I also wrote the following obituary after he passed away—Sumana Ramanan, 'Aslam Khan: A Musician Whom Mumbai Failed', 26 March 2018: https://mumbaimirror.indiatimes.com/mumbai/other/a-musician-whom-mumbai-failed/articleshow/63436912.cms.
5. I wrote an article about Madhukar Joshi on the occasion of his eightieth birthday—Sumana Ramanan, 'Upholder of a Great Tradition', *Mumbai Mirror*, 25 December 2018: https://mumbaimirror.indiatimes.com/opinion/columnists/sumana-ramanan/upholder-of-a-great-tradition/articleshow/67239004.cms.
6. 'What is fringe?', *Ashville Fringe Society*: https://www.ashevillefringe.org/what-is-fringe.

❖ Shore: 1969–72

7. I have used the translation in Magriel with du Perron, *The Songs of Khayal—Book Two*.

8. I have taken this phrase from an online recording of that rendition: https://www.youtube.com/watch?v=6RNV4zFZAX8.
9. In the initial portion of the khali, the tabla player does not produce any bass sound, which comes from the dagga. This is what distinguishes the khali from the bhari.
10. From Arun Kashalkar's unpublished poetry collection, translated from Marathi by Jerry Pinto.
11. The literal meaning of 'mandaarmala' is a garland of mandaar flowers. But the musical's protagonist is called Mandaar and the story is about his life.
12. I got these details from the festival website, but as of 14 May 2025, the information was no longer available.
13. 'Sawai Gandharva Sangeet Mahotsav: New singers Kashalkar and Shreekhande colour the stage', *Kesari*, Pune, 18 November 1971. I have translated the headline and parts of the report from Marathi.
14. Dhaval Kulkarni, 'How a Hindu-Muslim royal romance inspired many a Marathi literary work', *India Today*, 13 January 2025: https://www.indiatoday.in/india-today-insight/story/how-a-hindu-muslim-royal-romance-inspired-many-a-marathi-literary-work-2664101-2025-01-13; Suprita Mitter, 'Play it again, for Marathi theatre', *Mid-Day*, 15 October 2015: https://www.mid-day.com/lifestyle/culture/article/marathi-musical-theatre-mumbai-guide-evolution-dnyanesh-pendharkar-17687173.

◆ Architect

15. Warren Senders pointed this out to me.
16. For an exploration of the tension between tradition and innovation and between reproduction and improvisation in North Indian art music, see John Napier, 'Novelty That Must Be Subtle: Continuity, Innovation and 'Improvisation' in North Indian Music', *Critical Studies in Improvisation/Études critiques en improvisation*, 1, no. 3, 2006.

7.

◇ Black Box

1. https://www.facebook.com/179477825548290/photos/a.179908048838601/605669936262408.
2. Hridayesh Arts, another, smaller firm, was founded in 2005.

3. See Aneesh Pradhan's *Hindustani Music in Colonial Bombay* for a detailed history of the ecosystem in Mumbai in this period. Tejaswini Niranjana's *Musicophilia in Mumbai: Performing Subjects and the Metropolitan Unconscious* also has a wealth of insights about this era.
4. Aneesh Pradhan's *Chasing the Raag: A Look into the World of Hindustani Music*, Chapter 1, has details about All India Radio's role in supporting classical music.
5. See Amrita Shah's *Telly-Guillotined: How Television Changed India*.
6. Arnab Chakrabarty, 'Arun Kashalkar: Meet the Zen Master of Hindustani Music', *Scroll.in*, 22 June 2017: https://scroll.in/magazine/840650/arun-kashalkar-meet-the-zen-master-of-hindustani-classical-music.
7. Pradhan, *Chasing the Raag Dream*, page xix.
8. Michael Pollan, 'In Defense of Food', *Michaelpollan.com*: https://michaelpollan.com/books/in-defense-of-food/.
9. Devina Dutt and Pepe Gomes, 'Eyes Wide Shut', *Aroop: A Journal of Arts, Poetry and Ideas*, Volume 4, 2020: https://www.therazafoundation.org/_app_data/article/aroop_vol_04.pdf.
10. Arnab Chakrabarty, 'Requiem for her masters', *Mumbai Mirror*, 6 March 2017: https://mumbaimirror.indiatimes.com/entertainment/music/requiem-for-her-masters/articleshow/57489063.cms.
11. T.M. Krishna, *A Southern Music: The Karnatik Story*, page 55.
12. Priya Purushothaman, 'In sync with taleem and tradition', *The Hindu*, 2 March 2018: https://www.thehindu.com/entertainment/music/in-sync-with-taleem-and-tradition/article22910853.ece.
13. Priya Purushothaman's book, *The Call of Music: 8 Stories of Hindustani Musicians*, 2025, has a chapter describing Shubhada Paradkar's own journey as a woman who learnt in the three traditional gharanas, including the Agra style, and how she grappled with gender stereotypes.
14. Chakrabarty, 'Arun Kashalkar: The Zen Master of Hindustani Music', *Scroll.in*.

❖ Backwaters: 1943–57

15. For a detailed essay on this subject, see Urmila Bhirdikar, 'The Spread of North Indian Music in Maharashtra in the Late

Nineteenth and Early Twentieth Centuries: Socio-cultural Conditions of Production and Consumption', *Music and Modernity: North Indian Classical Music in an Age of Mechanical Reproduction'*, edited by Amlan Das Gupta.
16. Shanta Gokhale, *Playwright at the Centre: Marathi Drama from 1843 to the Present*, page 18.
17. Ibid, page 32.
18. Ibid, page 32.
19. Ibid, page 32.
20. The festival's programme and other information about it are available in Akashvani's *Listener's Guide to Radio Sangeet Sammelan: Sunday October 28 to Saturday November 3, 1956*. I downloaded a copy of this from the Prasar Bharati website, but when I checked on 13 May 2025, it was no longer there on the website.

◆ Sport

21. Amit Chaudhuri, *Finding the Raag: An Improvisation on Indian Music*, page 53.
22. There are, however, stories of singers having participated in literal duels in various royal courts.
23. Warren Senders pointed me to an example of Peter Schickele, an American composer, music educator and satirist, commenting on Beethoven's Symphony no. 5 as though it were a sports event: https://www.youtube.com/watch?v=WR4CdKSeD-E.

8.

◇ **Counterweights**

1. Photo of the house full sign outside the Godrej Theatre: https://www.facebook.com/search/top?q=omkar%20dhumal.
2. https://www.ncpamumbai.com/management/.
3. https://www.ncpamumbai.com/timeline/.
4. M. Rahman, 'Row over proposed NCPA complex in Bombay', *India Today*, 20 September 1988: https://www.indiatoday.in/magazine/indiascope/story/19880930-row-over-proposed-ncpa-complex-in-bombay-797746-1988-09-29.
5. 'The NCPA at 50': https://www.tata.com/newsroom/heritage/ncpa-50-years-tata. Albert Almeida, a consultant at the chairman's office, confirmed this to me over email in June 2023.

6. https://www.ncpamumbai.com/timeline/.
7. Ibid.
8. Special Correspondent, 'LitFest director slams Karnad for targeting Naipaul', *The Hindu*, 4 November 2012.: https://shorturl.at/E1IuD.
9. This amount has appeared in media reports and Albert Almeida confirmed this to me over email in June 2023.
10. 'NCPA-Aims and Objectives', *Sahapedia*: https://www.sahapedia.org/ncpa-mumbai%E2%80%94-aims-and-objectives#lg=1&slide=0. The MoA does not carry the date of this document, but the word 'establish' suggests that this was the original MoA.
11. I had requested the NCPA for its most recent MoA, and it sent me a copy on 2 July 2025.
12. The council proposed the change in 2006 and it was approved by the deputy charity commissioner in 2008, according to a copy of the MoU.
13. Anil Dharker, 'Diary of a Visionary', *Serenade*, 2 March 2017: https://serenademagazine.com/diary-of-a-visionary/.
14. I interviewed consultant A in person in 2016 and had at least three follow-up interviews on the phone, including on 13 April 2022, on 23 March 2023 and 16 May 2023.
15. Ibid.
16. Tinaz Nooshian, Rema Gehi and Dhamini Ratnam, 'NCPA faces growth pains', *Mumbai Mirror*, 4 April 2013: https://timesofindia.indiatimes.com/entertainment/hindi/music/news/ncpa-faces-growth-pains/articleshow/19538295.cms.
17. Ibid.
18. Laura Battle, 'Raag time melodies', *Financial Times*, 22 September 2012: https://www.ft.com/content/68776f1c-0245-11e2-b41f-00144feabdc0.
19. Suman Layak, 'Homi Bhabha's house up for sale: Khushroo Suntook to spend the money to make NCPA a global brand', *The Economic Times*, 22 December 2013: https://economictimes.indiatimes.com/wealth/personal-finance-news/homi-bhabhas-house-up-for-sale-khusroo-suntook-to-spend-the-money-to-make-ncpa-a-global-brand/articleshow/27739916.cms?from=mdr.
20. I interviewed Parikh for about two hours in his Mumbai home on 22 March 2023.

21. He did this over email in June 2023.
22. Ibid.
23. Ibid. The NCPA had, however, made public some details about funds it received that are governed by the Foreign Contribution (Regulation) Act 2010, for three years, on its website: https://www.ncpamumbai.com/wp-content/uploads/2025/02/NCPA-FCRA-Accounts-FY-2023-24.pdf.
24. 'Deciphering Disclosure Obligations: High Court's Guidelines on RTI Applicability to Public Trusts–People Welfare Society vs The State Information Commissioner & Ors', *Indialaw.in*: https://www.indialaw.in/blog/civil/rti-applicability-high-court-guidelines-on-trusts/. Also see the following report: Arunima, 'Whether state-funded 'public trust institution' obligated to provide 'information' under RTI? Bombay High Court clarifies...', *SCC Online:* https://www.scconline.com/blog/post/2024/03/06/bom-hc-clarifies-right-to-information-obligation-public-trusts-state-funded-institutions-legal-news/.
25. Section 8 of the RTI Act lists these exemptions: https://indiankanoon.org/doc/758550/.
26. 'Compliances requires (*sic*) for the Charitable Trusts', point 5, *B.C. Shetty & Co.*, 17 October 2023: https://bcshettyco.com/charitable-trusts.php.
27. The NCPA's email sent me this information on 2 July 2025. I sent a follow-up query asking how many of the instructors were foreigners, but did not receive a reply. But a friend of mine said that her children had learnt mostly from teachers who were from Russia, Kazakhstan and Uzbekistan.
28. Nooshian, Gehi and Ratnam, 'NCPA faces growth pains'.
29. I interviewed employee A on the phone in 2016 and 2017.
30. I interviewed consultant B on the phone in mid-2016.
31. I first interviewed consultant C on the phone on 27 June 2025 and followed up with an email exchange.
32. Nooshian, Gehy and Ratnam, 'NCPA faces growth pains'.
33. The NCPA sent me an email on 2 July 2025 with this information, which I had requested on 23 April 2025. The email also said that the SOI Chamber Orchestra (as opposed to the SOI), had thirty-five members. In follow-up email messages, I asked the NCPA whether all thirty-five of them belonged to the SOI and how the

fifteen Indians were spread across the SOI and SOI Chamber Orchestra, but did not hear back from the organisation.
34. Ibid.
35. I interviewed employee B over the phone on 3 April 2019.
36. The NCPA's email sent on 2 July 2025.
37. Layak, 'Homi Bhabha's house up for sale: Khusroo Suntook to spend the money to make NCPA a global brand'.
38. Rajshri Mehta, 'Homi Bhabha's iconic bungalow sold for Rs 372 crore', *The Times of India*, 19 June 2014: https://timesofindia.indiatimes.com/city/mumbai/homi-bhabhas-iconic-bungalow-sold-for-rs-372-crore/articleshow/36779144.cms.
39. Layak, 'Homi Bhabha's house up for sale: Khusroo Suntook to spend the money to make NCPA a global brand'.
40. Nooshian, Gehy and Ratnam, 'NCPA faces growth pains'.
41. Guruji had shown me the invitation letter from the NCPA at some point, but later misplaced it. I remember the amount being Rs 40,000.
42. I interviewed Rao on 11 April 2023 in her office.
43. In its email reply to me on 2 July 2025, the NCPA said it could not share how much it was paying these teachers per student.
44. These were the advisers for Indian classical music at least until mid-2023. In July 2025, the NCPA sent me a mail mentioning only Mala Ramadorai's name.
45. Press Trust of India, 'Shrutinandan NCPA Centre for Excellence in Music Gears up for their First Showcase', *The Times of India*, 30 May 2023: https://timesofindia.indiatimes.com/shrutinandan-ncpa-centre-of-excellence-in-music-gears-up-for-their-first-showcase/articleshow/100622033.cms.
46. This group consisted of Ajoy Chakrabarty, Hariprasad Chaurasia, Jasraj, Rajan and Sajan Mishra, Shivkumar Sharma and Zakir Hussain, from the Hindustani stream, and M. Balamuralikrishna, Ravi Kiran, Sudha Raghunathan, T.N. Krishnan, T.V. Sankaranarayanan and U. Srinivas, from the Carnatic stream: https://web.archive.org/web/20090902155823/http://www.ncpamumbai.com/announcements/10-july-2009-indias-leading-music-maestros-meet-ncpa.
47. Prathyush Parasuraman, 'Nita Mukesh Ambani Cultural Centre: Culture as spectacle', *Frontline*, 20 April 2023: https://frontline.thehindu.com/columns/counter-culture-culture-as-spectacle-

prathyush-parasuraman-nita-mukesh-ambani-cultural-centre-aims-to-be-the-cultural-compass-of-india/article66732927.ece.

❖ Travels: 1958–64

48. *Annual Report 1954-55: Ministry of Education,* page iii: https://dspace.gipe.ac.in/xmlui/bitstream/handle/10973/29317/GIPE-045718.pdf?sequence=2&isAllowed=y.
49. *Annual Report 1958-59: Ministry of Education,* page 95: https://schoolbooksarchive.azimpremjiuniversity.edu.in/displaybitstream?handle=20.500.12497/6276&fileid=7181112d-35b7-42c3-ab2b-6a0d347a1280.
50. Translated from Marathi by Mustansir Dalvi. This is the first verse of the poem, available on marathikavitaa.wordpress.com: https://shorturl.at/UtVWP.
51. Translated from Marathi by a person who did not want to be named.

◆ Sound

52. These include Adbhut Kalyan, and in Carnatic music, Niroshta, although I do not know how often these are performed.

9.

◇ Society

1. See T.M. Krishna, *A Southern Music: The Karnatik Story.*
2. M. Rajshekhar, 'Under BJP-RSS Rule, Madhya Pradesh's Culture Department Stares at Moral, Artistic Decay', *TheWire.in,* 18 June 2022: https://thewire.in/political-economy/madhya-pradesh-culture-department-tenders.
3. For more details, see the following article I wrote about Hindustani music writing in the media—Sumana Ramanan, 'Missing a Beat', *The Caravan,* 1 December 2019: https://caravanmagazine.in/commentary/state-of-writing-hindustani-classical-music.

❖ Mountain: 1973–80

4. Basira Beardsworth, compiler, *Chishti Sufis of Delhi: In the Lineage of Hazrat Pir-Murshid Inayat Khan,* page 8; Sadia Dehlvi, *The Sufi Courtyard: Dargahs of Delhi,* page 30.

5. Dehlvi, *The Sufi Courtyard*, *Oxford Reference*, page 39: https://www.oxfordreference.com/display/10.1093/oi/authority.20110803095608764.
6. Dehlvi, *The Sufi Courtyard*, page 30.
7. https://en.wikipedia.org/wiki/Mu%27in_al-Din_Chishti.
8. The last Agra hereditary musician moved out of Ruby Mansion in 2025. See Malini Nair, 'After 90 years, Agra gharana has moved out of its home in Mumbai', *Scroll.in*, 8 February 2025: https://scroll.in/magazine/1078897/after-90-years-agra-gharana-has-moved-out-of-its-home-in-mumbai.

◆ Rope

9. The rudra veena player Bahauddin Dagar told me that even these can change minutely.
10. N.A. Jairazbhoy and A.W. Stone, 'Intonation in Present-Day North Indian Classical Music', *Bulletin of the School of Oriental and African Studies, University of London* Volume 26, Number 1, 1963, pages 119 to 132; Mark Levy, *Intonation in North Indian Music: A Select Comparison of Theories with Contemporary Practice*.
11. I owe this to an observation made by T.M. Krishna in a lecture-demonstration.
12. See Magriel with du Perron, *The Songs of Khayal—Book One*, Chapter 2, 'Notating Khayal' especially pages 94 to 97.

10.

◇ Garden

1. For a detailed discussion of Hindustani music pedagogy, see Dard Neuman, 'Pedagogy, Practice, and Embodied Creativity in Hindustani Music', *Ethnomusicology*, 56, no. 3, 2012, pages 426 to 449: https://www.researchgate.net/publication/259746995.

◆ Language

2. For a detailed discussion of this, see Robin Cooper, 'Abstract Structure and the Indian Rāga System', *Ethnomusicology*, 21, no. 1, 1977, pages 1 to 32: https://www.jstor.org/stable/850849.
3. Howard Lasnik, *An Invitation to Cognitive Science: Language, Volume 1*, edited by Daniel N. Osherson and Howard Lasnik, page 3.

4. The thirteenth-century *Sangita Ratnakara* by Sarangdeva describes many examples.
5. Persian art music has twelve dastgahs, each 'representing a complex of skeletal melodic models on the basis of which a performer produces extemporised pieces', according to a description of the book *The Dastgah in Persian Music*, by Hormoz Farhat: https://www.cambridge.org/us/universitypress/subjects/music/ethnomusicology/dastgah-concept-persian-music?format=AR.
6. V.J. Cook and Mark Newson, *Chomsky's Universal Grammar: An Introduction*.
7. I am referring to the raag's melody, not the lyrics of compositions.

11.
◆ City
1. I owe most of the ideas in this section to my guru, Arun Kashalkar.
2. Warren Senders told me that his guru, Shreeram G. Devasthali, a student of Gajananbuwa Joshi, used this analogy.
3. I owe this analogy, too, to Arun Kashalkar.

12.
◇ Carnival
1. Devina Dutt, 'Showcase: Tribute to a legend', *The Hindu*, 18 October 2016: https://www.thehindu.com/features/friday-review/music/Showcase-Tribute-to-a-legend/article12547642.ece.
2. Some of these interviews appear in the following article of mine—Sumana Ramanan, 'Sacred Ground', *Mumbai Mirror*, 16 October 2016: https://mumbaimirror.indiatimes.com/others/sunday-read/sacred-ground/articleshow/54875385.cms.
3. This and the next sections draw from the following article of mine—Sumana Ramanan, 'How a Maharashtrian Cattle Grazer Taught Himself the Intricacies of Hindustani Music', *Scroll.in*, 29 March 2017: https://scroll.in/magazine/830162/how-a-maharashtrian-cattle-grazer-taught-himself-the-intricacies-of-hindustani-music.
4. This and the next sections draw from the following article of mine—Sumana Ramanan, 'Higher ground: Farmers line up at a classical music festival in a Maharashtra village', *Scroll.in*, 8 November 2016:

❖ Susegado: 1996–97

5. 'Kishori Amonkar and Arun Kashalkar's singing delights Valkini-Bhati', *Gomantak*, 16 June 1997.

◆ Time

6. The exception is dhamar, which has 14 beats and is divided thus: 5-2-5-2.
7. Peter Manuel, *Thumri in Historical and Stylistic Perspectives*, pages 148 to 151. Although this book is about thumri, the variation in intervals is probably true for khayal as well. Tabla players also say that intervals minutely vary.
8. Martin Clayton, *Time in Indian Music: Rhythm, Metre and Form in North Indian Rag Performance,* page 76. He also made this remark in an online lecture *Exploring rhythm in Hindustani music: Theories, Methods and Disciplines* presented by the Manipal-Samvaad Centre for Indian Music on 26 November 2021. The lecture was eventually deleted.
9. The tabla player Praveen Karkare gave me these numbers.

13.

◇ Colours

1. These four renditions are available on the First Edition Arts YouTube channel.
2. Pandit Arun Kashalkar Raag Khat, Swar Sadhanotsav, 24 March 2019: https://www.youtube.com/watch?v=JxkQH3cPNhA.
3. Tejaswini Niranjana, *Musicophilia in Mumbai: Performing Subjects and the Metropolitan Unconscious*, page 20.
4. Ibid.
5. Ibid. 'Through this shared language, musical subjects found articulation for new notions of selfhood premised precisely on that which was shared,' she writes.
6. Niranjana, *Musicophilia in Mumbai*, page 39.
7. This section draws from the following article of mine—Sumana Ramanan, 'At the grassroots', *Mumbai Mirror*, 13 November 2018: https://mumbaimirror.indiatimes.com/opinion/columnists/

sumana-ramanan/high-notes-at-the-grassroots/articleshow/ 66598934.cms.
8. For more details about the forum, see my article—Sumana Ramanan, 'A flawed solution', *Mumbai Mirror*, 11 December 2018: https://mumbaimirror.indiatimes.com/opinion/columnists/ sumana-ramanan/a-flawed-solution/articleshow/67034838. cms.
9. For more details, see my article—Sumana Ramanan, 'A veteran, a festival and a RAW officer', *Mumbai Mirror*, 17 May 2016: https://mumbaimirror.indiatimes.com/opinion/columnists/ sumana-ramanan/a-veteran-a-festival-and-a-raw-officer/ articleshow/52302718.cms.
10. Ibid.
11. The information in this section is drawn from the following article I wrote—Sumana Ramanan, 'The Secret History', *Mumbai Mirror*, 10 May 2017: https://mumbaimirror.indiatimes.com/others/ sunday-read/the-secret-history/articleshow/58088327.cms.
12. See Aban E. Mistry, *Parsis and Indian Classical Music: An Unsung Contribution*, pages 76 to 78, 84. She also mentions other musicians and many students of well-known musicians even thought they may not have become professionals.
13. Aneesh Pradhan, *Hindustani Music in Colonial India*, pages 52 to 66.
14. This is the estimate I got from many prominent members of the community, including Ramkishore Mankekar, the Mumbai-based editor in 2025 of the *Kanara Saraswat Magazine*, and Jaishankar Bondal, a Delhi-based career diplomat who has been documenting his community's heritage.
15. I wrote an article about this—Sumana Ramanan, 'The big footprint of a small community', *Mumbai Mirror*, 31 March 2016: https://mumbaimirror.indiatimes.com/opinion/columnists/ sumana-ramanan/the-big-footprint-of-a-small-community/ articleshow/51587084.cms.
16. Gaurang Kodical, Jayavanth Rao and Lalith J. Rao, compilers, *Directory of Chitrapur Saraswat Musicians & Dancers*, Kanara Saraswat Association – Kala Vibhag, Mumbai, 2006, page 9 and individual entries: https://drive.google.com/file/d/0B6AwxWg8 DVRFbk45ZUU2SFNhX2M/view?resourcekey=0-SIOR qXdott7zgpRvww0KVA.

17. The following articles describe this project in detail—Malini Nair, 'Before Indian classical music loses its diversity, an online project is rushing to archive it', 19 July 2023, *Scroll.in:* https://scroll.in/magazine/1052782/before-indian-classical-music-loses-its-diversity-an-online-project-is-rushing-to-archive-it; Gouri Dange, '2,000 hours of Indian classical music', *Frontline,* 12 October 2023: https://frontline.thehindu.com/arts-and-culture/a-monumental-project-to-create-a-digital-archive-of-indian-classical-music-and-performing-arts/article67411704.ece.
18. Sakshi Mehra, 'A DDA flat baithak brings intimacy back to Indian classical music. Beyond scale, spectacle', *ThePrint.in,* 16 August 2025: https://theprint.in/ground-reports/dda-flat-vasant-kunj-baithak-upstairs-indian-classical-music/2722206/.

❖ Beauty: 1998–2000

19. This is the recording of that Megh rendition: https://www.youtube.com/watch?v=BRUFwstHrWQ. Its quality is not great, so using headphones is advisable.

◆ Drama

20. Sometimes, a singer might use more than one avartan for one round of improvisation, especially within fast and medium-paced compositions, whose avartans are short. But a singer might occasionally also do so in a slow composition. In all these cases, the singer treats the start of the first avartan and the end of the last one as one big avartan.
21. I use the word 'song-text' to include any text set to music, including meaningless syllables, such as the ones found in taranas. By contrast, I use the word 'lyrics' to refer to text that is in a human language. In other words, lyrics are one kind of song-text.
22. I owe the term 'return to the familiar' and the observation that it has echoes in human life to Warren Senders.

14.

◇ Reception

1. Renuka Suryanarayanan, 'Morning raags set the tone', *The Hindu,* 22 September 2016: https://www.thehindu.com/features/friday-review/music/Morning-raags-set-the-tone/article14617774.ece.

2. Chakrabarty, 'Arun Kashalkar: Meet the Zen Master of Hindustani Music', *Scroll.in*, 22 June 2017: https://scroll.in/magazine/840650/arun-kashalkar-meet-the-zen-master-of-hindustani-classical-music.
3. Sumana Ramanan, 'Mystery of the Maestro', *Mumbai Mirror*, 3 April 2016: https://mumbaimirror.indiatimes.com/others/sunday-read/mystery-of-the-maestro/articleshow/51664525.cms.
4. Interview with Chinmoy Khaladkar, who also messaged me a translation of Bhimsen Joshi's quote.
5. Nandan Wandre sent me the audio recording of Purandare's comments in Marathi, which Mukul Kulkarni translated into English.
6. This was a magazine brought out on the occasion of Guruji's 75th birthday in May 2018.
7. Chakrabarty, 'Arun Kashalkar: Meet the Zen Master of Hindustani Music'.
8. Ibid.

❖ Arun, Mandaar, Ravi: 2001–05

9. Wikipedia, Jyotirlinga: https://en.wikipedia.org/wiki/Jyotirlinga.

◆ Quality

10. I borrowed this phrase from the Harvard College Writing Program: https://writingprogram.fas.harvard.edu/expos-20.

15.

◇ Cult

1. This vowel can be thought of as a continuation of the 'a' at the end of the previous word. It serves a musical purpose, not a semantic one.
2. Interview with Tina Brown, 'Philip Roth on the Future of the Novel', *The Daily Beast*, 23 September 2009: https://www.thedailybeast.com/philip-roth-on-the-future-of-the-novel.
3. Ibid.

◆ Weave

4. For this section, I have drawn from a presentation by Bhavik Mankad: https://baithak.org/appreciating-indian-classical-

music/laya-in-indian-classical-music/?fbclid=IwAR3XitNmag-QFAhcmF777R-ZvRENYy_7hu3TydtC2zshxTEmv4YHTMPFlRY. This presentation itself is based on the ideas Vamanrao H. Deshpande's *Indian Musical Traditions: An Aesthetic Study of the Gharanas in Hindustani Music*, Chapter 5, 'Two Gharanas at the Two Ends'.
5. Ibid.
6. The intervals between beats have sub-beats, which the percussionist expresses in a number of ways to suit the singer's stated preference, gharana and real-time improvisation.
7. I owe this insight to Arun Dravid.
8. There are exceptions, such as the late Padmavati Shaligram, who often used a leisurely pace.

16.

◇ Boutique

1. Vidya Rao, a thumri singer, writer and editor, explained this to me.
2. This was organised by *beej*, a dance organisation co-founded by Sanjukta Wagh.
3. Joshy Jesline, John Romate, Eslavath Rajkumar & Allen Joshua George, 'The plight of migrants during COVID-19 and the impact of circular migration in India: a systematic review', *Nature*, 14 October 2021: https://www.nature.com/articles/s41599-021-00915-6.
4. Basharat Peer, 'A Friendship, a Pandemic and a Death Beside a Highway', *The New York Times*, 31 July 2020: https://www.nytimes.com/2020/07/31/opinion/sunday/India-migration-coronavirus.html.
5. Sumant Kumar and Avinash Bhai Patel, 'The death of migrant workers in India during the first wave of COVID-19 pandemic', *Mental Health and Social Inclusion*, 26 September 2023: https://www.emerald.com/insight/content/doi/10.1108/mhsi-08-2023-0086/full/html.
6. Peer, 'A Friendship, a Pandemic and a Death Beside a Highway'.
7. Saurabh Kumar, 'Second wave of COVID-19: emergency situation in India', *Journal of Travel Medicine*, 28, no. 7, 2021: https://academic.oup.com/jtm/article/28/7/taab082/6284095.

♦ Story

8. I owe the observation about this contrast between Gwalior and Agra singers to Bhavik Mankad.

17.

◇ Puzzle

1. Muzaffar Alam, *The Mughals and The Sufis: Islam and Political Imagination in India 1500–1750*.
2. I first wrote to Dard Neuman, a scholar of Hindustani music at the University of California, Santa Cruz, whose online lecture I had attended. Neuman then put me in touch with Mohammadi.
3. This doctoral dissertation has more information on Qudsi: Sami-uddin Ahmed, 'Haji Muhammad Jan Qudsi of Mashhad: His Life, Times and Work', Aligarh Muslim University, 2002: https://core.ac.uk/download/pdf/144525871.pdf.
4. This is more or less a literal translation. The poet is likely to have used many words metaphorically in ways specific to that era.
5. Janaki Bakhle, *Two Men and Music: Nationalism in the Making of an Indian Classical Tradition*, page 99.
6. Max Katz, 'Institutional Communalism in North Indian Music', *Ethnomusicology*, 56, no. 2, 2012, page 280.
7. Ashok Ranade, *On Music and Music of Hindoostan*, pages 2 to 30 and 38, whose reference I came across in Katherine Butler Schofield's *Music and Musicians in Late Mughal India*, page 14, footnote 56, where she writes about 'Ranade's authoritative but overlooked evidence ... that hereditary musicians frequently used writing as an essential supplement to the embodiment and memory.'
8. Max Katz, 'The Scholarly Ustad: Muslim Musicians and their Textual Traditions' and Dard Neuman, 'Heterodoxy, Hybridity, and the Politics of the Popular in Post-1857 Hindustani Music', *Manipal-Samvaad Centre for Indian Music*, 8 August 2021: https://www.youtube.com/watch?v=q6Qs5OJLq3c&t=7s; Katherine Butler-Schofield, 'The Illiterate Ustad and Other Myths: Writing on Music in the Late Mughal World', *Ashok Da Ranade Memorial Trust*: https://www.youtube.com/watch?v=-7yajYkhKc8' and *Music and Musicians in the Late Mughal Period*.
9. Butler-Schofield, *Music and Musicians in the Late Mughal Period*, page 15.

10. As of July 2025, the website was being revamped.
11. Balamohan Shingade, 'What does it mean to sing Hindustani music while Hindutva attempts to co-opt the tradition?', *Scroll.in*, 22 October 2024: https://scroll.in/article/1069830/what-does-it-mean-to-sing-hindustani-music-while-hindutva-attempts-to-co-opt-the-tradition.
12. The literature is replete with such examples, such as the famous one of Hassu and Haddu Khan clandestinely listening to Bade Mohammad Khan.
13. Neuman, *The Life of Music in North India: The Organization of an Artistic Tradition; Studying India's Musicians*, page 99.
14. Justin Scarimbolo, 'On the secretive ustad: Pride among musicians and patrons in North India', *Indian Theatre Journal*, 4, no. 1, 2020, page 59. Also see Scarimbolo's doctoral dissertation, 'Brahmans Beyond Nationalism, Muslims Beyond Dominance: A Hidden History of North Indian Classical Music's Hinduization', University of Santa Barbara, 2014: https://escholarship.org/content/qt4gh1g3v3/qt4gh1g3v3_noSplash_c046ac58b5c831e956197d0971279407.pdf. In this dissertation, he says he 'challenges two key assumptions that structure nearly all historical accounts of modern North Indian classical music: (1) that Muslim musicians imposed a "secretive" and "jealously guarded" monopoly over the field from the seventeenth to the twentieth centuries and (2) that upper-caste Hindus eventually penetrated this monopoly only by the late nineteenth and early twentieth centuries under the protective umbrella of a nationalist musical reform movement,' page xv.
15. Das Gupta, 'Reflections on the Early Khayal', page 1.
16. Barlow and Subramanian, *Music and Society in North India*, page 1781.
17. Neuman, *Studying India's Musicians*, page 83.
18. M.N. Srinivas, *The Cohesive Role of Sanskritization and Other Essays*.
19. Nicholas Dirks, *The Hollow Crown: Ethnohistory of an Indian Kingdom*.
20. Nirmala Joshi, 'Compositions of Ustad Zahoor Khan (Ramdass)', *Sangeet Natak Akademi*, October 1959: https://indianculture.gov.in/compostitions-ustad-zahoor-khan-ramdass.

21. Sam Dalrymple, *Shattered Lands: Five Partitions and the Making of Modern Asia*, page 4.
22. *Religions Interactions in Mughal India*, edited by Vasudha Dalmia and Munis D. Faruqui.
23. William Dalrymple, 'Introduction: The Indosphere', *The Golden Road: How India Transformed the World*, pages 1 to 22.
24. Ibid, page 17.
25. Stephen Dale, *Indian Merchants and Eurasian Trade*, 1600-1750, pages 45, 58 to 60, 66, 112.
26. Vijay Tendulkar, 'Muslims and I', *Sabrang*, 9 January 2016: https://www.sabrangindia.in/article/muslims-and-i-vijay-tendulkar.
27. Gyanendra Pandey, *A History of Prejudice: Race, Caste and Difference in India and the United States*, page 2.
28. Ibid.
29. https://www.facebook.com/photo/?fbid=10160065772284638&set=a.96508614637.
30. Scroll staff, 'Sexual harassment allegations: Musician Akhilesh Gundecha steps down from Bhopal music school post', *Scroll.in*, 5 September 2020: https://scroll.in/latest/972286/sexual-harassment-allegations-musician-akhilesh-gundecha-steps-down-from-bhopal-music-school-post. After the Sansthan's internal complaints committee found the two musicians 'at fault', Akhilesh Gundecha filed a writ petition in the Madhya Pradesh high court refuting the committee's findings. In response, in June 2022, a dozen women filed an intervention application in the high court accusing the Gundechas of sexually harassing them, and urged action against the brothers. This application also accused Umakant Gundecha, who sang as a duo with Ramakant.
31. Alan W. Watts, 'Quotable Quotes', *Goodreads.com*: https://www.goodreads.com/quotes/95450-life-is-like-music-for-its-own-sake-we-are.
32. Pico Iyer, *The Art of Stillness: Adventures in Going Nowhere*, page 12.
33. Deccan Herald News Service, 'The tale of Shah Turkman Bayabani', *Deccan Herald*, 11 February 2014: https://www.deccanherald.com/content/385780/tale-shah-turkman-bayabani.html.
34. Mayank Austen Soofi, 'Delhi's Belly: Turkman, the survivor', *Mint*, 30 October 2014: https://www.livemint.com/Leisure/7iRp6cYdnNKndK4hyC0uhN/Delhis-Belly--Turkman-the-survivor.html.

♦ **Word**

35. Magriel with du Perron, *The Songs of Khayal—Book One*, page 201.
36. Ibid, page 202, 203; Trivedi, *The Emergence of the Hindustani Tradition*, page 112.
37. Das Gupta, 'Reflections on the Early Khayal', *ResearchGate*, page 6.
38. Sheila Dhar, *Raag'n Josh*, page 216.
39. Magriel with du Perron, *The Songs of Khayal—Book One*, page 202.
40. Ibid, page 101.
41. Ibid.
42. Ibid.
43. Her renditions of compositions about different social issues appear in a playlist 'Mere Khayal Se' on her YouTube channel *Radhika Joshi – Official*. One of her presentations on her project to create modern khayal compositions, at Ahmedabad University, is available online: https://drive.google.com/file/d/16ODkCjVItkudsXtW9JDuWmWnMrOcOIkQ/view.
44. I could not find renditions online of him singing his compositions. But Radhika Joshi has sung his composition on consumerism in Episode 7 of a playlist 'Mere Khayal Se' on her YouTube channel *Radhika Joshi – Official*.
45. His rendition of this fast composition can be found on his YouTube channel *Achintya Prahlad*, under the title 'Raga Harikamboji, in Hindustani style'. The composition begins a little after thirty-two minutes.
46. Aniruddh D. Patel, 'Music and the Brain: The Music of Language and the Language of Music', *Library of Congress*, 24 July 2009: https://www.youtube.com/watch?v=2oMvtw4aeEY&t=1090s.
47. Kartik Prasad set me thinking about the relation between human language and music.
48. T. M. Krishna, *A Southern Music*, page 277.

18.
◇ **Voice**

1. Oliver Craske, 'Finding the Raga by Amit Chaudhuri: a passion for Indian music', *The Guardian*, 29 April 2021: https://www.theguardian.com/books/2021/apr/29/finding-the-raag-by-amit-chaudhuri-a-passion-for-indian-music.

2. Ibid.
3. Samyukta Ranganathan, 'Exploring the Relationship Between Voice Disorders in Indian Classical Music and the Guru-Shishya Parampara Through an Understanding of the Autonomic Nervous System', *Voice and Speech Review*, 4 August 2024: https://www.tandfonline.com/doi/pdf/10.1080/23268263.2024.2374698. For this study, Samukta analysed several articles on the guru-shishya parampara using a qualitative research method in the social sciences called Constructivist Grounded Theory, or CGT.

❖ Light: 2001–14

4. From Arun Kashalkar's unpublished poetry collection, translated by Mukul Kulkarni.

◆ Feeling

5. I owe this formulation to Warren Senders.

19.

◇ Flame

1. 'Woody Allen on Life', *Filmfestivals.com*: https://www.youtube.com/watch?v=5yVPS8XBoBE.
2. Pico Iyer, *The Half Known Life*, page 5.

◆ Spiral

3. Exceptions include raags such as Adana, Paraj and Sohini, whose home base itself is the taar shadja.
4. Exceptions to this sequence include the formats of some branches of the Jaipur gharana, which sing the second verse right after the first verse, choosing to later independently project the taar shadja.

Interviews

I BEGAN INTERVIEWING ARUN KASHALKAR IN FEBRUARY 2016 and continued to do so until the end of June 2025, amassing hundreds of hours of recordings. In this period, I also recorded almost all of his music lessons that I attended. When it came to the key events in his life, I interviewed him several times, both to confirm the facts and elicit more details. Whenever possible, I double-checked the facts with primary sources and/or at least one other person.

Below, I have listed most of the other people I interviewed for the biographical part of the book, i.e. about the period before I got to know Arun Kashalkar, covering the years 1943 through 2015, which makes up the second strand. A few people on this list of over one hundred and fifty people are connected mainly to Arun Kashalkar's senior students, whose time learning from him also feature in the biographical portion.

I interviewed numerous others about the Indian classical music scene and its ecosystem, but I have not included them in this list because I have directly quoted many of them in the first strand, which pertains to my journey through the fringe culture. I have also not included in this list a few people whom I spoke to exclusively for the third strand, where I describe some basic concepts about khayal, because I have credited these individuals, where relevant, within the text or in the endnotes.

I have listed everyone below in alphabetical order by their first names and have also provided their birth years, to indicate the time periods through which they have lived. While interviewing three of them, I had noted down their ages, not birth dates. I could not reach one of them while the other two subsequently passed away, so I have prefixed their birth years with '~', to indicate that they are estimates. I also missed taking down the birth years of two people in the last category and was unable to reach them in the months leading up to the book's publication. I have inserted '***' in place of their birth years.

Family (ten): Adwait Kashalkar (1978), Ashish Kashalkar (1973), Dhanashree Kashalkar (1947), Kusum Wagh (1950), Prakash Kashalkar (1945), Sharada Palshikar (1952), Shrikant Kashalkar (1945), Subhash Kashalkar (1947), Ulhas Kashalkar (1955), Vikas Kashalkar (1950).

Students (forty): Ajay Risbud (1979), Akshay Vardhave (1995), Anandita Basu (1968), Anjali Joshi (1994), Asavari Gondhali (2004), Ashish Verma (1982), Ashwini Keshvan (1980), Bhavik Mankad (1991), Chetan Sharma (1978), Deepti Namjoshi (1985), Harshad Kamble (1992), Jayashree Gadagkar (1950), Kartik Prasad (1980), Kasturi Deshpande (1991), Kavita Joshi (1979), Ketaki Chaitanya, née Shetye (1991), Kiran Joshi (1963), Kirtee Gondhali (1984), Krishnna Natarajan (1975), Madhavi Jahagirdar (1972), Madhura Godbole (1985), Mandaar Valuskar (1982), Medha Dhawale (1972), Mukul Kulkarni (1980), Mukund Dev Sahoo (1988), Neha Purohit (1999), Omkar Dhumal (1992), Prabhakar Manchekar (~mid-1930s), Ravindra Parchure (1979), Sachin Surve (1977), Sanjith Pai (1981), Shekhar Damle (1957), Shirish Bapat (1954), Shreekar Kulkarni (1995), Smita Wagh (1956), Sugandha Sainath, née Laturkar (1987), Tushar Khanolkar (1972), Vikas Katre (1961), Vishal Moghe (1984), Yogesh Jahagirdar (1970).

Performing musicians and others closely involved with music (sixty-nine): Alka Deo Marulkar (1951), Amarendra Dhaneshwar (1951), Amit Chaudhuri (1962), Anand Shidhaye (1945), Anant Joshi (1976), Apoorva Gokhale (1973), Arnab Chakrabarty (1980), Arun Dravid (1943), Arun Kulkarni (1938), Aslam Khan (1940), Chandrashekhar Mahajan (1961), Deepak Raja (1948), Gopal Wadegaonkar (1942), Hema Deshpande (1963), Jayant Khot (1957), Jayashree Patnekar (1944), Kailash Patra (1967),

Kishore Navsalkar (1950), Lalith Rao (1942), Madhukar Joshi (1938), Maruti Patil (1953), Megha Prabhudesai* (1951), Mugdha Bhat-Samant (1975), Narayan Bodas (1933), Nayan Ghosh (1956), Pallavi Joshi (1976), Pratima Tilak (1967), Praveen Karkare (1971), Pravin Kaslikar (1984), Milind Raikar (1965), Omkar Jambhekar (1991), Prasad Chavan (1982), Prasad Jambhekar (1969), Premanand Amonkar (1966), Pournima Dhumale (1969), Prachla Amonkar (1972), Rafat Khan (1958), Raja Miya (1954), Rajesh Kelkar (1966), Ramakrishna Parsekar (1972), Ramdas Bhatkal (1935), Ranjani Ramachandran (1976), Ravindra Gangurde (1961), Sandhya Kathavate (1957), Sangita Agnihotri (1966), Sanjana Kaushik* (1995), Sharad Jambhekar (1939), Sharad Sathe (1932), Shashikant Athale (1968), Shashikant Tambe (1938), Shrikant Waikar (1950), Sveta Kilpady* (1977), Shyamrang Shukla (1954), Shrikrishna 'Babanrao' Haldankar (1927), Shruti Gokhale* (1965), Shubhada Paradkar (1957), Siddhesh Bicholkar (1985), Sukhada Kane (1961), Suresh Degwekar (1943), Suresh 'Bhai' Gaitonde (1932), Tulsidas Navelkar (1948), Vibhav Nageshkar (1955), Vinayak Pradhan (~1932), Vinayak Soman (1966), Vinod Digrajkar (1956), Vivek Joshi (1957), Vrinda Mundkar (1954), Yadnesh Raikar* (2000), Zunain Khan (1971).

* People in the lists above who learnt from Arun Kashalkar for a period or intermittently.

Music lovers and others (thirty-four): Adwait Haldankar (1962), Asavari Haldankar (1964), Bhalachandra Meher (1943), Chandra (1965), Chandrashekar Agarkar (1936), Chinmoy Khaladkar (1971), Devendra Shetye (1962), Datta Gumaste (***), Gautam Haldankar (1960), Gunwant Thakre (1944), Jairaj Phatak (***), Jyothi Kothare (1984), Krishna Godbole (1935), Kshipra Vishal (1982), Madhukar Chakradev (~1940), Manoj Vaidya (1977), Mukund Athavale (1954), Mukund Deshpande (1931), Nandan Wandre (1980), Neelam Karmalkar (1952), Nilima Kilachand (1944), P.V. Kamat (1934), Padmakar Tole (1936), Patanjali

Maduskar (1952), Pramod Jog (1951), Prasad Ambardekar (1977), Prasad Vanarse (1969), Sarada Bulchand (1978), Sujit Kulkarni (1966), Sukumar Kamble (1955), Usha Haldankar (1935), Vasant Upalanchiwar (h1941), Vikas Karmalkar (1951), Vithal Nadkarni (1949).

Note: Several of Arun Kashalkar's family members and students are also performing musicians.

Bibliography

1. Primary sources

Newspapers
- *The Times of India* (English).
- *Gomantak* (Marathi).
- *Kesari* (Marathi).
- *Loksatta* (Marathi).

Documents of the Indian government and state-run institutions
- All India Radio, *The Indian Listener*, April–July 1957.
- All India Radio, *Radio Sangeet Sammelan*, 1956, 28 October–3 November.
- Ministry of Education, *Report 1954-55*.
- Ministry of Home Affairs, *Census 2011*.

Arun Kashalkar's private papers
- Academic certificates.
- Leaflets and brochures of concerts.
- Notes about music.

Other written material
- *Pandit Arun Kashalkar (Rasadas): Amritotsav 2018*: A magazine of articles on Arun Kashalkar by a wide array of people, published on the occasion of his seventy-fifth birthday (in English, Hindi and Marathi).

Audio recordings
- Arun Kashalkar's concerts, renditions and lessons with Gajananbuwa: from Arun Kashalkar's collection and those of Ajay Risbud, Mukul Kulkarni, Prasad Ambardekar, Ravindra Parchure, Vikas Karmalkar and Yogesh Jahagirdar, among others.

- Recordings on www.gajananbuwajoshi.com.
- YouTube recordings of a variety of musicians.

Photographs
- Arun Kashalkar's private collection and those of his students.

Database of primary sources
- Katherine Butler Schofield and David Lunn, 'The SHAMSA database 1.0—Sources for the History and Analysis of Music/Dance in South Asia, c. 1700-1900,' *Zenodo*, 2018.

Secondary Sources

Books and articles about the origins and evolution of khayal:
- Amlan Das Gupta, 'Reflections on the Early Khayal', in *Poetics and Politics of Sufism and Bhakti in South Asia: Love, Loss and Liberation*, Hyderabad: Orient BlackSwan, 2011.
- Joep Bor, Françoise 'Nalini' Delvoye, Jane Harvey, Emmie Te Nijenhuis, editors, *Hindustani Music: Thirteenth to Twentieth Centuries*, New Delhi: Manohar Publishers & Distributors, 2010.
- Jon Barlow and Lakshmi Subramanian, 'Music and Society in North India: From the Mughals to the Mutiny', *Economic and Political Weekly*, 42, no.19, 2007.
- Katherine Butler Schofield,
  - » 'Chief musicians to the Mughal emperors: the Delhi kalāwant birādarī, 17th to 19th centuries, revised edition (2015); earlier published in *Dhrupad, its future: Proceedings of the 2013 ITC SRA (West) seminar*, NCPA: Mumbai, 2013.
  - » 'Did Aurangzeb Ban Music? Questions for the Historiography of His Reign', *Modern Asian Studies*, 41, no. 1, 2007.
  - » *Music and Musicians in Late Mughal India: Histories of the Ephemeral, 1748-1858*, South Asia Edition, New Delhi: Cambridge University Press, 2024.
  - » 'Reviving the Golden Age Again: "Classizisation," Hindustani Music, and the Mughals', *Ethnomusicology*, 54, no. 3, 2010.

- Madhu Trivedi, *The Emergence of the Hindustani Tradition: Music, Dance and Drama in North India, 13th to 19th Centuries*, Gurgaon: Three Essays Collective, 2012.
- Vilayat Hussain Khan, *Sangeetajnon ke Samsmaran* (in Hindi), New Delhi: Sangeet Natak Akademi, 1959.

Books and articles about khayal from the late nineteenth century onwards:
- Amlan Das Gupta, editor, *Music and Modernity: North Indian Music in an Age of Mechanical Reproduction*, editor, Kolkata: Thema Books, 2017.
- Aneesh Pradhan,
  » *Hindustani Music in Colonial Bombay*, Gurgaon: Three Essays Collective, 2014.
  » *Chasing the Raag Dream: A Look into the World of Hindustani Music*, Noida: HarperCollins Publishers, 2019.
- Daniel M. Neuman,
  » *The Life of Music in North India: The Organization of an Artistic Tradition*, Chicago: University of Chicago Press, 1990
  » *Studying India's Musicians: Four Decades of Selected Articles*, New Delhi: Manohar Publishers & Distributors, 2015.
- Govindrao Tembe, *My Pursuit of Music*, translated from Marathi by C.R. Kuddyady, Mumbai: Bharatiya Vidya Bhavan, 2014.
- Janaki Bakhle, *Two Men and Music: Nationalism in the Making of an Indian Classical Tradition*, Ranikhet: Permanent Black, 2005.
- Justin Scarimbolo,
  » 'Brahmans Beyond Nationalism, Muslims Beyond Dominance: A Hidden History of North Indian Classical Music's Hinduization', Doctoral Dissertation, *Alexandria Digital Research Library*, University of Santa Barbara, 2014.
  » 'On the secretive ustad: Pride among musicians and patrons in North India', *Indian Theatre Journal*, 4, no. 1, 2020.
- Kumar Prasad Mukherji, *The Lost World of Hindustani Music*, Delhi: Penguin Books, 2006.
- Max Katz, 'Institutional Communalism in North Indian Classical Music', *Ethnomusicology*, 56, no. 2, 2012.

- Namita Devidayal, *The Music Room*, Gurgaon: Penguin Random House, 2008.
- Sheila Dhar, *Raga'n Josh: Stories from a Musical Life*, Delhi: Permanent Black, 2005.
- Tejaswini Niranjana, *Musicophilia in Mumbai: Performing Subjects and the Metropolitan Unconscious*, New Delhi: Tulika Books, 2020.
- Wim Van Der Meer, *Hindustani Music in the 20th Century*, The Hague: Martinus Nijhoff Publishers, 1980.

Books about khayal vocalists and specific gharanas
- Ashok Da. Ranade, *Some Hindustani Musicians: They Lit The Way*, New Delhi: Promila & Co., Publishers in association with Bibliophile South Asia, 2011.
- B.R. Deodhar, *Pillars of Hindustani Music*, translated from Marathi by Ram Deshmukh, Bombay: Popular Prakashan, 1993.
- Chetan Karnani, *Listening to Hindustani Music*, Bombay: Orient Longman, 1976.
- Gajananbuwa Joshi, *Atmacharitra va Violinchya Gati* (Marathi), Mumbai: V.V. Ketkar, 1971.
- Manasi Joshi-Singh, *Bowing the Vocal Chords: Pandit Gajananbuwa Joshi*, Pune: Utkarsha Prakashan, 2012.
- Mohan Nadkarni, *The Great Masters: Profiles in Hindustani Classical Vocal Music*, New Delhi: Rupa & Co., 1999.
- N. Jayavanth Rao, *Sajan Piya: A Biography of Ustad Khadim Hussain Khan*, Bombay: Sajan Milap and N. Jayavanth Rao, 1981.
- Priya Purushothaman, *The Call of Music: 8 Stories of Hindustani Musicians*, Gurugram: Hachette, 2025.
- Ramanlal Mehta, *Agra Gharana: Tradition, Musical Philosophy & Repertoire*, translated from Hindi by Arijit Mahalanabis, State College, Pennsylvania, USA: Society for Indian Music and Arts, 2017.
- Sakuntala Narasimhan, *The Splendour of the Rampur-Sahaswan Gharana*, Bangalore: Veenapani Centre for Arts, 2006.
- Sangeet Samrat Khansahab Alladiya Khan, *My Life: As Told to His Grandson Azizuddin Khan*, translated from Hindustani, with an

introduction, by Amlan Das Gupta and Urmila Bhirdikar, Kolkata: Thema, second edition, 2012.
- Tejpal Singh and Prerna Arora, *Ustad Amir Khan: Pioneer of Indore Gharana*, translated from Hindi by Meena Banerjee, Kolkata: Thema, 2017.

Books and articles about khayal's aesthetics and pedagogy
- Amit Chaudhuri, *Finding the Raga: An Improvisation on Indian Music*, New York: The New York Review of Books, 2021.
- Chetan Karnani, *Form in Indian Music: A Study in Gharanas*, Jaipur: Rawat Publications, 2005.
- Dard Neuman, 'Pedagogy, Practice, and Embodied Creativity in Hindustani Music', *Ethnomusicology*, 56, no. 3, 2012.
- Deepak Raja, *The Musician and His Art: Essays on Hindustani Music*, New Delhi: D.K. Printworld, 2019.
- John Napier, 'Novelty That Must Be Subtle: Continuity, Innovation and "Improvisation" in North Indian Music, *Critical Studies in Improvisation*, 1, no. 3, 2006.
- Martin Clayton, *Time in Indian Music: Rhythm, Metre and Form in North Indian Rag Performance*, Oxford: Oxford University Press, 2000.
- Robin Cooper, 'Abstract Structure and the Indian Rāga System', *Ethnomusicology*, 21, no. 1, 1977.
- Shrikrishna (Babanrao) Haldankar, *Aesthetics of Agra and Jaipur Traditions*, translated from Marathi by Padmaja Punde and Shrikrishna (Babanrao) Haldankar, Mumbai: Popular Prakashan, 2001.
- Vamanrao H. Deshpande, *Indian Musical Traditions: An Aesthetic Study of the Gharanas in Hindustani Music*, Bombay: Popular Prakashan, 1973.

Books about khayal compositions
- Nicholas Magriel with Lalita du Perron, *The Songs of Khayal—Book One and Book Two*, New Delhi: Manohar Publishers & Distributors, 2013.

Online talks about khayal

- Max Katz, 'The Scholarly Ustad: Muslim Musicians and their Textual Traditions', *Manipal-Samvaad Centre for Indian Music*, YouTube, 2021.
- Dard Neuman, 'Heterodoxy, Hybridity, and the Politics of the Popular in Post-1857 Hindustani Music', *Manipal-Samvaad Centre for Indian Music*, YouTube, 2021.
- Katherine Butler-Schofield, 'The Illiterate Ustad and Other Myths: Writing on Music in the Late Mughal World', *Ashok Da Ranade Memorial Trust*, YouTube, 2021.

Books and articles about dhrupad and thumri

- Lalita du Perron, *Hindi Poetry in a Musical Genre: Thumri Lyrics*, Milton Park: Routledge, 2007.
- Peter Manuel,
    - » 'The Evolution of Modern Thumri', *Ethnomusicology*, 30, no. 3, 1986.
    - » 'The Intermediate Sphere in North Indian Music Culture: Between and Beyond "Folk" and "Classical"', *Ethnomusicology*, 49, no. 1, 2015.
    - » *Thumri: in Historical and Stylistic Perspectives*, Delhi: Motilal Banarasidass Publishers, 1990.
- Ritvik Sanyal and Richard Widdess, *Dhrupad: Tradition and Performance in Indian Music*, New York: Routledge, 2004.
- Vidya Rao, '"Thumri" as Feminine Voice', *Economic & Political Weekly*, 25, no. 17, 1990.

Books about Carnatic Music

- Lakshmi Subramanian, *From the Tanjore Court to the Madras Music Academy*, New Delhi: Oxford University Press, 2006.
- Sanjay Subrahmanyan, with Krupe Ge, *On That Note: Memories of a Life in Music*, Chennai: Westland, 2024.
- T.M. Krishna, *A Southern Music: The Karnatik Story*, Noida: HarperCollins Publishers, 2013.

Acknowledgements

WHILE WORKING ON THIS BOOK, MY FIRST ONE, I HAVE FELT at different times enlightened, gratified and energised as well as frustrated, anxious and exhausted. Through the ups and downs over the six years that I took to finish it, I have been lucky to have had the love, friendship, goodwill and help of many people. Gratitude to:

C.S. Rajan, for planting the seed by suggesting that I write a book about Maharashtra's classical music culture, and later, for an unconnected reason, inviting Arun Kashalkar to sing in my backyard; and Sarada Bulchand, for her role in bringing about an earlier concert, which led to this one.

Aman Khanna, Anjum Hasan, Geetha Venkataramanan, Pooja Sen, Sonal Shah, Supriya Nair and Vinod Jose, for carrying or editing various articles of mine about classical music; Meenal Baghel and Naresh Fernandes, editors par excellence and dear friends since the time we began our journalism careers, for seeing merit in my writing and boosting my spirits; Naresh, also for his thoughtful feedback on portions of the manuscript; Dipesh Chakrabarty, for teaching me to be alert to hidden histories; Stephen Langfur, for deepening my appreciation of beauty in writing and sharpening my craft; and Ramachandra Guha, for vital bits of advice.

The Raza Foundation and its managing trustee, Ashok Vajpeyi, as well as the Dr. Ashok Da Ranade Memorial Trust and its trustees, including Aneesh Pradhan and Anjum Rajabali, for awarding me grants and the privilege of being associated with them; the Sangam House writing residency, and its two stalwarts, Arshia Sattar and Trupti Prasad, for amazingly combining a focus on the big picture and an attention to detail; my dear co-residents, Felipe Franco Munhoz, Francesco Leto, Özge Calafato, Seema Punwani and Vidya Rao, for making my time there magical; Dhruvatara Sharma Churai and Priyanka Sarkar, for doing a great job of herding a rowdy bunch;

Rohit Tamang and Jahid Mohammed, for stocking the pantry and making sure that Jamun House was spotless; and Vidya, additionally for checking my translations of compositions.

Jerry Pinto, for instantly offering to translate two Marathi poems into English; Mustansir Dalvi for translating a verse from a Marathi poem; Gouri Dange, for getting another verse translated; Sumantra Ghoshal, for looking over my translation of an Urdu couplet; and Mayank Shekhar Jha, Paritosh Pandya, Priya Purushothaman and Srijan Deshpande, for giving me contacts, phone numbers and sources.

Each one of my guru bandhus and bahinis, for enriching our community, even if I could not interview all of them for want of time and could not include many of them in this book for want of space and because, at some point, I had to curb the proliferation of names; in particular, Ashish Verma, for helping me translate many composition titles; Krishnna Natarajan, for sharp observations on a draft and support; Bhavik Mankad and Vikas Katre, for feedback on the music strand; and Praveen Karkare, for lucidly explaining rhythmic concepts to me and checking portions in the book concerning rhythm.

Especially Kartik Prasad, for being my interlocutor throughout and insightful feedback on a draft; Mukul Kulkarni, for translating into English several primary sources, a poem and titles of songs from Marathi, for checking all the music notation and always being there to help with anything that I needed; Yogesh and Madhavi Jahagirdar, for being valuable sounding boards, especially in the early, uncertain stage; Devayani Jahagirdar, for her drawings; and above all, Arun Kashalkar, or Guruji, for his enormous patience, bottomless generosity and rare depth; Dhanashree Kashalkar, or Kaku, for fuelling the music; and the rest of the Kashalkar family, for their time and co-operation.

Shireen Mistry, who brought her hawk eye to some chapters of a very early draft, Tina Nagpaul, for her fellowship, and the rest of the Literature Live! team, for sharing my love of books and raucous discussions; the Network of Women in Media, India, for solidarity, and the Shillong tour group, for their warm response on a cold night to a presentation that I did based on a part of the book; Devina Dutt, for generously sharing her insights about the Hindustani music ecosystem based on years of experience; and Pepe Gomes, for his suggestions.

My dear friends Munis Faruqui and Clare Talwalker, for nuanced feedback on an important chapter; Dard Neuman, for reading two key chapters; and the brilliant and utterly generous Warren Senders, for reading the whole manuscript once, and then, of his own accord, again going through half of it, pushing me to think more clearly, sharing his insights, approaching my writing, in his words, 'as alternately the smartest possible and dumbest possible reader', and overall, showing the manuscript tough love. At Westland, Pallavi Mohan, for her careful editing; and my publisher and commissioning editor, Ajitha G.S., for her patience, sensitivity, hugely perceptive feedback and investment in this book from start to finish.

Longstanding friends, including the TIFR tribe, such as Aruna Dhir, Jyoti Singh, Sujata Paulose, for showing interest in this project, and Mangala Manohar, for her company; the Eternally Young gang, School is Cool set, Brandeis bunch and BIS beauties, for their positive energy and enthusiasm for what I do; Kiranavali Vidyashankar, for modelling strength and sharing her knowledge of Carnatic music; Sanjukta Wagh, for exemplifying artistic integrity and wonderful discussions about dance and music; and Anita Guha, Harini Narayanan, Sumati Surya and Sachin Vaidya, for always cheering me on.

My home support, in Mumbai, Rosy Phursunge, for her delicious meals, and Radha, for keeping my environment clean, and their counterparts in Bengaluru, Suma and V. Tamilazhagi; and my excellent trainer, Harshitha R., for keeping me fit. My aunts and uncles, for showering their affection on me and always wishing me well, including Bhanu Jay, Ganga and T.J. Sivakumar, T.J. Ravishankar and Usha and V. Subramanian; my cousins Nivedita Subramanian and Sucharitha Cintron, for sisterhood; my mother-in-law, Moham

Radhakrishnan, for helping run my household in the final stretch; my mother, Anuradha Ramanan, for her unwavering support and showing me what grit and discipline are, and my father, S. Ramanan, for encouraging me always to find my own path and proofreading a few chapters; and my loving children, Ritvik Ramanan Radhakrishnan and Samhita Ramanan Radhakrishnan, for teasing me about how long I was taking to write this yet always buoying me up, and dipping into some chapters amidst their busy lives.

My three pillars: my sweet sister, Kavita Ramanan, for her eternal support, always sympathetic ear and making time amidst her insane schedule to respond to some chapters; my aunt, Usha Subramanian, again, for her incisive comments on several drafts and being an inexhaustible source of moral support; and my beloved husband, Jaikumar Radhakrishnan, for casting his penetrating eye on the manuscript, his fine judgement, sense of humour and making this book possible.

Sound and Image

Raag renditions
Hitherto unreleased recordings of Arun Kashalkar's raag renditions, many of which the book mentions, will be available on Arun Kashalkar's YouTube channel, *Arun Kashalkar* (@arunkashalkar6610), under the playlist 'The Secret Master'. Where applicable, the description below the recording will refer to the relevant page(s) of the book. Subscribe to the free channel to keep up with the uploads.

Compositions
A searchable database of Arun Kashalkar's compositions, including their notation and renditions by him and his students, is available at archive.arunkashalkar.com. This database will be regularly augmented. Lifetime access to this database is available for a fee of Rs. 3,000 as of October 2025. This may be subject to change.

Images
Archival photographs linked to the book, with captions, will be uploaded on a section of Sumana Ramanan's website, www.sumanaramanan.in.

www.ingramcontent.com/pod-product-compliance
Lightning Source LLC
Chambersburg PA
CBHW050257010526
44107CB00033B/1414/J